From *A Song of the English*
1893

Fair is our
(Humble ye, my
For the
He ha
He hath smote for us   ا all the Earth!

—Rudyard Kipling

His appearance was certainly that of a hairdresser's dummy; but in the great demoralization of the land he kept up his appearance. That's backbone. His starched collars and got-up shirt-fronts were achievements of character.

—Joseph Conrad, *Heart of Darkness*

Humanity is waiting for something other from us than such an imitation, which would be almost an obscene caricature.

For Europe, for ourselves and for humanity, comrades, we must turn over a new leaf, we must work out new concepts, and try to set afoot a new man.

—Frantz Fanon, *The Wretched of the Earth*

Acknowledgment for permission to reprint previously published material:

From *Telling the Truth about History* by Joyce Appleby, Lynn Hunt, and Margaret Jacob. Copyright 1994 by Joyce Appleby, Lynn Hunt, and Margaret Jacob. Used by permission of W.W. Norton & Company, Inc.

From *Orientalism* by Edward W. Said, copyright 1978 by Edward W. Said. Used by permission of Pantheon Books, a division of Random House, Inc.

From Samuel P. Huntington's Keynote Address. *Cultures in the 21st Century: Conflicts and Convergences* (1999). Used by permission of The Colorado College.

GOODLY IS OUR HERITAGE

Children's Literature, Empire, and the Certitude of Character

Rashna B. Singh

The Scarecrow Press, Inc.
Lanham, Maryland • Toronto • Oxford
2004

SCARECROW PRESS, INC.

Published in the United States of America
by Scarecrow Press, Inc.
A wholly owned subsidiary of
The Rowman & Littlefield Publishing Group, Inc.
4501 Forbes Boulevard, Suite 200, Lanham, Maryland 20706
www.scarecrowpress.com

PO Box 317
Oxford
OX2 9RU, UK

British Library Cataloguing in Publication Information Available

Library of Congress Cataloging-in-Publication Data

Singh, Rashna B.
  Goodly is our heritage : children's literature, empire, and the certitude of
character / Rashna B. Singh.
     p. cm.
  Includes bibliographical references (p.   ) and index.
  ISBN 0-8108-5043-5 (pbk. : alk. paper)
  1. English literature—19th century—History and criticism. 2.
Imperialism in literature. 3. English literature—20th century—History
and criticism. 4. Children's literature, American—History and criticism.
5. Children's literature, English—History and criticism. 6. National
characteristics in literature. 7. Minorities in literature. 8. Colonies in
literature. 9. Racism in literature. I. Title.
PR468.I49S57 2004
820.9'358—dc22

                                                              2004006282

To my nanny, Mary Thompson, who helped to raise me.
And to my aunt, Ketayun M. Gilder, M.D.,
Who did so much for me.

But glad to have sat under
Thunder and rain with you,
And grateful too
For sunlight on the garden.

—Louis MacNeice, "The Sunlight on the Garden."

Contents

Acknowledgments   ix

Prologue   xi

Introduction   xxxv

1   Foundations   1

2   Fundamentals   67

3   Touchstones   113

4   The Blyton Books   199

5   Across the Atlantic   245

Epilogue   293

Bibliography   317

Index   331

About the Author   341

Acknowledgments

I would like to thank my forbearing editor, Sue Easun; my forbearing family—husband Rajindar, son Samir Indar, and daughter Namrita Shirin; those friends, colleagues, and students who contributed suggestions and asked the hard questions; Edward Picard and Anthony Dial for technical assistance when my computer and/or my computer expertise failed me. I have learned so much from listening to lectures by eminent scholars such as Howard Zinn. I would like to thank Professor Zinn for setting the record straight on so many matters and for responding to my enquiry.

This is a book about children's literature. I would also like to acknowledge those who inculcated in me a love for literature in my childhood, those who inspired me to love words, and those who insisted that I learn to use them appropriately. My parents, Dhan and Shirin Batliwala, often gave me books for my birthday and allowed me to read undisturbed for hours on end. Between the ages of seven and eleven, I lived in a small town in rural Bengal. My parents would take me to the Oxford Lending Library in Calcutta, a considerable distance away, to feed my hunger for books, and there I received enthusiastic advice from the two librarians. The only school in this small town was inadequate, so I was tutored privately by Mrs. Christiana, who taught me well indeed. For five years after that, I attended a boarding school, where my teachers were demanding but motivating. To those teachers—Mahendrie Hensman,

Nargis Gupta, Shakuntala Bhalla, W. J. Macmahon, K. I. Thomas, H. S. Sisodia, Mohammed Naeem, and others—and our librarian N. Mohan Raj, at the Lawrence School (Lovedale) in the Nilgiri hills of southern India, I also owe a debt of gratitude. So many of the staff at the school were colorful personalities and enlivened our school-days with their stories and tall tales: our matron, Miss Cheverton, and her ghost stories; Mrs. Richtor, the hospital matron, and the salts she used to cure everything; Hanif, the tailor, and his life stories; Maryayah . . . the list goes on.

On a recent trip to India, I reunited with many childhood friends and reaffirmed "the great solidarities of friendship." To the play-mates and friends of my childhood and youth—Mamta and Shalini Saran, Roma Anand Singh, Tandra Choudhury Saha, all my Lovedale classmates and friends, and all my Mount Holyoke college friends, scattered all over the world—so many nations, so many na-tionalities, "for the good times," thank you.

> The sunlight on the garden
> Hardens and grows cold,
> We cannot cage the minute
> Within its nets of gold
>
> —Louis MacNeice,
> "The Sunlight on the Garden."

Prologue

Human character, individual and national, is traceable solely to the nature of that race to which the individual or nation belongs.

—Robert Knox, M.D.
The Races of Men: A Fragment (1850)

The proper study of mankind is man, said one of England's most renowned men; and as the "boy is the father of the man," it may not be amiss to draw the attention of our young readers to the boyhood, if we may so term it, of England, and in tracing the progress of our island home from the time when it first became known down to the present time, in which it stands "the cynosure of neighbouring eyes," to note the not unimportant part boys have played in the formation of that national character which is now considered the type of true manliness, and which is the true cause of England's moral as well as physical supremacy over the other nations of the earth.

—From *Boys of the Empire* (1888)

In March 1983, President Ronald Reagan referred to the Soviet Union as the "evil empire." Almost two decades later, another U.S. president, popularly believed to be Reagan's ideological successor, also employed the word "evil" and applied it to enemy countries, this time Iraq, Iran, and North Korea. "States like these, and their terrorist allies," said George W. Bush in his first State of the Union address, "constitute an axis of evil, arming to threaten the peace of the world" (January 29, 2002). In both cases, their language created something of a global furor. In both cases, we saw the president of the most powerful nation in the world take a reductionist approach to complex and precarious world politics by choosing a word straight out of the lexicon of children's literature.

Such an approach was no accident but a carefully calculated appeal to our most primal fears, the fear of what is "outside over there." It is a fear of looming danger, of imprecise threat, of ontological evil, of the wild things. The word "evil" turns up with startling regularity in the discourse of U.S. politicians. Three other words that recur with equal predictability are "primitive," "barbaric," and "savage." Retired Air Force Lt. Gen. Tom McInerney referred to the kidnappers of American journalist Daniel Pearl as savages and barbarians. Congressman Richard Neal of Massachusetts, in a graduation address, reminded his audience that those who perpetrated the attack on September 11, 2001 come from cultures centuries behind those of the West (Holyoke Community College, June 2002). On September 11, 2001, *Time* magazine reported that Dick Gephardt stood with the Speaker of the House, Dennis Hastert, as he promised that both parties "will stand shoulder to shoulder to fight this evil" (34). And Condoleezza Rice, defending President Bush's plan to invade Iraq, insisted on the evil nature of Saddam Hussein. Evil is the adjective of choice to describe whichever foreign leader is in disfavor, whether it be Muammar Gadafi, Fidel Castro, or Saddam Hussein.

"Evil" is a word favored by the mainstream media as well. The cover of *Newsweek*, December 24, 2001, carried the headline "After the Evil" in big bold, black letters across the top, imprinted on the white of Osama bin Laden's turban. Bin Laden's portrait is blurry. The beard dominates, a smudge of black with purple and green tones. His eyes are hidden; his mouth leaks through like a smear of blood. In other portraits, his sensual lips snarl out at us. He is sometimes cast in a red glow, as he is in an illustration in the October 1 issue of *Time*. In yet another depiction, this time in the December 31, 2001 issue of *Newsweek*, bin Laden is portrayed in a black-and-white painting. His visage is cracked; practically the only colors visible are the trace of yellow in one eye and the red between his lips and around his mouth. He stares out at us like a wolf that has just bloodied his lip on his kill. "How He'll Haunt Us" is the headline. Lance Morrow's essay in the September 11, 2001, issue of *Time* uses the word "evil" repeatedly: "evil business," "evil mischief," "evil possesses an instinct for theater," "evil may vastly magnify its damage by the power of horrific images." The attack on the Pentagon and the World Trade Center towers in New York City, on September 11, 2001, was a dastardly act of evil; there is no question of that. But instead of an honest investigation into the identity of the perpetrators, or a realistic exploration of their motives for the purpose of preventing another assault, we are offered an evil genie straight out of picture books for children. The stark simplicity of the depiction obfuscates any real attempt at analysis. The attacks can then be ascribed to a single face, a single source of evil. In the December 31, 2001 issue of *Newsweek*, an article on the videotape that allegedly shows bin Laden chuckling at his handiwork is advertised as *Beyond Bin Laden*, and yet it never gets beyond bin Laden.

In the article, written by Evan Thomas and John Barry and entitled *Evil in the Cross Hairs*, we are presented with a portrait of an evil giant: "Osama bin Laden chuckles contentedly over slaughtering his own men along with several thousand Americans" (Thomas and Barry 2001, 10). The article is accompanied by a grainy picture from the videotape. "In the hearts of many Americans, bin Laden's smirking and gloating, at once evil and banal, inspired an overwhelming desire for revenge," we are told (10). The December 24, 2001 edition of *Newsweek* describes the video transcript of bin Laden as the voice of evil (13). In the November 26, 2001 edition of *Newsweek*, we read that the president calls bin Laden "the evil one" (Evan et al. 2001, 30ff.). To pit, even in print, the mighty forces of a superpower against one man, however malevolent, is to award him supernatural status. Doubts and conspiracy theories, we are told, are only in the minds of Middle Easterners. And so *Newsweek* presents both the American and the Middle Eastern mind as monolithic structures, simple and linear in their thought processes. A survivor, on seeing the videotape, is quoted in the December 24 issue of *Newsweek* as stating (justifiably, of course) that "the events of September 11 were the purest evil." Like everyone else, she wants a face and a name for that evil: "evil whose name is Osama bin Laden," she continues (4), as if the epistemology of evil were that simple, that easy.

In the October 1, 2001 issue of *Time*, the Taliban law enforcers are described as men in black turbans with kohl-rimmed eyes (McGeary 2001, 43). The magazine, in discussing the Taliban, is rife with references to "inscrutable" regimes, "savage wars," "shadows," "mysterious leaders," and "fanatically loyal" followers (42). In discussions of global politics, we often find the West set up in opposition to the rest. It was easy to install Osama bin Laden as the icon of the political underworld because his countenance summoned so easily metonymical associations with the storybook villains of the Orient. There is discussion of whether he might be delivered to the West, thereby dragging down the entire East with him in the tug of war between good and evil, with the West hefting mightily on the side of good. The Taliban's destruction of the Bamiyan Buddhas, which was a despicable and retrograde act, is presented as something that can only occur in a backward Eastern country as though Western colonial powers were not responsible for the destruction or despoliation of many famed Eastern monuments—for example, the caves at Elephanta, an island off India's west coast, where the Portuguese took aim at ancient sculptures for target practice. Lord William Bentick, who became the first governor-general of India (1828–1835), thought it would be a good idea to break up the Taj Mahal and ship its marble back to England to be auctioned! Only the low prices fetched on the marble market from other monuments saved the Taj. While hands are wrung, justifiably, for the loss of the Bamiyan Buddhas, the destruction of the Babri mosque in India by Hindu fundamentalists drew far less global outrage, and the destruction of historic Sikh *gurdwaras* (temples) in Afghanistan during U.S. bombardment none at all, not even a notice in the newspapers.

In the international political arena, egregious acts that originate in the United States or in Western Europe are almost always reported as the result of an abeyance or at worst an absence of judgment. Egregious acts that originate in the lands of the East are almost always reported as the result of an absence or at least an abeyance of morality.

The agenda of power is always invisible—or at any rate, indiscernible—to those in power. The destruction, oppression, atrocities, and deception—as much a part of the history of the United

States and so many European countries as they are of any in the East—are waived in this lofty pronouncement by Michael Elliot in the October 1, 2001 issue of *Time*: "History tells us this at least: when nations take upon themselves a global responsibility to rid the world of a shameful practice, they had better prepare for the long haul" (Elliot 2001, 21). In the battle between good and evil, it is best to use as spokesman someone from the other side who has crossed over, as it were. So it is indeed a Muslim journalist and commentator, Fareed Zakaria, who resolves that the Saudi monarchy must stop "flirting with fanaticism" and "rein in its religious and educational leaders" (Zakaria 2001b, 26); it is Zakaria who asks, "What can be done to reform the Arab world?" and who tells us "how to save the Arab world," assuming the moral high ground as his birthright, who speaks of a "fiery culture," completely missing the irony implicit in his statement, and who exhorts the United States to "drain the swamp" of Islamic extremism.

Imagery is sometimes used instead of words. George W. Bush resolved to smoke the terrorists out of their caves, thereby conjuring up a mental picture of a primitive and barbarian people. Before his handlers hushed him, Bush called the war on terror a crusade, a crusade against that old enemy, evil, an enemy with which Superman, Batman, Spiderman, He-Man, and (the latest comer) Harry Potter have all done battle. George W. Bush and all of America are now engaged in this battle. They are, of course, on the side of good. In the October 1, 2001 issue of *Time*, President Bush is reported to have termed it "civilization's fight" (20). In his article "The Case for Rage and Retribution" written for the special issue of *Time* that followed the attacks of September 11, 2001, Lance Morrow also sees it as civilization's fight: "The worst times, as we see, separate the civilized of the world from the uncivilized. This is the moment of clarity. Let the civilized toughen up, and let the uncivilized take their chances in the game they started" (50).

In a picture of the fallen twin towers in the September 14, 2001 issue of *Time*, a large cross foregrounds a scene of smoke and destruction. "Holy War" proclaims the caption. "As large swaths of lower Manhattan were turning to dust, farther uptown, at First Presbyterian on Fifth Avenue, the faithful gathered to hear the Rev. Jon Walton's service of mourning and lament." On September 11 itself, many TV stations showed split screens with the towers crumbling and people running for their lives on one side and Palestinians cele- brating on the other. The dichotomies of television are not subtle. But the rhetoric of evil is fluid, adaptable, compliant. It can be trans- ferred back and forth from one enemy to another, from one antago- nist to another. It has been hurled back at the United States just as it has been hurled by the United States.

When Social Darwinism, eugenics, racial theory, colonialism, technology, and power collude, it is a daunting alliance. All that re- mains is to harness the imagination. A *New York Times* article (June 16, 2002) indicates that four of the most lucrative movies of 2002 have been *Spider-Man, Star Wars: Episode II, Harry Potter and the Sor- cerer's Stone,* and *The Lord of the Rings: The Fellowship of the Ring* (Scott 2002, 26). All have in common the battle of empires, the struggle be- tween the forces of Good and the forces of Evil. That such a theme should be wildly popular in the wake of September 11 is no coinci- dence.

These films and others like them feed what the *Times* calls "a hunger for fantasy" (Scott 2002, 26). Although allegories, they are quite different from the moralistic and realistic (though ahistorical) allegories of the western genre, especially the John Wayne Westerns. Some Westerns—those with Clint Eastwood, for instance, and even a few with John Wayne—expose the fact that the struggle between the two sides was not that simple and clear-cut. There was an ambi- guity, sometimes a sense of guilt, certainly the possibility of empa- thy. But in the political arena, there can be no compromise between good and evil. "Star Wars," the *Times* article points out, "arrived not only in the midst of the malaise that followed Vietnam and Water- gate, but also at a time when the stalwart heroic movie genres, the war movie and the Western, could no longer in good faith sustain narratives of simple virtue" (26).

Nowhere are political and economic motives masquerading as ideology more effectively exposed than in Abdul R. Jan Mohamed's definition of the Manichean allegory, still so ubiquitous in the con- text of contemporary politics:

> The dominant pattern of relations that controls the text within the colonialist context is determined by economic and political impera- tives and changes, such as the development of slavery, that are exter- nal to the discursive field itself. The dominant model of power—and interest—relations in all colonial societies is the Manichean opposi-

tion between the putative superiority of the European and the supposed inferiority of the native. This axis in turn provides the central
feature of the colonialist cognitive framework and colonialist literary
representation: the Manichean allegory—a field of diverse yet inter-
changeable oppositions between white and black, good and evil, superiority and inferiority, civilization and savagery, intelligence and
emotion, rationality and sensuality, self and Other, subject and object.
(Gates 1985, 82)

One of the most famous (or now notorious) expositions of oppositional thinking or "the binary categories of Western meta-
physics" (Appleby, Hunt, and Jacob 1994, 212) is Samuel
Huntington's treatise on the clash of civilizations. In a keynote address in 1999, delivered at a symposium held at Colorado College
entitled "Cultures in the 21st Century: Conflicts and Convergences,"
Huntington summarizes some of his main ideas on the subject. He
sees the twenty-first century as the century of cultural conflict,
whereas the twentieth century had been one of ideological conflict.
Culture counts, he says, with consequences for good and evil (2).
And yet his rhetoric does not quite befit a new millennium as he falls
back on the old dichotomies of good and evil, terms left undefined.
The binary thought process is further revealed as he continues to define culture in a series of oppositions: "Scholars have also measured
societies along a number of other cultural dimensions and classified
them in terms of individualism and collectivism, egalitarianism and
hierarchy, pluralism and monism, activism and fatalism, tolerance
and intolerance, trust and suspicion, shame and guilt, instrumental
and consummatory, and a variety of other ways" (2). Unwittingly,
Huntington exposes a central colonial dilemma when he says,
"Now, however, modernization is a global phenomenon. All cultures are becoming modern, and in this sense one difference between the West and the rest is disappearing. Modernization,
however, does not necessarily mean Westernization. There is much
evidence, instead, that modernization strengthens existing cultures
and hence perpetuates the differences among them" (4). Huntington
does not clearly define what he means by modernization, but it
could be that, despite his denial, he sees it as synonymous with
Westernization.

When the colonized can speak the language, practice the social
norms, and adopt the culture of the colonizer, they become more

alert to social and legal inequities. "You taught me language," Caliban tells Prospero, "and my profit on't / Is, I know how to curse" (Shakespeare, *Tempest*, act 1, sc. 2). Huntington's lexicon betrays him when he ends his point with this pronouncement: "In the shorter term, modernization generates the resurgence of non-Western societies and cultures" (Huntington 1999, 4). Resurgence is a signifier. It is a loaded word redolent with implications beyond its actual meaning, implications of danger and evil.

Huntington compares economic data on Ghana and South Korea from 1960, indicating the similarity of their economic profiles at that point of time but their divergence since, as South Korea became an industrial giant while, in Huntington's words, "Ghana still remained Ghana" (5). Huntington asks how one can account for this difference in performance and acknowledges that many factors were undoubtedly responsible, but he settles on one. "I became convinced" he states, "that culture was a large part of the explanation. South Koreans valued thrift, savings, and investment, hard work, discipline, and education. Ghanaians had different values" (5). Huntington then shies away and does not so much as attempt to list those values. But what's really significant here is that he is speaking not of culture but of character and ranking countries according to a Western scale of virtue and value. That there might be a cost to all this progress, or that Ghanaians might not see the situation in quite the same way as he does, does not seem to occur to Huntington.

Huntington's vision of the future is one of confrontation and polarization: "For the first time in history, global politics is both multipolar and multicivilizational" (8). But shortly thereafter he drops the pretence of *multi* and speaks entirely in bipolar terms: "The most important axis in world politics will be the relations between the West and the rest" (8). In the original essay where he expounded this theory, *The Clash of Civilizations*, first published in the summer 1993 issue of *Foreign Affairs*, Huntington attributes this phrase to Kishore Mahbubani's article *The West and the Rest*, published in *The National Interest* in 1992. Mahbubani calls for "a comprehensive new strategy," pointing out that the exportation of Western values to the non-West does not constitute such a strategy but will only serve to "aggravate already serious problems" (3). There is nothing futuristic about Huntington's scenario. It is a scenario of the past and has already been addressed by Albert Memmi in his seminal work *The*

Colonizer and the Colonized. Memmi refers to "the famous and absurd incompatibility between East and West, that antithesis hardened by the colonizer, who thereby sets up a permanent barrier between himself and the colonized" (1965, 152).

Huntington's title owes more perhaps to Churchill, as we shall see shortly. Huntington refers to the challenge to America's core culture (which he essentially sees as European and Protestant) by "devotees" of multiculturalism (13). Again, his choice of word is a giveaway. "Devotees" is an Orientalist word, usually applied to the worshippers of deities regarded as arcane. We don't speak of the devotees of Christ but we do of the devotees of Krishna. The connotations and associations of the word are intended and become a reader cue. Just how derivative Huntington's argument is becomes evident when we read the following passage from a book called *New England Frontier: Puritans and Indians, 1620–1675* by Alden Vaughan, published in 1965, itself anachronistic in its view of the conflict between the Puritans and Indians as a clash of civilizations. The passage is quoted in a piece entitled "Indians" by Jane Tompkins:

> The root of the misunderstanding [about Puritans and Indians] . . . lie[s] in a failure to recognize the nature of the two societies that met in seventeenth century New England. One was unified, visionary, disciplined, and dynamic. The other was divided, self-satisfied, undisciplined, and static. It would be unreasonable to expect that such societies could live side by side indefinitely with no penetration of the more fragmented and passive by the more consolidated and active. What resulted, then, was not—as many have held—a clash of dissimilar ways of life, but rather the expansion of one into the areas in which the other was lacking. (Gates 1985, 64)

Huntington ends his speech with peculiar logic. Admitting that America is a multiethnic and multiracial society, he asks, "If it also becomes a multicultural society, lacking a common core culture, what will hold it together?" (13). The usual answer, he tells us, is the Declaration of Independence, the Constitution, and other documents—the American creed of liberty, equality, individualism, democracy, the rule of law, private enterprise. But then, in a final gesture of arrogance, he claims these values as "the product of the original unifying culture" and wonders how abstract political principles can hold this society together if that culture were to disappear. The possibility that other societies and other cultures or, God forbid, other civilizations might share these values or might even have engendered them is never raised. It does not seem to even occur to Huntington. These values are then entirely contingent and dependent on race, for which the word "culture" in this context is but a euphemism.

So what he is saying in essence is, "Assimilate. Become like us or lapse into barbarism." Huntington sees civilization as premised on culture, not on conquest or force or politics or power. Race and religion are, for him, the cornerstones of culture. His final statement is a warning against the return of the barbarian hordes:

> The issue for Americans is whether we will renew and strengthen the culture, which has historically defined us as a nation or whether this country will be torn apart and fractured by those de-termined to undermine and destroy the European, Christian, Protestant, English culture that has been the source of our national wealth and power and the great principles of liberty, equality, and democracy that have made this country the hope for people all over the world. That is the challenge confronting us in the first years of the 21st century. (13)

Huntington tells us that people often criticize his argument on the grounds that it is a self-fulfilling prophecy, that somehow because he says that clashes between civilizations exist and may intensify, he is arguing that they should occur (12). No, Huntington is not doing that, but his way of seeing the world is retrograde and harks back to colonialism, to good and evil fantasies. It ignores the complexities of history, the contingencies of economics, and contemporary political contexts. It is ultimately reductionist and, in a sense, racist, or at least racial, reducing conflict to difference rather than issues. The lofty term "civilizations" can obscure what is really at the center of Huntington's argument: national character. However, the purpose of this disquisition is not Huntington bashing but to reveal how deeply ingrained and resilient is his discourse. It masquerades as analysis but is in actuality atavistic in its thought patterns and processes.

Huntington's intellectual ancestry is derived from the likes of John W. Burgess, formerly professor of political science and consti-tutional law at Columbia University, whose treatise, *The Foundations*

of Political Science, was published in 1933. There is a somewhat startling affinity in what they propound. Burgess's basic contention is
that when physical geography, political organization, and ethnography correspond, it results in a completely national state, which he
describes as the strongest and most perfect form of modern political
organization (Burgess 1933, 22). There is a difference in the political
character of nations. Some nations are more capable of political organization than others. This is not only a difference in political character, however, but in the "psychologic character of nations" (35).
Nations that are less politically endowed should be subject to those
that are more politically endowed when it comes to state organization. That is both "natural and necessary," according to Burgess (35).
The Teutonic nations, he feels, are especially endowed with the capacity for establishing national states, "are especially called to that
work," and, therefore, are entrusted "with the mission of conducting
the political civilization of the modern world" (45).

Like Huntington, Burgess sees ethnic diversity as bearing the
potential for pollution and division. He writes:

> The further conclusions of practical politics from this proposition
> must be, that in a state whose population is composed of a variety
> of nationalities the Teutonic element, when dominant, should
> never surrender the balance of political power, either in general or
> local organization, to the other elements. Under certain circum-
> stances it should not even permit participation of the other ele-
> ments in political power. It should, of course, exercise all political
> power with justice and moderation—it is these very qualities of the
> Teutonic character which makes it *par excellence* political. It should
> also, of course, secure individual liberty, or civil liberty, as we term
> it here, to all; but, under certain circumstances, some of which will
> readily suggest themselves to the mind of any observing Ameri-
> can, the participation of other ethnical elements in the exercise of
> political power has resulted, and will result, in corruption and con-
> fusion most deleterious and dangerous to the rights of all, and to
> the civilization of society. (Burgess 1933, 46)

What it all comes down to is, once again, character.

Burgess insists upon a political mission for the Teutonic nations,
characterizing it clearly as a colonial policy. It is difficult for North
Americans to accept this, he acknowledges, since they forget that
they owe their own existence to this type of policy and balk at any

suggestion of interference in the affairs of other states. But they forget that the greater proportion of the globe is inhabited by people who have not succeeded in establishing civilized states and, in fact, entirely lack the capacity to do so and would be doomed to barbarism or semibarbarism unless the political nations step in and take over the work of state organization for them. This becomes the manifest destiny of the Teutonic nations, and Burgess's rallying call is disquieting in the context of the current policy of "regime change," or of changing the world as President George W. Bush put it grandiosely at his news conference of April 13, 2004. Interference in the affairs of barbaric or even partially barbaric populations is a calling that must be achieved by "any means necessary," for, says Burgess in an astonishing and almost amusing statement, "There is no human right to the status of barbarism" (47).

Another intellectual ancestor is none other than Winston Churchill. Aside from his memorable and highly eloquent essays and speeches where racial referents slip in and out without abashment, we may observe his use of the Manichean allegory in a single short story, *The Story of the Malakand Field Force* (1898). It is a story set, ironically enough, in the very same theater where President George W. Bush commenced his battle against evil: Afghanistan. The story is replete with references to ferocious Zulu, wily redskins, "wild and merciless fanaticism," "savages," "vendettas," "blood feuds," "miserable superstition," "barbarous people," and the "strange half light of ignorance and superstition." Everything is in excess in the Orient: "abundant crops," "copious rains," "numerous population." While women craft rude ornaments, men sit of an evening, smoking their hookahs or water pipes, or cleaning their guns, and speak of the "careless bravery" and "strange sports" of the white officers they have followed. They marvel at the punctual arrival of their pensions, and at the judges, collectors, commissioners, and other manifestations of "the comprehensive grasp of that great machine," the British Empire.

The very imagery of a machine and the rationality evoked by judges and commissioners suggest the opposition between civilized people and primitive people. British rule is "the advance of civilisation." Churchill pays extensive tribute at the end of the story to individual acts of heroism by Indian soldiers, to their coolness and courage, acts that reflect on the glory of their regiments—but their skill on the battlefield is attributed to "natural propensity" rather than "military knowledge." He says, "Their tactics are the outcome of their natures. All their actions, moral, political, strategic, are guided by the same principle." He marvels "that in the undeveloped minds of these wild and superstitious sons of the mountains, there lie the embryonic germs of economics and practical philosophy, pledges of latent possibilities of progress" (Churchill 1898). The Afghan tribesman are contrasted not only with the British but with the earlier Buddhist residents of the area who, when barbarism had "submerged Europe," were placid, thriving, industrious, and intelligent, "devoting their lives to the attainment of that serene annihilation which the word nirvana expresses." Churchill thus sees civilization as cyclical, concluding, "that the sun of civilisation can never shine all over the world at once." Clearly he sees it shining brightest on the British people and their empire at that period of time.

Churchill consistently refers to Europeans as modern and civilized peoples struggling against those whose "system of ethics . . . regards treachery and violence as virtues rather than vices" and whose code of honor is "so strange and inconsistent, that it is incomprehensible to a *logical* mind" [my italics]. He comes to the following conclusion about the ability of the white man to grasp the ways of the Afghans: "But a civilised European is as little able to accomplish this, as to appreciate the feelings of those strange creatures, which, when a drop of water is examined under a microscope, are revealed amiably gobbling each other up, and being themselves complacently devoured." After a while he starts to sound like a more elegant George Bush (or perhaps Bush just sounds like a less elegant Winston Churchill) as he sets in opposition "the strong, clear light of Rationalism and human sympathy" against the fanaticism, ignorance, warlike nature, and intolerance of the Oriental population, specifically those of the Mahommedan [sic] religion. The following passage deserves to be quoted in its entirety, so reminiscent is its rhetoric of modern-day perorations on the "war on terror." It also brings to mind popular perceptions of Muslim peoples in the contemporary Western world:

> But the Mahommedan religion increases, instead of lessening, the fury of intolerance. It was originally propagated by the sword, and ever since, its votaries have been subject, above the people of all other creeds, to this form of madness. In a moment the fruits of patient toil,

the prospects of material prosperity, the fear of death itself, are flung aside. The more emotional Pathans are powerless to resist. All rational considerations are forgotten. Seizing their weapons, they become Ghazis—as dangerous and as sensible as mad dogs: fit only to be treated as such. While the more generous spirits among the tribesmen become convulsed in an ecstasy of religious bloodthirstiness, poorer and more material souls derive additional impulses from the influence of others, the hopes of plunder and the joy of fighting. Thus whole nations are roused to arms. Thus the Turks repel their enemies, the Arabs of the Soudan break the British squares, and the rising on the Indian frontier spreads far and wide. In each case civilization is confronted with militant Mahommedanism. The forces of progress clash with those of reaction. The religion of blood and war is face to face with that of peace. Luckily the religion of peace is usually the better armed. (Churchill 1898)

The "clash of civilizations"—Churchill virtually uses the phrase. The struggle between civilization and barbarity, or good and evil or necessitates an oppositional structure in which we must know clearly where we are situated. It is not difficult, for while the enemy may be ill defined he is always easily recognized. He is never one of us, always the other, antithetical to everything we are. In his address to Congress shortly after the September 11 attack, President Bush clearly stated that everyone must take sides: "You are either with us or you are against us." No ambivalence, no shades of gray, no ambiguities are permitted. Even if the issues are not as clear-cut as we would like, allegiance is. You are with us or you are against us. You are on the side of good or on the side of evil. This is the fundamental polarity. On the side of good is civilization; on the side of evil is savagery. Civilization is ordered; savagery is chaotic. Civilization is structured; savagery is random. Civilization is light; savagery is dark. Civilization occupies space; savagery is void. Civilization is linear; savagery is circular. Civilization is historical; savagery is denuded of history. Civilization is rational; savagery is superstitious. Civilization is ordered; savagery is anarchic. Civilization is self-possessed; savagery is fecund. Civilization is articulate; savagery is silent or inchoate. Civilization is intellectual; savagery is instinctual. Civilization is clothed; savagery is naked or at least clothed differently. Civilization is soul; savagery is body. Civilization is spiritual; savagery is carnal. Civilization is scientific; savagery is superstitious.

Civilization is progressive; savagery is regressive. Civilization is familiar; savagery is foreign. Civilization is subject; savagery is object. Civilization is us; savagery is them.

On all sides, the problems of the world are presented and represented to us as a series of oppositions. Islamic extremism is in opposition to Western tolerance. Although Osama bin Laden tells us the entire world is divided into two regions—one of faith and another of infidelity. Heroic firefighters are contrasted with maniacal cowards; Palestinian gunmen [violent] are in opposition to Jewish settlers [peaceful]. When children are killed or injured in an Israeli raid it is the result of collateral damage, never intentional malice as it is where the Palestinians are concerned. An article in the December 31 issue of *Newsweek* persuades us that Mohamed Atta's fanaticism stems not from his political beliefs but from his cultural beliefs: "To Atta, the boxy building [the apartment building in Cairo into which his family had moved] was a shabby symbol of Egypt's haphazard attempts to modernize and its shameless embrace of the West" (Isikoff and Klaidman 2001, 43). We are offered no source for this statement and, since Atta blew himself up along with his victims, it cannot be confirmed or denied. Postcolonial critic Homi Bhabha notes:

> The discriminatory effects of the discourse of cultural colonialism, for instance, do not simply or singly refer to a "person," or to a dialectical power struggle between self and Other, or to a discrimination between mother culture and alien cultures. Produced through the strategy of disavowal, the *reference* of discrimination is always to a process of splitting as the condition of subjection: a discrimination between the mother culture and its bastards, the self and its doubles, where the trace of what is disavowed is not repressed but repeated as something *different*—a mutation, a hybrid. (Ashcroft, Griffiths, and Tiffin 1995, 34)

In *Off with their Heads*, Maria Tatar observes that "While the literature we read as adults . . . traditionally registers its disapproval of conformity and idealizes resistance to social regulation, the literature we read to our children by and large stands in the service of productive socialization" (1992, xvi). Mainstream media reporting of important news stories frequently come within the latter category. It is, one might argue, on a continuum with children's literature. How we see the world is first represented in the books we read as children and extends into the accounts we read as adults. Just as self must depend on other for definition, civilization must search out its converse. There can be no crossover. As long as the sides are kept separate, antithetical, and discrete, the other side can be kept in check. But to avert the threat to its survival, civilization cannot simply contain or even control savagery; it must conquer it.

Many important novels in the twentieth century—*The Heart of Darkness, A Passage to India, Lord of the Flies* among them—deal with the issue of restraints. What happens to the civilized person who is outside the context of civilization and how can that person be restrained from sliding back into savagery? *Robinson Crusoe* (1719), which will be discussed in a later chapter, shows us on the other hand an Englishman who, in spite of every opportunity and even compulsion, does not revert to savagery but becomes instead a one-man outpost of civilization, somewhat shaggy, but never barbaric. When savagery is linked to race, class, or gender, the conquest must be both physical and ideological, a hegemony of presence and perspective. The metaphor for civilization is the city; the metaphor for savagery is the forest or bush or veld or desert. "To colonize does not mean merely to construct wharves, factories, and railroads," wrote Le Marechal Lyautey, commissioner general of the *Exposition Coloniale et Internationale de Paris*. "It means also to instill a humane gentleness in the wild hearts of the savannah or the desert" (Chandler 1931, 1). Following the First World War, France was the greatest colonial power in the world, its holdings comprising forty-seven nations. It was time to impress upon the French people the value of their colonies to their country and this was the purpose of the international exposition held in Paris in 1931 (Chandler 1931, 1). What was especially significant, however, was that the exposition sought to display a commonality among Western colonial powers. The *mission civilisatrice*, which was at the core of French colonial policy, was extended to all of Europe and even to the United States.

Writing for *l'Illustration*, Pierre Deloncle states, "At a time when certain intellectuals and political parties are freely talking of a failure or a 'decline of the west,' the colonial exposition at Vincennes comes at a ripe moment to affirm that the great European nations (and the United States with them) are not in the least disposed to ac-knowledge this failure or to renounce the civilizing mission that have undertaken [*sic*]" (Chandler 1931, 2). Such reasoning allowed France to proclaim herself both an empire and a republic, Britain to believe that it was simply acting in loco parentis on behalf of its colonies until they came of age, in other words, civilized enough to rule themselves, and the United States to hearken to the bidding is-sued in Kipling's famous poem to "take up the white man's bur-den." After all, the United States already regarded its westward expansion as a civilizing mission, an expression of its manifest des-tiny to tame the wilderness, just as Europeans had done in Asia, Australia, and Africa.

The nations that exhibited at the international exposition also betrayed two primary purposes for colonization. On the one hand, they proudly put forth their civilizing mission, their endeavors to improve the quality of life for their subject peoples, which they demonstrated through a display of schoolhouses, medical equip-ment, and means of transportation. On the other hand, they dis-played what was arguably the true raison d'être—rubber, coffee, precious metals, exotic foodstuffs, and other raw materials—which were presented along with statistics that indicated their value for the master countries (Chandler 1931, 4). The only non-European nation to exhibit as a colonial power was the United States. The French ex-hibit was naturally the most extensive and occupied center stage, but the *Exposition Coloniale Internationale de Paris* was a concerted ef-fort not only to educate the French nation about the importance of their colonies, which was its purported primary goal, but also to demonstrate and express the commonality of the Western cause, or of the white race, as they embarked on a civilizing mission or con-tinued their engagement in it:

> In this light, the *exposition coloniale* takes on the air of an elaborate justification: a proof, to herself and to other colonizing powers, that the task of bringing civilization to the uncivilized is a task undertaken by Europe and America. Attacked from the left for their paternalistic and exploitative attitudes, and by the right for a failure of nerve, French supporters of the colonial enterprise looked upon the exposition as an opportunity to furnish proof to the world that colonialism was accomplishing its noble goals. (Chandler 1931, 2)

The ideology that lay behind the *exposition coloniale* was then that of albinism, the founder of which was Carlyle. In his seminal book *The Sociology of Colonies* (1949), Rene Maunier tells us:

> According to him [Carlyle] the distinguishing virtue of the *Gentleman*, which ought thereafter to be sought and ensued by every man worthy of this title, is: power. He sings the praise of the *Ruler*, the man who reigns over others, the directing-man, who is the true aristocrat; the praise of the man who is able to find scope for his energy, able by exercising to confirm and renew it. In this he agrees with Stendhal, but he is the first to deduce from these premises conclusions of an imperial nature. It is he who was the first to speak of "dominating" and of "dominated" peoples. It was he who preached a universal despotism, for the *virtue* and the *advantage*— to be attained at the same time and in the same way—of the white peoples. (Maunier 1949, 34)

There could not be a clearer conception than this of the way in which power and an imperial destiny are considered the outcome of character, individual character as well as conglomerate, racial conglomeration in this case, but national in other interpretations. The antithesis between the civilized and the rest is not simply cultural; it is religious, it is scientific, it is geographical, it is biological, and it is decidedly racial.

We see an exemplification of this in *Uncle Tom's Cabin* (1852), where Harriet Beecher Stowe, despite her belief in emancipation and her sensitivities to the suffering of the enslaved, presents the contrast in physical as well as social terms as she describes Topsy and Little Eva, the daughter of Topsy's master:

> There stood the two children, representatives of the two extremes of society. The fair, high-bred child, with her golden head, her deep eyes, her spiritual, noble brow, and prince-like movements; and her black, keen, subtle, cringing, yet acute neighbor. They stood the representatives of their races. The Saxon, born of ages of cultivation, command, education, physical and moral eminence; the Afric, born of ages of submission, ignorance, toil and vice! (266–67)

Reflected in this passage is the prevalent notion of the time that an individual was not only a product but also a representative of his or her race. The individual is then die cast, programmed by race. Such is not the raw racism of St. Clare's father, Eva's grandfather, who was just and generous to those of his own race but considered the Negro the intermediate link between man and animals. Stowe's is a racialized rather than a racist perspective and consequently she can envisage a time when the dark races can free themselves from the bondage of birth:

> If ever Africa shall show an elevated and cultivated race,—and come it must, some time, her turn to figure in the great drama of human improvement,—life will awake there with a gorgeousness and splendor of which our cold western tribes faintly have conceived. In that far-off mystic land of gold, and gems, and spices, and waving palms, and wondrous flowers, and miraculous fertility, will awake new forms of art, new styles of splendor; and the Negro race, no longer despised and trodden down, will, perhaps, show forth some of the latest and most magnificent revelations of human life. Certainly they will in their gentleness, their lowly docility of heart, their aptitude to repose on a superior mind and rest on a higher power, their childlike simplicity of affection, and facility of forgiveness. In all these they will exhibit the highest form of the peculiarly *Christian life*, and, perhaps, as God chasteneth whom he loveth, he hath chosen poor Africa in the furnace of affliction, to make her the highest and noblest in that kingdom which he will set up, when every other kingdom has been tried, and failed; for the first shall be last, and the last first. (197)

We will soon see just how Christian, in the truest sense, is this prediction and just how charitable is this view when compared to another—perhaps more prevalent—view of the dark races, published as a treatise on race a year before *Uncle Tom's Cabin*.

While the so-called dark races were viewed as oppositional, the East was often viewed as complementary, as Edward Said points out in *Orientalism*. But the East too was often seen in oppositional terms. As Said tells us, "the Orient has helped to define Europe (or the West) as its contrasting image, idea, personality, experience" (Said 1979, 1–2). Despite the military power of Islam after the death of the prophet, its cultural force, and its religious strength, Gibbon could write that the Muslims were "coeval with the darkest and most slothful period of European annals" (Said 1979, 59). The dominance of the Ottoman Empire constituted a constant threat to European civilization: "Not for nothing did Islam come to symbolize terror, devastation, the demonic, hordes of hated barbarians," says Said (59). If you could control the image, the representation, as he indicates, you could control the Orient itself and so the subject then becomes "not so much the East itself as the East made known, and therefore less fearsome, to the Western reading public" (60). On the other hand, Islam was seen as a civilizing influence in Africa, the culture and laws it introduced as being superior to that of the primitive natives.

In a crisis such as the one engendered by the terrible attacks on September 11, 2001, the task of the government is to render the enemy as fearsome as possible. Through its various authorized media outlets that sometimes shed even their pretence of independence and integrity, or are simply incorporated into a shared ideology and thus become not much more than stenographers, the government must demonize the enemies of the state, especially when it senses public support for its policies slipping. Overnight, the American public must be convinced that a Saddam Hussein or an Osama bin Laden, despite earlier links to the United States, is evil incarnate. The enemy made known becomes a single face: brown skin, black beard, turbaned head, leering at the grief of good citizens who watch in disbelief and horror as the twin towers collapse in the background.

Over and over again, the same image is broadcast, superimposed on the destruction. It becomes the face not only of the enemy but also of the East itself and, in retaliation, hundreds of innocent people who bear even a vague resemblance are attacked, harassed, and, in some cases, killed. The face is then not simply an image but, in the semiological sense, a symbol. It is projected in opposition to the twin towers, which it was responsible for bringing down. The towers symbolize planning, structure, organization, the institutions and appurtenances of a civilized society: people in business suits, transactions, telephones, fax machines, computers, and elevators—in other words, everything that is ordered, modern, progressive, technical, urbane. The face, on the other hand, symbolizes savagery, chaos, primitive thinking, retrogressive views, evil. For now it is foregrounded. It has triumphed. For now. But the battle against evil will resume.

Edward Said tells us in *Orientalism* how the prophet was consistently defiled in the Middle Ages:

Onto the character of Mohammed in the Middle Ages was heaped a bundle of attributes that corresponded to the "character of the [twelfth-century] prophets of the 'Free Spirit' who did actually arise in Europe, and claim credence and collect followers." Similarly, since Mohammed was viewed as the disseminator of a false Revelation, he became as well the epitome of lechery, debauchery, sodomy, and a whole battery of assorted treacheries, all of which derived "logically" from his doctrinal impostures. Thus the Orient acquired representatives, so to speak, and representations, each one more concrete, more internally congruent with some Western exigency, than the ones that preceded it. It is as if, having once settled on the Orient as a locale suitable for incarnating the infinite in a finite shape, Europe could not stop the practice; the Orient and the Oriental, Arab, Islamic, Indian, Chinese, or whatever, become repetitious pseudo-incarnations of some great original (Christ, Europe, the West) they were supposed to have been imitating. Only the source of these rather narcissistic Western ideas about the Orient changed in time, not their character. (1979, 62)

The practice persists. Pat Robertson recently referred to Mohammed as a pedophile because one of his wives was a pubescent girl. And on the *60 Minutes* show of October 6, 2002, Jerry Falwell declared the prophet "a terrorist," setting off riots that resulted in a hundred deaths in India alone. More recently, Army Lt. Gen. William G. Boykin is reported to have said in regard to a Somalian warlord, "I knew that my God was bigger than his. I knew that my God was a real God, and his was an idol." Boykin also proclaimed that the enemy in the war on terrorism was Satan, and that God had put President George W. Bush in the White House (www.CBSNews.com, October 21, 2003).

In the wake of the September 11 attacks, Edward Said was called upon repeatedly by every U.S. newspaper and TV channel of note to "explain" the Islamic mind or the way that Muslims think. Leaving aside the fact that he's not Muslim, although indeed erudite on many aspects of the politics and cultures of the region, the presumption that he could explain or interpret the terrorists' thought processes was preposterous. Said refused to participate in this process of simplification or to pontificate on the mind of the Muslim as if it were a monolithic subject:

During the present crisis, I didn't want to be tokenized or made to represent the "other" point of view, despite my long involvement

> as an advocate of Palestinian rights and the many books and arti-
> cles I have written on cultural misunderstanding, ignorance, and
> misrepresentations of Arabs and Islam. What could I know about
> the crazed fanatics who committed suicide in the slaughter of in-
> nocents? And why indeed was there this extraordinary assump-
> tion that from my university office I had some special insight into
> the smoldering twin towers? (2002, 69)

Others are not as reticent and soon fill the vacuum. Christopher
C. Harmon, for instance, the author of *Terrorism Today* and an adjunct fellow of the Claremont Institute, makes the following pronouncement in which, for all practical (or rather, ideological)
purposes, the word "terrorist" can be substituted by the word
"Muslim." "Terrorists are our enemies," he declares, not stopping
to specify which terrorists he is talking about or what that word
constitutes, "and the enemies of all who understand the short glorious word 'democracy' and the simple phrase 'rule of law.' Their
approach to political life and competing interests turn not upon
truths acknowledged by human reason, but upon bullets fired to
punctuate declarative sentences" (2).

Ignoring the declarative nature of his own sentences, Harmon
continues: "Like pirates, terrorists are enemies of mankind. They
should be hunted down anywhere and everywhere by all civilized
states and given capital punishment. Moreover, their safe havens
and state supporters are in violation of every respectable tradition of
international law, and even the softer strictures of the UN Charter"
(2). It is perhaps this last claim that is the most telling. The United
States itself has frequently flouted international law and even the
softer strictures of the U.N. Charter. Noam Chomsky and others
have gone so far as to claim that many U.S. foreign policy actions
have been nothing short of terrorist in both nature and intention.
Harmon's outcry is far from atypical. Seldom in the mainstream media is the nature of U.S. policy or practices seriously analyzed, exposed, or debated. What is important here is not whether that policy
and those practices have been right or wrong. The point is that there
is an entire nation, barring certain key intellectuals and an assort-
ment of radicals and malcontents, who are ignorant of and indifferent to the role of their nation in an international context. That the
mainstream media can ignore with impunity this failing on their

part to inform the public tends to indicate its participation in a political agenda that is assimilated and disseminated with little, if any, mediation, intervention, historical or social perspective, or critical judgment.

One of the most serious and sensitive scholars of international politics, Eqbal Ahmad, states in an interview conducted by David Barsamian and recorded in a volume entitled *Confronting Empire* that comments such as *New York Times* columnist Thomas Friedman's that terrorists "are driven by a generalized hatred of the United States" is "nonsense." "This is not analysis," states Ahmad. "This is witchcraft" (99). Witchcraft also resurfaces as the modern-day McCarthyism used to silence debate and dissent. The magic word has become 9/11 and all that the fateful events of that day set in motion. Instead of unlocking old holds, it has locked the world into a new hold from which there seems to be no release.

Much has been written on this subject by critics far more expert than I. Suffice it then to say this: representation trumps reality, fictions supercede facts, language shapes event, and sign governs information. Of course, neither Western nor white nor colonial powers are alone in the production of information, but the best propaganda is that which is not recognized as such, where the matrix is so deeply embedded in the consciousness and what is not said takes on more significance than what is said. Knowing then becomes a negotiation between nation and narrative and all knowing becomes allegorical. Patterns of sublimation begin in childhood. So do binary and hierarchical thinking. The child must be trained to see in oppositions and on a scale of order. The child must be trained to think through repetition, through the use of rhetorical tropes, through representational modes, through the discourse of negation. It is an epistemology in which we are schooled early on. The story of nation and people, race and culture, begins as the bedtime story.

Introduction

This book will look at literature for children as an imagining agency that worked with and within the colonial agenda. It will examine the typology of character in selected writings for children, with the focus on those works still circulating, and investigate how constructions of character became cultural imprints that served a functional purpose in the wider context of race and power, a context that will be referred to again, when relevant, in the course of the discussion. In fact, character sometimes becomes a code word for a particular political agenda. My use of the term *character* is not intended to be scientific or technical, character as opposed to personality or temperament. My use is intentionally broad based and unspecific. I am using the term as it was understood and interpreted in a national and political consensus, as it betrays the inner logic of societal constructions, as a hermeneutic term. What I am searching for in this study is the moral and intellectual consensus to which Antonio Gramsci referred when he said that hegemony flows not from the barrel of a gun but from moral and intellectual consensus. It is the politics of "hearts and minds," the predominance obtained by consent rather than by force (Femia 1987, 24), in this case, the consent implicit in character as a socially constructed notion.

Gramsci puts forth the notion that social or class supremacy is manifested in two different ways: "domination or coercion" and "intellectual and moral leadership" (Femia 1987, 24). Character comes

within the latter category; it is based on both external and internal social controls, external in a limited manner through rewards and punishments, but internal in a more significant manner through the
internalization of prevalent norms. "And whereas," says Femia in ex-
pounding on Gramsci's thought, "'domination' is realized, essentially,
through the coercive machinery of the state, 'intellectual and moral
leadership' is objectified in, and mainly exercised through, 'civil society,' the ensemble of educational, religious and associational institutions" (24). Such institutions play a key role in the formation of
character. Femia goes on to note the solid economic roots that Gramsci insisted upon, for if hegemony is "ethico-political," it must also be
economic and have its foundation "in the decisive function that the
leading group exercises in the decisive nucleus of economic activity"
(24). This is precisely the juncture between colonialism and character.
Character construed as ideal is assenting behavior that upholds the
prevailing political and economic structure.

It should be quite evident that any number of books could have
been included in this study, but a selection had to be made. Although I offer postcolonial readings of these texts, that is not my primary aim. I intend to examine how character building became one
instrument of colonial discourse and practice, and children's literature one instrument of its inculcation. My context is British colonialism with one foray into the pioneering movement of the American
West. Books that may warrant a postcolonial reading but are not
within my purview will not be included: Macdonald, for instance, or
Grahame or Milne. Besides, other critics have successfully attempted postcolonial readings of all three. Nor will I include books
such as *Tom Sawyer*, *Huckleberry Finn*, or *Little Women*, where notions
of character undoubtedly play a major role, but not necessarily in
the context of empire. Inevitably, my selection will be limited and
even somewhat arbitrary. Selections invariably are, almost by definition. No doubt there will be criticism of what I left out and what I
put in. There are many more works than I am able to include that
would help me make my point, over and over again. My main intention, however, is not simply to show that character building was
part of the colonial agenda but to illuminate how they interface in
children's literature, especially in literature that is still being read.
My interest is not only in the past but also in the present. They are,
of course, coupled, as the epilogue will attempt to show.

Although not all the books I include in my study are still being read, many are immensely popular and are offered to children by teachers and parents alike as "classics." In *The Nimble Reader: Literary Theory and Children's Literature*, Roderick McGillis points out that it is only recently that critics have begun to take children's literature seriously, and one consequence of the new critical approach through which it has been studied is the creation of a canon (1996, 44). A canon committee was formed within the Children's Literature Association and *Touchstones: A List of Distinguished Children's Books* put out in 1985. The only selections in my study that are no longer widely read are those in the chapter on the American West. Still accessible in the collections of any established town library, they are meant to be representative of the resources that would have been available to young readers during the period of their publication. The ideas and images they embody are still in wide circulation, if not the books themselves.

Some titles are being reintroduced after having been out of print for years and years. For instance, PrestonSpeed Publications in Pennsylvania has recently reissued many titles by G. A. Henty, which is why I am including some of his books in my study. Predictably, they are offered uncritically. The publisher actually claims to be "delighted" to offer these works to a whole new generation of adults and young people. So not only is Henty's ideology still being propagated, it is being propagated intentionally and for a precise purpose that will be discussed in a later chapter. That the historiography of empire was seldom challenged on either side of the Atlantic, until recently, is indicated by the following statement from Admiral E. R. Zumwalt Jr. of the U.S. Navy:

> My interest in Henty came from my father, Dr. Elmo Zumwalt, Snr., of Tulare, California, who had read all of his books as a young boy in the turn-of-the-century years. He wisely motivated me to begin reading them at the local Tulare library when I was 10, and I voraciously devoured all of them.
>
> I consider that they taught me more about history than I learned from more academic texts, and were key in motivating me for a life of adventure when I grew up. (Butts 1992, 65)

Arthur M. Schlesinger Sr. (1888–1965), the well-known social historian, recognized the influence of Henty's works on his choice of career. His son, Arthur M. Schlesinger Jr. (1917–), winner of two Pulitzer Prizes in history, comments, "My father exposed me to Henty at an early point, and I read book after book with enjoyment and fascination. Such knowledge as I have of ancient Egypt, the republic of Venice, India, southern Africa, the rise of the Dutch republic, the struggle for Chilean independence, the Franco-Prussian War, the Boxer rebellion, and many other historical episodes, had its roots in Henty." What is amazing is not so much the willingness to accept Henty's writings as historical but to accept his historiography. Lester Pearson, former Canadian prime minister, comments in his *Memoirs*,

> The Sunday School library encouraged similar interests. From its shelves I learned of life and adventure through . . . G. A. Henty. Henty was, I must admit, the author whom I knew best among all English writers until I went to college. His exciting stories based on history's more romantic episodes stirred my imagination mightily and, I suspect, had much to do with my liking and concentration on history in my educational progress. When years later I travelled extensively abroad as Canada's Secretary of State for External Affairs, there was hardly a place I visited which I had not known through that prolific but now almost forgotten writer of adventure for boys. (www.prestonspeed.com)

In this study I am dealing with character as a self-concept, not character as the "other" construed it. But one of the most odious effects of colonialism was to compel upon the colonized a self-concept that did not grow from within but was forced from without. Children who are neither Western nor white have all too often internalized the construction of character explored here. I have, with some exceptions, avoided blatantly jingoistic works, works that trumpet the heroic deeds of empire without abashment. They are too transparent for my purposes, and few of them are being read these days. Such stories certainly commemorate the character traits that constitute an ideal empire builder, but in a manner so celebratory and so exaggerated that they become little more than paeans to the British Empire, their mode propagandistic and their purpose patent. I do touch briefly on Henty, Ballantyne, and Marryat because their books have been reissued, or have remained in print, and are therefore still in circulation. As Jacqueline Rose comments in *The Case of Peter Pan; or, The Impossibility of Children's Fiction*, the boy's adventure story "was always part of an exploratory and colonialist venture which assumed that discovering or seeing the world was the same thing as controlling it" (1984, 9). I am more interested in those works that, while not exactly subtle, are less overt, where the qualities of character are not so much proclaimed as encoded.

In their essay on "The View from the Center: British Empire and Post-Empire Children's Literature," Peter Hunt and Karen Sands say,

> Just as the concept of "empire" saturated British culture, so virtually all (English-language) histories of children's literature agree that children's books, always fundamentally involved in reflecting and transmitting culture, were the witting or unwitting agents of the empire-builders. This was true of *all* writing, not merely the stories designed for the boys who were to be the empire-builders: it affected girls' stories, school stories, religious stories, and fairy stories. None of this is in dispute: the extent and nature value of that affect, however, has not been examined, precisely because it is so apparently obvious. (Hunt and Sands 1996, 40)

This book focuses on the nature value rather than the extent of the affect. The extent of the affect is probably inestimable and often intangible. In examining the nature value, with particular attention to character, one is examining qualities that, while not exclusively English, were often regarded as exclusively English by the English and harnessed, consciously and willfully, in the service of their empire. It is important to note this. It is indicated by the many conceptualized references to national character in the period of empire. It is also important to note that the choice of texts in my study is meant to be illustrative rather than exhaustive, representative rather than comprehensive.

What are these books really teaching children in terms of how they should be and how they should see? With these questions in mind, my desired audience is not only students and scholars but also mothers and fathers, teachers, and teachers of future teachers. For this reason, I have tried to keep this book simple and straightforward, not because people outside academia are incapable of comprehending the twisted route to meaning that academics often like to take, but because they tire of it. I have attempted, without obfuscation or unnecessary digression, to read the constructions of character in selected texts for children and to demonstrate that these too were social constructions that both reflected and furthered an imperialistic, expansionist agenda. Speaking of the school story, specifically of the stories of Frank Richards (a pseudonym for Charles Hamilton), Jeffrey Richards states, "The stories for over fifty years dramatised and endorsed the public school values and virtues, endorsing those characteristics which the British believed sustained their empire and justified their role as the world's policemen—team spirit and fair play, duty and self-sacrifice, truth and justice" (Butts 1992, 12).

Many excellent studies of children's literature in the context of empire have recently emerged, most notably M. Daphne Kutzer's *Empire's Children: Classic British Children's Books* (2000). Although we share an interest in particular texts and agree on the importance of children's literature as a transmitter of imperial and cultural values (see Kutzer, xxi), our foci are different. I focus on character, while Kutzer is more broad based. Kutzer also selects different texts to study, although we overlap on a few. Another important study of children's literature in the context of empire is *Imperialism and Juvenile Literature* (1989), edited by Jeffrey Richards. This is a detailed and comprehensive study and contains important contributions on Ballantyne and Henty as well as the boys' papers, flying and hunting stories, and girls' fiction. Generations of children read these types of stories. My own brothers had a few Henty titles on their shelves, years after India's independence, well-meaning gifts from family friends who had either never thought through their implications or were not fazed by them.

My work is corollary to both Kutzer's and Richards's whose studies are well worth the investigation by the reader who wants to delve further into this subject. Jacqueline Rose's work, *The Case of Peter Pan; or, The Impossibility of Children's Fiction*, and Karin Lesnik-Oberstein's *Children's Literature: Criticism and the Fictional Child* (1994) are important theoretical contributions to the field. They are especially important because children's literature has not generally been considered a serious critical subject, so studies have tended to be descriptive, thematic, or historical: source books, guides, or that sort of thing. Similarly, Perry Nodelman's study of narrative theory in regard to picture books, *Words about Pictures: The Narrative Art of Children's Picture Books* (1988), provides sophisticated critical analysis of a literary genre that most critics would scoff at taking seriously. Rose and Lesnik-Oberstein compel us to examine texts written for children, or those read mostly by them, as corollaries to adult literature rather than rudimentary versions of it. Both texts ask us to consider not just the literature but also the child, or rather the constructed child, and the interplay of socioeconomic, political, and cultural influences that are brought to bear when a child encounters a text. Rose states unequivocally, "There is no child behind the category 'children's fiction', other than the one which the category itself sets in place, the one which it needs to believe is there for its own purposes" (1984, 10).

Lesnik-Oberstein examines the interrelationships among the child, the story, and the criticism. *Voices of the Other: Children's Literature and the Postcolonial Context* (2000), edited by Roderick McGillis, is another important contribution to the field. It is a collection of essays by writers from Australia, Canada, China, Germany, the United Kingdom, and the United States that examines both colonialism and postcolonialism. In addition, the collection edited by Dennis Butts, *Stories and Society: Children's Literature in Its Social Context* (1992), has proven eminently useful. The purpose of my work is to study how character is projected, expressed, and embodied in selected children's fiction and how this construction served a colonialist agenda. Once again, it is not an open-ended postcolonial reading of children's literature, even if my approach may be perceived as postcolonial in the sense McGillis sets forth in his introduction: "The postcolonial critic, then, has a responsibility to read works of literature for their stated and unstated assumptions about the other. To put this another way, the activity of the postcolonial critic is political; he or she intervenes in the ways cultures construct persons" (2000, xxviii). I attempt to examine the cultural construct of children's literature as expressed through notions of character. In doing so, I am forced to confront the assumptive aspects of the canon and its underlying system of structural relations as well as subversive codifications. Children's literature is not only a material but also an ideological industry.

Enid Blyton and the Mystery of Children's Literature by David Rudd (2000) is another work that parallels my own. His is an extensive study of this highly influential writer, to whom I have devoted a chapter but, again, my focus is more on her constructions of character. Throughout this study, I am forced to use many broad, all-encompassing, and comprehensive terms, terms that are sometimes more ample than accurate. These include: "white," "Western," "Asian," and "African." Such terms preclude complexity and do not leave room for exclusion or exception. They are always used with this awareness and simply as a matter of convenience. The use of "British" as opposed to "English" has produced much debate and discussion. In the context of empire, however, they become virtually exchangeable. The term "colonial" in this work is, unless otherwise stated, a reference to British colonialism.

Character is complex. It comprises a person's mental and moral qualities, reputation, traits, habits, quirks, and even, at times, beliefs. While personal and national character were considered closely linked, and while character was considered something determined by race, a society could fret about its deterioration, as we have seen. Many influences go into the formation of character: family, culture, gender, personal experience, religion, and so on. Every culture, every society attends to character, attempts to inculcate it in their young, and affords it importance. Although the conception of ideal character may vary, there is also some overlap, so some of the traits privileged in one culture may also be privileged in another. Conversely, some cultures rate certain traits far more highly than do others. A recent study in the United States draws a correlation between quiet people and violence. Considering the general distrust or disfavor with which people who are reserved or reticent are often received in this society, the conclusions of this study are not entirely surprising. A recent *New York Times* article (July 26, 2002) tells of the pitch being made by the mayor of Schenectady, N.Y., who is white, to attract Guyanese immigrants to his city. He describes them as "hard-working, entrepreneurial and tidy" (Kershaw 2002, 18), all aspects of the self-image of white immigrants.

Writing in *Harper's* magazine (September 2003) of the effect of public education in crippling children's minds and spirits, John Gatto, a former teacher in New York schools and author of *The Underground History of American Education*, refers to a book published in 1918 entitled *Principle of Secondary Education* by Alexander Inglis. Inglis breaks down the actual purpose of modern schooling into six basic functions: adjustive or adaptive (reflexive obedience), integrating (conformity), diagnostic and directive (determining each student's proper social role), differentiating (appropriate training for that role), selective (improving the breeding stock), and propaedeutic (managing this social structure). This, says Gatto, is the purpose of mandatory public education in the United States. Henry Giroux expresses similar concerns about the corporate model of teaching in an article in *Z Magazine*, entitled "Youth Panic and the Politics of Schooling."

Character education functioned similarly in the framework of empire. It was a fifth column used to preclude dissent or insurgence. Edward Mack writes in *Public Schools and British Opinion 1780–1860*: "From the very beginning character has seemed, on the whole, more important to the English than learning. Wykenam's belief that manners or character make the man was probably less an axiom of Public School education when it was first formulated than it is today, but masters, parents, and boys have cared, all through Public School history, as much if not more about character than about anything else" (1938, 30). In this study, I am concerned not so much with how character is formed as with how it is conceived and constructed, reflected and represented. I am concerned not so much with its history or its evolution as with its presence and its purpose within the colonial context. I am concerned with how it becomes part not only of moral education but also of a political and social program and how writing for children, consciously or unconsciously, services that program. The "politics of 'hearts and minds'" begin in childhood. Children's literature is then the place to begin.

1

Foundations

Here is the stuff that is read somewhere between the ages
of twelve and eighteen by a very large proportion, perhaps an actual majority, of English boys, including many
who will never read anything else except newspapers;
and along with it they are absorbing a set of beliefs which
would be regarded as hopelessly out of date in the Central Office of the Conservative Party. All the better because it is done indirectly, there is being pumped into
them the conviction that the major problems of our time
do not exist, that there is nothing wrong with *laissez-faire*
capitalism, that foreigners are unimportant comics and
that the British Empire is a sort of charity-concern which
will last for ever. Considering who owns these papers, it
is difficult to believe that this is unintentional.

— George Orwell, *Boys' Weeklies*

I have lived in many countries, and talked in several languages: and found something to esteem in every country
I have visited. But I have never seen any nation the equal
of my own. Actually, such is my belief, Mr. Orwell!

— *Frank Richards replies to George Orwell*

Race underlies much of binary thinking. Color is primal: it is one of the first things we learn to distinguish in infancy, and whether or not racial distinctions are entirely dependant on color, it has been used to categorize those differences. Regarding other races as inferior to theirs is not a sanction exclusive to people of European descent. Color underlay the Aryan caste system, and the Chinese clearly expressed their sense of racial superiority in regard to foreigners. But race was an essential part of the ideology of European colonialism and was harnessed for specifically political purposes. "Albinism" refers to the doctrine of the white man, as we have seen. Carlyle connected the notion of the "gentleman" to an imperial nature and the exercise of power. The gentleman is not only someone who is polite and polished, but someone who knows how to take charge and use his authority to do his duty.

It was David Hume, however, who, as Henry Louis Gates points out in his introduction to a collection of essays in *"Race," Writing, and Difference*, in the middle of the eighteenth century, "gave to Bosman's myth the sanction of Enlightenment philosophical reasoning" (Gates 1985, 10). Bosman was a Dutch explorer who published a myth in the very early part of the eighteenth century, a myth that he claimed to have heard from the Africans he "discovered." The myth was that while God created black as well as white men simultaneously, blacks were allowed "the first Election" and chose gold, leaving the knowledge of letters to white men. In return for their avarice, God established whites as their masters in perpetuity (Gates 1985, 10). In his essay "On National Characters" (1748), Hume confesses his suspicion that the Negroes in particular, but all other species of men as well, were naturally inferior to whites. To support his theory, Hume makes this astonishing claim: "There never was a civilized nation of any other complexion than white, not even any individual eminent either in action or speculation" (Gates 1985, 10). An example of the latter, put forth from Jamaica as "a man of parts and learning," Hume dismisses as a parrot. Gates reminds us how pervasive such a viewpoint was. It was picked up by a thinker as notable as Kant who (in *Observations on the Feeling of the Beautiful and Sublime*, 1764) develops these ideas in discussing "National Characteristics," claiming that the divide between the black and white races is as great in terms of mental capacities as it is in color. "Kant, moreover, is one of the earliest major European philosophers to conflate color with intelligence," says Gates (1985, 11), while it was Hegel, echoing Hume and Kant, who claimed that Africans had no history because they had no systems of writing and were unable to write in European languages (Gates 1985, 11). Writing, Gates points out, is the visible sign of reason and, after the "Enlightenment," the faculty of reason was used as the watershed that separated civilized and un-civilized society (Gates 1985, 8).

Reduced to the simplest terms, as it often was by those who pro-pounded it, the argument was this: a superior race has the right, in-deed the duty (or, further, the responsibility) to rule over an inferior one and bring the light of civilization into the darkness of their sav-agery. At the turn of the last century, in 1899, Rudyard Kipling de-livered his famous injunction to the United States, a nation he saw as fraternal with his own. In response to the American takeover of the Philippines after the Spanish-American War, Kipling calls upon Americans to assume their share of the responsibility of race:

> Take up the White Man's burden—
> Send forth the best ye breed—
> Go bind your sons to exile
> To serve your captives' need;
> To wait in heavy harness,
> On fluttered folk and wild—
> Your new-caught, sullen peoples,
> Half-devil and half-child. (Kipling 1980, 323)

John Buchan, one the chief apologists of the British Empire, who was also a Member of Parliament and finally governor-general of Canada, put it succinctly. The difference between white and black, he says in his novel *Prester John* (1928), is "the gift of responsibility" (264). In 1894, Benjamin Kidd, author of *Social Evolution*, spoke of "the altruistic spirit underlying our civilisation" and "the conscien-tious discharge of the duties of our position towards the native races" (Winks 1963, 79). He then goes on to make this extraordinary statement: "We have respected their rights, their ideas, their reli-gions, and even their independence to the utmost extent compatible with the efficient administration of the government of the country." That it was Britain's right to rule over "fluttered folk" and "sullen peoples" was a widespread and deeply ingrained conviction, not simply a piece of governmental propaganda. It penetrated deep into the consciousness of the people at all levels and was communicated in a variety of ways. Rene Maunier points out that imperialism has not remained unchanging. One type of imperialism has succeeded another, each emphasizing the political, the economic, or the moral aspect as expedient (Maunier 1949, 31).

The four principles of imperialism as propounded by Carlyle are aristocracy, energy, mysticism, and utilitarianism. Aristocracy means that domination should be the privilege of those who are both strong and righteous. Energy refers to the idea that the exercise of power is desirable in itself and demands action: "all expansion is sound and good, for it deploys the energy of the strong" (Maunier 1949, 34). Mysticism means a divine mission to augment the affairs of the world, a divine mission of power and duty. Finally, utilitarianism is none other than biological utility. "*Selection* is for the Englishman *election*," says Maunier (1949, 35).

One of the most effective means of dissemination of the imperial ideal was, of course, popular literature, and it was especially effective in the literature written for the young. G. A. Henty, Captain Marryat, Francis Brett Young, and John Buchan were only the best known of a number of authors who not only chronicled the achievements of empire builders for scores of schoolboys but also celebrated their character (see Singh 1988, 12). George Alfred Henty (1832–1902) fought in the Crimea in the 1850s and served as a war correspondent in West Africa, Ethiopia, Austria, France, Italy, Spain, and the Balkans. His prodigious output of three to four books a year made him one of the most influential and significant writers in this particular genre of adventure stories about the empire. Henty's heroes were deeply embedded in the consciousness of English children, boys in particular. Through roughly ninety books, Henty transported schoolboys to the far reaches of the British Empire, taking them *With Clive in India* (1884) or *With Moore at Corunna* (1898), *With Wolfe in Canada* (1887), or *With Roberts to Pretoria* (1901) and *With Kitchener in the Soudan* (1902). Apart from the historical context, there is little to distinguish one work from another. The theme they have in common is character.

Henty's heroes established the norm for imperial character. For those who did not belong to the race and, most particularly to the nation, it was a norm that was out of reach. But for the British schoolboy it was eminently accessible. All he had to do was emulate the hero's character, to be like Yorke Harberton in *With Roberts to Pretoria*: "a good specimen of the class by which Britain has been built up, her colonies formed, and her battlefields won—a class in point of energy, fearlessness, the spirit of adventure, and a readiness to face and overcome all difficulties, unmatched in the world" (Winks 1963, 57).

The reward for such character is respect and an awareness of being engaged in a noble endeavor. It is to shoulder one's share of the white man's burden, to discharge one's duty in bringing hope to the benighted, succour to the weak, and government to the lawless. The exemplary British virtues of valiant battle, always tempered by the principles of fair play, are celebrated in every single story. The result is a life of fulfillment, for, as A. P. Thornton points out, "Henty's books have as happy an ending as books can well have" (Winks 1963, 58). What Henty and the others were chronicling was not simply history but also, inadvertently, the historicity of a worldview.

In 1897, a high-water period for European colonization, when the British Empire in India was secure and British and other European colonies in Africa were being established, people did not mince words when referring to the "lesser breeds." In April of that year, an English newspaper called the *Social-Democrat* published a story called *Bloody Niggers*. Its author was a socialist and Scottish aristocrat called R. B. Cunningham Graham, and in using the term *Niggers* in his title he was simply shedding the politeness in print that was customary and using a term that was quite acceptable in daily conversation. Graham's piece was in the tradition of Jonathan Swift's *A Modest Proposal*. What he did was to bring to the surface, without obfuscation, the prevalent social and scientific beliefs of the time. The British race he says with heavy sarcasm (and also lyricism) is a race of "limited islanders, baptised with mist, narrowed by insularity, swollen with good fortune and wealth" (Lindqvist 1996, 82). God has chosen them to rule over mankind, and the Romans and Greeks were but preparation for them.

The lower races of Africa, Australia, America, and the South Sea Islands are all essentially "niggers" or "bloody niggers" (see Lindqvist 1996, 82). But when culture and nation enter the equation, color is no longer the only criterion, for some European strains were regarded as other kinds of niggers: "European niggers." The archetype of the nigger is the African. God must have been in a bad mood when he created that continent, is Graham's ironic claim, or why would he have peopled it with races doomed to be ruled and replaced by other races? It would have been better to have made them English in the first place so as to save Englishmen the bother of exterminating them. What rights do niggers have? None, because they have no guns. Their land, cattle, and fields, even their wretched household utensils belong to the English, who also have the right to their women, to abuse physically, impregnate, or infect with syphilis. The British, he says, get exercised about the genocide perpetrated by the Turks and others, all but their own victims, whom their empire drowns in blood.

Graham's satire came to my attention through an excellent little book by a Swedish writer, Sven Lindqvist, called *Exterminate All the Brutes*, which he describes as "One man's odyssey into the heart of darkness and the origins of European genocide." Lindqvist's title is taken of course from Kurtz's famous pronouncement in *The Heart of Darkness*, and he tells us that Graham and Conrad became friends and corresponded with each other about their work (1996, 83). His is a sobering study of the systematic, highly theorized but entirely specious nature of "scientific" racism that was based on ridiculous and outrageous hypotheses. Yet these hypotheses were widely accepted and wholly believed by many of the best minds of the time, because they were put forth as scientific theories and treatises.

Race underlies not only binary thought patterns but also imperial ideology, as Lindqvist's book so amply illustrates, an ideology that engendered some of the most egregious incidents of savagery the world has known. It is ironic then that the races to be exterminated with impunity were seen as savage. Race had been regarded as one of many factors that influenced human culture. After Darwin, it became the definitive one (Lindqvist 1996, 130). In *Telling the Truth about History*, Joyce Appleby, Lynn Hunt, and Margaret Jacob show us how Darwin's scientific genius could not detach itself from his cultural context:

> The social attitudes of an imperial and market-oriented society in which continuous reform seemed possible were woven through Darwin's science.
> On one hand Darwin the materialist could conceptualize human equality—simply the equality of all atoms—randomly se-

lected; the inheritance of acquired characteristics was incompatible with random selection. But Darwin the British gentleman could also effortlessly imagine that moral superiority, a characteristic so fortuitously acquired by Westerners, particularly by men, might even be inherited: "the low morality of savages . . . their insufficient powers of reasoning . . . weak power of self-command . . . this power has not been strengthened through long-continued, perhaps inherited habit, instruction and religion." Darwin's racial and sexual views permeated his discussion of the origin of species and especially of the descent of man. (Appleby, Hunt, and Jacob 1994, 184)

The same was true for many other scientists at the time, putting an end to the myth of pure science and, as Appleby and colleagues point out, bringing about our contemporary disillusionment with the heroic model of science: "Science has lost its innocence. Rather than being perceived as value-free, it is seen as encoded with values, a transmitter of culture as well as physical laws" (Appleby, Hunt, and Jacob 1994, 16).

Children's literature is not entirely innocent either and must acknowledge its role as an encoder of values and transmitter of culture and, when such values or culture betray bias, it must accept the culpability of its participation. The political and ideological dimensions of children's literature are not just an accident or a harmless by-product but an integral part of its purpose. The exploitation of children's literature in Nazi Germany is an egregious example. In *Children's Literature in Hitler's Germany*, Christa Kamenetsky points out that propaganda took the guise of idealism and "Nazi ideology inevitably resulted in a peasant and ancestor cult that were both endowed with National Socialist meanings and objectives" (1984, 41). Nor were picture books exempt from censorship or official review. Picture books, such as those of Elvira Bauer, which show the Jew as repellant and mean while the German appears noble, or contrast ugly Jewish children with active, cheerful, and healthy German ones, were an integral part of the Hitler Youth indoctrination program (Kamenetsky 1984, 166–67).

It would surely not be too far-fetched to compare these images with those that appear in a number of British publications for children that offer a similar contrast between the colonizer and the colonized or to compare the Nazi folk education program with the character education so rampant in publications for British children. The difference is, of course, that the German program was far more formalized and official. The similarity is that both served a political agenda. The cultivation of character was critical to the well-being of the empire. Character was considered one of the chief criteria for natural selection in a wider context, an economic, social, and political context. That the qualities of character attributed to the white races, the Saxons especially, also served an imperialist agenda is no coincidence. The qualities of character with which the white race was presumed endowed by nature were most clearly illustrated by depicting the benighted races that lacked those traits.

That the colonized races, regardless of history and geography, were seen as sharing a common inventory of characteristics is a dead giveaway. For instance, the famous Victorian explorer Richard Burton wrote about the African: "He is inferior to the active-minded and objective . . . Europeans, and to the . . . subjective and reflective Asiatic. He partakes largely of the worst characteristics of the lower Oriental types—stagnation of mind, indolence of body, moral deficiency, superstition, and childish passion" (Gates 1985, 198). Patrick Brantlinger, whose essay "Victorians and Africans" addresses this pictoriography, indicates,

> The development of physical anthropology and of "ethnology" as disciplines concerned with differences between races was reinforced from the 1860s on by Darwinism and Social Darwinism; these "sciences" strengthened the stereotypes voiced by explores and missionaries. Evolutionary anthropology often suggested that Africans, if not nonhuman or a different species, were such an inferior "breed" that they might be impervious to "higher influences." (Gates 1985, 201)

In *The Descent of Man* (1871), Darwin indicated his belief that between the primates and civilized man are intermediate forms such as gorillas and savages. But they are both dying out and, in the not too distant future as measured by centuries, he predicted, the savage races will be exterminated and replaced by the civilized races of man (Lindqvist 1996, 107).

One of the earliest studies of racial difference appeared well before Darwin, however. It was called *The Races of Men: A Fragment* (1850) and written by a scientist called Robert Knox, who had studied anatomy with the famous French scientist and naturalist Georges Cuvier. Knox attempts to show anatomical differences between the dark and the light races. For instance, he claims that the brain of the former, although not of different size, is of a different quality: "The texture of the brain is, I think, generally, darker, and the white part more strongly fibrous" (1850, 151). But his experience, he admits, is limited. In fact, it is based on an autopsy of only one corpse, in which Knox found a third fewer nerves in the arms and legs than in a white man of corresponding size. This claim would be laughable today and easily disproved by any college anatomy student, but it would have been taken seriously by most of Knox's contemporaries who were in a rush to prove their mental, moral, and physical superiority over those they ruled and thus justify not only colonization but also its cost: the horrific acts of violence that so often accompanied it.

Such theorizing, of course, continues into the present day with speculation about why blacks don't make good swimmers or golfers. (Jack Nicklaus is reputed to have said that they have different muscles that react in different ways.) The emphasis on black bodies, of course, is carefully designed to minimize the potential of black minds or black character. In *The Bell Curve*, Charles Murray and Richard J. Herrnstein as good as advise black people to concede victory to whites in the mental sphere while rightfully claiming their due in the physical sphere. Eugenics is still alive and well. For those who wish to pursue further just how absurd pseudoscientific theorizing about black bodies can become, Sandra Gilman's study, "Black Bodies, White Bodies" in *"Race," Writing, and Difference* makes fascinating reading.

Knox rails against the hypocrisy of statesmen, historians, theologians, and journalists who try to cover up the racial and racist underpinnings of conquest. He sees nothing wrong in perceiving or judging in racial terms, only in being dishonest about it. Race, says Knox, is the great question, in fact the most important question (1850, 11). This is followed by one of the unexpectedly forthright statements that he puts forth from time to time: "Empires, monarchies, nations, are human contrivances often held together by fraud and violence," he says (12). What he scornfully refers to as "nature's democrat" he defines as "the respecter of law when the law is made *by himself*" (16). Knox does not beat about the bush when it comes to exposing the true nature of government. As a result, we can sometimes be distracted momentarily from his shocking, even obscene, pronouncements on the nature of the dark races. Knox resolves not to shy away from the issue of race as so many others have done. His is not a theoretical study but an empirical one, working from the present toward the past. As in Conrad's *The Heart of Darkness*, we see in Knox an essential contradiction.

Accompanying the utter denigration (in the case of Knox) and distaste (in the case of Conrad) for the darker races is an open, honest, and almost avant-garde awareness of the true purposes of colonialism:

> Successive races of men appear on the globe; the space they occupy is of course too small for them, whether it is England or France, New York or Calcutta, Moscow or Rome (I mean ancient Rome)—they find the space always too narrow for them; from Point de Galle to the Himalaya, from the Bay of Bengal to the Persian Gulf, it is always too confined. At times the plea is commerce, legitimate commerce; Hindostan and China are grasped at; it is quite legitimate—we do not want their territory, we only want to trade with them. At other times the premeditated robbery is glossed over with a religious pretence—the conversion of the heathen—a noble theme for declamation. A national insult will also serve the purpose, as at Algiers. A wish to serve Africa forms the excuse for an expedition to the Niger, the real object being enslaving the unhappy Negro, dispossessing him of his lands and freedom. I prefer the manly robber to this sneaking, canting hypocrisy, peculiar to modern civilization and to Christian Europe. (1850, 38)

The injunction to love our neighbors as ourselves, Knox tells us, is an admirable one, except that race gets in the way. If you ask the Dutch Boor [*sic*] what the source of his contempt and hatred of the Hottentot, the Negro, or the Caffre is, the answer will be race. Ask him what is their warrant, their right to reduce these races to slavery and bondage, to rob them of their lands and enslave their children, he will, if he is an honest and straightforward man, point to the firearms suspended over his mantelpiece and say "There is my right!" The statesmen of modern Europe dissemble, claiming treaties, protocols, alliances, and principles, but the result is the same: robbery, plunder, seizure of others' lands (1850, 39).

The most interesting aspects of Knox's book for the purposes of this study, however, are not his rantings about race, nor even his exposure of imperial intent and his antipathy to its hypocritical claims.

More pertinent in this context is the second paragraph of the preface where there is a clear statement of the contention that underlies my book: the contention that character was perceived as closely allied and associated with race. According to Knox, "Human character, individual and national, is traceable solely to the nature of that race to which the individual or nation belongs" (1850, 7). Elsewhere he states that all aspects of human character, individual, social, or national, can be traced "to the all-pervading, unalterable, physical character of race" (23). Much of Knox's book sets out to confirm this connection. Character, according to him, is not only resolutely but also eternally tied to race. It is immutable and cannot be influenced by climate or context. As an example he puts forth the Irish Celt and the Saxon-English who have not amalgamated in seven hundred years of absolute possession, the Cymbri of Wales who remain as they were, and the Caledonian who still lingers unaltered on the wild shores of his lochs and friths, eking out a meager subsistence from the narrow patch of soil left him by the austere climate of his native land. "Transplant him to another climate, a brighter sky, a greater field, free from the trammels of artificial life, the harnessed routine of European civilization; carry him to Canada; *he is still the same*; mysterious fact" (21).

Knox then takes up the example of the *habitans* of French Canada: "Seignories, monkeries, jesuits, grand domains; idleness, indolence, slavery; a mental slavery, the most dreadful of all human conditions. See him cling to the banks of rivers, fearing to plunge into the forest; without self-reliance; without self-confidence. If you seek an explanation, go back to France; go back to Ireland, and you will find it there: it is the race" (21). Race is destiny; it is the sole determinant of character. Even in the free United States, according to Knox, the Celt is distinct from the Saxon and does not understand what the latter means by independence. "With me," claims Knox, "the Anglo-Saxon in America is a Saxon, and not a *native*: the Celt will prove a Celt wherever he is born, wherever he is found. The possible conversion of one race into another I hold to be a statement contradicted by all history" (22). History is no chapter of accidents in Knox's view, but distinctly attributable to race (23).

As to the Celtic character, Knox appeals to his Saxon brothers to judge the accuracy of his estimate: "Furious fanaticism; a love of war and disorder; a hatred for order and patient industry; no accumulative habits; restless, treacherous, uncertain: look at Ireland. This is the dark side of the character. But there is a bright and brilliant view which my readers will find I have not failed to observe" (27). Knox does not elaborate, however. He then makes an extremely revealing point: "As a Saxon, I abhor all dynasties, monarchies and bayonet governments, but this latter seems to be the only one suitable for the Celtic man" (27). So race determines character and character, in turn, must determine how a people are to be governed. The significance of this statement in the colonial context is obvious.

The influence of climate or circumstance on character, Knox dismisses as "neatly-formuled untruths" (31). The round head of the Turk is not a result of his wearing a turban or the small hands of the Hottentot a result of a scarcity of food. He dismisses such claims as the Dutch being dull and phlegmatic because they live among marshes, attributing them instead to "miserable, trashy, popular physiologies" (31). In all climates and under all circumstances, "the Saxons are a tall, powerful, athletic race of men; the strongest, as a race, on the face of the earth. They have fair hair, with blue eyes, and so fine a complexion, that they may almost be considered the only absolutely fair race on the face of the globe" (43). Knox admits that they are not a well-made or proportioned race, however, with the trunk being disproportionately large in comparison to the limbs. What is most important, however, is that they are impervious to climate but follow instead "the law of hereditary descent": "Two hundred years of Java, three hundred years of southern Africa, affect them not. Alter their health it may, and does, withering up the frame; rendering the body thin and juiceless; wasting the adipose cellular tissue; relaxing the muscles and injuring the complexion, by altering the condition of the blood and secretions; all this may be admitted, but they produce no permanent results" (44). Once a Saxon, always a Saxon, however embattled.

Knox's beliefs have all been upturned by contemporary theories on race, which have determined that race is largely a social not a biological category. In *Human Biodiversity: Genes, Race, and History*, Jonathan Marks tells us that while racial differences are very significant, they are not significant biologically. Marks gives us this example: If a person from central Africa were to produce offspring with someone from Western Europe, the children will almost invariably identify themselves and be classified as black, but of course the children participate equally in the ancestry of both parents and will represent both their gene pools (1955, 111). Marks says:

> Where racial categories are important in terms of the treatment one receives upon assignment, a great deal of significance is placed on what may be a small genetic contribution. The problem is that the categories are discrete, while the ancestries of people are not. It is the discreteness of these racial categories, in defiance of the biology of the people who are being classified that makes racial categories fundamentally non-biological. They are social constructs. (1955, 112)

Knox is unwilling to concede even the effect of climate on complexion, saying that the Saxon is fair not because he lives in a temperate or cold climate, but because he is a Saxon. A case in point, according to Knox, is that the "Esquimaux" (Eskimo) are nearly black despite living amidst eternal snows. The Tasmanian is even darker (if it is possible, he adds) than the Negro, despite living in a climate as mild as that of England. "Climate has no influence in permanently altering the varieties or races of men; destroy them it may and does, but it cannot convert them into any other race; nor can this be done even by act of parliament" (44). Knox then ascribes even more specific character traits to the Saxon race. The Saxon is plodding, more industrious than any other race, a lover of labor for labor's sake. He is generous, mechanical, a lover of order and punctuality, neatness and cleanliness. In terms of these qualities, no race can compare. He also respects wealth and comfort, and his genius is applicative rather than inventive. The Saxon's taste in the fine arts and music is practically nonexistent, having no musical ear and capable of mistaking noise for music. Saxons prefer instead pursuits such as prize fighting, bull baiting with dogs, sparring matches, horse racing, and gymnastics.

Knox's pronouncement on the Saxon race is echoed in countless characterizations in both adult and children's literature written in the period of British colonialism and thereafter, characterizations of adventurous, restless, eager, energetic, and daring boys and men: "When young they cannot sit still an instant, so powerful is the desire for work, labour, excitement, muscular exertion. The self-esteem is so great, the self-confidence so matchless, that they cannot possibly imagine any man or set of men to be superior to themselves"

(45). "Accumulative beyond all others," Knox adds with disarming honesty, "the wealth of the world collects in their hands" (45). Knox also notes that no race (perhaps) outdoes the Saxon in an abstract sense of justice and a love of fair play. The "perhaps" is a concession to fairness, since he is Saxon himself. But then in another display of his disarming honesty he adds that their love of fair play applies *"only to Saxons"* (47) and does not extend to other races. Justice and fair play are key ingredients in the British perception of their national character. The Saxons tend toward expediency and away from theory, according to Knox. Their ruin has been their selfish nature and their inability to offer the very freedom they cherish to others. In an honest appraisal of his own race, Knox goes on to examine the faults that have been their undoing:

> Hypocrisy and unscrupulous selfishness are blemishes, no doubt, in the Saxon element of mind; they lead to sharp practices in manufactures, which have, somehow or other, a strange connection with dishonesty; they give to Saxon commerce a peculiar character, and to Saxon war a vulgar, low, and mercenary spirit, cold and calculating; profitable wars, keenly taken up, unscrupulously followed out. The plains of Hindostan have been the grand field for Saxon plunder: the doings there are said to be without a parallel in history. (1850, 61)

Knox subscribes to two contending principles: the Newtonian view of the law of unity of the organization and what he terms the law of deformation, which he also describes as the law of individuality, of species. Just as he denies the influence of context or climate on character, he denies the possibility of any change or admixture arising from intermarriage. There are two reasons for this: the innate hostility between races and the fact that the stronger race will prevail and obliterate all traces of the weaker one. Knox does not modulate his view of intermarriage. One can practically feel the venom pouring forth as he says:

> By interrmarriage [*sic*] an individual is produced, intermediate generally, and partaking of each parent; but this mullato [*sic*] man or woman is a monstrosity of nature—there is no place for such a family: no such race exists on the earth, however closely affiliated the parents may be. To maintain it would require a systematic

course of intermarriage, with constant draughts from the pure races whence the mixed race derives its origin. Now, such an arrangement is impossible. Since the earliest recorded times, such mixtures have been attempted and always failed; with Celt and Saxon it is the same as with Hottentot and Saxon, Caffre and Hottentot. (1850, 66)

It is with regard to the "dark races of men" that Knox unleashes the full force of his invective. The struggle between the fair and the dark races he calls "the old tragedy" (149) and he goes on to frame that struggle in a succession of oppositions: "the strong against the feeble; the united against those who knew not how to place even a sentinel; the progressists against those who stood still—who could not or would not progress" (149). Look around the globe, he says, and it is the same story. The dark races stand still while the fair progress. How else can a company of London merchants lord it over a hundred million colored men in Hindustan? Or the Celtic race prepare to seize Northern Africa or the British to annex New Zealand?

Knox is convinced that there is a physical and consequently psychological inferiority in the dark races. This has to do more with the quality of the brain than its size. He then enumerates the differences he has observed. First, the dark races are less strong physically than the Saxon and Celt. Second, the size of their brain is inferior, not only in comparison with these two races, but also in comparison with the Sarmatian and the Slavonic. Third, the form of the skull differs and is differently situated on the neck. The texture of the brain is darker with the white part more fibrous. Whereas the convolutions of the upper surface of the two hemispheres are nearly symmetrical in the brains of the dark races, in the fair races it is the reverse. Finally, says Knox, the whole shape of the skeleton differs from theirs, as do the forms of almost every muscle of the body. He then plunges into detail about the size and the setting of the jaw, the bones of the nose, and so on.

Knox admits that it is not easy to answer the question of who constitutes the dark races of ancient and modern times. He asks if the Copts, the Jews, the Gipsies [sic], the Chinese can be considered dark races and concludes that "Dark they are to a certain extent; and so are all the Mongol tribes—the American Indian and Esquimaux—the inhabitants of nearly all Africa—of the East—of Australia" (153).

Since the Saxon will not mingle with any dark race or allow owner-ship of land, the only option will be to exterminate them: "Extinction of the race—sure extinction—it is not even denied" (153). This is Knox's portrait of the Hottentots of South Africa:

> Of a dirty yellow colour, they slightly resemble the Chinese, but are clearly of a different blood. The face is set on like a baboon's; cranium small but good; jaws very large; feet and hands small; eyes linear in form and of great power; forms generally handsome; hideous when old, and never pretty; lazier than an Irishwoman, which is saying much; and of a blood different and totally distinct from all the rest of the world. The women are not made like other women. (1850, 156–57)

"As for the Negro and Negroland," says Knox, "Central Africa, as yet untrodden and unknown," does he even need description? "Is he shaped like any white person?" he asks. "Is the anatomy of his frame, his muscles, or organs like ours? Does he walk like us, think like us, act like us?" (161). Knox answers his own questions: "Not in the least" (161).

The past history of the African races is simply a blank according to Knox, and he does not hold out any hope of their ever becoming civilized. The true Negro he acknowledges does seem to have quali-ties of a high order and might even reach a certain point of civiliza-tion. It is here that climate plays a role, for the Celtic and Saxon races cannot acclimatize to lands such as Central Africa or Central America and must therefore resort to enslaving the colored man and thus live in continual fear of his vengeance. Knox dismisses what he calls the idle, foolish, and almost wicked notions of the black man being de-scended from Cain. It is not simply in color that the black man differs from the white but in everything: "He is no more a white man than an ass is a horse or a zebra: If the Israelite finds his ten tribes among them I shall be happy. But what has flattened the nose so much—altered the shape of the whole features, the body, the limbs?" (163). Repulsion to-ward the racial characteristics of black people was endemic and is re-flected in the fiction of the period, even into the twentieth century. In Buchan's *Prester John*, the hero—white, of course—refers to the "pre-posterous negro lineaments" of "niggers." (1928, 32).

Knox awards less attention to the "Other Dark Races," saying that little is known of the dark races of Asia, even those of "In-dostan." India has not altered since the time of Alexander the Great, he explains, which means it has not progressed or changed for twenty-three or twenty-four centuries. The experiment being conducted by the East India Company in educating two young Brahmins will amount to nothing, for "it is one thing to cram a young head with book learning, but quite another to improve the natives of Indostan, who have stood still in the face of European civilization so long, unaltered and seemingly unalterable" (1850, 164).

Knox acknowledges that the Chinese were acquainted with the magnet, the art of printing, the making of gunpowder, and with most useful domestic and mechanical arts, but they could never turn any of these inventions to great account, he contends (188). Like the Indians, they remained stationary. He then concludes that their arts must have belonged to some other race from which China borrowed without comprehension. Knox's representation of the Chinese bears elaboration because of the ease and nonchalance with which he dismisses one of humanity's greatest civilizations:

> Their religion is a puzzle; their morals of the lowest; of science they can have none, nor is it clear that they comprehend the meaning of the term. A love for science implies a love of truth: now truth they despise and abhor. I do not believe there is an individual Chinaman who could be made to comprehend a single fact in physical geography. So profound was their ignorance, their want of foresight and of common sense that they could not send a single person to Europe so as to give any information about the armament which ultimately overthrew and plundered them. An English or French engineer possesses more practical knowledge than the united *savans* of their empire. (1850, 188)

In response to the contention that they were recording eclipses while Europe was in the Dark Ages, Knox replies that the recording of eclipses calls for no great effort of the mind (189). To those who point to their canals and bridges as proof of their civilization, Knox's response is to point out that by that criterion the bee, the wasp, and the ant should all be considered civilized. Mere mechanical art is no proof of high intelligence, he says, and finally dismisses them as a nation without a true history, devoid of all principle, "essentially a nation of liars" (189).

Knox spends much less time and energy on the Arabs, the Australian and Tasmanian races, the Malay, the many tribes of Hindustan, or the natives of Madagascar, Borneo, Sumatra and the Eastern Isles. "The reason," he says, is simple: "Scarcely anything positive is known of them" (190). He notes, however, that the reproductive organs in the Tasmanian are said to be quite peculiar in both the man and the woman and that it has been reported that the Australian woman ceases to be productive after intermarriage with one of the fair races. In regard to the American races, Knox's proposition is that they were in descent when the Europeans first landed, gradually becoming extinct. Having passed through countless periods of existence, they were just living on the crumbs of a past generation, for this is the race that built and inhabited Copan. The chief characteristic of the American copper-colored race, according to Knox, is a flat or depressed forehead. Once again, in regard to the Americas, he comes up with one of his witty and revealing invectives: "Whilst I write this the Saxon race is at work in America, clutching at empires. The go-ahead principle (meaning want of all principle) is at work" (168). Knox refers to the futility of importing bonded labor and reiterates his contention that the white man cannot colonize a tropical country. It must revert to those races whose constitution is adapted to the climate. He rebukes those who think they continue to lord it over the Negro (a race he concedes can be energetic) as they do over feeble races like the Hindus or Chinese with a few European bayonets, levying taxes and land-rent and holding a monopoly of trade, furnishing them with salt at fifty times its value. "Why not call everything by its right name?" he asks and this is one of the main arguments of his book.

Knox's intention is simply to describe the various characteristics of the races, establish a hierarchy in terms of those characteristics, and expose the hypocrisy of those who will not make the connection between character and race or who believe that those characteristics can be modified, adapted, or bettered. This is Knox's final solution:

> I here conclude this brief and hasty and imperfect sketch of the dark races. No one seems much to care for them. Their ultimate expulsion from all lands which the fair races can colonize seems almost certain. Within the tropic, climate comes to the rescue of those whom Nature made, and whom the white man strives to destroy; each race of white men after their own fashion: the Celt, by the sword; the Saxon, by conventions, treaties, parchment, law. The result is the same—the robbing the coloured races of their lands and liberty. (1850, 210)

It is a typical Knox statement, a combination of honesty and heterodoxy. The most forbidding aspect of Knox's work is that it cannot be dismissed as the ramblings of a racist or as an outburst from a man whose brain is half-cocked. Not only would his pseudoscientific conclusions have been considered respectable, they would have been considered rational and acceptable as well. "After Darwin, it became accepted to shrug your shoulders at genocide," says Lindqvist (1996, 130). Racism was espoused by many reputable citizens, scientists and lay alike. Indeed, it was part of mainstream thought. On January 19, 1964, the Anthropological Society in London arranged a debate on the extinction of the lower races. It was argued that more highly developed races must displace less highly developed ones. The moral and intellectual superiority of the Anglo-Saxon race will prevail. The disappearance of the lower races was only a question of time (Lindqvist 1996, 131–32).

A. R. Wallace, the codiscoverer of the theory of evolution, explained that extermination was just another name for natural selection. "Contact with Europeans leads the lower, mentally underdeveloped peoples of other continents to inevitable destruction," says Wallace. The European's superior physical, moral, and intellectual qualities mean that he reproduces himself at the expense of the savage, "'just as the weeds of Europe overrun North America and Australia, extinguishing native productions by the inherent vigour of their organisation, and by their greater capacity for existence and multiplication'" (Lindqvist 1996, 132). On March 27, 1866, Frederick Farrar gave a lecture on "Aptitude of the Races in the Ethnographical Society," Lindqvist tells us. He divided the races into three groups: savage, semicivilized, and civilized. The Aryan and the Semitic he placed in the last group, the Chinese in the second, as they had once been brilliant but suffered from "arrested development," while the so-called savage races belonged, of course, to the first group. The savage races, said Farrar, are without a past or a future, doomed to extinction even as races far nobler than they have been doomed before them. Not one single man of note has been produced out of their "teeming myriads" and, if they were to be wiped out by a catastrophe, they would leave behind no trace other than their actual physical remains. Farrar calls them "irreclaimable" savages because the only way in which they are influenced by civilization is to disappear before the face of it. Many races have already disappeared and many more are doomed to go under: "Because darkness, sloth, and brutal ignorance cannot co-exist with the advance of knowledge, industry, and light" (Lindqvist 1996, 135).

Then, of course, there is Herbert Spencer, who incorporated Darwin's theory of speciation into his own understanding of the ebb and flow of civilizations, societies, and social institutions. It is Spencer who provided the picturesque phrases with which we understand Darwin's concepts: "the survival of the fittest" and "nature red in tooth and claw" (Ann Arbor Science Collective 1977). Spencer saw nature working through a "purifying process" by which animals kill off those of their kind who are sickly, aged, or malformed, also operating in human society: "The poverty of the incapable, the distresses that come upon the imprudent, the starvation of the idle, and those shoulderings aside of the weak by the strong, which leave so many 'in shallows and in miseries,' are the decrees of a large, far-seeing benevolence" states Houghton (see Winks 1963, 62). "Incapable," "imprudent," "idle," and "weak" implicate traits of character rather than physical, social, or economic conditions as causation for calamitous circumstances. It is significant that Spencer should look for natural selection in terms of character, and it indicates how character became one of the criteria, in addition to intelligence and physique, for natural selection and the survival of the fittest. For, when Spencer speaks of human nature, he speaks not only of biology but also of character.

The great patriarch of racist theories, sometimes known as the Father of Racism, was Joseph-Arthur, Comte de Gobineau. Like Knox, Gobineau believed that there are innate inequalities among the various human races. His contentions are very similar to those of Knox, despite the fact that Knox challenges him on a few points. Gobineau's *Essai sur l'Inegalite des Races Humaines* was published in 1854. Like Knox, Gobineau believes the racial question to be the central one, the key to all other issues. There is little need to go into Gobineau's theories (if they can be dignified by that term) in detail. There is a great deal of overlap with Knox.

In brief, Gobineau divides the world into three basic races. The "negroid" is the lowest and is placed at the foot of the ladder. The essential feature of this race is its animal character that is exemplified by the shape of the pelvis and is stamped on the Negro from birth while it foreshadows his destiny. His intellect will always be limited and his mental faculties dull or nonexistent, but he possesses an intensity of desire, and thus of will, that may be called terrible. The Negro's senses, especially taste and smell, are developed to a further extent than in the other two races. This is the proof of his inferiority. He eats voraciously, excessively, and without discrimination: "his inordinate desires are satisfied with all, however coarse or even horrible" (1854, 135).

The Negro is unstable, capricious, and cannot be tied down. As a result, he cannot distinguish between good and evil. He single-mindedly pursues his desires. And "Finally, he is equally careless of his own life and that of others: he kills willingly, for the sake of killing; and this human machine, in whom it is so easy to arouse emotion, shows, in face of suffering, either a monstrous indifference or a cowardice that seeks a voluntary refuge in death" (1854, 135). If we think about the Nazi extermination of six million Jews or the five to eight million deaths that were a direct result of the slave labor enforced in the Congo during the rule of King Leopold of Belgium, the patent falsehood of Gobineau's application of such traits to any one racial group becomes apparent. In his stunning account of this horrific period, Adam Hochschild comments in *King Leopold's Ghost* that, although statistics about mass murder are hard to prove, if this number turns out to be even half as high, that would make the Congo "one of the major killing grounds of modern times" (3). Gobineau does concede, however, that the Negro is not a mere brute, because behind his low receding brow, in the middle of his skull, there are signs of a powerful energy even if it is directed to crude objectives (135).

The "yellow race" Gobineau describes as the exact opposite of this type. The skull points forward, not backward; the forehead is wide and bony, often high and projecting. The shape of the face Gobineau sees as triangular with the nose and chin devoid of the coarse protuberances that is characteristic of the Negro. The race is prone to obesity and to apathy. He lacks the strange excesses common to the Negroes. He has feeble desires, is more stubborn than violent, and his materialism, although constant, is restrained. He is rarely a glutton and far more discriminating in his choice of food. He is mediocre and can comprehend whatever is not too deep or sublime. He is utilitarian and respects order. He is practical and adaptive but not inventive. He understands the value of limited freedom. This race constitutes an ideal middle class, but can never be leaders or creators.

With excitement that practically exudes from the page, Gobineau announces "We come now to the white peoples" (137). The qualities he itemizes with regard to the white race are reflected repeatedly in the children's books that constitute the subject of this study. That is why the racial theories of Gobineau and others are so important and so significant in this context. This is what he says about the "white peoples:"

> These are gifted with reflective energy, or rather with an energetic intelligence. They have a feeling for utility, but in a sense far wider and higher, more courageous and ideal, than the yellow races; a perseverance that takes account of obstacles and ultimately finds a means of overcoming them; a great physical power, an extraordinary instinct for order, not merely as a guarantee of peace and tranquillity, but as an indispensable means of self-preservation. At the same time, they have a remarkable, and even extreme, love of liberty, and are openly hostile to the formalism under which the Chinese are glad to vegetate, as well as to the strict despotism which is the only way of governing the Negro. (1854, 137)

That the theories of Knox and Gobineau were pervasive and internalized by a wide spectrum of the population, not just those who considered themselves scientists, can be seen by comparing the above passage to similar passages in G. A. Henty's or John Buchan's novels, passages that enumerate these very characteristics as consummate in their heroes.

Indeed, in many of the works considered in this study, in British colonial writing in general, and in works about the American West, the qualities of "energy," "perseverance," "courage," "physical power," "order," and so on are celebrated. It is then no great leap to see the notion of character that appears in children's literature of the Empire as being part of the same context as the racial notions of Gobineau, Knox, and others. Gobineau goes on to make an outrageous claim. He states that since the white races experience an extraordinary attachment to life, they value their own lives and those of others more and, further, they are more sparing of life. If they are cruel, it is consciously so, unlike the Negro. They understand the concept of honor with all its concomitant civilizing influences, a concept unknown to both the yellow and the black man. This is written in the year 1854, a period when many egregious acts of oppression, violence, and injustice had already been committed by white colonizers and by which time the Atlantic slave trade had already peaked.

The white people's intellect is incomparable, of course, but when it comes to the senses, they are inferior to the others, although vigorous in physical structure. But this works out well in the end, because they are therefore "less tempted and less absorbed by considerations of the body" (Gobineau 1854, 137). The racial theorists of nineteenth-century Europe were often talking about racial character, not simply about race as physicality. But, of course, according to their theories, character was determined by race. They did not take into account cultural factors in the formation of character traits; they dismissed or were skeptical about climate and environment as influences. David Brion Davis indicates that while Oliver Goldsmith attributed the Negro's differences to climate, he could still describe the entire race as "stupid, indolent, and mischievous" (1966, 456). Thus differences were perceived as being both environmental and biological. Davis says, "Environmentalists repeatedly associated cultural traits with the Negro's supposed physical deformity" (457). It was Montesquieu, Davis tells us, "who made it a fashion to exaggerate the influence of climate" (457) whereas David Hume had acknowledged the influence of cultural environment and social role on human character. Twelve years after the first appearance of his essay "Of National Characters," however, in 1754, Hume added a long note that was more assenting about a possible link between climactic influence and national character, especially in extreme climactic zones such as polar and tropical latitudes. Yet Hume also suspected that Negroes were naturally inferior to whites because they had produced no civilized nations, no noted artists or scientists or leaders or warriors. Like Jefferson later on, Hume could conceive of a natural or innate inferiority over one that was the result of environment (Davis 1966, 457).

History was discredited. Context did not count, nor did social circumstance. A person's character was determined by biology; there was nothing that could alter it. "The assumption of a universal, fixed, and narrow human nature implies genetic homogeneity for whatever loci underpin that nature" (Marks 1955, 257). Even an admixture of the races would not help, because Gobineau agrees with Knox that when the races are mixed the great get lowered, although he does admit some good results. If there had been no crossbreeding between the races, "the yellow and black varieties would have crawled for ever at the feet of the lowest of the whites" (Gobineau 1854, 138), and that would have precluded some of the advantages that follow the mixture of blood, such as an increase in artistic sensibility. In fact, Gobineau attributes to their "civilizing instincts" the impulse of the chosen peoples (the white race) to mix their blood with that of others (111).

In his important book, *Imagined Communities*, Benedict Anderson points out that the attitude toward miscegenation among later imperialists was very different from that propounded by the early nineteenth-century Colombian liberal Pedro Fermin de Vargas, who proclaimed in his "policy on barbarians":

> To expand our agriculture it would be necessary to hispanicize [*sic*] our Indians. Their idleness, stupidity, and indifference towards normal endeavours causes one to think that they come from a degenerate race which deteriorates in proportion to the distance from its origin. . . . *It would be very desirable that the Indians be extinguished, by miscegenation with the whites, declaring them free of tribute and other charges, and giving them private property in land.* (Anderson 1991, 13–14).

Anderson adds emphasis to highlight Fermin's notion that the Indian is ultimately redeemable by impregnation with white, "civilized" semen, and the acquisition of private property (1991, 14). This is a very different way of thinking, he points out, from the preference for full-blooded natives over half-breeds in which the British indulged. What the British propounded as imperial policy was what Anderson calls "mental miscegenation" (91). Although imperialism was exercised on every plane—political, social, and especially economic—it was cultural imperialism to which the British most readily confessed, perhaps because they regarded Anglicization as a boon beyond all others. Macaulay, for instance, in his famous *Minute on Education* (1835), advocated for English education over the vernacular with the aim of creating a class of persons who would be Indian in blood and color (that unfortunately was beyond the imperial scope) but English in terms of taste, opinion, morals, and intellect. In his ineffable arrogance, he claimed that a single shelf of a good European library is worth the entire native literature of India and Arabia. As Anderson remarks in his note, "We can be confident that this bumptious young middle-class English Uvarov knew nothing about either 'native literature'" (91).

The character of white people then becomes the standard by which all others will be judged, just as it is in the case of appearance, where, Gobineau says, "Those who are most akin to us come nearest to beauty" (1854, 113). Gobineau refers to his respect for a scientific authority and claims to remain within its obligations at all times (104). Specious theories such as his were transcribed from the arena of science, where they claimed to abide, and imported into the arena of politics by the likes of Lord Cromer, British consul general in Egypt who, Leila Ahmed points out, had "believed quite simply that Islamic religion and society were inferior to the European ones and bred inferior men" (152). Ahmed quotes Cromer as enumerating the ways in which European men are superior to "Oriental" ones: "The European is a close reasoner; his statements of fact are devoid of ambiguity; he is a natural logician, albeit he may not have studied logic; he loves symmetry in all things . . . his trained intelligence works like a piece of mechanism. The mind of the Oriental on the other hand, like his picturesque streets, is eminently wanting in symmetry. His reasoning is of the most slipshod description" (152). There is an analogous passage in E. M. Forster's *A Passage to India* (1924). As Fielding leaves India, he ruminates on how "He had forgotten the beauty of form among idol temples and lumpy hills; indeed, without form, how can there be beauty? Form stammered here and there in a mosque, became rigid through nervousness even, but oh these Italian churches!" (Forster 1924, 282). While writing picture postcards to his Indian friends, Fielding frets that they will miss the joys of form that he experiences and this "constituted a serious barrier." They would see "the sumptuousness of Venice" but "not its shape." Although Venice did not constitute Europe, "it was part of the Mediterranean harmony" and the Mediterranean, says Forster preposterously, "is the *human* [my italics] norm" (282).

Racial differences then extend beyond physique and physiognomy, beyond intellect and ability; they extend to perception and to character. Race is seen as influencing the way in which the individual interacts with his environment. As far back as 1894, Benjamin Kidd complained of "the spectacle of the resources of the richest regions of the earth still running largely to waste under inefficient management" (Winks 1963, 79). The same argument is made today, especially in regard to the Middle East where the management of oil resources is a critical and volatile issue. But Gobineau and Knox are obsolete, it might be argued. No one takes them seriously any more. Their theories have not only been discredited, they are considered laughable. Not so fast. Imperialist ideology and Social Darwinism remain bedfellows—it's just that no one wants to resurrect the old terms. David Duke, Jerry Falwell, and Pat Robertson are only the more mainstream and quasi-respectable voices of intolerance and religious supremacy: This is what Jerry Falwell advocates as the Muslim solution: "We should invade their countries, kill their leaders, and convert them to Christianity" (Pollitt 2001, 9). Most recently, he came out on the CBS television show *60 Minutes* to proclaim, with all the conviction and ignorance of his bully pulpit, that Mohammed was "a terrorist," a conclusion he claimed to have reached after careful consideration (*60 Minutes*, October 6, 2002).

Think back to what Huntington is saying. Read between the lines. Think about the political strategy to play up racial and cultural differences between the United States and its enemies, differences dressed up by lofty references to "our way of life." Character counts and it is still being connected to race. On July 9, 2002, President Bush delivered a speech about corruption in corporate America where he saw character (or the lack of it) as the main culprit. He does not blame the system or the ideology but a simple lack of morality, a simple failure of character. On that same day, Sean Hannity of Fox News made sinister references to dark strangers entering our homes in reference to the kidnapping of a white child. The accused perpetrator was white; dark was obviously used metaphorically, but the damage was done. In another segment, in reference toward police brutality, caught on videotape, toward a young black male, Hannity turned to the African American commentator who was visibly upset by what he had just seen and said something to this effect: "If you can be rational for a minute . . ." Hannity also asked him to stop jumping up and down. A day later, Bill O'Reilly, also of Fox News, and another barometer of popular perception, stated that the president must protect us from evil (July 10, 2002). "The association between cultures and crania continues," as Marks comments (1955, 74). And between culture and character, one might add. Appropriating a character type and attaching it securely to a particular people then becomes a political agenda. Marks says, "The study of intelligence and its heredity was initially an attempt to give a biological explanation for the cultural dominance of Europeans. Intelligence and morality were tightly bound to one another" (Marks 1955, 246). And so were character and morality.

Just how deeply ingrained notions of character are, however, can be seen in an example offered by critic David Spurr in his book *The Rhetoric of Empire* (1993). Spurr points out an instance of retrograde thinking in, of all people, Susan Sontag. In her narrative *Trip to Hanoi*, Sontag relates the struggle of the Vietnamese to defend themselves against bombardment by the United States. The book is also an "interior journey" toward an understanding of Vietnamese culture. At one point, Sontag contrasts the Vietnamese with the neighboring nations of Laos and Cambodia. The influence in those countries, she states, is Indian or "Southern," an eclectic blend of Hinduism and Buddhism. On the other hand, "Vietnam presents the paradox of a country sharing the same severely tropical climate but living by the classical values—hard work, discipline, seriousness—of a country with a temperate or cold climate" (Spurr 1993, 40). So deeply embedded in Western consciousness and discourse is the association between race and character that even someone as iconoclastic as Susan Sontag has internalized it. True, the reference to race is in the guise of climate, but cold and temperate climates are usually associated with white people and "classical" is a term that has been appropriated to describe *their* ancient cultures. If someone as enlightened as Sontag can succumb to this type of deterministic thinking, or if it is so subliminal that she is not even aware that she is participating in it, then what hope is there for the likes of Hannity and O'Reilly? As Spurr remarks, "The point is not to make a Stanley out of Susan Sontag, but to show that her discourse incorporates the classic colonial standards of Western civility—hard work, discipline, sexual continence—in passing judgment on the darker races. Sontag's imagination colonizes Vietnam as an outpost of classical *American* values, free from the Southern or Indian influences of the sensuous, exotic east" (41).

Character determinism, as it might be termed, then becomes the context within which we are led to understand—or rather, misunderstand—ourselves. Our self-concept is developed not only through our own experiences and environment, it is also handed down—handed down not necessarily by our own society but by the dominant one whence it is accepted and internalized. Aside from physical self-reliance, principles and morals are among the first things we teach children. The values that are imparted to the child are derived from the group as well as the family, though of course individual development cannot be discounted. The upper-middle-class, Western-educated elite of colonized nations internalized the connection between culture and character so prevalent in the literature of colonialism and so pervasive in contemporary epistemological formations. They then began to despise those traits that they believed were innate to both their race and their nation, traits that were the reverse of the ruling Europeans' characteristics. For example, as Leila Ahmed indicates, Qassim Amin, a French-educated Egyptian lawyer, assumed and proclaimed "the inherent superiority of Western civilization and the inherent backwardness of Muslim societies," writing that the latter were ignorant, lazy, and backward. Within Muslim societies, however, differences were to be found, with the Turk being "clean, honest, brave," while the Egyptian was "lazy and always fleeing work" (Ahmed 1992, 155). Mister Johnson in Joyce Cary's novel by the same name refers to "our" standards and "our" institutions. Even though he is intended to be an object of ridicule, he represents countless colonial subjects who seriously identified themselves with the colonizer. E. M. Forster shows us that character determinism was so deep that it could cause a complete misreading of a situation. In *A Passage to India*, the Indian doctor, Aziz, pulls off his collar stud and offers it to the English teacher, Fielding, who has just stepped on his last one. Aziz insists that it is a spare, although he wrenches it off his own collar in an act of generosity and friendship. Later this becomes evidence to the British bureaucrat, Ronny Heaslop, of the Indian "inattention to detail" and of "the fundamental slackness that reveals the race" (Forster 1924, 82).

Marks comments, "We define a racist study as one in which the individual is judged on the basis of group membership, and the qualities attributed to the group are therefore considered to be represented in the individual. It involves subsuming the biology of the individual to that of the group to which it belongs (or is attributed)" (1955, 103). He tells us that the first biologist to acknowledge that cultural dominance was simply the result of historical contingencies, and not an indicator of biological superiority, was the English Marxist Lancelot Hogben (Marks 1955, 74). Additionally, Franz Boas conceptually divorced biological history from cultural history (Marks 1955, 75) and questions of human history from the gene pool (73). Marks notes that Boas "did not hold that there were no significant biological differences among peoples, or that 'races' did not exist—only that they did not suffice to explain the variation in attitudes and behavior encountered around the world. They were worthy of study, but not as an explanation of cultural differences; those were the result of different histories, not different biological backgrounds" (73).

What this amounts to is a confusion of biological and cultural categories, says Marks: "To the extent that there may be genetic variation for behavior, specific behaviors cannot be linked to specific genotypes with any degree of certainty" (269). And yet that is just what we keep doing. Today we call it racial profiling. It is even a part of our popular mythology, the perceptions of the playground. A young black child is expected to excel at basketball, while the Chinese child is expected to excel at mathematics, for example. Post–September 11, George W. Bush and his wife, Laura, were judged not only by their actions but also by the character they revealed in the wake of that tragic event. According to the December 3, 2001 issue of *Newsweek,* Laura Bush is said to have spoken "soothing words to the nation." Her steadiness helped her husband. "She couldn't have been more calm, resolved, almost placid, which was a very reassuring thing," he said (24–25). So she was the nurturing mother of the nation.

As for the president himself? We are told that "After the wanderings of that first, fog-filled day, he has been a model of unblinking, eyes-on-the-prize decisiveness. . . . He has been eloquent in public, commanding in private" (25). And when he visited the ruins of the twin towers, he was a model of masculinity and resolve but also of compassion. Bush, as represented in these magazines, betrays the classic characteristics of the empire builder. A *Time* (October 1, 2001) article speaks of Bush's "plainspoken style," "powerful voice," "clenched-jaw poise," "frontier attitude," and the "rallying cry" he issued (21–22). He is firm, determined, resolved, tough, and courageous. Readers of the December 3, 2001 issue of *Newsweek* are told of "The traits that produced success so far—lofty self-confidence, a simple view of history, a willingness to delegate, a reliance on a small band of advisers and on his own charm" (26). The magazine article speaks of Bush as being "jocular," "feral," a "born gang leader," "proud of his management style," "a fighting machine," a man "on the muscle," "full of resolve," "destined to win," for whom there is "no looking back" (28). We see him hunting pheasants with No. 41, his father, as they "talk family, dogs and how the bass are doing in Crawford Pond," presumably in that order (Sidey 2001, 35).

Here, in a contemporary context, we see a direct and deliberate association between character and nationality. We are told in the September 24, 2001 issue of *Time* that "He [the president] picked up a bullhorn, slung his arm around one rescue worker and spoke to the others—and to the world—with a grace that was both convincing and, somehow, *unmistakably American*" [my emphasis] (49). Every action bespeaks resolve, fortitude, and strength. Even his father noticed. "George is so strong," this issue of *Newsweek* quotes the forty-first president as saying of the forty-third. "I told him that I did not know how he got through that speech without showing more emotion" (35). The powers-that-be have been "jolted" into "making tough calls, not ducking them," we are assured in the December 31, 2001 issue of *Newsweek* (30). Other verbs also suggest powerful, energetic, muscular action: "grapple," "galvanized," "marshal" (24, 48, 54). In contrast, the enemy is cast in shadows, lurking in darkness, operating in secret and by stealth, not in command centers but in caves, training in what *Newsweek* terms "the dark arts" (23). This is semiotic language. The terms are metonymic, imagistic, multivalent, and covertly political. And what is being spoken of is not simply individual character but genotype.

In his book *The New Man in Soviet Psychology*, Raymond A. Bauer makes this important point: "The theories of psychologists and prevailing political and social ideas act upon each other. The findings of psychological research carry political and social implications and influence social and political ideas, just as social and political ideas influence the areas of interest of the psychologist and often condition his basic assumptions" (1952, 3). Bauer relays Bertrand Russell's facetious observation that even the experimental animals used by psychologists seem to reflect the national character of the experimenters. Russell said, "Animals studied by Americans rush about frantically, with an incredible hustle and pep, and at last achieve the desired result by chance. Animals observed by Germans sit still and think, and at last evolve the solution out of their inner consciousness" (Bauer 1952, 3). Each nation assumes a national character but that, of course, is a construction that would collapse very easily when confronted with individual disposition and experience. Nevertheless, the notion persists that a discrete national character can be defined and demarcated. Bauer comments, "In fact, it can be said without qualification that, although there is some variation in the consistency of such assumptions from situation to situation in various societies, even for the most heterogeneous of societies it is possible to identify a dominant set of such assumptions, and that they are an essential element in understanding the nature of that society" (1–2). It is these assumptions that this study considers rather than the actual constitution of a national character that, in the final analysis, is a chimera.

An article in the *Washington Post* dated Saturday, August 24, 2002, indicates the mistrust of Muslim child-care providers that followed in the wake of September 11. Parents were often reluctant to place their children in the care of women who were linked to the tragic events of that date merely by the fact that they shared the same religion or ethnicity as the alleged perpetrators. In the wake of a terrorist incident, ethnic character is immediately implicated, a connection that is not made in the same way where white people are concerned. Immediately after the bombing in Oklahoma City, a young white man with a blonde buzz cut and more than a passing resemblance to Timothy McVeigh could probably have walked into an agency anywhere in the United States and rented a Ryder truck with no hint of suspicion—but hundreds of men with barely a passing resemblance to the September 11 hijackers were evicted from aircrafts and detained at airports.

Even after the most rancid theories of biological determinism fell out of favor or were not publicly espoused by more humane or liberal thinkers, especially as the nineteenth century gave way to the twentieth, the conviction that there was such a thing as character determinism persisted. After all, this was not as invidious a notion as outright racism. Character could be improved, developed, inculcated. The colonized peoples had to be trained to overcome their natural proclivity in terms of behavior. They had to be taught how not to be lazy, inefficient, untidy, chaotic, dissolute, dishonest, duplicitous, superstitious, childlike in some cases, devilish in others. Until then, and until they learned to govern their lands and themselves by the rule of law (i.e., the law of the colonizer), to govern in a disciplined, fair, and rational manner, their lands would be held in trusteeship. This was the double mandate advocated by Lord Lugard in 1922 (Osterhammel 1997, 110). Colonialism was a political and economic trusteeship—political because the requisite character traits were still not developed and economic because a subsistence economy must be replaced by a market economy, and that too would require the traits of energy, entrepreneurial spirit, and so on. Thus the relationship, far from being perceived as oppressive, was seen as productive, far from being perceived as exploitative, was seen as supportive.

Character became one of the foremost rationales for the continuation of colonialism in its later stages. The inculcation of productive, responsible, and accountable character traits in the colonized was a far more humanistic proposition than the exercise of power, the imposition of force or the exploitation of economic resources. It was no more than a parent would do for a child. Jürgen Osterhammel comments

> If we seek a more general consensus for colonialist thought in its late phase after 1920, when straightforward biological determinism gradually fell out of favor in scholarship, we find the notion (still widespread today) that there is an African, Oriental, Indian (or whatever collective unit is chosen) *character*, which disqualifies non-Europeans from association with Europeans on an equal footing. The lay psychology of colonial expatriates, applied on an everyday basis and continually reaffirmed by the mechanism of the self-fulfilling prophecy, was based on a series of characterological generalizations: the "natives" were said to be lazy, shiftless, cruel, playful, naive, dissolute, duplicitous, incapable of abstract thought, impulsive, etc. However, serious scholarship has also operated with judgmental antitheses. So-called Orientalism is based on the mental operation of distancing inversion, in which "the Orient" is held to be the antithesis of Europe in every respect— static, lacking history, incapable of self-reflection, etc. (Osterhammel 1997, 109)

Most nations have a clear sense of their identity, their purpose, their mission, and their destiny. And most nations have a defining era during which they believe that identity was realized or that destiny was fulfilled. For Britain, the Second World War served that function on an interim basis and the British Empire on an enduring basis. During such periods a clear sense that character is destiny emerges and that character is molded not merely by experience but also by biological determinants. Across the Atlantic, pioneering efforts and westward exploration and settlement enabled Americans to fulfill their character destiny.

It is important to note that British national character is clearly differentiated in much of this writing, even though the white race in general is considered superior to other races. Like Churchill, many nineteenth-century writers also believed that races declined and fell or rose to fulfill divine intention. "Of all the races upon earth now, the English race is probably the finest," declared Charles Kingsley in 1859 in an address to the Ladies Sanitary Association (*Sanitary and Social Essays* 1892, 258–59). It is a young race, he says, and its potential has still not been developed, so one of the duties of its members is to help the increase of the English race. God decrees the differences between the races, although all are equally loved. Some races are chosen as leaders. In *The Idea of Race*, Michael Banton states, "At the end of the nineteenth and in the early twentieth century the British saw race relations in an imperial context as involving them with backward races overseas. Social Darwinism flourished both in this context and in discussions of the relations between social classes at home. Similar patterns were present in the United States" (1978, 96).

The British posited courage against cowardice, strength against weakness, virility against effeminacy, exertion against languor, principles against corruption, morality against degeneracy, hard work against sloth, adventure against caution, endurance against capitulation, duty against disaffiliation, loyalty against infidelity, and the outdoors against the indoors. They saw themselves as doers, not talkers. Benjamin Kidd described the British as one of "the energetic races of the world" (Winks 1963, 79). Reviewing *Desmond's Daughter* (1916), a novel by Maud Diver, a British novelist who wrote prolifically about India, the *Times Literary Supplement* appreciates its espousal of "the aphorism that the true test of manhood is not 'I think, therefore I am,' but 'I act, therefore I am'" (250). Another British novelist of India, Edward Thompson, comments on the tendency of Indians to wax rhetorical rather than to get anything done (see Singh 1988, 200ff.). It is a muscular model of imperial ideology. Spurr synthesizes it aptly: "The distinctly British version of colonial discourse promoted, by contrast, a set of secular and quasi-religious ideals borrowed from the humanism of high culture: a natural aristocracy, a muscular Christianity, the racial superiority of the Anglo-Saxons, and, to use a phrase often invoked in Parliament, 'the trusteeship of the weaker races'" (1993, 114).

Character was how the British triumphed. It was how they gained and ruled their vast empire. It was what made them superior. Character is the British legacy to the world, civilized and un. We are told this over and over again in colonial writing, writing for both adults and children. For a fuller examination of representations of Indian character and the mirror image the British saw in themselves, readers are referred to my earlier work, *The Imperishable Empire: A Study of British Fiction on India*.

A reviewer in the *Times Literary Supplement* could comment, in reference to *A Farewell to India* (1931) by Edward Thompson, "The Englishman has been too mindful of his probably genuine superiority" (42). In *Sons of the Empire*, Robert H. MacDonald describes how Lord Baden-Powell used his publication, *Scouting for Boys*, to promote heroic history, an important tool in the education of recruits. He encouraged the flying of the flag, the presentation of small pageants to illustrate historical scenes, and trips to the museum to view models of Waterloo and Trafalgar. He even suggested episodes he thought suitable for staging, one of them being a script for the storming of Delhi "which made a point of English audacity and martial sacrifice," and he adopted Sir Henry Newbolt's poem about a confrontation between the hero of the mutiny, John Nicolson, and a rebellious native leader, Mehtab Singh. After lecturing Singh on the meaning of empire and the mystery behind it, Nicolson tells him, "You forget that you are dealing with a Briton—one of that band who never brooks an insult even from an equal, much less from a native of this land" (MacDonald 1993, 173). Character determinism is how Britons believed they held the world.

Nicolson's words bring to mind an incident that occurred shortly after the attacks of September 11. My husband and I walked into a Wal-Mart store in Colorado Springs, a city we were visiting just one month after the attack. A man in a somewhat worn camouflage uniform approached my husband and addressed him aggressively as a "man from Afghanistan." Gesticulating with his index finger, my husband corrected him, saying that he was from India, not Afghanistan. The man responded: "I don't care where you are from. And don't point at me. I am an American." Bumper stickers, advertisements, T-shirts, buttons all announce "Proud to be an American." References are made to "the American way." The attacks of September 11 are posited as an attack not only on America as a nation but on the American way of life, on American freedom, on American democracy and secularism, and on American character. You hear people say on TV, "We are Americans." What any of this really means is never specified, never defined, because we are supposed to know. And we do. It is a reference to character. It is as though the ghost of Baden-Powell speaks and tells the people to fly the flag, except this being America, the appropriateness of the place or time is disregarded and flags stream out of cars, blaze out of pickup trucks, flutter in flower pots, hang out of windows and over mailboxes. They are sported on apparel, decorate office doors, pinned to lapels, and flutter in the corner of TV screens.

In listening to George Bush, Dick Cheney, and members of their government demand the righteousness of "regime change" in Iraq, one recalls Baden-Powell's words, put into the mouth of his favorite hero, Captain John Smith of Pocahontas fame: "Our mission is to *clean* the world," he has him say in a play that appeared in *Scouting for Boys* (MacDonald 1993, 169). Even in the year 2003, commentators talk about which parts of Iraq have not yet been pacified, a term straight out of the lexicon of colonialism. Author Niall Ferguson writes in the *New York Times Magazine* (2003) that Americans lack empire-building qualities. Ferguson points out that Britons regarded participation in empire building as a national duty. In contrast, Americans lack the stamina and the appetite for it. Even in a contemporary context, character is viewed as the key element in empire building.

Character was part of the popular mythology of imperialism just as stories (in print or transmitted orally) of action and adventure were. The colonies were the best testing grounds for masculinity, a great place for a boy or a very young man to come of age. "The border," says the chief commissioner in Maud Diver's *Lonely Furrow* (1923), "is the finest anvil I know for hammering out men" (299). Another of Diver's characters, a Colonel Wyndham, comments in *The Unsung* (1945) "the military virtues are the bed-rock virtues" (198). To him heroism, for which war provides a theater, compensates for the horror that it also spawns. Elsewhere, when a mother confides her concern about her son's sensitive, bookish nature, Colonel Wyndham prescribes India, if possible the frontier. Maud Diver's novels were paeans to the watchdogs and builders of the empire, "the decent, average Englishmen on the spot" caring only for "the Job Well Done" as the brother of Mathew Arnold, William Delafield Arnold, described his compatriots in his novel on India, *Oakfield* (1854). In a speech at the Imperial Institute in London made on November 11, 1895, Joseph Chamberlain spoke of the power of character in ordinary Englishmen who have risen to the responsibilities of race. The connection between character and nationality is made directly:

> I think . . . of the way in which a number of young Englishmen, picked as it were haphazard from the mass of our population, having beforehand no special claims to our confidence, have nevertheless controlled great affairs, and with responsibility placed upon their shoulders have shown a power, a courage, a resolution, and an intelligence, which have carried them through extraordinary difficulties—I say that he indeed is a craven and a poor-spirited creature who despairs of the future of the British race. (Winks 1963, 81)

The colonies afforded an opportunity not only for adventure but also for service. In 1887, Sir Henry Stewart Cunningham satirized this ideal in a novel called *The Coeruleans: A Vacation Idyll*:

> India was a stage, on which "the great Liberal Cause" was being exhibited in a phase of rapid progress for the edification of Asia and mankind: that freedom of the press was accomplishing its beneficient mission; that public opinion was successfully combating administrative abuses, and trial by jury judicial oppression; that a great nation was rallying for self-assertion; that with the development of institutions, as near as possible as those in force at Westminster, the future of India, as a prosperous, enlightened, and orderly member of the community of nations was assured. (vol. 1, 56)

Again, one of the chief modes by which this national coming of age might be achieved was character development. Even the most benign or loving portrayal of Indians or Africans in colonial novels contrasts their lack of efficiency, order, and physical prowess with that of the Englishman. Joyce Cary's *Mister Johnson* (1939) presents us with a clownish, chaotic character, the Nigerian antithesis to the efficient, purposeful, and organized—if somewhat obsessed—Englishman. George Orwell's *Burmese Days* (1934), a work highly critical of the British Empire both in terms of its principles and its practices, presents a portrait of an Indian doctor "panting up hillsides slippery with bamboo leaves and blazing his gun at nothing" (45) in the company of his English friend Flory. Maud Diver, referred to earlier, reiterates the contention that "Temperament is Destiny" in her novel *The Great Amulet* (1908) and reminds her readers repeatedly that it is by character, as demonstrated in men like General Desmond, "brave, upright, and of an understanding heart, that England holds India" (*Desmond's Daughter* 1916, 310). The Empire demanded service and sacrifice, which were given to it freely by the best it bred.

In his study of colonial relationships, *Prospero and Caliban*, Octave Mannoni comments, "European civilization and its best representatives are not, for instance, responsible for colonial racialism; that is the work of petty officials, small traders, and colonials who have toiled much without great success" (24). This was a popular perception among colonial era writers such as Diver. Only "Tommys" beat natives, she says, thereby connecting character firmly to class as well as to race. *Pukka* sahibs or true gentlemen behave decently; even the natives know that. In *Ships of Youth* (1931), one of General Desmond's subordinates asks anxiously: "Hazur, when are all the pukka Sahibs coming back to India as before the Great War? Too often now they send us sons of *bunnias* [small-scale businessmen] and *vakils* [lawyers] other than the warrior caste" (123). In *Burmese Days*, Orwell says of Ellis, a boorish, racist, crude Englishman, that he was one of those Englishmen who should never be allowed to set foot in the East (1949, 23). That there was a good and bad character type for the purposes of colonizing was a widely held belief.

The concept of character encountered in British colonial fiction, although androcentric for the most part, was not entirely gendered. Diver, for instance, dislikes an aggressive or domineering woman but, on the other hand, has no patience with women who are weak or whimpering either. Her ideal woman is General Desmond's wife, Honor Desmond, who can ride a horse as well as any man but can also nurse a sick person tenderly. She can combine strength and courage with "that superb completeness of surrender which is the distinctive mark of a strong woman's love" (*Captain Desmond, V.C.*

1907, 371). In other words, the woman must share some of the qualities of ideal British manhood but must know her place in the hierarchy. More on this in a later chapter.

Diver often refers to the responsibility of the ruling race, a concept she takes very seriously. She is unforgiving toward those who forget it. Responsibility involves not only a firm hand but also a fair one, not only maintaining order but also taking care of subordinates. One did one's duty without giving it too much thought and without asking too many troublesome questions, like Flory in *Burmese Days* or Fielding in *A Passage to India*. It was an attitude bred in the public schools and in the ranks of the scouts. One of the headmasters of the famous public school, Harrow, puts it this way "The business of a school is to work and get on with its life without bothering about whys and wherefores and abstract justice and democratic principles" (Mack 1973, 124–25). An Indian ruler in Edward Thompson's novel *So a Poor Ghost* (1933) is upset because the English tend to treat India simply as one big public school, with themselves as the housemasters and the Indian rulers as the prefects, upon which the main British character in the novel offers "Three cheers for Dr. Arnold of Rugby!" He adds, "He set the Empire on the right lines!" (48).

The heart of England is the middle classes, observes E. M. Forster in "Notes on the English Character," and the heart of the middle classes is the public school system: "With its boarding-houses, its compulsory games, its system of prefects and fagging, its insistence on good form and on *espirit de corps*, it produces a type whose weight is out of all proportion to its numbers" (Forster, 1936, 3). Forster refutes the authenticity of the famous remark, attributed to the Duke of Wellington, that "the battle of Waterloo was won on the playing-fields of Eton." He notes that the remark is inapplicable historically and was never made by the Duke of Wellington, who was an Irishman anyway. But this is nothing to public school products who "go on quoting it because it expresses their sentiments; they feel that if the Duke of Wellington didn't make it he ought to have, and if he wasn't an Englishman he ought to have been" (Forster 1936, 5). The world into which these schoolboys will venture, Forster reminds us, is not made up entirely of public school men, nor even of Anglo Saxons, but of a wide variety of peoples.

Of the vast corpus of literature that the British wrote about their colonies, India in particular, four broad categories emerge: adventure, romance, mystery, and domestic life. The first constitutes the largest. Young British boys thrilled to the exploits of colonial heroes in books by G. A. Henty and Captain Marryat, in boys' magazines, and in papers. Such works were seen as an important part of character education and still are. A website devoted to the works of Henty sets out the following statement under the category of "Personal Character":

> Finally, and of greatest importance, G. A. Henty lived during a time in which honesty, integrity, hard work, courage, diligence, perseverance, personal honor and a strong Christian faith were greatly valued. This was especially true of members of the British armed forces, of which Henty was a part. As a consequence, Henty's heroes are models of these virtues of personal character—and always owe their successes to these characteristics.
>
> The young reader identifies with Henty's heroes while he is vicariously reliving their experiences as he reads. These heroes become, for the duration of the story, his peers and examples—and, children learn, almost entirely, by example.
>
> American and British educators a century ago were as much concerned in building good character in their students as they were in imparting to them academic knowledge. This accounts for the great popularity of Henty's works during that golden period of education. (Jagt 2002)

Bertrand Russell took a very different view of the matter. In 1914, he wrote to *The Nation* complaining about boys' books, which he said, encouraged the mad rush into war. This was a "blood lust," a reversion to "atavistic instincts," which had been encouraged by that "whole foul literature of glory" and by "every text-book of history with which the minds of children are polluted" (MacDonald 1993, 16).

Across the Atlantic, the same role was played by popular fictions of the American West. It is no coincidence that a prototype movement of the Boy Scouts that predated its actual founding in the United States took the American pioneer as its model and called itself the Sons of Daniel Boone (MacDonald 1993, 13). Open air and physical exercise became a fetish. They were seen as the antidote to the pollution and problems of inner-city conditions. MacDonald tells us that "The fresh-air theory fitted in easily with the goal of national regeneration, and connected both to the imperial program and to the ideal of the frontier" (24). John Buchan celebrated in his stories a clean, vigorous lifestyle, the life of the country where you rise early and take a cold bath and take to fog and damp as your natural environment, as opposed to the decadent life of the urban dweller. One might even claim that the goal was not simply national regeneration but the regeneration of the white race, and what better stage for it to play out than a potential colony, as yet unconquered. MacDonald quotes a writer called Fred Burnham who, in 1893, saw Matabeleland as one of the last great adventures of empire, a "mingling of the adventurous and hardy from every corner of the world. If there was a single colony of the British Empire that was not represented, I have yet to hear of it" (65). Burnham refers to Australians, Americans, Dutch, and a veritable coalition of the white races, and describes the effect on character of life in an outpost of empire, adding, "The Honourable Sirs and Lords who joined us, fought with us, starved with us, and died as men should, doing their bit, were the least materialistic of all and often generous to their own undoing. Even our rotten wasters and ne'er-do-wells became for a time heroic and dependable" (65).

In *The Character Factory* (1984), Michael Rosenthal provides a chart that indicates the specific national inefficiencies of character that scouting was supposed to address and correct. Character training was part of the primary purpose in its founding and continues to be so. From the very beginning, Rosenthal tells us, scouting was seen as a solution to the moral, physical, and military weakness that was perceived as a national crisis, especially after the Boer War. Scouting was intended to provide for the less privileged what public schools provided for the more privileged: character training in the service of a national agenda. This was no "disembodied, altruistic exercise," says Rosenthal, "but a thoroughly political act with significant social consequences" (1984, 7). This was a movement specifically designed to produce acceptance of one's place in life, blind patriotism, submission, discipline, and the subservience of self to community (7). It was a movement that envisaged the regeneration of the nation and national efficiency, but was also calculated to ensure the stability and self-interest of the upper classes (7).

Along with scouting, one of the most effective means of the dissemination of what I will call character ethics were the periodicals or papers produced specifically (and separately) for boys and girls. The boys' papers, which in the nineteenth century were only a penny or two apiece, regaled young lads with stories of adventure. These stories drew on two main sources: British history and colonial exploits. The import of character development and its significance for the nation and the empire is made unequivocally clear in the following passage from *Boys of the Empire*, a periodical published in 1888. Underlying the periodical's mission and purpose is the belief that in the boy must be laid the foundation for the man:

> The proper study of mankind is man, said one of England's most renowned men; and as the "boy is the father of the man," it may not be amiss to draw the attention of our young readers to the boyhood, if we may so term it, of England, and in tracing the progress of our island home from the time when it first became known down to the present time, in which it stands "the cynosure of neighbouring eyes," to note the not unimportant part boys have played in the formation of that national character which is now considered the type of true manliness, and which is the true cause of England's moral as well as physical supremacy over the other nations of the earth. For as the early thoughts, actions, and habits of the boy give some idea of what his future destiny will be, so does the beginning of a great nation impress all who behold its rise with wonder and admiration. But the beginning of all nations must be ever buried in obscurity, or, at all events, blended with fables and legends from which it is no easy task to disinter the truth.
>
> The transmutation of English boys from uncouth savages, with long, flowing locks, tattooed limbs, and wolf-skin covering, into polished young gentlemen with clear skins, broad-cloth suits, and mouths filled with the wisdom and excellence of past ages, has not been effected in a single day. (no. 1, chap. 4, p. 12)

The argument that underlies my book is made amply clear in this pronouncement. Character counts and must be consciously promoted, and while character needs careful nurturance, its origins are predetermined by race. The allusions to physical characteristics make that clear. Every culture has a concept of ideal character or at least of idealized traits to be fostered, but few cultures are as mindful, deliberate, or purposeful about it as the British in the period of Empire. To correlate success in a campaign with traits of character or to claim for it a national purpose is not unique either, but few cultures are as persistent or decided about it. "There are national faults as there are national diseases," comments E. M. Forster in "Notes on English

Character." No national character is complete, he acknowledges: "We have to look for some qualities in one part of the world and others in another. But the English character is incomplete in a way that is particularly annoying to the foreign observer" (Forster 1936, 15).

The emphasis on character in the literature for children at the time of the British Empire was meant to serve the colonial agenda. Though not as structured or comprehensive as scouting, it functioned in much the same way. Character formation was considered one of the most important tools of the civilizing mission of colonialism and one of the main building blocks of a successful empire. Character is clearly connected to nation and to race, which at the time were often regarded as synonymous. Tablets in the cloisters of Westminster Abbey, for instance, "Commemorate the work of all those men and women of the British race who served Malaya 1786–1957" or "the work of men and women of our race who laboured to serve the people of the Sudan." Race resulted in a particular temperament, and temperament was considered destiny. This was one of the key instruments of British colonial ideology and was consistently used to justify its right to the domination of lesser peoples. Individual achievement and glory were closely identified with national achievement and glory. Heroes were not just individuals, they were representatives of their nation and race.

In an editorial note, the editor of *Boys of the Empire* refers to the penny weeklies of his schooldays, which boys read surreptitiously, ashamed of their fascination with these poorly written journals and with their illustrations of brutal deeds. They appealed to the most sordid instincts of the boys, according to the editor, and their determination to keep them hidden from parents and teachers fostered deceit. So it is his purpose to offer the boys of the present generation reading material that can be read openly and proudly, unlike the furtive reading of the past which "conveyed no lesson of manliness and honour, encouraged no healthy patriotism, and taught nothing that was permanently useful" (1: 1, 23). That he was engaged in a *mission civilisatrice* would seem to be indicated by the following claim:

> After all, boys are pretty much the same in nature and aspiration in all countries under the British Flag. They enjoy the same great inheritance, they are animated by the same spirit of pluck and honour which has made our Empire what it is, and whether they dwell in our own islands, in city or in village, in the backwoods of

Canada and Australasia, in India or in South Africa, or in any one
of the distant outposts of British civilisation; whether they wear
the white collar of our public schools or the tan coat of the colonial
farmstead, they are all bound together by the same ties of loyalty
and duty and responsibility. (1:1, 23)

He is referring, however, to British boys who live in the distant outpost of Empire. The apparent inclusiveness is therefore deceptive. The
editor's aim is to nurture and strengthen the spirit of patriotism and
loyalty and, further, through the agency of the Empire League, to
unite in a spirit of fellowship "those who are destined in the coming
years to carry on the glorious traditions of the British race" (1:1, 23).
The members are not being asked to make any great sacrifices of time
or energy, or to enter into any major obligations, but simply "to undertake by some direct personal effort to make themselves in all respects worthy of their proud position as sons of the Empire" (1:1, 23).

With that aim, the editor intends to put out "a rattling good paper" every week and to give boy readers "exactly what they like, and
not what he thinks they ought to like" (1:1, 23). And what is that? Adventure, of course, for all boys love adventure. It will be supplied
partly in the form of fiction contributed by leading writers and partly
in the form of thrilling narratives from real life. School life at home
and abroad, sports and athletics, the achievements of champion players in national games, the hobbies and pastimes of boys, advice on
various activities such as the keeping of home pets and the collecting
of stamps and coins, the home workshop, seasonable pursuits, and
an exchange mart will constitute the rest of the magazine.

Boys of the Empire was the official organ for the Boys' Empire
League, whose stated purpose was "to promote and strengthen a
worthy Imperial spirit in British-born boys." The motto for the league
was "Many Countries but One Empire." Among its patrons were the
Duke of Marlborough and other titled nobility. Membership in the
league was open to all "British-born" boys over ten years of age who
could join by electing a secretary and sending their names through
him, in the case of a school group, or, by simply sending his name and
entrance fee directly, in the case of an individual. The league's rules
are telling and indicate that it was yet another school for character:

Every Member undertakes, by some direct effort, to make himself
a fit and worthy representative of the British race at home and

abroad. He should count it his greatest privilege, as it is his highest duty, to show by his moral standard, his physical development, his intelligent knowledge of the Empire, his loyalty to British Institutions and to the Queen, that the British race is worthy of its proud position in the world.

Every Member promises to treat all foreigners with Christian courtesy, and in the true spirit of "noblesse oblige" to remember in his dealings with them the traditions of the British race for honesty, manliness, and high courage, and to try to do nothing that would lower his country in their eyes.

Members promise to read at least one book every year dealing specifically with one of Her Majesty's dominions across the seas, and as far as possible with the co-operation of their teachers, to specialise in acquiring a knowledge of the country and its people. Suitable books will be indicated.

Members of the League are expected to look upon each other as comrades, irrespective of what their political views in a party sense may be, and to unite in a common feeling of true pride in the Empire, and a determination to uphold its glorious history. (*Boys of the Empire* 1:1, 19)

The founders of the Boys' Empire League, "intent on stimulating manly effort to some true purpose, and specially to bring the opportunities and duties of Imperial Citizenship within the reach of all British Boys," devised a scheme whereby the two boys who gain the highest marks in an examination will be awarded a free start on a farm out west. This competition was open to all boys between the ages of sixteen and nineteen years in England, Scotland, Ireland, and Wales. The prize included free kit, free passage, and free location with a selected farmer in Northwest Canada (*Boys of the Empire* 1:1, 13).

In a regular series in this paper, an author called Sandow teaches boys breathing, calisthenics, and other methods to make them "robust and healthy, strong and irresistible, not only physically, but mentally and morally" (1:1, 6). Among the prescriptions is a morning tub or, for those who cannot manage this, "a cold douche of water down the spine or a rapid sponge over" (1:1, 6). Once again, the avowed purpose is not simply the strength of the individual, but the strength of the empire. Sandow says,

I never write with greater zest or pleasure than when I sit down to write for boys, and it is particularly so in this instance, where I write for Boys of the Empire, for it is your duty as sons of the Empire to make yourselves strong and healthy.

The standing of an Empire depends upon the grit and strength of its men and women. You know it is to the British love of sport and exercise that we owe the standing of the nation. (1:1, 6)

Over and over the message is hammered home. The boys of the empire have an obligation to develop their physical, mental, and moral character not simply for their own personal improvement but for that of the empire. General Baden-Powell himself, in an article entitled "The Boy Scout," lists as the main key to success in scouting, "pluck and self-reliance" (*Boys of the Empire* 2:1, 39). The secret of these two qualifications, he tells the boys, "is *confidence* in yourself" but cautions them that "pluck must not be confused with rashness and foolhardiness." He adds, "Coupled with your pluck and self-reliance, you must have discretion," explaining that discretion is not a readiness to back out if there is danger, but "sufficient cool-headedness to see how, by using your pluck and self-reliance, you can go into the danger and get through it all right" (2:1, 39).

In the boys' papers it would be difficult to distinguish entertainment from edification. The Religious Tract Society founded the *Boy's Own Paper* in 1879, again for the purpose of counteracting the "pernicious influence" of the penny dreadfuls, as they were known. Stories of conquest are told in a manner that would undoubtedly thrill a young boy, yet are unmistakably meant to drive home important lessons. A feature on Robert Clive, in an issue of the *Boy's Own Paper* published in 1899, takes us in the midst of an assembly gathered by the governor to plan the defeat of French forces led by Joseph François Dupleix in the showdown for sway over the Carnatic in India. Robert Clive is called upon to offer his opinion and proposes, to the shock of those assembled, a bold assault on Arcot, the seat of the Nabob who is supported by the French. In a voice like a "trumpet blast," he appeals to his startled audience "in words of fire, to show themselves Englishmen, and not tamely to let slip, for fear of a few insolent French adventurers, a chance of action and of victory that might never return" (1091:22, 146). No sooner is bravery mentioned than it is branded as British, and the same goes for a number of other qualities. We hear Clive assuring a recalcitrant corsair that he would be safe under the English flag because an Englishman never breaks his word (1097:22, 242). Other cultures might claim the same qualities of course, but seldom are they so specifically appropriated. Which British boy would not be inspired to seek glory in the colonies by the description of the attack that follows?

> A few nights later a tremendous thunderstorm broke over Arcot and the country round it; and the few inhabitants who had not marched south with Chunda Sahib to the hoped-for plunder of Trichinopoly—already terrified by the fury of the storm—were doubly so by the strange, ghostly sights and sounds that seemed to attend it.
>
> One man had heard, in a momentary lull of the tempest, the measured tramp of an army coming from the east, though it was well known that no armed force lay in that quarter; and even had there been any, it would never have chosen such a night for its march. A second had caught a fitful glitter of steel flickering through the dark jungle, as of swords or spears held aloft by many men. A third had seen plainly, in a sudden glare of lightning, a line of ghostly figures gliding fast through storm and rain and darkness, in the dress of the white-faced English of Madras, who, as everyone knew, were cowering behind their walls many miles away." (1091:22, 146)

Far from cowering, of course, the English were marching toward Arcot, which they captured with little resistance. From that day on, the young readers are told, Robert Clive was known among his native soldiers by no other title than "Sabat Jung" or "The Daring in War." It was a name that was soon to be famous through all of India (1091:22, 146).

In another piece, written approximately a year later in the form of a letter, the writer comments on how Clive made good, despite the predictions of his family, and vindicated himself to his ornery father who is reputed to have said, "Well, it seems that booby *has* got something in him after all!" (1095:22, 209). How amazed all his family were to see their "naughty, idle, passionate Bobby come home as one of the most famous men alive, with all England hurrahing over him" (1095:22, 209). Clive, boys are told, nobly relinquished his command to Major Lawrence on the latter's return to duty "and for a bold, self-reliant fellow like him, who had always been impatient of any kind of authority," this was seen as "simply splendid," as was the fact that he would not accept a sword of honor, set with diamonds, from the company unless Major Lawrence also received one (1095:22, 209). It's all about character.

In the boys' papers, character is celebrated not only through tales of derring-do, but also in interviews, letters, and other more prosaic formats. A "chat" with the late prime minister of South Australia, the "Hon. J. A. Cockburn, M.D. Lond., Now Agent-General for the Colony," written by a "B.O.P. [Boy's Own Paper] special commissioner," opens with this comment: "Boys from our public schools who have character, a moderate capital, and brains, can do well in South Australia" (1094:22, 202). The prime minister goes on to talk about the magnificent climate, ample land, and mineral and natural wealth of the colony. These assets and amenities are open to those who long for a colonial life, and for them the country offers excellent prospects, with one qualification. "Only," says Dr. Cockburn, "young men going out must have grit, pluck, and endurance; and these have made Australia what it is" (1094:22, 203). Similarly, in a *Boys of the Empire* article entitled "How to Emigrate," William Weeks advises "Through the unsettled state of South Africa I do not think there is an opening there for any but fighting men" (1:21). And, in a subsequent issue, E. C. Buley tells boys "How We Won Our Colonies." It is a predictable story: "Little of our Empire has not been won by dint of struggle and bloodshed. In America, in India, and in Africa we have had to fight for our heritage, and the possession of those places has only been yielded to us after the expenditure of much human life and treasure" (1:24, 475).

Every issue of the *Boy's Own Paper* begins with a section entitled *A Bold Climber; Or, For An Empire*, which then comprises various stories, mostly adventurous and heroic in nature. Pictures of "Our Public School Football Teams 1899–1900" are interspersed throughout as are various pictures of English triumphs—for instance, one entitled "A Pirate's Stronghold," where bare-limbed peasants stand in obvious contrast to "a stately procession of English ships of war sweeping majestically over the smooth, shining sea, the foremost of which bore an admiral's flag" (1096:22, 226). Readers are thus invited to note the contrast not only between the backward and the progressive, but also between the anarchic and the ordered. Not every section of the magazine is onerous, however. Boys are offered puzzles from India, wire working, instruction in pen-and-ink sketching, in *How to Preserve a Caterpillar* or *How to Build a Sailing Dinghy*. Inside covers in these journals depict scenes from various battlegrounds, the flags of the empire, or the insignia of famous British regiments.

The Rev. J. Vaughan, M.A., warns against the "immense importance" attached to games and the great popularity of athletic pursuits: "Among boys at school the royal road to distinction is to excel
in cricket or football or athletic sports. A brilliant 'bat' or a swift
bowler soon becomes a hero among his fellows; while a boy un-
skillful at games runs the risk of being looked down upon as a 'duf-
fer'" (1091:22, 154). There is no question that athletic pursuits and
games are awarded preeminence, and the connection between skill
at sports and skill on the battlefield clearly seen. It is this very preeminence and popularity that probably launched the Rev.
Vaughan's warning. In his chapter on "The School Story" in *Stories
and Society: Children's Literature in Its Social Context*, edited by Dennis Butts, Jeffrey Richards notes that organized games were used as
a powerful means of social control and character formation to
counter vandalism and indiscipline. "Sport was used to direct energy and aggression into productive channels. It promoted manliness and chivalry through the ideas of team spirit, leadership,
loyalty, bravery, fair play, modesty in victory and humility in defeat" (Richards 1992, 6).

In the December 9, 1899, issue of the *Boy's Own Paper*, in an article entitled "An Unrecorded Expedition," Walter Louis notes,

> No nation can chronicle less [*sic*] reverses against their troops than
> Great Britain; the total known can be almost counted on the fingers
> of a hand. Twice have those sturdy mountaineers the Afghans de-
> feated, but it is a wild tribe on the West Coast of Africa who can
> boast that three times have they worsted the troops sent against
> them. Like the Afghans, they annihilated an expedition, then
> checked the advance of a second, and after a lapse of twenty-five
> years again drove back a large force, requiring a strong punitive
> expedition before they were reduced to submission.
>
> In the expansion of our great Empire numerous expeditions
> have had to be sent out to quell or stay the hand of the surround-
> ing and savage tribes, who, unchecked before the arrival of British
> civilisation, chafe under the restrictions placed upon their lawless-
> ness, their horrible customs, and despotism. The expedition
> against the Mandingoes is one of the many that is unrecorded save
> in a passing notice in the press "that an expedition sent out to pun-
> ish a lawless tribe had received a severe check, but that a larger one
> had completely restored peace and tranquility." (1091:22, 148)

Louis proceeds to elaborate on the British role in mitigating the slave trade through the employment of their cruisers. When two envoys are sent to remonstrate and warn of interference should the practice continue, they are treated with great disrespect according to Louis, and sent the following reply: "Say that the Mandingoes have always been an independent tribe, owing no allegiance to an European, and will brook no interference from any" (1091:22, 148). Qualities cherished as part of their own self-image are seen as nothing short of impudence in "lesser peoples," unless they have accepted British sway, in which case such qualities are appreciated as mirroring their own.

Across the page from this article, a full-page color illustration underscores the connection between intrepidity in battle and intrepidity in sports and games. It depicts a robust football game in full swing on a village green with the captain calling out "Played, Sir!" (1091:22, 149). Pictures of "Our Public School Football Teams 1899–1900" are interspersed throughout the paper and portray groups of impassive boys sitting or standing in affectedly masculine stances, legs apart, hands resting on thighs or folded across chests, bodies tense and rigid, eyes expressionless and lips unsmiling. In an issue dated April 16, 1833, of the earlier journal, *Boys of the Empire*, we read that "It was their earnestness in national sports which enabled the British boys, when they grew up, to gain easy victories over the clumsy crossbow men; and this same earnestness would, in case of war, enable our brave boys to conquer all foes" (11:9, 172).

When the races are held in contrast it is not simply their physical features that are being compared but their temperaments. Cool-headed Englishmen, whose ships sail into the bay in an orderly fashion and in "a stern silence" that contrast "so startlingly with their size and strength, and the deadly purpose on which they were bent," are compared to "their impulsive and childish enemies with a weird sense of supernatural power" (1096:22, 226). In such cases, we are told, the "nervous, excitable Asiatic is always prone to strike first, from sheer inability to bear the strain of suspense" (1096:22, 226). In another instance, "the feverish, undisciplined fury of the East, soon hot and soon cold" is contrasted with "the cool, steadfast courage of the West" (1096:22, 227). In every siege, battle, confrontation, or encounter, boys are invited to view the British and their colonial subjects as oppositional—oppositional not simply as combatants during the period of conquest, but oppositional above all in terms of character and temperament.

That this binary distinction is based on race becomes entirely clear when we compare the depictions of white subjects, those of self-governing colonies: the Cape, Canada, Australia, and New Zealand. These subjects are allowed into the family: "In all of them the British flag flies high, the inhabitants are still sons and daughters of the British Empire, and even though born under the Southern Cross or near the Polar Star, they speak of this soggy little island in the grey North Sea as the land of Home" (1098:22, 261). In contrast, Indians are consistently portrayed as uncivilized, their rulers as cruel and brutal. In not-so-subtle visual semiotics, an illustration depicts a dark skinned, bare-legged man running down steps, hands clapped to his ears, hair on end, eyes popping out of their sockets, a stricken, terrified expression on his face. "Another victim of the Nabob's cruelty," proclaims the caption. Clive stands confidently in another illustration, hands on hips, one knee thrust forward, half-facing another Englishman. The Indians are in profile, portrayed as shadowy silhouettes, shaded dark, while the facial features and eyes of the English soldiers are clearly discernible (1096:22, 225).

It is one of Robert Clive's followers who sets up the comparison between Clive and his enemy: "Were 'the Daring in War' [Clive] to come against him, assuredly he and all his rabble would fall down at the mere sound of the mighty one's name" (1099:22, 275). The cruelty of Siraj-ud-Daula, "the crowned ruffian" (*Boy's Own Paper* 1099:22, 275) is alluded to repeatedly. There is mention of Tipoo's Tiger, now in the Victoria and Albert Museum, and a similar one that belonged to Siraj-ud-Daula, another enemy of the British. Tipoo's Tiger is a mechanical organ of painted wood that, when wound, emits grunts and groans. That such accounts of cruelty were no idle agency is indicated in Stanley Wolpert's *A New History of India*. Wolpert refers to J. Z. Holwell's authorship of the "Black Hole Tragedy" as an account "which would ignite generations of British schoolboys with passionate indignation and outrage against the 'uncivilized natives' of India" (Wolpert 2000, 179). On the other hand, British oppression is quickly and easily justified in the pages of these journals. In a *Boys of the Empire* piece called "The Mystery of Ram Dakwallah," R. T. Simpson writes, "The sowing of indigo is only oppressive to the Bengali because of the strict supervision necessary to be exercised over its cultivation by the European planter and his native servants" (1:24, 464). It is for the planters that the boys' sympathies are invited: "Little know in England of the great indigo industry in Bengal, the adventurous life of the planter, his troubles and anxieties." Pity the poor planter who must endeavor "to induce unwilling natives to sow indigo for him" (1:24, 464).

The boys' papers had large weekly print runs, 665,000 copies for the *Boy's Own Paper* alone. Further, two or three boys shared each copy (Richards 1989, 5). Their influence cannot be underestimated, and the image they projected of the state of the empire was uniform. Everywhere you look in the pages of the boys' papers, the empire is ordered, fair, just, and enlightened. Everywhere you look, the Pax Britannica is being upheld. Everywhere you look, "the steady march of civilisation has planted the white man during the past twenty years in countless settlements throughout the land of the lakes and prairies right up to the Rocky Mountains, and beyond, even to the verge of the Pacific Ocean" (1099:22, 283). F. H. Williams, the author of this particular piece, entitled *Indian and Canadian Sketches*, then goes on to enumerate the "fruitful results of the Government's resolution of the Indian problem," noting that "In the year 1871 the 'Great White Queen' concluded treaties with her Indian subjects, whereby their claim to the soil was for ever extinguished, on the following terms" (1099:22, 283). The terms, as laid out, seem completely reasonable and fair. While it would be ingenuous to expect a paper intended primarily for English boys (though also read by boys in other parts of the empire) to provide them with a critical look at the imperial practices of their country, what they are fed is decidedly and often gratuitously propagandistic.

Similarly, in *Boys of the Empire*, indigenous peoples are seen as little more than animals, with an instinctive but not intelligent understanding of land use, while the white man's appropriation is not only productive but also progressive: "It is pretty generally understood that thoroughbred savages, who are possessed of lands, throughout the length and breadth of which abound grass, fame, water and timber, look with a fearfully malignant eye on the encroachments of the white race. Lords of such a domain, they are happy; bereft of it, they are quite as miserable as it is possible for any human being to be" (23:366). Not all the stories in these journals are drawn from the empire—there are stories of the Saxons, of the Kentish men, of eighteenth-century England, of Flanders, and of the Scottish borderlands, for instance. The material and moral progress of England through the ages is traced in *Boys of the Empire*, as we are reminded in the passage quoted earlier that "The transmutation of English boys from uncouth savages, with long, flowing locks, tattooed limbs, and wolf-skin covering, into polished young gentlemen with clear skins, broad-cloth suits, and mouths filled with the wisdom and excellence of past ages, has not been effected in a single day" (1:12).In one particular piece in the *Boy's Own Paper* at the turn of the century, there is a sustained attack on the Chinese that recalls the raw racism of Knox's assaults. It indicates just how pervasive such racial "theories" were and the extent to which they percolated into writing for children. In "John Chinaman, and What John Bull Owes Him," the author, Angus R. H. Mackay, B.A., T.C.D. is ruthless. This is the introduction to the Chinese that he provides for the young reader:

> Let us look first of all at the man as he is. His head is a different shape from ours, his eyes and his nose are at different angles, and his hair is twisted into a form which the rest of the world regards as the reverse of beautiful. To lose that carefully twisted pig-tail is the greatest disgrace a Chinaman can suffer.
>
> By nature he is indolent, an arrant liar, and an inveterate thief. His house is a filthy den, and his streets are so narrow that two chairs, which is his only substitute for a carriage, cannot pass one another, but the one must back into a shop or dwelling-house to let the other go by. (1092:22, 165)

"He writes," Mackay grudgingly acknowledges, "but the 5,000 characters at his disposal can hardly be said to compose an alphabet, as the letters used are in themselves more of the nature of descriptive pictures" (1092:22, 166). As for his conversation, it is carried on in monosyllables. He has abundant books and reveres them, "but their language is rude and clumsy" (1092:22, 166).

The brutality of John Chinaman is renowned, proclaims Mackay: "No nation on the face of God's earth, with any pretence to civilisation, has ever arrived at the grades of torture to which the Chinaman has for centuries been accustomed" (1092:22, 166). Both their tortures and their punishments are brutal. Having demolished the physical, mental, and moral character of the Chinese, Mackay proceeds to acknowledge their inventions, discoveries, and achievements: the printing press, the compass, gunpowder, paper, silk, tea, and china being the chief of them. Yet the English are well ahead of them "in all points of real civilisation" because they have made steady progress while John Chinaman "has, hare-like, curled his head under his pig-tail, and gone to sleep" (1092:22, 166). Mackay acknowledges their debt to the Chinese in these words:

> Among the nations of the world there is none which appears more utterly foreign to the Anglo-Saxon than the slant-eyed, pig-tailed people of Pekin [sic] and Canton. And yet the Anglo-Saxon owes this strange-looking, strange-mannered, and strange-tongued Celestial a debt which cannot be estimated in coin. Every newspaper which is daily in our hands, all social gatherings where tea is drunk, and every lady rustling in her silks, is debtor to John Chinaman. (1092:22, 166)

Turning to the *Boy's Own Paper* of a later date (1924–1925) in order to see what the preoccupations of empire are as it approaches its concluding era, we find that interest in the empire remains strong: the pull-out section is on arms and badges used in the British Empire with an accompanying article later in the text. Along with the usual arts and craft or hobby pages, natural history information, school stories, and sports advice, we still find accounts of adventure from the far-flung reaches of the empire, but with this important difference. The tales tend to be of pure adventure: cowboy carnivals, encounters with poisonous snakes or hostile natives in the Matabele Country, rather than the triumphal recounting of historic sieges and battles that were so trendy at the turn of the century. While earlier issues did contain similar articles—on Maori burial caves, or a tiger hunt at Calcutta, a Cornish adventure or the Spanish-American War, even contributions by Jules Verne and W. H. Hudson—these were interspersed punctually with stories of colonial victories.

The young readers of *Boys of the Empire* and the *Boy's Own Paper* would have had no difficulty in recognizing (and claiming) those traits of character that were assumed to be distinctively British. In "The Feathers of Uaala: A Story of Central Africa" by W. C. Best-Randall from the *Boy's Own Paper*, we are told of a white man who was left to die (abandoned by another white man, "the unforgivable sin") in the fetid jungle maze of Natomba with only a couple of heathen native bearers to look after him. But the man, McAlister, did not die: "With the stubborn, rugged courage of his race, he had fought death, and Natomba too, and reached down to civilisation to hear reports of his death, and of Duprez's story of how, in trying to fetch help, the whole spoils of the expedition had been lost in crossing one of the swamps" (4: 47, 234). Because he is a friend to the white man who saved his life, their chief is described as regal in bearing and possessed of a deep intelligence behind his soft brown eyes: "It takes a real king to look the part dressed only in a blanket and a feather, but Uaala's carriage alone marked him as one born to regal honours" (4: 47, 234). The picture of Uaala bears out the description as he stands with regal poise before the rather scrawny and scruffy looking Duprez who, at the end of the story, finds that he is the dupe, and McAlister gets his revenge for having been abandoned by him. Another story, "On Safari: A Story of the African Bush" by Major G. C. Cooper, M.C., relates how the African Negro adores meat and will enjoy the flesh of any animal no matter how it died, fresh or stale, raw or cooked. "The occasional shooting of some sort of beast for your porters will keep them in great good humour. They over-eat themselves like children at a school-treat, and then curl up and sleep off the ill-effects" (4:47, 51).

Derogatory racial stereotypes abound in these stories. We meet "thick-lipped fuzzy-headed Matumis," a "semi-savage tribe" with a predictable love of colored cloths and cheap knives. In "Tales of Empire Explorers: An Australian Hero from Boys of the Empire," a story by someone called Firth Scott, we hear of natives who were not only numerous but also warlike, hostile, and savage, preying on white men out of a lust for revenge and vengeful hatred. (1:22). In other stories, boys are introduced to "savage Papuans," Romany who bear off a swooning white woman in a blanket, "sassy niggers," "Irish barbarians," a Jew who practices usury, "an old darky preacher," a "Parsee" with a "magnificent flowing beard," "dark-skinned Hindoos," "coffee-coloured rogues" who "will never tell you the truth," Mohammedans who are "picturesque ruffians," murderous thugs, and a "redskin" called Gliding Serpent who grunts "Ugh" from time to time. In an issue of *Boys of the Empire* published at the turn of the century, young readers are taken on a journey to Africa in an article entitled "In Dwarfland and Canibal [sic] Country: A Record of Travel and Discovery in Central Africa" by A. B. Lloyd, who terms his account "an important book of African travel."

By 1946–1947, the *Boy's Own Paper*, though still carrying stories of adventure from various parts of the empire from the Canadian backwoods to Cyprus, as well as the usual mix of sports features, articles on hobbies, animals and natural history, and mysteries, is far less jingoistic. It is interesting to note that the issue of August 1947, the month and year in which India became independent, makes no mention whatsoever of that event, even though India was the most highly prized colony of all and its independence began a domino effect that ended in the virtual dissolution of the empire. The issue of 1947 does, however, celebrate the World Scout Jamboree where, we are told, "Distinctions of colour, class, creed and race are forgotten by these young ambassadors in their enthusiasm and goodwill. Boys still show the world that the art of being good neighbours is not such a difficult matter after all" (22, 11). Advertisements now proliferate on the pages of this periodical, which has risen to ninepence in price. British products and craftsmanship are openly lauded. The stories still celebrate courage and risk taking but the enemy is more likely to be a black mamba than a member of a hostile tribe. Stories are still directed to "the boy who wants to go places and do things" (May 1947, 22). A small news article tells of three British boys who were among the thirty-six survivors of an air crash in the China Sea. After attempting to save trapped Chinese fellow passengers, they had to make their way through the night toward the coast of the Philippines, in rafts, drenched by the spray of waves. "Tributes were made to the courage and cool-headedness of the boys" who, although cold and miserable, worked with a will, and paddled and bled throughout the hours of darkness. Sixteen hours later they were spotted by rescue aircraft and picked up by an U.S. Army troopship. When they landed at Manila they received a great welcome and, five days later, braved flight again (May 1947, 24). A decidedly Christian current flows through the advice given to boys in this updated postwar version of the paper, its reduced dimensions enabling it to fit easily into a boy's coat pocket. The mind-set of some of the contributing writers to the boys' papers is revealed in the words of Frank Richards, author of the Greyfriars and St. Jim's series of school stories and editor of the *Magnet*. One of the most telling statements in his outraged retort to George Orwell's criticism of the boys' papers is his condemnation of Shaw, Ibsen, and Chekov as "duds" (Orwell and Angus 2000, 488).

That the boys of Britain were expected to own a clear sense of obligation not only to their country but also to their empire becomes clear from the copious references in the *Boy's Own Annual* to the glories of British triumphs overseas. No such wealth of reference may be found in the equivalent girls' periodical, the *Girl's Own Paper*. Even in 1900, whole issues go by with no reference to the colonies whatsoever. There are articles on *Practical Points of Law*, on *Pet Dogs and How to Train Them*, even on *Site, Base, Support, and Superstructure: A Contrast between Ancient and Modern Methods of Building*, on *An Agricultural Village* and *How a Girl Should Dress*, on *Finnish Embroidery* and on *A Girl's Flower Garden, and What She Can Do with It*. There are stories, of course, and poems. There are question-and-answer columns and Christian advice but only rarely an article that connects the girls to their counterparts in other parts of the empire. One such article appears in the December 29, 1900, issue. It is entitled "A Girls' High School in West Africa" by the Right Rev. Bishop Johnson who, his picture reveals, is an African. His opening sentences leave no doubt about his views on colonization: "One great advantage of the conquest of Western Africa has been the gift of education. It has not been altogether an easy piece of work, but at the same time it has been of inestimable good to those who have had the advantage of passing through these Institutions" (61, 196). This school, known as the Annie Walsh Institution, is situated, we are told, on a very high eminence with large and extensive grounds of its own. There are about 120 girls, of which only 50 are boarders. During the school day they don "European costume" but "are at first inclined to revel in their native attire and in the freedom to which they have always been used to" when they return home at night (61, 196). While the girls have given a good account of themselves in examinations and exhibitions, the teachers, one of whom is the daughter of Dr. Livingstone, lament their lack of interest in English games.

The bishop tells us that "There is an inclination among African children to shirk that which is difficult and troublesome, and leaving it for someone else to do" (196). Already he is identifying his people in Orientalist terms as African rather than by nation or ethnicity. The English headmistress comments that

> Evils that we thought crushed appear again and again; with the increase of new pupils there is generally an increase of evils of various kinds which require to be combated. We need much patience, loving-kindness, and firmness in order to check the wrong tendencies which, though small in themselves, are capable of developing into very serious offences. The toil has to be done with hands and knees quietly and patiently, perseveringly doing the same things day by day. (61, 196)

The bishop notes that educated African girls will be a very great factor in the future of the race as the Civil Service and other departments begin to offer increased opportunities for "natives" (61, 197). The bishop also notes that the *Girl's Own Paper* can be found in their library and "in everything that is English great interest is exhibited, and those white ladies who come out are expected to show a very high standard of Christian civilisation" (197). An accompanying photograph of the staff of the Annie Walsh School shows six African teachers, all in Victorian attire and, not surprisingly, looking extremely grim and uncomfortable as such attire must have been in a tropical climate. Five of the teachers stand in the back row, while one sits with the two English teachers in the front row.

Some of the short stories, such as "Visitors to the Bungalow" by Laurie Munro, contain the stock racial references of the time. It is the story of two English girls in India, one the daughter of a doctor who has been presented with an opal in return for curing a young man's toothache. Some crooks try to steal it but a monkey foils their plot by chewing up the stone. The young female readers of this issue would have learned that Hindus worship monkeys and that Carol was actually a bit nervous of Indians (61, 31), but little else about the country. A telling piece is one by James and Nanette Mason that pays homage to Queen Victoria upon her death, published in the February 9, 1901 issue of the paper. Much of it is a tribute to her character. "It quickly came to be recognised that, however inexperienced, she was well-meaning and high-principled" (61, 307). Among her qualities are listed unaffected simplicity, thoughtful kindness, quick sympathy, dignity, discretion and reserve, personal charm, prudence, deliberation and self-restraint, and freedom from prejudice. In noting the increasing proclivity of the prince-consort for politics, Victoria notes in a letter to her maternal uncle, King Leopold of Belgium, "We women are not made for governing, and if we are good women we must dislike those masculine occupations" (308). In fact, although Queen Victoria is referred to as "the greatest woman in position the world had ever seen" and "the central figure of the whole English-speaking race," (306), we are also assured that she always had very clear views as to the right and duty of the man to be the head of the household and agreed with Carlyle that "the man should bear rule in the house, and not the woman. This is an eternal axiom, the law of nature, which no mortal departs from unpunished" (308).

King Leopold of Belgium is referred to as "a man of conspicuous ability and long-sighted clearness of judgment" (306). In a tribute to "Our New Queen: Queen Alexandra" (February 23, 1901) we hear, "But her greatest charms with sensible people have undoubtedly been her attitude towards home life, her unobtrusive ways, her reluctance to express pronounced opinions even if she entertains them, her devotion to her husband and the remarkable tact with which she has played her part during all the many yeas that she has stood on the steps of the throne" (343). The article also relates a touching incident wherein the queen notices a tired-looking young girl standing in the hall of Marlborough House and, on gentle questioning, finds that she has brought with her children's garments that had been ordered sewn on the newly invented sewing machine. Noting the neatness of the work, the queen solicits the girl's confidence and finds that she is hoping to someday purchase a sewing machine of her own with which to support her invalid mother and earn for her more than bare bread. Whereupon the princess orders a food and wine basket to be sent home with her and, early on the morning of Christmas Day, the girl finds a handsome new sewing machine with a card attached to it bearing the words "A Christmas gift from Alexandra" (343). In case they miss the import of this story, the young female readers of the paper are told, "As a straw shows which way the wind blows, so a deed such as this may be taken as a sure indication of disposition and character" (343).

Queens and princesses serve as role models for young girls in terms of character development. There is an extensive article on Princess Elizabeth in one of the issues, which outlines how she is being groomed for the assumption of the throne:

> Her journey towards woman hood is not likely to be very easy, but from her parents she will learn what the Crown of England really

means and she will learn from them why our monarchy stands so firm. The British Crown has come to stand as an epitome of the best qualities of our race—stability, tolerance, integrity, a sense of duty to God and country. She is being well trained to bear the heavy responsibilities that will one day fall to her lot (61, 292).

Although the magazine includes humorous stories that betray the incompetence or simple-mindedness of women, especially in financial matters, it also includes articles that encourage women to expand their horizons. One, by a Mrs. Creighton in the April 6, 1901, issue, entitled "A Purpose in Life," exhorts women to look beyond housekeeping. The author describes housekeeping as "so often merely an excuse for wasting her time on the part of the incapable woman" (421), though she does warn them that "it is always well not to be too professional" (421). But whereas young men were being urged to serve their country and the cause of the empire in contemporaneous *Boy's Own* issues, young women were simply reminded of their responsibility for "the service of mankind" and asked "to think of their duties rather than of their rights." If they use their newly won liberty only to have a good time, states the author, or to amuse themselves, "if they neglect to hear the call to service, to fit themselves to bear their share of the world's burden, then women will miss the great opportunity which is now theirs of becoming fellow-workers, fellow-citizens with men, and of learning how to do that work which, in the great economy of the world, can only be done by them" (421). There is the occasional Australian story but, other than that, little mention of the empire or of the glories of England. Sometimes we are taken into other lands, as in a brief article on life in Turkey in the April 27, 1901 issue, which deplores "its shiftlessness, its neglect of cleanliness and comfort, its despairing acceptance of a condition of apathy, stagnation, and decay" (492). But, for the most part, the papers for girls stay close to home in comparison to those for boys.

For British boys, adventure was the coming-of-age ritual as they advanced toward manhood. Adventure was realized through military campaigns, especially in frontier outposts or rugged athletic pursuits fraught with danger, such as mountain climbing. In an article in *Gender and History* called "Domesticating the Frontier: Gender, Empire and Adventure Landscapes in British Cinema 1945–59,"

Wendy Webster points out that in her Christmas broadcast in 1952, before her coronation, Queen Elizabeth II spoke of the need "to keep alive that courageous spirit of adventure," a spirit which, she said "still flourishes in the old country and in all the younger countries of our Commonwealth" (Webster 2003, 86). Webster also points out that the film "The Conquest of Everest" opens with scenes of Elizabeth's coronation, with cheering crowds juxtaposed against images of newspaper headlines. After all, the two climbers were from Commonwealth countries, although it was Edmund Hilary, as a white man, who embodied the spirit of British adventurers. Webster states that "Most scholars date the demise of the adventure hero to the Western Front of 1914–1918, when the immobilisation, dismemberment and slaughter of trench warfare wrote the obituary of active masculinity in quest of military glory." After 1918, Martin Green argues, "the adventure of imperialism had lost intellectual and moral credibility" (85). Children's adventure stories, however, remained a homosocial world that still promoted the questing adventurer and explorer as hero.

The connection between qualities of character and national or racial identity is clearly delineated in the children's literature that was written in the era of the British Empire. In recent literature it is more subtly linked, with the connection sometimes indirectly stated and sometimes simply implied. In earlier stories, especially, race is construed not just as lineage but also as patrimony. National character becomes imbricated with individual character, manners with morals. In character ethics, the interweaving strands of politics, culture, race, history, and pseudoscience are clearly discernible. Since character was emphasized so strongly and so coherently by parents, teachers, public schools, scouting groups, books, papers, and magazines, children would naturally have considered it one of the most important aspects of their development. Having the "right" character then becomes as important as having the "right" attitude or point of view (both of which participated in character construction), or being of the "right" class or race, which was also connected. The inculcation of certain character traits was not an isolated, peculiar, or discrete aspect of personality development but intrinsic to a unified ideology of race. It was the duty, the responsibility—in fact, the obligation—of those of superior endowment to extend those advantages to the less fortunate. Resilience, raw courage, daring, endurance, hardiness, duty, loyalty, and sacrifice: these were the qualities that were considered the inheritance of a white, English especially, male child. To those who lack this birthright, he must extend his patronage and protection. To civilize the wilderness he finds around him, whether in the form of a vestigial landscape or the atavism of ancient cultures, then becomes his manifest destiny. He must not only dominate but also domesticate his environment. And while he may recognize and acknowledge the nobility of some of his subject peoples, it is a nobility that is instinctive and intuitive and therefore inferior to his own, which is the outcome of selective breeding, of lineage.

For instance, while the native of one of the colonies might act honorably, he does so by impulse rather than because of the rational sense of fair play so carefully nurtured in the Englishman. While colonizer and colonized may share athletic prowess and an understanding of manliness, the latter will lack the purpose and sense of service and of course the Christian sensibilities that underpin the actions of the former. Needless to say, character formation was seen as far more essential to the development of men than of women in the growth and maintenance of empire, but women were by no means exempt. Patience, purity, virtue, loyalty, persistence, thrift, and industry were among the attributes desirable for the female partner in the colonial enterprise.

Notions of character and their connection to nation were the direct successors of notions of biology and their connection to race. Neither notion, nor their resulting representations, was innocent. Whether conscious or unconscious, the focus on character in much of children's literature was part of a program, a political and social program that was driven by global concerns and market forces. In *Britannia's Children: Reading Colonialism through Children's Books and Magazines,* Kathryn Castle writes:

> The "crossover" between these two worlds, of school texts and leisure pursuits, was a common occurrence and helped to blur and merge the function of "instruction" and "entertainment." In a sense both worked together to fashion an Empire for the young. For the youngest pupils there was little difference between the stories in their readers and the papers or annuals they might read for pleasure. Stories by popular adventure writers appeared in both, and it was not uncommon for fiction writers to turn their hand,

like Kipling and Henty, to the history textbook. Senior pupils could break from preparation for examinations which stressed the military successes of Empire and find famous military men recounting their experiences in periodical features such as "Great Sieges in History" or "Pictures from the Book of Empire." Activities such as the Boy Scouts and Girl Guides, the Duty and Discipline Movement, Empire Days and the other agencies of socialization stressed values which were echoed or advertised in both school and leisure materials, and again served as bridges between the more and less formal agencies of children's instruction. (1996, 6)

Although each of the major colonial powers indulged in an idea of itself that was different and distinct from the others, they also shared a faith in the importance of character and recognized its role in nation building and the ideology of empire. That there were obvious commonalities in their conceptions of their national character is telling. It points toward a shared experience of privilege and a shared history of power, an unwritten and unspoken collusion in the employment of racial imagery, in myth making, and in the production of imperial propaganda.

The discourse of character formation became necessary to the discourse of empire. As children read tales of adventure and exciting exploits, they envied those who were engaged in them and aspired to emulate them some day. Books were breeding a new generation of empire builders who, even as they thrilled to the inherent dangers involved, imbibed the qualities necessary for successful engagement. Children's literature thus colluded, consciously or not, in the process and propagation of the national narrative and the exploits of those whom it inspired. What emerged is a coherent construction of character that is closely allied to race, and, occasionally, to class. This became the prototype for generations of children who aspired to roles of leadership and control.

It is the emphasis on character in so many children's books and its employment on behalf of a political agenda that first propelled this study. I noticed not only the degree of attention afforded to character traits but also the congruence of those traits. Whether we are dealing with books written or set at the end of the nineteenth century, in the early part of the twentieth century, or in the middle of the twentieth century, a notional child emerges that embodies the idealized traits of character that was so much a part of the British sense of self. This child is not simply an ideal, however; he (it is usually though not always a he) is also a teaching tool, a teaching tool for self-development, so that a young reader might strive to acquire similar traits in himself and better gauge his place in the world.

A volume published in 1928 by the Macmillan Company is particularly revealing. From the preface we know that it was one of many that provided lists of best stories for the use of parents and teachers. It is called, quite directly, *A Guide to Literature for Character Training* and written by Edwin D. Starbuck. The book is indeed a project of the Institute of Character Research of the University of Iowa. In 1919, the author tells us, the Character Education Institution at Washington, D.C., offered a prize of $20,000 for the best statement of methods of character training in the public schools. In almost every state, committees of educators were appointed and twenty-six of them submitted plans. The plan submitted by the Iowa Committee won the prize and resulted in the publication of their book (1928, ix).

Character training has become a popular political cause and contemporary educational trend as well. The state of Utah presently incorporates it into its curriculum as a formal policy. The Governor's Music and Education Program celebrating the 2002 Olympic Winter Games in Salt Lake City actually used the old saying: "Character is destiny" in its website.

The Value and Character Education Implementation Guide of the Georgia State Department of Education, dated August 1977, includes patriotism in its character curriculum. Patriotism is defined as support for the U.S. constitution and love for the United States of America. So far, so good. But when they add "with zealous guarding of the authority and interests" (http://chiron.valdosta.edu), it introduces an element of empire into the equation.

Books such as *Personal Character and National Destiny* by Harold B. Jones are popular across a wide spectrum. Jones argues the role that strong personal character plays in allowing an individual to overcome nearly any form adversity. It is an old argument, one that writers of empire often used and one that may be met with in Henty's idea of heroism. But Jones focuses on qualities and values that he sees as quintessentially American: self-reliance and self-achievement, faith, honesty, perseverance, and so on. In his review of the book on the publisher's website, Gary Quinlivan, dean of the Alex G. McKenna School at Saint Vincent College and adjunct scholar of the Acton Institute, writes, "Economic personalism, the normative philosophical origin of the study of economics, once again proclaims that religion and its shaping of personal character is the prime determinant of national destiny. Jones' book is a wake-up call" (www.paragonhouse.com).

Character training is neither new nor exclusive to the British and American contexts. Bauer points out that with the approach of the Second World War, the Soviet system began to emphasize the individual's responsibility to the state. In 1941 and 1942 character training began to be stressed in education and educational psychology to a greater extent than before. Articles by both psychologists and educators on "strength of character" and loyalty to the state began to appear (1952, 130). Character education and training almost invariably conform to the exigencies of the political situation and the pressing needs of the nation. Bauer, whose book was published in 1952, tells us that there had been considerable pressure on Soviet psychologists to study the "New Soviet Man" to determine how his particular character traits are formed within the conditions of Soviet society. Both character traits and the conditions under which they develop were defined for the psychologist. If it were possible to conduct empirical research that clearly demonstrated the connections between the two, Bauer points out, the psychologist who achieved this would become an official hero overnight (169). British imperialism, however, was addressing a racial and national rather than an experiential basis for character development.

"Literature," Starbuck reminds us, "is the great transformer of all our values" (1928, 17). However, "While a piece of literature may be pregnant with ethical implications, it should carry them gracefully" (16). Writers should neither talk up nor down to children. To be effective they should be nondidactic. Stories socialize, says Starbuck, "and there is health and sanity in that" (9). But the storyteller is not simply an entertainer or moralizer. "She is through her art an organizer of the human race—its past, present, and future. It is not simply that she is called to coordinate rich and full personalities in her children. She is called to a far greater service. She is to integrate her charges into an age-old body of tradition" (9). So storytelling is bound to character development, which, in turn, is bound to tradition. The role of character development played by literature is direct. It helps adjust the personality, rebuild the "plastic lower-self materials into a higher selfhood of refined tastes, insights, and high purposes and recenters the self in a world of ideal values" (18). Starbuck recognizes that some of the old stories, such as fairy tales, have emerged from what he terms "primitive" civilizations, but the values of "courage, chivalry, joy in life, and sense of honor" that they teach are basal (3).

An updated version of Starbuck's book is *Building Character through Literature: A Guide for Middle School Readers* by Rosann Jweid and Margaret Rizzo, which is advertised as "a literary guide for parents and educators who have embraced the concept of character education." The writers are quoted on the back of the dust jacket as saying that "As educators, parents, and politicians continuously search for ways to rebuild our youths' values, a book like this is key to developing character strength." In the preface, the authors inform us that with violent incidents increasing in our schools, society is asking who will be responsible for teaching the values that will eliminate violence. Character education has become an important issue for parents, educators, and community leaders, an issue that is being seen as the responsibility of not just the family but also of every part of society. The authors' purpose is laid out thus: "Our primary purpose is to introduce novels that show strength of character with guidance for discussions that can raise character issues. Our intention is that the reader will be able to identify with the character issues that appear in the book and develop the ability to evaluate them, determining those worthy of emulation" (v).

The titles Jweid and Rizzo include are wide ranging and include many old favorites, as well as new ones, such as *Harry Potter and the Sorcerer's Stone*. I will address the section on *The Secret Garden*, since this book will be discussed later in my study, and the author's approach indicates that such stories are seldom problematized for children. None of the questions for discussion refers to race or gender. Children are asked to consider the circumstances of Mary's childhood in India and how this upbringing may have affected her personality and behavior, but the circumstances (being orphaned or being indulged by the servants) is not the same as the context (being a white child in a colonial society who takes the superiority of her race and the rights attendant upon it for granted). None of the questions deals with Mary's treatment of her ayah or asks children to consider why she could not treat the servants in her uncle's manor in England in the same autocratic and arrogant way. Significantly, children are asked instead how Colin treats servants. So, in this book that is devoted to character education, Colin's petulant mistreatment of English servants is to be noted, while Mary's despicable treatment of Indian servants is disregarded. Daphne Kutzer notes in *Empire's Children* that Burnett's *A Little Princess* "has not suffered at the hands of censors, despite its problematic portrayal of Indians" (11). The same is true of *The Secret Garden*, where the problematic portrayal of Indians is routinely ignored.

The "teaching story" is, of course, an old concept and not limited to a single culture. African and Asian civilizations have used it widely: Buddhist Jataka Tales and Sufi stories are evident examples. Character education is still one of the main purposes of teaching children about heroes. For instance, in schools, during the annual lesson on Martin Luther King on the anniversary of his birth, his character is emphasized over his political actions. In a review of recent publications about Martin Luther King and the civil rights movement, Anthony Walton writes in *Harper's*:

> She [a second grade child] has been taught that Dr. King's life and career are a quintessential American story—a narrative full of struggle and reversal, but one in which truth and justice ultimately triumph. The story goes something like this: At one time, white Americans mistreated black Americans, but because of the vision, humanity, and leadership of Martin Luther King whites saw the error of their ways and made the changes in society necessary to rectify the situation. The narrative has a clear and clean "arc," as they say in Hollywood. It focuses on an identifiable hero and has a satisfying ending. It is a tale of the sort useful in the passing on of culture and morality to children. (2002, 67)

The "founding fathers" of the United States of America, Thomas Jefferson especially, are presented as uncomplicated heroes. The complexities and contradictions of Jefferson's character and actions, the contrast between his words and his deeds, are not simply slurred over, they are entirely neglected. Heroes are presented as monochromatic and monolithic. The "politics of 'hearts and minds'" begin in childhood. Children's literature is then the place to begin.

2

Fundamentals

The project of a total history is one that seeks to reconsti-
tute the overall form of a civilization, the principle—
material or spiritual—of a society, the significance common to all the phenomena of a period, the law that accounts for their cohesion—what is metaphorically the
"face" of a period.

—Michel Foucault, *The Archaeology of Knowledge and the*
Discourse on Language

It is not enough repeated at earnest gatherings of students of children's fiction who are not themselves children that their subject-matter is necessarily produced,
circulated and administered *by adults*, without this being
in any way an infringement of children's rights. Given
this condition, however, and given the excellent commitment of those producers and administrators of the fiction
to their own taste and judgment, it follows that understanding the texts in hand is a matter of answering the
question, what values are here being urged upon our
children by means of this narrative? After all is said and
done about the indeterminacy of the effects of fiction,
about the self-referring and involuntarily self-subverting
text, the death of the author and the invention of meaning, it remains true that our narratives are our readiest

> and most popular way of theorising the world, and that
> we mark our preferences amongst them in terms of our
> key distinctions of worth.
>
> —Fred Inglis, *Social Class and Educational Adventures*

The first imprinted images that most children see are the pictures in a picture book. The adjectives that are often used to describe these pictures are lavish: "gorgeous," "lustrous," "lush," "brilliant." The pictures are designed to captivate the child and, equally, entrance the parent. They err on the side of excess in this effort, holding out to both parent and child the promise of sheer sensual satisfaction, of visual satiety. Illustration competes with text in pursuit of the reader—or rather, the gazer—and in many instances, illustration overcomes text. They invite a prolonged gaze. Picture books are a depository for images that will become an intrinsic part of a system of signifiers. The text may be minimal or even absent altogether, but it is implicit in the illustrations. In picture books, the illustrations often serve to decode the text, instead of the other way around. Perry Nodelman in *Words about Pictures: The Narrative Art of Children's Picture Books* comments, "All of our conceptions of meaning relate to such structures, so that to 'see' objects is to match the actually meaningless images of them that our eyes provide with the categories we have already established" (1988, 8).

Picture books establish categories that we will revisit over and over again. When Osama bin Laden appeared on our television screens repeatedly after the events of September 11, 2001, we recognized him, not because we had seen his particular visage but because we had seen his typology: in the genie, or in the villainous Jabar in Disney's *Aladdin*. A tall Caucasian with a blonde buzz cut and blue eyes, a Timothy McVeigh, on the other hand, could not be part of this continuum. "How does Orientalism transmit or reproduce itself from one epoch to another?" asks Edward Said in *Orientalism* (Said 1979, 15). Images are one of the most potent means of transmission. Illustrations in picture books most often seek their source in what is perceived as luxuriant, even exotic, rich, certainly copious: the natural world, faraway countries with their costumed characters, marketplaces, urban centers, celebrations of all kinds. Perhaps the richest source of all, for a visual banquet, is the East. For as long as it has been a construct of the West, the East has held promise of mystery and of opulence. Subsequent awareness of famine, poverty, and scarcity has not quite succeeded in dislodging this metonymic association, at least not in the realm of picture books. The association is pictorial, certainly, but it is also epistemological.

In the early period of the British Empire, the word "India" was practically a metaphor for riches, making its appearance as such in Shakespeare's *Henry VIII*, for instance:

> to-day the French,
> All clinquant, all in gold, like heathen gods,
> Shone down the English; and to-morrow they
> Made Britain India; every man that stood:
> Show'd like a mine. (act 1, sc. 1, 18–21)

Novels of the mysterious East were published at a steady clip and included stories of mystery, occult events, strange rites and rituals, the quest for lost jewels, and lush landscapes where danger lurked. Words such as "splendor," "jewel," "pearl," "mystery," "treasure," or "curse" abound in titles. The focus was not only on the mystifying but also on the bizarre, not only on the exotic but also on the odd. The Romantic poets fused the sumptuous with the spiritual, the mysterious with the beautiful, but maintained the mythology of the Orient, painting it in poetic expressions that evoked an ample and abundant geography, a landscape of indulgence that extended even to lifestyle:

> In Xanadu did Kubla Khan
> A stately pleasure-dome decree:
> Where Alph, the sacred river, ran
> Through caverns measureless to man
> Down to a sunless sea. (Coleridge, *Kubla Khan* 1–4)

Keats' *Endymion*, Shelley's *The Indian Serenade*, Moore's *Lalla Rookh*, and Southey's *The Curse of the Kehanna*, among others, also contributed to an epistemology of the East that became established, even entrenched, in the Western imagination (Singh 1988, 11–13).

Equally rooted in this epistemology was the notion of the East as inchoate, a place where evil lies closer to the surface, a more primal, even primitive, place where a vague and somewhat vestigial menace can barely be contained:

> It was perhaps their presentiment that in a primordial land irrational and malevolent influences were most potent, that led the British to accentuate the bizarre and grotesque aspects of India. The persistent comments on heat, dust, dirt, and disease are not merely reactions to the alien aspects of the environment; they are also attempts to articulate and manifest its threat. The emphasis on the monstrous betrays the underlying fear. (Singh 1988, 216)

The East then becomes the place where the wild things are. And picture books provide for the child an early geography of the mind that corresponds to a perceived physical geography, the jungles where wild animals live. A correspondence is established between an internal landscape of fear and an external landscape of perceived threat.

Roland Barthes, in reference to a story in *Paris Match*, where Africa is regarded through a European child's eyes, writes "Ultimately the Black has no complete and autonomous life: he is a bizarre object, reduced to a parasitical function, that of diverting the white man by his vaguely threatening *baroque*: Africa is more or less a dangerous *guignol*" (1979, 37). Places and peoples outside the safe space of the familiar, the ordered, the domestic, the known, are either purely pictorial or detached from the dimensions of humanity afforded those within the scope of the familiar. They are then, to varying extents dehumanized, inviting observation but not empathy or identification.

Although Maurice Sendak's classic picture book *Where the Wild Things Are* (1963) does not specify a location, it portrays a landscape rife with malevolence, albeit on a child's scale. Clearly, the landscape depicted is tropical, luxuriant with excess, one that encroaches on the cozy, comfy containment of Max's room. Just as the pictures famously expand, so does the forest with all its metonymic associations of the fecund and the feral. "That very night in Max's room a forest grew / and grew—," the book tells us. But the forest does more than grow in Max's room; it invades it. Furthermore, it seems to be growing out of the floor and rug, in the room itself, suggesting a subterranean terror that surfaces in much the same way as the horror in Conrad's *Heart of Darkness*, not as an external threat but as a menace that lurks within, ready to molest the civilized world.

The unbridled menace of the forest stands in clear contrast to the controlled cultivation of the plant in the flowerpot. Ultimately, even the ceiling is hung with vines, and the walls of Max's room merge with the world all around, suggesting the ultimate futility of cordons around civilization. It is, in fact, Max who initiates the offensive by donning a wolf suit and participating, as it were, in the wildness that lies in wait, silently around us—a sort of children's version of Mr. Kurtz and his reversion to savagery. Max sails off through night and day voluntarily, as explorers and colonizers were wont to do, and when he comes to where the wild things are, we find that it is quite evidently a tropical place, a place with terrible creatures. The reiteration of the word "terrible" in this context resounds with Conradian echoes. Naturally, Max, with the instincts of his race, seeks to control the wild things. "BE STILL!" he commands. And he *tames* [my italics] them with the magic trick. It is the pacification of the savages through the imposition of a superior civilization. And they, the terrible wild things, acknowledge Max's manifest destiny by making him "king of all wild things." The wild things themselves are almost the prototypical "half-devil and half-child" of Kipling's verse. Their grins veer between malice and mischief, their actions between aggression and acquiescence.

There is some ambiguity here, however, since they first term Max "the most wild thing of all." This recalls the "claim of distant kinship affirmed in a supreme moment" that Marlowe mentions in *Heart of Darkness* (1902, 73). In the illustration that follows Max's coronation there is no text, and we see him simply as one of the wild things himself, baying at the moon in the darkness, his wolf suit outfitting him perfectly for his environment. The next illustration is also devoid of text and depicts Max as a willing and enthusiastic participant in the "wildness." In the illustration that follows, however, the smirks of the wild things, which are as silly as they are scary, fade somewhat as Max establishes his superiority and claims his divine right by riding on the back of one of them, who glances up at him from the corner of his eye with a look of obvious displeasure. Max simultaneously asserts and loses control, ordering "the wild things off to bed without their supper" but then feeling like a lost and lonely little boy.

Max's departure is strangely, almost humorously, reminiscent of the departure of Kurtz in *Heart of Darkness*, where the natives "broke and ran . . . leaped . . . crouched . . . swerved" (Conrad 1902, 97), where they "stamped their feet, nodded their *horned heads* [my emphasis], swayed their scarlet bodies" and where "they shouted periodically together strings of amazing words that resembled no sounds of *human* [my emphasis] language" (Conrad 1902, 96). Sendak's wild things have, of course, horns on their heads. Similarly, as Max gets ready to leave, "The wild things roared their terrible roars and gnashed their terrible teeth and rolled their terrible eyes and showed their terrible claws" but Max, ignoring their pleas to remain and their declarations of devotion, boards his private boat and bids them good-bye. Consider also this description of the reception the natives award the military hero in Maud Diver's *Desmond's Daughter*:

> Then only did the cheering crowd disperse; and the Afridis went back to their hills, quite unaware that, for Sir Theo Desmond, their spontaneous tribute was an imperishable memory—the finest victory he had ever won. And, in honouring the man, they honoured equally the race that breeds such men; confirmed afresh, in their own unique fashion, the unquestioned fact that England holds her supremacy in the East as much by the power of individual character as by the power of the sword. (1916, 566)

Max returns to the night of his very own room, a different night this, a night devoid of danger, where his supper awaits, his room cozy and orderly once more. His room is a sanctuary from the wild things. Max is still a child, but his short-lived experience of domination foretells a time when he might be willing to exchange the safety of his domestic environment and sail across seas to assert his superiority once more. Of course, the fact that his supper was still hot suggests that the entire episode was a dream or the projection of subconscious fear, the id perhaps. Where the wild things are is an atavistic world, prehistoric perhaps, or simply primitive, beyond the ken of civilization. The wild things are "them"; Max belongs to "us." In *Orientalism*, Edward Said states,

> Theses of Oriental backwardness, degeneracy, and inequality with the West most easily associated themselves early in the nineteenth century with ideas about the biological bases of racial inequality. . . . To these ideas was added second-order Darwinism, which seemed

to accentuate the "scientific" validity of the division of races into advanced and backward, or European-Aryan and Oriental-African. Thus the whole question of imperialism, as it was debated in the late nineteenth century by pro-imperialists and anti-imperialists alike, carried forward the binary typology of advanced and backward (or subject) races, cultures and societies. (206)

This division is made clear in *Where the Wild Things Are*. Where the wild things are is *Outside Over There*, the title of another of Sendak's books that is interesting in this context. It is sometimes regarded as part of a trilogy with *Where the Wild Things Are* and *In the Night Kitchen*, which preceded it. "Outside over there" are the great empty spaces of the world, ripe for exploration and ready to be fertilized by the seeds of Western civilization. But, it must be cautioned, it is a world that can compel civilized beings—a Max, a Mr. Kurtz—to regress into participation in its primal impulses, to revert to tooth and claw. It is a world that submits to the Western world of civilization, as long as the latter is vigilant. In *Outside Over There* (1981), the wild things are projected as goblins. They come for the baby when no one is watching, when vigilance levels are low. Papa, the usual protector, is away at sea. Mama is in the arbor, seemingly remiss in her duties. Her melancholy manner distracts her from her maternal obligations. She sits idly, staring off into the distance, her bonnet dangling casually from one hand while the other lies relaxed in her lap. Behind her, her baby wails, clutched in the arms of her older sister, Ida. Neither seems able to get her attention. The goblins crouch in the far corner of the picture, watchful and ready, the ladder they hold between them signifying their intentions. They are apparently unseen or invisible, since they are literally under the nose of a large and fierce German shepherd that does not seem to see or smell them.

In the next scene, Ida is playing her horn to rock the baby still, but she has her back turned and does not watch her. "*So* [my italics] the goblins came." They leave behind a fake baby made of ice. Ida, realizing what has happened, goes in pursuit—but she makes "a serious mistake." She goes out of the window backward into the "outside over there," hooded (like the goblins) in her mother's rain cloak. It is a serious mistake because it suggests the possibility that she has entered their world. It is interesting to note here that witches were sometimes depicted seated backward. Dorinda Neave, in an article entitled "The Witch in Early 16th-Century German Art" refers to the belief that in Satan's realm everything was reversed from the natural or usual order (Neave 1988, 5). Like Max, Ida has escaped the constrictions of civilized society. Her backward approach indicates a misdirected move, one that removes her from the restraints of civilization. As she passes the robber caves, she hears her Sailor Papa's song but does not turn around. If she did, she would "catch those goblins with a tune / she'd spoil their kidnap honeymoon." The goblins have stolen the baby to be their bride.

The mention of bride, wedding, and honeymoon admit the possibility of sexual associations. This becomes especially significant in light of the fact that the colonized country, India was often imagined as a siren: seductive, something that lures you and does not let you go. The goblins are featureless at first glance, but they are not faceless. Their faces are unmistakably black. And on close inspection, under a bright light, they have faint but grotesque features. Their hands, however, are white, suggesting perhaps their proclivity to entice, to beckon others (white people, specifically) into their darkness. They do that by appealing to the darkness within each of us, for each of us harbors the capacity to enter into a state of chaos. Ida is suddenly referred to as "Ida mad." Later she becomes "Ida sly" as she turns into a siren herself, entrancing the goblins with a tune, eventually playing the very tune that sends sailors wild out on the ocean in the moonlight, the siren song. The goblins dance themselves into frenzy, but one baby lies "crooning and clapping as a baby should" and that is Ida's. She lies "cozy in an eggshell."

Again, as in *Where the Wild Things Are*, the cozy and the contained are juxtaposed with the feral and the anarchic. The images that follow pick up on that theme. Ida hugs her baby tight and follows the stream that twists through the meadow like a path, up the ringed-round hill to the arbor. All these references are pastoral, if not actually domestic. They are also images of containment and interiority, despite the outdoor landscape. We see a man (presumably Papa?) sitting in a cottage-like structure with red tile roofs and white curtains tied back at the windows. The door is open and he seems to be playing a piano. In the arbor her mother is waiting with a letter from her father assuring them that he will be home one day and asking Ida to watch the baby and her Mama for her Papa who loves her always.

Not only are the roles reversed and Ida invested with adult responsibility, but she is now no more mad Ida or foolish Ida or terrible Ida but brave, bright Ida, having redeemed herself, like Max, by her return to civilization, to order and to control.

In Sendak's famous picture books, as in the great novelists of the British Raj, the impetus for regression from civilization comes from the inside. It is not so much an external encroachment but rather a response to an external encroachment: "In Forster's *A Passage to India* there is the echo, which annihilates the significance, even the substance of all things, immense and trivial. In Bates' *The Jacaranda Tree*, we sense the presence of an incubus that drives the doomed to their destinies. In King, it is evil incarnate. In Scott there are the familiar bogeys of isolation, dislocation and loss. The spoilers are not external, uncontrollable factors, but human beings" (Singh 1988, 216).

Accompanying that acknowledgment is awareness that although the "wild things" are everywhere, in an alien, almost vestigial land they rise more readily to the surface to entice us. The word "terrible," so emphatically repeated in *Where the Wild Things Are*, stems from "terror" which, in turn, recalls "The horror, the horror" made famous by Conrad in *Heart of Darkness*. Ultimately, in the hands of a sophisticated author, the horror is a landscape of the mind, universal in locus but localized in topography. The association between vestigial landscapes or atavistic cultures and Asian or African geographies then becomes ineffaceable. Picture books make an early but tenacious contribution to this connection.

Critics initially feared the effect that *Where the Wild Things Are* might have on children, both because of the fearsome aspect of the wild things and because of the warning issued by the famous child psychologist Bruno Bettelheim that it might reinforce a child's fear of being deserted (Sonheim 1991, 11). Ultimately, Max is deserted not by his mother—who, after all, has a hot supper awaiting him—but by civilization, a desertion that he initiates. His mother perhaps symbolizes that civilization, as the hot supper and now normal state of his room symbolize its reinstitution. Bettelheim accuses Sendak of misrepresenting how to deal with "destructive fantasies" (Sonheim 1991, 12). But Max's destructive fantasies unlock far more than a child's imagination; they hark back to a fear of the foreign, of primitivism and savagery, of the uncontrolled. The interiors of our minds become a place of fear that takes on the topographical features of lands with dense jungles and deep rivers. It is a topography that has been explored by the major writers of the British Empire: Conrad, Kipling, Forster, and Naipaul among them.

It may be a universal tendency to envisage evil as something outside over there, beyond our ken, ready to ambush our superior sensibilities when the restraints have been loosened. Our external threat becomes internalized, lurking in the deepest recesses of our beings. Tony Morrison refers in *Playing in the Dark* to "Americans' fear of being outcast, of failing, of powerlessness; their fear of boundarylessness, of Nature unbridled and crouched for attack; their fear of the absence of so-called civilization; their fear of loneliness, of aggression both external and internal" (1992, 37). All these fears find expression in *Where the Wild Things Are*. Max temporarily crosses the boundaries and escapes from civilization into savagism. As the illustrations expand to finally fill the entire page, so too are the margins of civilization blurred. But ultimately the civilized world calls Max back and the inherently civilized nature of his being responds. Some of Sendak's books—*We Are All in the Dumps with Jack and Guy*, for instance—indicate a strong social conscience on the writer's part. It is not so much that he is purposefully promoting some sort of racial agenda but that he participates in a perceptual mind-set that is old and tenacious. We can certainly leave open the possibility, however, that Maurice Sendak had a point or a purpose that was beyond the pale of a simple children's story in *Where the Wild Things Are* and *Outside Over There* and that our associations have been charily engineered accordingly.

Like Max in *Where the Wild Things Are*, Peter Pan in J. M. Barrie's undying classic assumes the role of cult leader. He becomes "the Great White Father" and has "braves" prostrating themselves before him and, again like Max, "he liked this tremendously" (1928, 104). In a reversal of the Pocahontas/John Smith situation, he saves Tiger Lily. The more sinister side of this famous figure is buried in the endless theater productions and movie versions that suppress anything murky and make it a simple, saccharine-laden fairy tale. And yet there is much that is murky in *Peter Pan*, to start with the ambivalent, even Oedipal attitudes toward motherhood. I would agree with Jacqueline Rose's assessment when she says "*Peter Pan* is sometimes scoffed at today for the excessive and cloying nature of its innocence. It is in fact one of the most fragmented and troubled works in the history of children's fiction to date" (1984, 11). Rose focuses on the sexual aspects of the story, insisting quite rightly that it cannot be absolved by describing the work as fantasy, for, as Freud discovered, sexuality works above all at the level of fantasy. What interests me in this work are the tensions between order and chaos, civilization and savagery, reality and fantasy that we encounter in so much of the writing of empire.

Peter Pan, as a work, has had several metamorphoses. It was not originally intended for children but first appeared as a story within a story, in a novel for adults by Barrie called *The Little White Bird; or Adventures in Kensington Gardens* (1902). The Peter Pan chapters were extracted from the novel and published separately with elaborate illustrations by Arthur Rackham as *Peter Pan in Kensington Gardens* (1906). The first theatrical version was produced two years earlier. Many different writers worked up the narrative version, since Barrie himself resisted doing so and, when he did, failed completely (Rose 1984, 6). *Peter Pan* is not a politically correct work; its rude racial references have been a source of embarrassment for some producers. A community production in Amherst, Massachusetts, for instance, transformed the redskins into sprites in a misguided attempt to sanitize the work and render it more palatable politically.

Throughout *Peter Pan*, the overt and covert are in strife, as are surface and subterranean. The home under the ground for which Peter measures the children combines the cozy and civilized: teatime, fireplace, the washing with the wild and the feral, or at least the primitive: a mud floor, a rough and simple basket hung up for the baby, and the underground location itself. As in Max's room, there is encroachment on the inside from the outside, an encroachment the children can barely control: "A Never tree tried hard to grow in the center of the room, but every morning they sawed the trunk through, level with the floor. By tea-time it was always about two feet high, and then they put a door on top of it, the whole thus becoming a table; as soon as they cleared away, they sawed off the trunk again, and thus there was more room to play" (1928, 76). The curtain that shuts off the home from Tinker Bell's private apartment, furnished fashionably and lavishly, is the flimsy barrier between the civilization the apartment represents and the "nameless fear" Mrs. Darling senses.

Peter Pan's mother, unlike Wendy's or Max's, is not awaiting his return with a warm welcome. There is clear indication of emotional (or sexual?) abuse. On hearing him utter a hollow groan, Wendy runs toward him thinking he is in pain. "It isn't that kind of pain," Peter replies "darkly." In response to her question, Peter tells Wendy that she is wrong about mothers:

> They all gathered round him in affright, so alarming was his agita-
> tion; and with a fine candour he told them what he had hitherto
> concealed.
> "Long ago," he said, "I thought like you that my mother would
> always keep the window open for me; so I stayed away for moons
> and moons and moons, and then flew back; but the window was
> barred, for my mother had forgotten all about me, and there was
> another little boy sleeping in my bed." (1928, 115)

We might also recall what Tootles says about the ladies who came to him in dreams. "Pretty mother, pretty mother," he would say and then shoot them. Max returns home, but Peter Pan has perpetually escaped the bonds of time, place, and propriety.

The world of conventions is one that Wendy's family is acutely aware of, and although she and her brothers escape it, their flight is only temporary. Wendy's father, Mr. Darling, "had a passion for be-ing exactly like his neighbours" (1928, 3), their nursery was con-ducted correctly, there are many references to what is "good form" and what is not, and to the importance of "fitting" (75–76). Their sin-gle servant, Liza, is referred to in the plural, as "the servants," again for the sake of appearances. And when John and Michael realize that by joining the pirates they would have to forswear their loyalty to the king, they turn away from temptation. Wendy hopes that they will all die like English gentlemen and, indeed, the boys all end up living like English gentlemen. The twins, Bibs and Curly, become staid office-goers, carrying little bags and umbrellas, Michael be-comes an engine driver, John is a family man, Slightly marries a lady of title and becomes a lord, while Tootles becomes a judge. Wendy is almost ashamed to allow Peter to see the sedate matron she has be-come. They all eventually participate in Victorian propriety; it is only Peter Pan who permanently escapes its constraints and refuses to compromise, although allowing Wendy and her progeny brief forays into Neverland.

While Peter Pan addresses Captain Hook as a "dark and sinister man" (1928, 154), there is a darkness in his own character as well. When Wendy tries to talk to him about old times, she finds that new adventures have caused him to forget the old ones. He has even forgotten who Captain Hook is. "Don't you remember," asks Wendy, "how you killed him and saved all our lives?" And Peter Pan "carelessly" replies, "I forget them after I kill them" (176), a dark and sinister statement in itself. James Hook is described as a "not wholly unheroic figure" (158) even though he is a "black-hearted" pirate. Black and dark are used so persistently in conjunction with Captain Hook that it is hard to avoid the racial connotations. But Captain Hook is not black, nor a redskin; he is a white man and, as such, still part of the civilized world, renegade though he may be. Most telling of all is when the author, although not inviting sympathy for him, affirms that Hook "was true to the traditions of his race" (155). "The man was not wholly evil," we are told (130). He loves flowers and sweet music, plays the harpsichord, and is affected by the beauty of nature. He has a "better self," a touch of the feminine in his "dark" nature, as do all the great pirates, but it is not always in mastery.

In his final moments, Hook returns in imagination to his youth, to the playing fields of long ago when he was a more righteous person as symbolized by the fact that all his attire was right. His dying wish is to provoke Peter into doing something that is bad form and he finally succeeds. When Hook asks Peter as they duel "who and what art thou?" Peter answers that he is youth and joy, a little bird that has broken out of the egg. Immediately the reader is told that this is nonsense (155). Peter's victory over Captain Hook produces not exultation but insomnia and nightmares. On discovering that Wendy has grown up and has a baby, he steps toward the sleeping child with his dagger upraised but he does not strike; he sobs instead, and this time Wendy does not know how to comfort him as she did when she was a girl. Peter Pan remains one of the wild things; at the end he is described as a "tragic boy" who shrinks from the light because it reveals reality. His realm is Neverland, an alien place outside over there.

From Freudian readings to cultural fetish, *Peter Pan* will continue to be reinterpreted. Like so many Victorian and Edwardian authors, J. M. Barrie explores the edges of "civilization" and peers into the chaos that lies beyond. Conformity to custom, conservative behavior, good form—these are the barriers that must be erected to keep the darkness, the "nameless fear" at bay. When the children return home, they are safe and snug within the walls of civilization while Peter Pan peers in "at the one joy from which he must be forever barred" (171). Peter remains on the outside looking in. Like the children, the reader returns to the safety of the inside, the stability of British order. Peter, however, remains in the hinterland, not only the boy who would not grow up but also the child who would not conform.

In "Home and Family: English and American Ideals," Gillian Avery comments: "Later Victorians, often remembering the sternness of their own upbringing and the moral pressure put upon them, tried to make amends by peopling their books with irresponsible nursery scamps and pickles. But their mischievous escapades nearly always took place with a secure background of protective parents and nurses" (Butts 1992, 41). An exception to Avery's point may be Charles Kingsley's *Water Babies*. No "secure background of protective parents and nurses" exists for the grubby little chimney sweep although, in clear contrast, the angelic little girl that Tom describes as "the little white lady" has a stout old nurse who sleeps in the next room. Tom is virtually an orphan: one of his parents is dead and the other is in Botany Bay. Tom expects to have to take care of himself since he does not remember ever having had a father. His only protection comes not so much from human beings (with the possible exception of the Irishwoman) but from the forces of nature. *Water Babies* is a complex and fascinating work, some of it intended for adults rather than children. Kingsley's concern for the underprivileged emerges in his descriptions of Tom and the oppression and trials he must endure just to survive, but that concern was grounded in his religious and social beliefs. Kingsley wrote, "We must touch the workman at all his points of interest. First and foremost at association—but also at political rights, as grounded both on the Christian ideal of the Church, and on the historic facts of the Anglo-Saxon race" (Banton 1978, 66).

Water Babies is rich in the referents of race. As in *Peter Pan*, the negative associations of black are set against the positive associations of white. Tom is "a little ugly, black, ragged figure, with bleared eyes and grinning white teeth" (1889, 18). He is "a little black ape" (18). That the reference is not entirely innocent may be noted when one considers Kingsley's statement that "the black is more like an ape than a white man—he is—the fact is there; and no notions of an abstract right will put that down" (Banton 1978, 67). In contrast is the room in which the beautiful little girl lies. Tom enters this room by mistake, lost in the "pitchy darkness" of the large and crooked chimneys of the old country house he has been sent to work in. The room is all dressed in white. The window curtains are white, the bed curtains are white, the furniture is white, and the walls are white. The little girl, whose cheeks are almost as white as the snow-white pillow upon which rests her head, hair spread out like threads of gold, lies under a snow-white coverlet.

White connotes race but also moral choice. "Those that wish to be clean, clean they will be; and those that wish to be foul, foul they will be" (1889, 11), the Irishwoman tells Mr. Grimes, Tom's master who frequently beats him up. Kingsley acknowledges that Jesus died for the Negro as well as for the white. In Tom's dream, physical and moral cleanliness are coupled as he hears the little white lady crying to him, "Oh, you're so dirty; go and be washed," and the Irishwoman, who serves as a sort of chorus, saying "Those that wish to be clean, clean they will be" (39). Tom is certainly mischievous, but he is not evil. His dirt washes off once he plunges into the stream and becomes a water baby, whereas Mr. Grimes will perpetually remain Mr. Grimes: grimy inside. Clean and dirty take on not only a moral significance but also an ecological one. The river is clear and cool as it runs its course through the countryside but dank and foul as it flows through the town.

The book presents children with lessons in prehistory (pterodactyls), natural history (metamorphoses and spawning), marine biology (sea cucumbers and golden combs), the geography of discovery (elephants and giraffes and Cannibal Islands), ecology (wasteful and dirty practices like letting sewage run into the sea instead of using it for fertilizer like "thrifty reasonable souls"), scientific discovery (Huxley, Faraday, Darwin, and others), Darwinism (selection and competition), and even Social Darwinism as when the salmon tell Tom that the trout allowed themselves to become degraded. Because the trout were lazy, cowardly, and greedy and chose to poke about in little streams and eat worms and grubs, they are properly punished for it: "they have grown ugly and brown and spotted and small" (Kingsley 1978, 86). A trout actually had the impudence to propose to a lady of their *race* [my italics], in other words, a salmon. Kingsley's concern with sanitary reform, Banton claims, relates to his racial philosophy in two ways. He believed that poor sanitation and poor health contributed to the degradation of races, exemplified in *Water Babies* by the trout who are "degraded in their tastes" (Kingsley 1978, 86). He also believed that inward nature was reflected in outward appearance, as this was the era of phrenology, as Banton points out (70). The trout were once just like the handsome and stately salmon but because of their poor character, they have deteriorated in appearance as well as in morals.

Kingsley reserves his worst invective, however, for mankind. They not only spear the poor salmon right out of the water but turn on each other with shouts and blows and words that make Tom shudder and feel sick, "for he felt somehow that they were strange, and ugly, and wrong, and horrible" (Kingsley 1978, 92). Their fighting is savage and desperate and, as a result, Tom is very glad that he is a water baby and has "nothing to do any more with horrid dirty men, with foul clothes on their backs and foul words on their lips" (93). That we do not have visible proof of a phenomenon or a process or being does not mean that it does not exist. The redeeming power is of the imagination and the numerous quotations from Wordsworth and Coleridge throughout the book affirm this belief.

The imaginative, social, and political nexus in children's literature may not be conscious, intentional, or ideological. There is no doubt that there will be those who will scoff or be outraged at the merest suggestion that a children's book, especially a much loved classic such as *Where the Wild Things Are*, could be anything other than that, a children's book. How could one possibly read so much into those lovable monsters or those entrancing illustrations? To counter that charge I will offer Susan Lehr's well-articulated statement in *Battling Dragons: Issues and Controversy in Children's Literature*: "I cannot imagine anyone seriously arguing that authors of children's books, whether past or present, operate in a political and ideological vacuum and pursue their artistic vision without constraint or limitation. Like other cultural artifacts, children's literature is a product of convention that is rooted in, if not determined by, the dominant belief systems and ideologies of the times in which it is created" (Lehr 1995, 159). Whether the connections are intentional, the agenda planned, or the ideology reflective is hardly the point.

What we are talking about here are metonymic associations that operate insidiously and subliminally but powerfully, nevertheless. As Perry Nodelman comments "Indeed it is part of the charm of many of the most interesting picture books that they so strangely combine the childlike and the sophisticated—that the viewer they imply is both very learned and very ingenuous" (1992, 21).

Few children's stories have been as metonymic or as political as *Little Black Sambo* (1899). It is a book that has come to practically symbolize racial stereotyping in children's literature, and the chief reason is the illustrations. The illustrations clearly suggest Africans, distorted and exaggerated in feature in most (though certainly not all) versions. American versions of *Little Black Sambo* that were published in the 1920s, 1930s, and 1940s were especially responsible and Bannerman could not maintain control since she had lost the copyright. In 1947, a critic asserted that "the original illustrations use all the usual stereotypes found in malicious cartoons of Negroes . . . the thick lips, the rolling eyes, the bony knees, the fuzzy hair" (www.pancakeparlour.com). The tigers, however, and the use of the Indian term *ghi* (the clarified butter that the tigers turn into) denote India. In her biography of Helen Bannerman, *Sambo Sahib*, Elizabeth Hay writes, "Among the more substantial complaints were charges that the pictures showed stereotypes or caricatures of black people, that the book showed black people in primitive jungle settings, and that the name Sambo had derogatory overtones for black people because it had come to be used in a generic way for any Negro" (1981, 155). So, aside from the confused geography, the caricatures are what have drawn condemnation for *Little Black Sambo*.

Take away the illustrations and the giveaway names, however, and leave only the text, and we have a story of a little boy who knows how to think on his feet. It has been a beloved story, perhaps because it is an empowering one. Some critics have even seen Sambo as a black hero, years ahead of the dumb black characters generally portrayed at the time. Hay talks about the appropriation of Bannerman's texts by other publishers, chiefly because her copyright claims were rather weak (1981, 156). Editions with illustrations by others far outnumbered in sales those editions that contained the author's own illustrations (155). Hay's study constitutes a staunch defense of Bannerman and her intentions, but she admits, "Some of the pictures are horrifying. No wonder people took offence" (156). Hay points out that Bannerman, not being a trained artist, tended toward caricature in style. While Hay's defense of the original impetus of the Sambo story and of Bannerman's relatively benign illustrations is entirely legitimate, she perhaps pushes too far when she claims "individualistic parents" for him (158). After all, his parents are Mumbo and Jumbo, and mumbo-jumbo is a phrase we use for gibberish, when the sounds or individual components of language do not make sense separately. Alternatively, the term may apply, loosely, to any "Negro" idol, fetish, or bugaboo. Hay also exhaustively researches Sambo's name and how it came to be the generic name applied to a black male as Jock or Mick is for a Scotsman and an Irishman respectively.

Even as she claims that the book was one of the very few then available that even acknowledged the existence of black people, Hay admits that it had, in all its versions, "a very powerful impact on people's instinctive images" (1981, 159). Of course, it's not clear what Hay means by instinctive images. Does she mean that it provoked an automatic association between black people and primitivism? Or does she mean by instinctive that these images have been instilled in us to the point of producing an instinctive metonymic response? The point remains: a charming tale, much loved by generations of white children, becomes controversial because it is illustrated with gross caricatures of black people. Yet this is a story about a little black boy escaping from tigers, a story that is supposed to celebrate courage and resourcefulness. Hay's take on the ambiguous setting of the tale is as follows:

> Why then did a person who was both well travelled and scholarly write a book which contains aspects of both Africa and India? The explanation is that she was writing, not for publication, but for her own daughters. She wanted to set her story somewhere far away and exotic; she chose an imaginary jungle-land and peopled it with what were to her daughters a far-away kind of people. To have made the setting India would have been too humdrum and familiar for them. Then, because she had a liking for terrifying tigers, she brought them in as the villains. She was far too good a naturalist not to be aware that tigers are found in India but not in Africa; no matter. Her jungle-land was an imaginary one, and tigers, which for her were symbolic dragons, were essential to the story. (Hay 1981, 29)

So we have a generic jungle setting with a generic black boy who has a generic and derogatory name used mostly for black boys and men. Yet Hay goes on to say that Bannerman's motive was not to ridicule or demean people in any way, for she simply regarded all people as part of the human race (1981, 142). The nobility of Bannerman's impulses and the purity of her motives are not, however, being impugned here. The point is the effect and the influence of her depictions. And let us not forget that she was part of the colonizing class in India. The introduction to the early editions indicates clearly that she could not escape the worldview that came with that position: "Once upon a time there was an English lady, who had two small daughters. To amuse these little girls in India, where black children abound and tigers are everyday affairs, she used to now and then invent stories, for which, being extremely talented, she also drew and coloured the pictures. The Story of Little Black Sambo, which was made up on a long railway journey, was the favourite." Selma Lanes, in *Down the Rabbit Hole*, makes the somewhat extravagant claim that "Sambo was taken to everyone's heart precisely because he allowed us to acknowledge what we knew inside but avoided confronting: that black people were human beings just like us. In loving Sambo unreservedly, in some way every white had the feeling that he was also accepting the black man as a fellow human being" (Hay 1981, 160). Of course, to her, American and white are one and the same thing. It is evident that her "us" does not include black Americans, for surely it came as no surprise to them that they were human!

The ambiguity of the setting and of Sambo's identity is exactly what allows the identification with the primitive, an identification that may have been well intentioned but is nevertheless insidious, and reiterated, for generations of white children, a prototypical association of black with jungles and jungles with primitive, a network of connections that continued to operate in their minds long after childhood was over. This network of associations is not the result of *Little Black Sambo* alone, of course, but of a number of picture books, books that have come to be regarded as classics. As we have seen in the prologue, in describing the terrorists (and, by extension, the communities they come from) as oppositional, Bush and his cabinet essentially employ picture-book or comic-book dualities to reconstruct a colonialist epistemology. It's a basal and binary mode that divides the world into good or evil, civilized or barbarian, us or them, those who live in caves or jungles and those who live in cities and houses. Sure, an Osama bin Laden would be equally likely to employ such divisive rhetoric, but his words would be validated by a much smaller group of people, whereas the words of President Bush would be invested with authority because they are spoken from a position of legally constituted power. Such would be, in Foucault's words, "a regime of truth" (Rabinow 1984, 74). Such rhetoric reiterates not only colonial discourse but also the lexis of children's literature, a lexis that juxtaposes subjugated peoples with primitivism or primordial landscapes. In these political utterances we see what Roland Barthes, in his classic *Writing Degree Zero and Elements of Semiology,* calls "a familiar repertory of gestures, a gestuary, as it were, in which the energy expended is purely operative, serving here to enumerate, there to transform, but never to appraise or signify a choice" (Barthes 1953, 13).

Julius Lester's retelling of the Sambo story, *Sam and the Tigers,* which was published in 1996, with illustrations by Jerry Pinkney, attempts to rescue a tale that he has remembered since he first read it at the age of seven. The biggest challenge for them both, he writes, was history. "Many whites had loved *Little Black Sambo* as children and were afraid their love of it made them racists now. That is not so. Many blacks, angered and shamed, resolved that it be thrown in the garbage. For many years so had I" (Lester 1996). Lester and Pinkney attempt to shift the focus of the story to the child, who is now known simply as Sam, the child as a hero, to make it the story of "the young black child who could outwit tigers." Their version is much more lavishly and lovingly illustrated. Interestingly, while the tigers are much larger, more realistic, and far more fierce, the forest, which in earlier American versions of *Little Black Sambo* are sometimes reduced to a single but highly semiotic palm tree, are far more lush, yet somehow friendly. Sometimes one is reminded more of northern woods than of tropical jungle, though the palm does make an appearance. In one scene, Sam and his parents stand in a cottage garden more reminiscent of England than of Africa. On closer observation of the "jungle," one finds the trees have visages that gaze on the action taking place before them with a variety of expressions. This not only "humanizes" them but also neutralizes their threatening aspect.

Lester makes a conscious decision to use what he describes as "the southern black storytelling voice," which means that there are elements of dialect in the language and that the association between Sam and black Americans is not only reiterated but in fact subverted. The black people in Lester and Pinkney's version are far more "civilized" and refined than the caricatures of earlier versions. They are completely humanized, their expressions are subtle and varied, and they project intelligence and warmth. They are a far cry from the grotesque cartoon characters of yore, and thus the book's objectives are achieved. But the setting remains ambiguous, "Sam-sam-sa-mara," provoking an Orientalist association, while the introduction of Brer Rabbit and African Elephants further fuse its elements into a "fanciful" (Lester's word) mix.

The Story of Little Babaji is another retelling of the Sambo story; in this case, the names of the characters are changed to "authentic Indian names," the author's note on the text tells us. The authentic names, appearance, and attire of the characters certainly offset some of the controversy. Although the setting is never identified, it is clearly India. The details are carefully adapted to this setting with one exception: the pancakes, which are not exactly a popular Indian breakfast food! However, the book is an example of how the essence of the story has been extracted from its questionable casing without coopting it in the process.

Countless children's picture books associated with India have the jungle as their setting because of the universal childhood fascination with wild animals, and the connection between India and the jungle has thereby become an obstinate one. As a result, it is the jungle that is popularly identified as Indian topography in the popular imagination, not mountains or even deserts to any great extent. Let us take a typical example. In a story entitled *Basil Brush in the Jungle* by Peter Firmin, Basil the fox builds a cage and then looks for a wild animal to put into it. Calling for a taxi, he and his friend Harry the mole determine to go to the jungle to find one. When the taxi driver announces that he will take them to the airport, Basil asks, "Are there any wild animals at the airport?" (1979, 11). The taxi driver answers that there are not, and they must take an airplane to India for "that is where the jungle is" (11). The narrative then informs young readers that the airplane took them over the sea, over the forests, over the deserts, and over the mountains to India, "where the jungle is," and adds "it was very hot in India" (14). As their search for a suitable wild animal to house in the cage unfolds, the people we see are an Indian umbrella seller in the street clothes of the region and a ferry man in peasant garb, sporting a turban and a beard. In the end, the ferryman locks Basil in the cage and says, "There you are. Now you have a wild animal in your cage" (42). He advises Harry to unlock the door when he gets home, because the fox is too wild for our jungle! The jungle as topography thus becomes the jungle as trope, its inhabitants noble savages locked in a time warp, as is the country in the one-dimensional representation offered by the majority of picture books.

Nowhere is this connection made so clearly and coherently than in the much loved Babar books. Ariel Dorfman has written a brilliant critique of the Babar story as archetypal imperial myth, so it would be redundant and repetitive to attempt a detailed analysis here. But much before I read Dorfman, it had struck me that *The Story of Babar* and subsequent Babar books serve as exemplar. In them, we see the *mission civilisatrice* as transformative myth. We follow the adventures of a baby elephant as he goes from being a lovable but wild creature of the forest to an urbane citizen, a transformation wrought by the civilizing influence of French colonization and, by extension, that of other European powers as well, on primitive peoples. The Old Lady, who virtually adopts Babar and becomes his mentor, might be taken to represent Mother France and her benevolence. Babar returns to his country, where he is chosen king. Much like the citizens of the colonies who have been educated in the mother country but return to lead and enlighten their native lands, Babar's subjects are clothed, civilized, and learn to partake of high culture. Once again, a child makes the association between tropical landscapes, naked or scantily dressed people, and primitivism on the one hand and metropolitan settings, European raiment, and civilization on the other.

While the opening scene of *The Story of Babar* projects a peaceful, idyllic scene that is violently shattered by the obviously Western hunter, this act becomes, in the larger scheme of things, a destructive but necessary act that brings about a greater good. The Old Lady signifies not just the benign but in fact the benevolent nature of colonialism. She gives Babar whatever he wants. In the scene where she watches Babar's departure from her balcony, she not only commands a fine view but also signifies her superior status. Her words "my little Babar" suggest strongly the proprietary nature of her feelings for him. One is reminded of Queen Victoria and her interest in Prince Duleep Singhji, the last Sikh ruler of the Punjab, who was a great favorite of hers. In an essay in the journal *Nishaan*, David Jones tells how the queen kept Prince Duleep Singhji close on state occasions in spite of opposition from British aristocrats and European diplomats alike. She even invited him into her family circle at Osborne and sketched him as he played contentedly with her children (2000, 49). The Old Lady similarly takes Babar into her house, where he dines and exercises with her, and they go for automobile rides together.

The resemblance between Queen Victoria and the Old Lady is hard to resist in another instance. In 1898, Queen Victoria explained to Lord Salisbury the importance of not making the colonized feel like a conquered people, in other words, of noblesse oblige. "They must of course *feel* that we are masters, but it should be done kindly and not offensively" (Spurr 1993, 32). The Old Lady is always kind to Babar. She is not proprietary so much as maternal, or rather grandmotherly. Of course, we are dealing with French colonialism here, not British, but there is a commonality in the discourse. The notion of tutelage (*la tutelle coloniale*) is closely aligned to the British notion of trusteeship or guardianship, which was part of the British construction. David Spurr comments, "The queen's letter to her prime minister points to another paradox of colonial discourse: the desire to emphasize racial and cultural difference as a means of establishing superiority takes place alongside the desire to efface difference and to gather the colonized into the fold of an all-embracing civilization" (32). The French considered their colonies an intrinsic part of the French Republic, and the imperial ideal was one of assimilation. The French system has been defined as "that system which tends to efface all difference between the colonies and the motherland, and which views the colonies simply as a prolongation of the mother-country beyond the seas" (Roberts 1929, 44).

In "Babar and the French Connection: Teaching the Politics of Superiority and Exclusion," an essay in a collection called *Critical Perspectives on Postcolonial African Children's and Young Adult Literature* (1998), Claire-Lise Malarte-Feldman and Jack Yeager attempt to read the first three Babar books in the context of the French *mission civilisatrice*. The first three Babar books were written by Jean de Brunhoff himself before his premature death from tuberculosis at the age of thirty-eight. His son Laurent subsequently continued the series. It is a perceptive reading, and falls in line with many other readings of Babar as a colonial narrative, not only Dorfman's and Herbert Kohl's but Harry Payne's and also Patrick Richardson's essay "Teach Your Baby to Rule," which considers the play of power politics in this children's "classic."

Malarte-Feldman and Yeager's reading of the Babar stories as specific to the *mission civilisatrice* may, however, be challenged. For instance, they claim that Celesteville's "perfect layers . . . represents the epitome of Cartesian order, a monument to the virtues of [school] work and play" and the same is true of the symmetry of French gardens, "a clear representation of Versailles" (1998, 73). However, British colonial architecture, public works, and the layout of their towns are also testament to their struggle to build bulwarks against what they perceived as the bedlam of the colonies, to stanch its chaos and to reflect through their own edifices their counterpoised rationality. In the scene where the Old Lady is left alone standing on a balcony, sadly watching the retreating figures of Babar in his little car, Arthur and Celeste trailing behind, as they go down the boulevard, we are struck by the orderly procession of trees, marching alongside the avenue in pairs, contained in concrete circles along the concrete sidewalk. In *The Imperishable Empire: British Fiction on India*, I refer to the British perception of India's comminatory powers, its ability to disrupt suddenly and irrevocably the sanity and equilibrium of the British establishment:

> Hence the unremitting references to her destructive power, her ravenous appetite. The neatly intersecting roads and sensibly planned civil station in Forster's A *Passage to India*, the insistence on precedence and protocol in Bates' novel, are suggestive of the British attempt to subjugate or at least to contain the anarchy of the environment. The accountant in Conrad's *Heart of Darkness*, with his got-up shirtfronts in a remote jungle station, is analogous. (Singh 1988, 214)

In the city, the palm trees of Babar's native habitat, visible in the opening scene, have been domesticated and are now but a tame potted palm before which Babar's portrait is taken. And so the potted palm and the trees within their concrete circles suggest containment of the jungle. In *Babar Comes to America*, all the artifacts of civilization from Harvard to Heinz ketchup are available, inadvertently looking ahead, perhaps, to neocolonialism and the new Pax Americana.

It is necessary, says Dorfman, to remind the reader of "a few uncomfortable historical facts" (1983, 18). *The Story of Babar* was written in 1931, when the countries of Africa were still colonies: "In contrast to his tiny admirers—first they were French, then British, then North American—he is dealing with a naive country that has not evolved along with him and continues to be primitive, tribal and naked" (19). On meeting his cousins, Arthur and Celeste, Babar is overjoyed, but hurries to clothe them and take them to eat cakes—in other words, to civilize them. Babar is not happy in exile; he misses his people. What he wants is to assimilate to Western ways, not to live apart from his people, and so he returns. Now it so happens that the king of the elephants dies from eating a poisonous mushroom, and Babar is chosen king in his place, not on account of his accomplishments, nor even his lineage, but on account of his assimilation alone: "My good friends, we are seeking a King," proclaims Cornelius, an elephant elder, "Why not choose Babar? He has just returned from the big city, he has learned so much living among men, let us crown him King" (Brunhoff 1931, 38).

Malarte-Feldman and Yeager offer an insightful reading of the scene in *Le voyage de Babar* where the little elephants are learning math, which they take to symbolize Western science. Education in the French system will allow them to participate in the larger enterprise of empire where "learning, work, goodness, and perseverance overcome ignorance, laziness, cowardice, and fear by the sheer force of their moral power, recalling once again the underpinnings of and justification for the French civilizing mission" (74). Babar marries his cousin (we are never told whether she had any choice in the matter) and the clothed king and queen appear before the naked but happy natives. The elephants are primitive in comparison to the French, but they are not savage. This is indicated by contrasting them with the Gogottes, a comical circus sort of people whose pointed horns and yellow skin certainly set them apart as "other." A child reading and rereading the Babar books would be left to identify backwardness with forests (palm tree forests, in particular), wilderness, and nakedness, while civilization and advancement would be associated with European cities, clothes, shops, cakes, and similar artifacts. Babar goes *From the Deep Woods to Civilization*, which, in fact, is the title of an autobiography by Charles A. Eastman (1916), an assimilationist Native American writer. The *Babar* stories constitute a type of ethnography of primitive peoples brought to the light of civilization through colonization.

Like Dorfman, one can read into the Babar books not simply a subtext, but what Barthes calls a second-order language:

> This universal semantization of the usages is crucial: it expresses the fact that there is no reality except when it is intelligible, and should eventually lead to merging of sociology with socio-logic. But once the sign is constituted, society can very well re-functionalize it, and speak about it as if it were an object made for use: a fur-coat will be described as if it served only to protect from the cold.
>
> This recurrent functionalization, which needs, in order to exist, a second-order language, is by no means the same as the first (and indeed purely ideal) functionalization: for the function which is represented does in fact correspond to a second (disguised) semantic institutionalization, which is of the order of connotation. The sign-function therefore has (probably) an anthropological value, since it is the very unit where the relations of the technical and the significant are woven together. (Barthes 1953, 42)

Dorfman points out that in the Babar books the nebulous nature of the location of the jungle is deliberate. It allows and extends a more spatial and semiotic association. "The land of the elephants," Dorfman says, "stands for Africa without overly representing it, without actually using the name, which might precipitate an overly painful identification" (1983, 23) or, one might add, an overly limiting one. For, just as in the Sambo story, it is not the jungle as location that is significant but the jungle as sign.

For schoolteachers and general readers, Herbert Kohl's essay "Should We Burn Babar? Questioning Power in Children's Literature" (1995) is useful, if somewhat simple in comparison to Dorfman's. Kohl takes up the important question of what do with books such as the Babar books: whether to set them aside as collector's items, to consign them to children's literature research libraries, or, alternatively, to allow children to read them but to teach them to read critically and in context. Kohl reflects on the impact of *Babar* in his own perceptions:

> In *Babar* the reader learns that there are different classes of people and the Rich Lady is of the better (that is richer) class and that elephants are not as good as people, but might be if they imitate people. Was I aware of those distinctions as a child? Did I learn to admire the rich from reading the book? Did I also learn about the inferiority of creatures from the jungle (people included)? I can't be sure, but I do think that from my early reading I got the impression that people who served the rich weren't as good as the rich. (Kohl 1995, 7)

This was in direct opposition to the notions he picked up from his neighborhood and home, especially from his unionist grandparents, who talked about the rich disparagingly.

Kohl suggests that there are several ways to look at the Old Lady's generosity. She can be seen as patriarchal or as a caring and sympathetic woman providing an alternative to the patriarchy, a Jane Addams of her time, perhaps, welcoming immigrant elephants and helping them adjust to a new land. While he claims that both ways of looking at the Old Lady can be supported by the text, he seems to veer toward the former although, one must point out, there's something patriarchal about a Jane Addams, too.

One of Kohl's most perceptive points about *Babar* is expressed in the following passage:

> In de Brunhoff's illustrations the civilized elephants have personal identity and distinction; the natural elephants are portrayed as indistinguishable from each other. Here we see where the power is when the wild and the civilized make contact. Every time I looked at the book as a child, I felt there was something here that wasn't right. The mothers weren't being treated fairly. They should have been the ones in the car and the children should have been running behind, or they should all have been together in the car. Yet that wouldn't work either, since the idea of dressed and naked elephants riding together seemed embarrassing to me. That illustration was and is painful for me to look at. (1995, 10)

In terms of character and behavior, Kohl suggests that the transference of power by Babar to Cornelius through his hat "suggests to children that blind acceptance of authority is good behavior" (1995, 20). While many believe that children should not question adult authority, states Kohl, the presence of illegitimate authority or legitimized authority that acts in illegitimate ways mandates that children should know how to question authority. "One compelling reason for not reading *Babar* is that it makes a thoroughly undemocratic way of governance seem natural and unquestioned," he claims (21).

Jean Perrot provides an angry refutation of Kohl's arguments in his essay "The French Avant-Garde Revisited: Or, Why We Shouldn't Burn Mickey Mouse" (1998). Perrot sees Kohl as an "involuntary pawn" in "the cultural imperialist struggle" (Perrot 1998, 84). He especially points to his declaration: "I wouldn't ban or burn *Babar*, or pull it from libraries. But buy it? No. I see no reason to go out of one's way to make [it] available to children, primarily because I don't see much critical reading going on in the schools, and children don't need to be propagandized about colonialism, sexism, or racism" (28). Perrot's counterarguments seem to emerge from his own cultural and perhaps nationalist ideology, and his reading is somewhat ingenuous. It is left to the individual reader to decide which approach is the more convincing. Certainly, it would be absurd to think that a casual childhood encounter with Babar would be dangerous or even necessarily a contribution to colonialism, sexism, or racism, as Kohl claims. But Babar is part of a powerful intertextuality of children's literary works that reiterate and reinforce each other until the impressions that accumulate are no longer innocent or innocuous but part of the system of propaganda to which Kohl refers, intentional or not.

The Curious George books (1941) by H. A. Rey are part of this intertextuality. "The man" removes George from the jungle to a big zoo in a big city, promising him that he "will like it there" (*Curious George* 1941, 14), which is rather deceitful considering that George, a monkey, is being asked to abandon his native habitat and customary freedom within it. George's habitat is also described simply as Africa. Again, it is not necessary to be more specific. The semiotic function has been served. The man's first impulse as he sees George and considers him "a nice little monkey" is to say "I would like to take him home with me" (6), in much the same manner as the early explorers of the American continent took back native specimens to Spain or to England. "In a barbaric world such as this," Dorfman points out, "where everyone is naive and defenceless, Babar's proximity to the Western cosmos (the adult cosmos), to the illustrious center, now and in future episodes will become the foundation of his investiture, the fount of his regency" (1983, 21). One more example is worth mentioning, *A Bear Called Paddington* (1958) by Michael Bond, where the Brown family discovers in London's Paddington Station a stuffed bear with a sign around his neck reading: "Please look after this bear. Thank you." Like Curious George, Paddington is mischievous and adventurous, but more significantly, he is "from darkest Peru," clearly a metonymic reference to the African continent with which Peru is meant to share characteristics.

Another association between a mental and a physical landscape that recurs in picture books with some frequency is that between tropical features such as jungles, palms, mango trees, and so forth and nonsense words. An instance would be *Tingo Tango Mango Tree* (1995) by Marcia Vaughan, where the main character is an iguana called Sombala Bombala Rombala Roh, while the turtle is Nanaba Panaba Tanaba Goh, the bat Bitteo Biteo, and so on. Of course children enjoy nonsense syllables and rhyming words, and these may be found in a number of children's books. But the persistence of this association serves a discourse of nullification in which, as adults, we will continue to be engaged through many different media. It is the discourse of "the puzzling East" as Barrie calls it in *Peter Pan* (1991, 961). When Indians appear on *Sesame Street* they are often orientalized—a snake charmer blowing letters of the alphabet from his pipe, for instance— or nullified in other ways. For instance, an Indian mother serves her child coconut milk at bedtime. Not only is this inauthentic, it is nonsense. In *Empire of Signs*, Roland Barthes writes,

> The West moistens everything with meaning, like an authoritarian religion which imposes baptism on entire peoples; the objects of language (made out of speech) are obviously *de jure* converts: the first meaning of the system summons, metonymically, the second meaning of discourse, and this summons has the value of a universal obligation. We have two ways of sparing discourse the infamy of non-meaning (non-sense), and we systematically subject utterance (in a desperate filling-in of any nullity which might reveal the emptiness of language) to one or the other of these *significations* (or active fabrications of signs): symbol and reasoning, metaphor and syllogism. (1982, 70)

The associations established in picture books constitute the first meaning of the system that summons the second meaning with which readers will engage for the rest of their lives through the metonymic images in newspapers, magazines, and films.

The *Daily Hampshire Gazette*, a newspaper in western Massachusetts, portrays a group of Indians sitting atop a tree, like so many monkeys, listening to a political speech. There seems to be no other point to the picture but their perch. Another picture from the same newspaper depicts cows wandering the streets of New Delhi. There is no accompanying text, only a caption that asks, "Have you ever been to New Delhi?" The picture is itself the text. Similarly, a picture in the *Denver Post* portrays a group of Indian women, hands held up, fingers curled, as though they are about to draw their claws, tongues hanging out, eyeballs protruding. "Guffaws for good health" is the caption and there is a two-line explanation that they are members of the International Laughing Club celebrating World Laughers Day in the belief that fits of laughing can boost the immune system. An absurdist cast seems to be the only point to the picture. Throngs of protesters or mourners in the Arab world are consistently depicted as fanatical, frenzied, or shrill in direct opposition to the ordered, controlled expressions of Westerners. A *Newsweek Traveler* article analyzes "The Dark Side of Islam." Accompanying the article is a picture of Muslim men from North Africa kneeling in prayer, guns at their sides. The picture is truncated so that the men's faces are not shown. They are simultaneously decapitated and dehumanized. In *Condé Nast Traveler*, a travel magazine, Jerry Hall rises resplendent like a blonde Venus out of the darkness of a cluster of veiled women dressed in black and crouched around her. In the *New York Times*, there is a picture of the store where two Arab terrorist suspects were arrested in Lackawanna, N.Y., and, just coincidentally, there is a six-year-old Arab boy outside playing with a toy gun his grandmother gave him on his birthday. Every day in our daily newspapers the difference between the two worlds is visible: one controlled and orderly, the other anarchic and wild; one world constitutes meaning, the other nullity at best, dehumanization at worst.

Sambo, Mumbo, Jumbo, Oompa-Loompas, Sombala Bombala Rombala Roh—all contribute to a discourse of nullity. Nullity can result in a lack of empathy, in a loss of identification with the subject. The subject, even when human, is nullified as nonhuman. A contemporary example is our placid acceptance of the death of more than half a million Iraqi children as a result of the U.N.-sponsored sanctions imposed after the Gulf War of 1991. In the United States, at least, these children became, very easily, nameless, faceless forms without substance, surface without interior. We do not know their names, their hometowns, their favorite colors, and we do not care to know because we lost sight of their individual identities. We could not actualize or conceptualize these children because they had already been culturally distanced. Such distancing is political but it is also perceptual. One wonders for how long we would have stood by and watched healthy children slowly starve or sick children be deprived of drugs due to an official policy if those children had been, say, Swedish or Swiss rather than Iraqi.

Nakedness is another signifier and naked brown bodies figure in picture book after picture book about India or Africa. *Lakshmi, the Water Buffalo Who Wouldn't* (1969) is written and illustrated by an Indian, Mehlli Gobhai, but the authenticity of the tale is not the point here. A little village boy might very well be scantily clad in hot weather and thus it would be valid to depict him as such. But the intentionality is neutralized by the effect, and the effect is undoubtedly that the nakedness becomes a signifier. Its association with primitivism is assured, but connotations of carnality, even sexuality, might also be considered. The discourse of nullification also comprises caricatures of the mystic or exotic East as in *Swami on Rye: Max in India* (1995) by Maira Kalman, which features a pink-turbaned, chocolate-complexioned caricature of a dog (Max) Swami, complete with third eye, on the cover. The text unabashedly exploits every stereotype from the "Snake Charming School" to "the Magic Lantern." Once again, nonsense is used as a means of nullification. A woman, described as willowy and draped in a sari, offers Max "nectar of hummingbird hums, fire of fireflies, and cheese juice." A levitating man introduces himself as "Vivek Shabaza-zaza-za." He places his palms together in the gesture of *Namaste* and proceeds with the introduction "I am your genial genie, your garrulous guru, your suave swami." He then proceeds to summon forth the standard mystical speculation of the meaning of life.

The description of India that ensues goes beyond the well-worn street scene: crowded, confused, and chaotic, with vendors, soothsayers, carts, cows, and rickshaws. It is nonsensical, even absurd: "A woman carrying four baskets of fish on her head and four fish carrying a basket of women on their heads." What results is not the familiar nonsense of children's stories; it is a pure Orientalist catalogue of India as a wondrous but strange place, a convolution of curries, heat, ancient ways, truth-telling third eyes, gyrating dancers, snakes, cricket, sacred temples, the Taj Mahal, ahimsa, nirvana, karma, monsoons, the works! If irony is intended, most children will surely miss it. The text sets them up to ridicule Indians (even if ever so gently) as both sagacious and silly in much the same spirit as we do Kipling's Hurree Babu and his many spin-offs. Such books participate in a process of objectification that constitutes a form of cultural violence, for they encourage children to see their own cultures as normative while the cultures of countries such as India are not simply exotic but bizarre. This prepares children to participate in a system of structural relations wherein other cultures become mere commodities in the picture-book market.

Innocuous adaptations of folk tales can also reify images of primitivism and poverty, portraying India or vaguely situated African lands as backward but colorful and their people as primal but enchanting. This is perhaps why folk and fairy tales from Asia and Africa are favored over more modern parables. Their settings, which are either rural and rudimentary or royal and opulent, sustain prevailing stereotypes that would be dislodged by the substitution of urban or Westernized landscapes. It is interesting to note in this context that picture books published in India contain far more representations of modern or industrial India than those published in the United States.

Even a cursory glance through picture books that depict Africa reveal the essentially anthropological stance from which it is also approached. Rural, pastoral life is the main setting for most stories or accounts; many scenes picture huts or marketplaces. Wild and domestic animals abound, as do musical instruments, drums, games, masks, lamps, ornaments, pots, calabashes, gourds, body markings, head wraps, firewood and so on. We are told more about peoples than about people, about ways of life than about specific events. Representations are often stylized and exaggerated or exotic and colorful. As late as 1961, *Otto in Africa* describes the continent in terms that are not simply vague but imprecise: "After four days at sea Otto and Duke saw Africa. There was a small city to the south, a desert with a fort to the east, and mountains to the west" (Pene du Bois 1961, 16). They decide to land in the east, at a fort, where they are warned by the soldiers that Abou the Fierce and his bandits are about to attack. The region is obviously a French colony. Although that is not stated, the French flags and soldiers' uniforms make it clear. Abou the Fierce and his bandits are portrayed as Arabs with great big hooked noses and iniquitous grins, people who brandish guns and swords.

Such images don't go away easily. The images of a people or a place established at an early age in the mind of a child can result in a lifelong association that is difficult to disrupt. In *Among the Believers*, V. S. Naipaul describes how reminiscent a scene he stumbles upon in Afghanistan is of his early reading, how it brings back the images of his childhood: "The Afghan encampment had taken me back to the earliest geography lessons of my childhood, to the drawings in my *Home Far Away* text-book: men creating homes, warmth, shelter in extreme conditions: the bow-and arrow Africans in their stockades, protected against the night-time dangers of the forest; the Kirghiz in their tents in the limitless steppes; the Eskimos in their igloos in the land of ice" (Naipaul 1981, 177).

Picture books posit in the child's imagination an orientalist world, a world that is alternatively exotic and resplendent or primitive and quaint. The apparently benign images of the forty thieves with their fierce expressions, voluminous turbans, and poised daggers in *Ali Baba and the Forty Thieves* take on a more sinister aspect when the inevitable association with Osama bin Laden occurs post–September 11, 2001. All turbaned, bearded men are then drawn into a mire of metonymic associations that are both damaging and dangerous.

This is not to suggest that there are no picture books that go beyond such renditions. More and more, picture books are focusing on actual families or individuals and their stories rather than simply on colorful customs or splendid landscapes. But it will be a slow process both in terms of output and in terms of the displacement of old and stubborn images, especially because the "classics"— Kipling's *Jungle Stories*, the Babar and Tarzan stories, and others— continue to enjoy widespread circulation and popularity. Disney and comic books help, of course, to keep them in circulation. In a world where the U.S. Defense Department consults with Hollywood scriptwriters and producers to help generals think outside the box (*New York Times*, November 19, 2001), anything is possible.

Where does this all lead, what does it all add up to, and how is it connected to character? Essentially, this: picture books are the earliest expressions of an epistemology that constructs the world in terms of alterity. They effectively set up the dichotomies, dichotomies that can appear benign at first glance, mere contrasts, but can assume a more portentous aspect when a first principle is assumed: good or evil, civilized or barbarian, clothed or naked, town or jungle, us or them. Picture books are where the "Manichean allegory" is first established.

> Distinguishing between material and discursive practices also allows us to understand more clearly the contradictions between the covert and overt aspects of colonialism. While the covert purpose is to exploit the colony's natural resources thoroughly and ruthlessly through the various imperialist material practices, the overt aim, as articulated by colonialist discourse, is to "civilize" the savage, to introduce him to all the benefits of Western cultures. Yet the fact that this overt aim, embedded as an assumption in all colonialist literature, is accompanied in colonialist texts by a more vociferous insistence, indeed by a fixation, upon the savagery and the evilness of the native should alert us to the real function of these texts: to justify imperial occupation and exploitation. If such literature can demonstrate that the barbarism of the native is irrevocable, or at least very deeply ingrained, then the European's attempt to civilize him can continue indefinitely, the exploitation of his resources can proceed without hindrance, and the European can persist in enjoying a position of moral superiority. (JanMohamed 1983, 81)

It would seem nothing short of shocking or absurd to so much as suggest such a nefarious intention or role for children's picture books. After all, can there be anything more innocent? But we are not talking here of plots hatched in boardrooms or official strategies. We are talking about a structure of seeing, the effect of which is both insidious and long lasting.

The stock illustrations of the Sambo story set up an immediate opposition, one that belies the actual content of this story about a resourceful and quick-thinking black child. The intentional blackness of Sambo immediately invites a contrast with whiteness, just as Sambo's environment (wherein tigers roam) invites a contrast with the cozy room where the child might be reading the book. Similarly, *Where the Wild Things Are* urges us to think in binaries: wild things and tame or civilized things, order and anarchy, compliance and noncompliance. African and Asian lands and peoples are essentially represented antonymically to Western lands, with the subject positioned as object and projected in a series of contrasting images: black in contrast to white, exotic in contrast to everyday, strange in contrast to familiar, threatening in contrast to safe, and primitive in contrast to civilized. Whereas picture books clearly distinguish between the familiar and the fantastic in Western settings, they are fuzzier in Eastern settings. The familiar is available to the American child in countless books that act as counterfoil to folk and fairy tales, but this is not the case with books about Asia and Africa. A recent picture book about India, *Aani and the Tree Huggers* (1995) by Jeannine Atkins, is relatively rare. The focus there is not on any mythological aspect but on the political situation, and the characters are functional rather than representational.

Ezra Jack Keats' *The Snowy Day* (1963) received critical attention and acclaim for some of the same reasons. The black child is subject, not object, although his sometimes featureless face is problematic in its suggestion of a generic black child. The point becomes clear when we ask ourselves how many books about mainstream white families we have come across that concern their daily lives, habits, and/or social customs for their own sake. Such details are usually incorporated into the story, if they figure at all, whereas in stories about African or Asian families, the customs and everyday activities are the story. Perspective is often one-dimensional, essentialist, or indiscriminate; settings function semiologically. Sambo, Babar, and Curious George all dwell in settings that are neither specified nor located in any particular geography. Geographical features are not simply blended or blurred, they are abstracted and become little more than sketchy or sporadic articulation of landscape, mere props in the production of otherness. The same often holds true for people.

Picture books do not promote a political agenda; rather they are a part of it, however inadvertently. By offering the child a clear demarcation between his or her world and another's, they lay the foundation for binary modes of perception. This is certainly not to argue for the erasure or glossing over of differences in some misguided if noble impetus toward universalism or "color blindness" or some sort of imaginary sisterhood or brotherhood. It is to indicate that there are psychological and political as well as physical aspects of representation. It is to argue that picture books participate in a logocentric production of knowledge, in which prepackaged perception is inherent and integral:

> For if it is true that no production of knowledge in the human sciences can ever ignore or disclaim its author's involvement as a human subject in his own circumstances, then it must also be true that for a European or American studying the Orient there can be no disclaiming the main circumstances of *his* actuality: that he comes up against the Orient as a European first, as an individual second. And to be a European or an American in such a situation is by no means an inert fact. It meant and means being aware, however dimly, that one belongs to a power with definite interests in the Orient, and more important, that one belongs to a part of the earth with a definite history of involvement in the Orient almost since the time of Homer. (Said 1979, 11)

Picture books are paradigmatic in terms of the production and the reproduction of a particular knowledge. They position the reader as subject and the material as object; they both invite and preclude participation. The reader is the observer and only in a limited sense the interpreter. Rather than hermeneutic, the mode of response to picture books is voyeuristic, akin to viewing the world as diorama. Often picture books presume a separation between text and reader and to some extent preclude heuristic modes of knowledge. They set the stage for later children's literature, for syntagmatic associations, and for the discourse of duality.

Kohl's measured pronouncement on the proper employment of picture books that are multivalent in theme, intent, or effect is entirely valid:

> The challenge parents face is how to integrate encounters with stereotypes into their children's sensibility and help their children become critical of aspects of the culture that denigrate or humiliate them or anyone else. The challenge is also how to let children feel free to develop their own evaluation of cultural practices. Instead of prohibiting things that tempt children, this means allowing them the freedom to explore things while trusting them to make sensible and humane judgments. It also means being explicitly critical of books and TV and encouraging children to discuss questions of judgment and values. This might seem a bit abstract, but I have found that watching TV and ques-

tioning what one sees, that visiting a toy store and suggesting which behaviors certain dolls and toys are designed to influence, can begin as early as children can talk. Nor need it be a grim exercise. (1995, 15)

Similarly, Perry Nodelman in *The Pleasures of Children's Literature* cautions that identification can lead to manipulation. When children identify with a character by accepting their similarity to that character they are also being asked to reach certain clear conclusions about right and wrong behavior. Says Nodelman, "The subject position represents unarticulated and implicit ideologies" (1988, 138).

Although they are not picture books but early chapter books, despite Quentin Blake's line illustrations, Roald Dahl's much-loved stories will be considered in this chapter because some of them have become controversial for the same reasons as many picture books. *Charlie and the Chocolate Factory* (1964), in particular, has been criticized for its patronizing, disdainful, even racist portrayal of the Oompa-Loompas who patently are meant to represent immigrant workers. On first look, the Oompa-Loompas would seem an obvious example of nullification. They are diminutive, funny looking, imported from Loompaland, and "what a terrible country it is!" (1964, 73). Here, however, the nullification may be a careful ploy. The obvious identification of the Oompa-Loompas with low-paid immigrant workers would seem to betray a somewhat different intentionality. The Oompa-Loompas are portrayed as happy with their lot, for it allows them to live and work in conditions far superior to those in their homeland. Typical of those who employ and exploit cheap immigrant labor, Mr. Wonka is full of praise for his Oompa-Loompa tribe. "They are wonderful workers," he comments and adds, "They all speak English now" (71). And, of course, the Oompa-Loompas love dancing and music. Primitivism and nakedness or near-nakedness are clearly, even deliberately, associated: "They still wear the same kind of clothes they wore in the jungle. They insist upon that. The men, as you can see for yourselves across the river, wear only deerskins. The women wear leaves, and the children wear nothing at all" (71). Like the great white protectors of colonial times, Mr. Wonka has rescued these benighted tribal members from their "terrible" country, where the jungles are thick and infested by the most dangerous beasts in the entire world (69). The

poor people had to live in treehouses to escape these beasts—
"whangdoodles" and "hornswogglers" and "snozzwangers"—and
they were practically starving to death, subsisting on green caterpil-
lars and red beetles and eucalyptus leaves and the bark of the bong-
bong tree all mashed up together.

Mr. Wonka lures them with their favorite food, the cacao bean,
symbolic of the money and material incentives that are part of the
myth of immigration to a nation such as the United States. Although
the Oompa-Loompas would seem to resemble some sort of pygmy
tribe, Dahl further complicates the geography by depicting the skin
of at least one of them as rosy-white and his long hair as golden-
brown (1964, 83). "He wore the usual deerskin slung over his shoulder," (83) we are told, which suggests simply some sort of archetypal
primitive tribe.

Where is the homeland of the Oompa-Loompas? As in the
Sambo books, it is a mythical and archetypal jumble, but somewhere
in Africa is certainly what is suggested. Like the habitat of Babar or
Curious George, the Oompa-Loompas' country of origin is not specified. That's part of the point. They are generic immigrant workers
whose ethnic identification is not necessary to their exploitation.
Dahl's deliberate—in fact, transparent—reiteration of stock images
and stereotypes points to satire. The system of "guest" workers and
the exploitation of immigrant labor in an industrial, capitalist context
is what is being satirized. Although *Charlie and the Chocolate Factory*
was published well before the era of rampant globalization, it antici-
pates and disparages its excesses.

The manifest ease of colonial assumptions and appropriation is
signified by Veruca Salt, the girl who got everything she wanted, and
who demands *"Daddy!* I want an Oompa-Loompa! I want you to get
me an Oompa-Loompa right away! I want to take it home with me!
Go on, Daddy! Get me an Oompa-Loompa!" (1964, 76). Again, as in
the first Curious George book, we are reminded of how the early
colonialists of the Americas captured fine native specimens to take
back with them to display to their compatriots. One might also recall
the little girl who begs for a Native American baby in *Little House on
the Prairie*, but more on that in a later chapter. In addition, the story is
satirical of the rigidities of class and economic status in England. It is
also significant that Dahl has the Oompa-Loompas stare back across
the river at the children in the chocolate factory who are staring at

them, returning the gaze, so to speak! In fact, one of them points at the children and whispers something to his companions, which results in the entire group bursting into peals of laughter (72). Dahl worked for the Shell Oil Company in Africa; it is probable that this experience opened his eyes to the true nature of colonial authority and ambitions. Yet *Going Solo*, where he describes his experiences in Africa in most detail, is a characteristic colonialist account of adventures in a landscape replete with dense foliage, spiky thorn trees, burnt scrubland, deadly snakes, huge vultures, and foraging lions. Dahl was obviously the benign colonial, kind and supportive of his "boy," but not overtly questioning of either the purposes or the practices of colonialism. Dahl was part of a commercial enterprise, not the colonial administrative network, but of course they were connected. Included in *Going Solo* is a brief paean to the latter:

> The District Officers in Tanganyika were a breed I admired. Admittedly they were sunburnt and sinewy, but they were not gophers. They were all university graduates with good degrees, and in their lonely outposts they had to be all things to all men. They were the judges whose decisions settled both tribal and personal disputes. They were the advisers to tribal chiefs. They were often the givers of medicines and the saviours of the sick. They administered their own vast districts by keeping law and order under the most difficult circumstances. And wherever there was a District Officer, the Shell man on safari was welcome to stay the night at his house. (1986, 31)

The wacky characters he describes in the first chapter of his book ("The Voyage Out") belie this account. As one of them explains, "People go quite barmy when they live too long in Africa" (1986, 9). Dahl refers to the empire builders he encounters on the ship as he headed from London to Mombassa as comedians. They may, in fact, have been the inspiration for some of the eccentric characters in his stories. The British, he contends, maintain their sanity in a foul climate among foreign people by allowing themselves to go "dotty" (3). His accounts of their bizarre behavior is indulgent, certainly tolerant, even nonjudgmental:

> What I still remember so clearly about that voyage is the extraordinary behaviour of my fellow passengers. I had never before

encountered that peculiar Empire-building breed of Englishman who spends his whole life working in distant corners of British territory. Please do not forget that in the 1930s the British Empire was still very much the British Empire, and the men and women who kept it going were a race of people that most of you have never encountered and now you never will. I considered myself very lucky to have caught a glimpse of this rare species while it still roamed the forests and foot-hills of the earth, for today it is totally extinct. (1986, 2–3)

Through all his tales for children, however, runs a distinct dislike for authority that is arbitrary, gratuitously cruel, mean-spirited, and capricious. Roald Dahl emerged from a classic British background even though his family was Norwegian. His father wanted all his children to be educated in English schools, insisting that they were the best in the world and, after his premature death, Dahl's mother honored his wishes. Roald Dahl's autobiographical books, *Boy* (1984) and *Going Solo* (1986), indicate that his inspirations for the cantankerous, ornery characters who figure so prominently in his tales were drawn from the adults he encountered in his schooldays rather than from the English colonials he met in Africa. It was the family doctor who persuaded his mother that, even at nine, young Roald was not too young for boarding school. When he feigns an attack of acute appendicitis in order to get sent home, if only for a few days, the doctor reminds him that "Life is tough, and the sooner you learn how to cope with it the better for you" (1984, 99).

Significant for this study is the very different conception of children's character that emerges in Dahl's stories. In the forthcoming chapters we will confront repeatedly the stiff upper lip principle advocated by the doctor and so celebrated in British literature for children. In English children's classics, as well as in the writings of the most widely read English children's author of all, Enid Blyton, we meet a model of character that is essentially heroic. The British child, especially the male child, must be tough, strong, sturdy, robust, resilient, courageous, direct, trustworthy, and loyal. Instead, Dahl offers us youngsters who survive by their wits. Brain is more important than brawn. They are resilient and courageous, but it is a different kind of resilience and courage, born not of physical bravery but of mental adaptation. In book after book, a child rebels and triumphs over adults who are malicious, ruthless, or spiteful. This is achieved by outsmarting and outwitting them, by thinking up clever practical schemes to resist oppression, fight injustice, and obtain liberation. The children in his books are wily, sometimes devious by necessity. They can often be circuitous and, while they may be loyal, it is strictly on their own terms. They present a stark contrast to the incipient colonial builders we will encounter in the following chapters.

In *Boy* we see clearly where Dahl's conception and experience of vindictive adults came from. The adults who entered his life during his school years were in stark contrast to his enlightened father, his strong but loving and protective mother, his nanny, and many siblings. When his mother discovered that he had been unfairly caned as a boy of about nine, she confronted the headmaster who delivered the punishment and informed him that she would not allow such treatment, that they don't beat small children like that where she came from. That such memories stayed with Dahl when he wrote his imaginative tales becomes clear from his description in *Boy* of the headmaster of his subsequent school, St. Peter's, which he attended between the ages of nine and thirteen:

> I have already told you that *all* Headmasters are giants, and this one was no exception. He advanced upon my mother and shook her by the hand, then he shook me by the hand and as he did so he gave me the flashing grin a shark might give to a small fish just before he gobbles it up. One of his front teeth, I noticed, was edged all the way round with gold, and his hair was slicked down with so much hair-cream that it glistened like butter. (1984, 79)

The masters at the school were tough, Dahl tells us, and if you wanted to survive, you had to become pretty tough yourself. The boys were caned liberally and Dahl, like the others, feared the cane, which was not simply an instrument for beating but "a weapon for wounding" that "lacerated the skin" and "caused severe black and scarlet bruising that took three weeks to disappear" (120).

At Repton, the public school Dahl attended after St. Peter's, the prefects or Boazers as they were called there, could thrash them for leaving a football sock on the floor of the changing room instead of hanging it up on a peg. The Boazers had the power of life and death over the junior boys: "A Boazer could thrash us for a hundred and one other piddling little misdemeanours—for burning his toast at tea-time, for failing to get his study fire burning in spite of spending half your pocket money on fire-lighters, for being late at roll-call, for talking in evening Prep, for forgetting to change into house-shoes at six o'clock. The list was endless" (1984, 141). After each beating the victim was made to stand in the middle of the room and lower his pajama trousers so that the abrasion could be surveyed. The Boazers would then compliment each other for landing every lash in the same place or for delivering the lashings without drawing wet blood. This was clearly the infamous culture of British public schools, and in his writings Dahl rejects it unequivocally. Adults who exploit, hurt, or tyrannize hapless children, who abuse their authority and misconstrue their power, meet with dire but well-deserved fates.

To the children at St. Peter's, a grown-up was a grown-up, their age irrelevant, and all grown-ups were considered dangerous creatures (1984, 85). The masters were sadistic enough to leave the door to their common room open so that they could hear the sound of the cane clearly when the headmaster was administering punishment across the hall. That the common practice of flogging affected him deeply and lastingly, Dahl makes clear in *Boy*:

> By now I am sure you will be wondering why I lay so much emphasis upon school beatings in these pages. The answer is that I cannot help it. All through my school life I was appalled by the fact that masters and senior boys were allowed literally to wound other boys, and sometimes quite severely. I couldn't get over it. I never have got over it. It would, of course, be unfair to suggest that *all* masters were constantly beating the daylights out of *all* the boys in those days. They weren't. Only a few did so, but that was quite enough to leave a lasting impression of horror upon me. (1984, 145)

Dahl goes on to distinguish between "a few quick sharp tickles on the rump," of which he does not disapprove, and the sadistic flogging he witnessed both at St. Peter's and at Repton. Even the school matron was no warm and motherly figure, but a powerful and forceful woman who drops soap flakes into the open mouth of a snoring boy.

When a boy called Ellis has his enormous boil lanced without warning by the doctor who plunges the point of a scalpel deep into its center, he screams "like a stuck pig," only to be chided by the matron who admonishes him not to make a fuss about nothing. Pain, as Dahl points out, was something they were expected to endure. When Dahl himself almost has his nose ripped off his face in a car accident, he endures the trauma courageously. But what his stories describe is not so much the raw physical courage the British consistently lauded as part of their self-image, but a mental and moral courage. The public school ethic prevailed at Repton, as it did at the Rugby of *Tom Brown's Schooldays*, which will be discussed in a later chapter. Physical prowess was glorified and even the masters treated an athlete with the utmost respect and attention. They were, says Dahl, "the demigods, the chosen few" (1984, 162).

Dahl's resistance to the abuse of authority came early. He was a talented athlete who became captain of Fives as well of squash-racquets and normally would have been appointed a Boazer in recognition of his talents. But the authorities did not trust him because of his dislike of rules and his unpredictability. Perhaps his Norwegian heritage played into it as well, although Dahl does not mention it as a factor. He acknowledges that some people are born to wield power and exercise authority and he was not one of them. He agreed with his housemaster on this point, knowing that he would have been incapable of upholding the whole principle of being a Boazer by refusing to beat Fags.

Power and authority wielded without warrant, especially when accompanied by cruelty, are reviled in almost every one of his books. James in *James and the Giant Peach* (1961), the little boy in *The Witches* (1973), Sophie in *The BFG* (1982), George in *George's Marvelous Medicine* (1980), and, of course, Matilda in *Matilda* (1982) all outmaneuver and outsmart the adults who are preying on them, whether they be witches, giants, mean grandmothers, aunts, or parents. James's aunts, Aunt Sponge and Aunt Spiker, are not only selfish, lazy, and cruel but they beat him for no reason at all, deprive him of toys and books, and disparage him constantly. The Twits are disgusting people who do disgusting things to each other, capture birds for pie, and force their captive monkeys to do everything upside down and stand on their heads for hours on end. The farmers in *Fantastic Mr. Fox* (1970) are nasty, foul, and mean. The witches are terrifyingly malevolent and spiteful although they disguise themselves well as benevolent ladies. Dahl's seemingly misogynistic insistence in the opening pages that only women can be witches is consistent with the *Malleus*

Maleficarum of 1486, the leading authority on witchcraft for the next two centuries, which clearly identifies women as the chief practitioners of evil superstitions and witchcraft (Neave 1988, 4).

The oppressed are always children or animals. Dahl does introduce adults who are kind and caring—even if they are eccentric. The grandmother in *The Witches*, the teacher in *Matilda*, the parents and grandparents in *Charlie and the Chocolate Factory* and *Charlie and the Great Glass Elevator* (1978) are caring, generous, and understanding. The BFG is a lovable, sensitive, and compassionate giant. The insects in *James and the Giant Peach* are enormous and would generally be considered repulsive: an old green grasshopper, a spider, a centipede, an earthworm, and a silkworm. But they quickly reassure James that he is not their designated victim but one of the crew. They would never dream of hurting him, they reassure James, and remind him that they are all in the same boat. We see a solidarity among the oppressed that probably stems from Dahl's remembrance of his schooldays. "Small boys can be very comradely when a member of their community has got into trouble," he tells us in *Boy*, "and even more so when they feel an injustice has been done" (1984, 122). A boy called Highton at St. Peter's wrote to his father to report the injustice of Dahl's caning, since Dahl's father was not alive. Although nothing much came of it, Dahl never forgot the kindness shown by one small boy to another. That kindness is reflected in the insects' treatment of James, in Mr. Fox's generosity to his fellow animals, and in the concern of the little girl in *The Magic Finger* (1966) for the ducks her neighbors hunt.

What enables those who are the underdog to ultimately succeed is quick thinking, clever scheming, problem solving, cooperative effort, and calm outlook. In a culture that exalts courage, we actually have characters confessing that they are afraid, as does Charlie in *Charlie and the Great Glass Elevator*. As is often the case in Dahl books, there is a reversal. Here, those in authority act and sound like little children—the president actually pleads with his nanny not to make him drink milk and the ex-chief of the army is made to stand in the corner by the nanny, Miss Tibbs. Similarly, in *The Magic Finger*, the ducks and the hunters reverse roles, which results in the reformation of the latter. And in *The Twits* (1980), the Twits end up on their heads while the monkeys turn on their trainers. Dahl's books inscribe a very different concept of character from that of most British children's literature.

They relocate power and redefine authority. They empower children to act not by virtue of race or nationality but as individuals who draw upon their own inner resources. While there are certainly some dubious racial references—to weird African languages, for instance, knock-knock jokes that play on Chinese names, or the reddish-brown skin of the gruesome Bloodbottler giant—such references are not surprising given his time and background. More noteworthy for the purpose of this work is that Dahl subverts the prevailing paradigm of character.

Roald Dahl was, of course, predated by Lewis Carroll whose absurdist tale *Alice in Wonderland* (1865) was revolutionary for its time, focusing on entertainment rather than edification. Like Dahl's stories, *Alice* uses reversals and inversions, which compels the reader to question the normative and obliges him or her to adopt a relativist perspective. If physical dimensions are not fixed—Alice grows larger and smaller alternatively—then character is certainly not. Her emotional responses are in constant flux. Even identity is negotiable:

> "I've seen a good many little girls in my time, but never *one* with such a neck as that! No, no! You're a serpent and there's no use denying it. I suppose you'll be telling me next that you never tasted an egg!"
>
> "I *have* tasted eggs, certainly," said Alice, who was a very truthful child; "but little girls eat eggs quite as much as serpents do, you know."
>
> "I don't believe it," said the Pigeon; "but if they do, why, then they're a kind of serpent: that's all I can say."
>
> This was such a new idea to Alice, that she was quite silent for a minute or two, which gave the Pigeon the opportunity of adding, "You're looking for eggs, I know *that* well enough; and what does it matter to me whether you're a little girl or a serpent?"
>
> "It matters a good deal to *me*," said Alice hastily; "but I'm not looking for eggs, as it happens; and, if I was, I shouldn't want *yours*: I don't like them raw" (1865, 354). (Griffith and Frey 1996)

Alice in Wonderland forces both the adult and the child reader to acknowledge the critical dimension of perspective: spatial, temporal, and even moral. When Alice asks the Footman how she is to get in, he retorts, "*Are* you to get in at all?" (355). Alice herself considers "How puzzling all these changes are! I'm never sure what I'm going to be, from one minute to another!" (354).

Alice in Wonderland was completed in 1863. By that time, India had been declared a crown colony and the Empire was nearing its zenith. Surely it would not be too far-fetched to read a reference to empire in the exchange between Alice and the March Hare who reprimands her for her lack of civility in sitting down at a table without being invited (359). Certainly there is an antiauthoritarian bias that emerges in the depiction of the random and zealous tyranny of the queen and the rather foolish, besotted response of the king. Most important of all for this study of character constructions is the antiheroic nature of Alice who can be courageous and considerate but also recalcitrant and petulant.

Alice in Wonderland looks forward to the stories of Roald Dahl and, like them, is antonymic and iconoclastic. Elaine Showalter's point in *Sexual Anarchy: Gender and Culture at the Fin de Siècle* (1990) that many books written primarily for boys in the Victorian era "represent a yearning for escape from a confining society, rigidly structured in terms of gender, class, and race" may be applied to some of these works. *Alice in Wonderland* is one of the few that permits such an escape for a girl. Even Wendy in *Peter Pan* must maintain her girl role of playing mother while engaged in adventure and escape. Gendered roles are most clear in Beatrice Potter's *The Tale of Peter Rabbit* (1902) where his sisters are good little girls who listen to their mother, while Peter breaks free, his disobedience and defiance gaining tacit approval from his mother, who recognizes his adventures as a rite of passage toward adulthood.

In the next chapters we encounter works that are far more prescriptive and rigid in their notions of character and that promote a far more valorized character type.

3

Touchstones

The year 1897, in the annals of the British people, was marked by a declaration to the whole world of their faith in the higher destinies of their race. If a strong man, when the wine sparkles at the feast and the lights are bright, boasts of his prowess, it is well he should have an opportunity of showing in the cold and grey of the morning that he is no idle braggart. And unborn arbiters, with a wider knowledge, and more developed brains, may trace in recent events the influence of that mysterious Power which, directing the progress of our species, and regulating the rise and fall of Empires, has afforded that opportunity to a people, of whom at least it may be said, that they have added to the happiness, the learning and the liberties of mankind.

—Winston Churchill, *The Story of the Malakand Field Force*

God . . . has chosen to teach Rome one way and England another. He has chosen to make you an English woman, a member of the Church of England, English in education, character, brain, feelings, duties: you cannot unmake yourself. You are already a member of that Spiritual One body, called the English nation . . . consider whether you know what the Church of England is, what God's education of England has been, and whether the one or the

> other are consistent with each other. I say they are. I say
> that the Church of England is wonderfully and mysteri-
> ously fitted for the souls of a free Norse-Saxon race; for
> men whose ancestors fought by the side of Odin, over
> whom a descendant of Odin now rules.
>
> —Charles Kingsley, *Letters and Memories*

The texts that have come to be designated "children's classics" through the years, whether or not they were written primarily for children, may be considered among the main repositories for domi-nant cultural narratives. Any attempt to deconstruct such texts, whether that term is used loosely or in its specific Derridean sense, must also attempt to deconstruct the children to whom they were and are sold, sold in both the commercial and the ideological sense. The text as well as the vendor of the text presumes—in fact, postulates—a particular child reader, a reader who is then as much constructed as the children who are characters in the books themselves. Because both the text and the criticism of the text are addressed to those who hy-pothesize such a reader, the subject is not just the constructed child of the text but the constructed child for whom the text is intended, whether by author or by purveyor.

Jacqueline Rose in *The Case of Peter Pan; or, The Impossibility of Children's Fiction* contends that the child is not simply constructed but perhaps fictitious (1984, 10). The inevitable consequence is not just a silenced text but also a silenced reader. This is the reader who does not respond to the text in a prescribed or predictable manner, the reader who does not relate to the text at all, or the reader who re-jects the text, as a whole or in part, as worthy of being considered a "classic." As Karen Lesnik-Oberstein points out, "Deconstruction dissolves the polarity of subject and object: the critic is not an objec-tive observer or analyst of the object, but a participant, who is read as much by the text as the text is read by him. The deconstructionist does not view himself as a subject exterior to an object. Text and critic mutually and continually construct one another" (1994, 152).

Frances Hodgson Burnett's *The Secret Garden* (1912) reads the reader even as the reader reads the text. Critics, teachers, and par-ents alike commend this work as an enduring children's classic. It has never been out of print and is still widely read and recom-mended to children who are about the age of its main protagonist,

Mary. The fact that it is seldom problematized in cultural, social, or political terms tells us as much about its readers as it does about the text. It tells us that both reader and text participate in the same cultural narrative. John Rowe Townsend agrees that "it is perfectly possible to judge books for children by non-literary standards. It is legitimate to consider the social or moral or psychological or educational impact of a book; to consider how many children, and what kind of children, will like it. But it is dangerous to do this and call it criticism" (14). Dangerous for whom one might ask. Text or reader?

In the age of Harry Potter, *The Secret Garden* might have been as neglected as some of Burnett's other works—*Little Lord Fauntleroy* (1886) or *The Lost Prince* (1914), for example—given its somewhat slow pace and anachronistic context of colonial India and British aristocracy. Both *The Secret Garden* and *A Little Princess* (1906) have been kept alive as texts by theatrical and film productions, especially the former. This tale of the simultaneous awakening of a garden and of two young children has been retold, set to music, and consequently revived in countless local productions by amateur theatricals as well as in professional productions. In 1938 it was staged in England as a musical, although it had a short run. It came to Broadway from 1991 to 1993, winning a Tony award and going on the road successfully both in the United States and abroad.

Colonial India, in the vision of Frances Hodgson Burnett, who had never set foot in it, lacks entirely the rosy tints with which nostalgia, reminiscence, and longings for lost power colored it in so many contemporary and later accounts. Mary Lennox's vitriolic, even obscene, treatment of her servants in India and her cantankerous attitude toward the country might have exposed a less sentimental and more sordid side of the relations between the colonizer and colonized had Burnett in any way thought to problematize these issues. Instead, she allows Mary her high-handed ways with the Indian servants with no censure or intervention of the sort she consistently provides when it comes to the English servants. Then Burnett makes it clear that Mary's haughty ways will not long be tolerated. And yet haughty ways are tolerated from her cousin, Colin, the young lord of the manor. Burnett lets the reader know unequivocally that Colin can rant and rave and order everyone about like a "rajah" not only because of his social status or his gender, but because of his invalid condition, and the servants' consequent fear that any refusal or reprimand would jeopardize his health—whereas Mary's autocratic and far more obnoxious treatment of the Indian servants is allowed to stand as the natural order of things, as a matter of course, afforded by racial privilege rather than determined by character or circumstance.

Not only is any narrative mediation absent, but the author neglects to articulate the Indian servants' response while she so clearly articulates the English servants' response, as we will soon see. It probably does not even occur to her that they may actually have feelings, much less a voice. Critics participate in this silencing by failing to comment on it. For instance, Phyllis Bixler, whose work *The Secret Garden: Nature's Magic* (1996) is one of the most detailed on the subject, notes Burnett's adulation of aristocracy and royalty (80). She agrees with critics who claim that Colin simply exchanges "the tyranny of an invalid for the imperious ego of an estate master" with the apparent approval of the author (80). Yet, in her chapter on "Class and Gender" she fails, as do most critics, to comment on or even notice the imprint of class-consciousness in a colonial system where class is cross-fertilized by race. No mention is made whatsoever of Mary's outrageous treatment of her Indian servants, outrageous even in the colonial context where, while there was no presumption of equality, there was, according to many memoirs and journals, at least an expectation of essential civility, especially after the country became a crown colony. Annotative comments in regard to Mary's treatment of her Indian servants are conspicuously absent not only from the author but also from almost every critic. Mary's behavior, which is the direct outcome of a position of privilege, is sanitized by being described as spoilt. Bixler notes that "anyone who reads widely in the criticism of a text as complex as *The Secret Garden* is likely to discover that, having their own ideologies and personal interests, adult readers can be selective, too" (86). Her own occlusion is an example.

Similarly, Mavis Reimer, writing on *A Little Princess*, notes that one of the most significant methods of reinforcement and transmission of implicit messages is through the constitution of a reader by the text. She quotes Mary Poovey, who points out that the "structural paradigms" of a text "construct the reader as a certain kind of reader and position this reader in a particular relation to the system of connotations to which a text gives specific form and in which it therefore participates" (2003, 111–12). It is telling that Reimer herself seems to constitute and position a reader in precisely this fashion. The word that betrays this is "order" in the following sentence: "Burnett's story of Sara Crewe specifically invokes the context of India and Anglo-Indian relations. British power over India had been transferred from the East India Company to the Crown in 1858, in the wake of the restoration of order after the Indian Mutiny of 1857, events Burnett alludes to in *Sara Crewe*" (114). Reimer does not say "the order" but simply "order," thereby positioning her in a system of structural relations where the restoration of British colonial rule is conceived of as order.

Burnett does not invite the reader in any way to perceive Mary's manners, which are described as "imperious" and "Indian" in the same breath (Burnett 1912, 42), as the outcome of a system that not only sanctioned but in many cases mandated an imperious attitude. Mary fetches no censure from the author until she tries the same tactics toward the English servants:

> Mary listened to her [Martha, the young housemaid] with a grave, puzzled expression. The native servants she had been used to in India were not in the least like this. They were obsequious and servile and did not presume to talk to their masters as if they were their equals. They made salaams and called them "protector of the poor" and names of that sort. Indian servants were commanded to do things, not asked. It was not the custom to say "Please" and "Thank you," and Mary had always slapped her Ayah in the face when she was angry. She wondered little what this girl would do if one slapped her in the face. She was a round, rosy, good-natured looking creature, but she had a sturdy way which made Mistress Mary wonder if she might not even slap back—if the person who slapped her was only a little girl. (Burnett 1912, 25)

The loving attachment to their ayahs borne and testified to by generations of English men and women who had been raised in India in their early years is completely absent from Mary's relationship to her ayah. We are told in *Plain Tales from the Raj* (1975): "Archetypal ayahs are always 'very gentle, sweet-natured women with beautiful hands, very gentle and beautiful in their movements'" (Allen 1975, 22). Perhaps because Burnett did not herself come from a colonial family and had no Indian background, she did not understand how personal relationships so often belied political ones. As one old India hand recounts with regard to his servants: "They gave you the most wonderful service in the world and in return you felt that they were your people and that you jolly well had to look after them" (Allen 1975, 78).

Of course, it was a feudal relationship. Of course, love for one's ayah (as for one's mammy) did not alter the fact that she was bound in a state of servitude or slavery, as the case may be. Burnett's sketchy representations of interpersonal relationships in India depict such relationships as aloof and unsentimental. While this is certainly not how they were characterized in countless memoirs, she perhaps stumbles inadvertently on a larger historical truth, one that is recognized at the end of E. M. Forster's *A Passage to India*. Within a structure of inequality, a loving personal relationship will inevitably be affected or even precluded by the political pathology. That is why at the end of the novel, when the Indian doctor Aziz tells Fielding, an Englishman he has come to know and respect, that it is only when all the English have been expelled from India that they can be friends. When Fielding asks why they could not be friends right then, the answer is cosmological and comes from the earth and the sky: "No, not yet. . . . No, not there" (Forster 1924, 322).

Although the hierarchy of class is strictly preserved in Yorkshire, where *The Secret Garden* is primarily set, the classes can commingle, as they do within the framework of the friendship the children develop with Dickon, who is "only a common moor boy, in patched clothes and with a funny face and a rough, rusty-red head" (Burnett 1912, 97). Despite his humble position, Dickon is universally respected and admired, as is his mother, Susan Sowerby. It is the advice of this mother of twelve children that the lord of the manor takes, although she is a working-class woman, and it is she who secretly brings provisions to the children. A similar relationship with any of the Indian servants would be unthinkable to Burnett, although they did indeed exist, although chiefly in the context of childhood, or between an officer and his orderly.

Charles Allen comments, "Ayah was the open door through which contact with India was made" (1975, 22). But again, Burnett, lacking an India background altogether, would not have understood the depth of such relationships. What she does apparently know of India would have been common knowledge at the time, part of the prevailing mythology of empire, that it was everything that England was not, its diacritical contrast. *The Secret Garden* sets up a series of oppositions: life and death, light and dark, stasis and growth, sickness and health, black and white, Indian and English, sallow and rosy, thin and fat. This sort of binary thinking was a natural corollary of empire building. After all, if an oppositional difference could not be established between "them" and "us," then the purported moral basis for empire would be lost, leaving only an economic or political rationale.

The very first paragraph of *The Secret Garden* makes the distinction between the light hair of Mary and the dark faces of her servants. The fact that Mary was yellow in complexion is clearly associated with being born in India and always being ill. The fact that she was a fretful and ugly baby as well is also indirectly ascribed to the land of her birth. And so her care is allocated to her ayah as opposed to her mother. Until she has been in Yorkshire for a while, she is consistently characterized as thin. But once she, and later Colin, begin to "plump up" (Burnett 1912, 250), the word *fat* is used repeatedly and always positively, as it is associated with health. The fresh air of the garden and the outdoors is contrasted with the stuffy air of the room in which Colin has been self-confined for so many years.

Both appetite and fresh air are associated with the English moors, whereas "In India she [Mary] had always felt hot and too languid to care much about anything. The fact was that the fresh wind from the moor had begun to blow the cobwebs out of her young brain and to waken her up a little" (48). Running in the wind has warmed her blood and made her healthily hungry for the first time in her life. In contrast, the Indian climate (as it is generalized here) is not conducive to a healthy appetite, to vitality, or to caring about anything that grows. When Mary asks for a bit of earth in response to her uncle's question as to whether there was anything she wanted, he is reminded of his wife who fell from a branch in the garden and died, "someone else who loved the earth and things that grow" (119). The word *earth* is not used in a general sense here: Mary means English earth. In India, Mary tells him, she did not know anything about gardens. She was always ill and tired and hot. Sometimes she made little beds in the sand and stuck flowers in them. Even gardens symbolized stasis there. "But here it is different" (118). Here she watches the daffodils and lilies and snowdrops work their way out of the earth, "pushing up pale-green points because the spring is coming" (133).

This difference extends to health, to interest in growing things, and to involvement in outdoor activities. But most crucially, it extends to character. When Mary tells Dickon how other English children in India had teased her by chanting the old nursery rhyme, "Mistress Mary, quite contrary," he replies, sniffing a handful of rich black Yorkshire soil crumpled in his hand, "there doesn't seem to be no need for no one to be contrary when there's flowers an' such like, an' such lots o' friendly wild things runnin' about makin' homes for themselves, or buildin' nests an' singin' an' whistling, does there?" (109).

Topography is perceived as directly influencing character, certainly behavior. In E. M. Forster's *A Passage to India*, irritation is seen as exuding from the very soil. "Could one have been so petty on a Scotch moor or an Italian alp?" wonders one of the English characters as he observes how cross or wretched everyone in the group seemed. "There seemed no reserve of tranquility to draw upon in India. Either none, or else tranquility swallowed up everything" (1924, 78).

Mary's mother and Colin's mother are contrasts. The former was "a great beauty who cared only to go to parties and amuse herself with gay people" (Burnett 1912, 2). The latter was also a great beauty, but a kind and tender person who had won a place in the heart of the simple Yorkshire rustics who worked on the estate. By all indications, she would have been a wonderful mother to Colin and, according to Susan Sowerby, she still watches over him. There is, however, congruence between Mary and Colin. Both are tyrannical and self-centered initially, although Burnett reserves her harshest words for Mary, going so far as to describe her as "a little pig" (2), the very epithet Mary uses for her ayah, Saidie, "because to call a native a pig is the worst insult of all" (3). In India, Mary had not been an affectionate child "and had never cared much for anyone" (5) but in England "her cold little way" (38) and her "sour and cross" (40) demeanor give way to a newfound affinity for people, as she counts those she has come to like.

Similarly, her "imperious Indian voice" (42) is replaced by a soft, eager, and coaxing tone as she speaks to the robin in Ben Weatherstaff's presence. When Mary first speaks to Ben, she speaks as she would have "to a native, and had not known that a cross, sturdy old Yorkshireman was not accustomed to salaam to his masters, and be merely commanded by them to do things" (91). In addition to her personality, Mary's appearance, which is described as thin, sallow, and ugly (46), is slowly being transformed. The unconditional acceptance and obedience of the servants in India is replaced by the frank gruff manner of Ben Weatherstaff who tells Mary, "Tha' an me are a good bit alike. . . . We was wove out of th' same cloth. We're neither of us good-lookin' an' we're both of us as sour as we look. We've got the same nasty tempers, both of us, I'll warrant" (41). Both Mary and Colin are used to being waited on, Mary by "blacks" as Martha calls Indians (69) and Colin by the staff of Misselthwaite Manor.

The opulent Orientalist portrait of India that Mary paints, one of elephants and camels and "officers going to hunt tigers" (69) and rajahs, stands in sharp contrast to rugged Yorkshire, with its expanse of moors where wuthering winds alternate with "warm, sweet wafts" of sun (155), so unlike the hot oppressive sun of India. The scenery of Yorkshire is in direct contrast to that of India: "Never, never had Mary dreamed of a sky so blue. In India skies were hot and blazing; this was of a deep, cool blue, which almost seemed to sparkle like the waters of some lovely, bottomless lake, and there, high, high in the arched blueness, floated small clouds of snow-white fleece" (60).

In India new growth after the rains is riotous and uncontrolled. "Everything is hot, and wet, and green after the rains in India. . . . And I think things grow up in a night" (64), Mary tells Ben Weatherstaff, the old gardener, who replies, "The crocuses and snowdrops and daffydowndillys won't g'ow up in a night. Tha'll have to wait for 'em. They' poke up a bit higher here, and push out a spike more there, an' uncurl a leaf this day an' another that" (64). Nature is ordered and purposeful here; in India it is wild and unrestrained.

India is a persistent presence in the novel. It is a referent for Mary long after she leaves its shores, but it is a totally disembodied one. None of the Indian characters is given shape or voice other than by proxy. Perhaps Burnett shied away from direct characterizations because of her lack of familiarity with the country. Or she may have felt that shadowy or sketchy references and the vaguest outlines of Indian characters would suffice for the purpose they serve in the story. Unfortunately this seems to be the trend in productions of the musical version of *The Secret Garden* as well. Since the musical takes liberties with the book anyway, there is scope for reinterpretation and revision. Instead, most productions simply recycle the sorry old

Orientalist stereotypes and focus far more on the trappings than on the theme, which is not problematized at all. India becomes a bland backdrop in most of these productions. In a production I saw in Amherst, Massachusetts, the Indians, aside from some singing parts, were mostly mute, as they are in the book. They appeared sporadically and suddenly to wave their arms and strike strange poses in some sort of impersonation of spiritual beings, still the shadowy stick figures of so much colonial writing.

The only affectionate allusion Mary makes to India is her recollection of the lullabies her ayah would sing to her and which she then uses to soothe Colin. And, in probably the only correspondence that is established between India and England, Dickon's ability to charm animals is compared to that of Indian snake charmers. The country's central role in this story is to be a foil for almost everything in England: the climate and the seasons, the landscape and the flora, the people and the places. But what is especially interesting is the connection between climate and character that is so clearly established in this tale. This is a tale of transformation, one that is wrought essentially by the outdoors, by nature, by wholesome activity, and by wholesome people like Dickon. Not only is a garden brought back to life but Mary and Colin are transformed from sickly, pale, petulant, obstinate, and difficult children to "new creatures" (260), robust and rosy, laughing, with hearty appetites for both food and fresh air.

Previously, both children had been confined and had lived closed, claustrophobic lives. Colin's sickroom bears a correspondence to India in that it curtailed and severely limited his options. And, in a sense, India had been one vast sickroom for Mary. It had drained her of any vigor or vitality and had thus curtailed her movements as well. Colin at least had a window on the world through his picture books: "Shut in and morbid as his life had been, Colin had more imagination than she had, and at least he had spent a good deal of time looking at wonderful books and pictures" (210). Having lived shut up in a room in a great manor, Colin "had lived on a sort of desert island all his life and as he had been the king of it he had made his own manners and had had no one to compare himself with" (233).

Mary had been like that too, but since she has been at Misselthwaite, she has gradually realized her own lack of congeniality. Having come to this self-discovery, she naturally wishes to communicate it to Colin. Mary has come to find out, in the words of Susan

Sowerby, the eminently sensible and capable rustic Yorkshire woman, that the whole orange does not belong to her. And it is she, Mrs. Medlock predicts, who is likely to teach Colin that the whole orange does not belong to him either and to enable him to find out the size of his own quarter. It is Mary who brings "with her a waft of fresh air full of the scent of the morning" (196), who brings with her the spring, and who transmits to Colin the rejuvenating effects of fresh air. She, in turn, has been taught by Dickon: "Lie on your back and draw in long breaths of it," she instructs Colin. "That's what Dickon does when he's lying on the moor. He says he feels it in his veins and it makes him strong and he feels as if he could live forever and ever. Breathe it and breathe it" (197).

Similarly, when Colin has one of his monstrous tantrums, it is "savage little Mary" (176) who calms him down. First she threatens to frighten him by screaming louder than he can. She even warns him that he will scream himself to death and she wishes he would (175). She peremptorily orders the nurse to show her his back in order to prove to him that there is no lump there. The nurse and Mrs. Medlock, the housekeeper, are aghast and huddle near the door, staring at her with their mouths half open. In light of the fact that Mary has lived until now entirely in India, the word "savage" is noteworthy. Their confined environments have, however, turned both children into savages: "A nice, sympathetic child could neither have thought nor said such things, but it just happened that the shock of hearing them was the best possible thing for this hysterical boy whom no one had ever dared to restrain or contradict" (176).

Mary's loneliness prior to her discovery of the garden and her friendship with Colin and Dickon is one of the things that made her sour and cross, but India is the major reason. In fact, whenever Mary grows contrary or obstinate, it is associated with being "imperious and Indian" again (101). The air of the moors is credited with Mary's transformation:

> Every morning she awoke in her tapestried room and found Martha kneeling upon the hearth building her fire; every morning she ate her breakfast in the nursery which had nothing amusing in it; and after each breakfast she gazed out of the window across to the huge moor, which seemed to spread out on all sides and climb up to the sky, and after she had stared for a while she realized that

if she did not go out she would have to stay in and do nothing—
and so she went out. She did not know that this was the best thing
she could have done, and she did not know that, when she began
to walk quickly or even run along the paths and down the avenue,
she was stirring her slow blood and making herself stronger by
fighting with the wind which swept down from the moor. She ran
only to make herself warm, and she hated the wind which rushed
at her face and roared and held her back as if it were some giant
she could not see. But the big breaths of rough fresh air blown over
the heather filled her lungs with something that was good for her
whole thin body and whipped some red colour into her cheeks and
brightened her dull eyes when she did not know anything about it.
(Burnett 1912, 44)

The air of the Yorkshire moors restores her appetite and replaces the
yellow tint of her complexion with a rosy one. The racial connota-
tion of yellow is unavoidable. The air also makes Mary a far more
amiable and agreeable person. Such air was not available to her in
India. It was available to Colin in England, but he shut it out.

Ultimately, Burnett's book is not only about the resurrection of a
hidden garden or about the restoration of the strength and spirits of
two children who had languished in somewhat different ways and
for different reasons. It is an ode to all the elements that come together to produce a true English child: a love of fresh air, an enjoyment of exercise, ebullient good spirits, a voracious appetite, a
generosity of spirit, fortitude and resilience, moral fiber, a capacity
to roam, to discover, to find adventure, to unearth secrets, the very
qualities fêted in the Blyton books, in *Tom Brown's Schooldays* (1857),
in all celebrations of English character. These qualities are nourished
by the very soil of the land and nurtured by the winds that blow
across it. Burnett tells us categorically "There is no doubt that the
fresh, strong, pure air from the moor had a great deal to do with it"
(1912, 67). The wind not only gives children an appetite but fighting
with the wind stirs the blood. And the same things stir the mind. In
India, Mary "had always been too hot and languid and weak to care
much about anything, but in this place she was beginning to care
and to want to do new things" (68). Magic transformations are common in stories for children, but here it's her new environment that is
making her feel decidedly less contrary. Wordsworth and the other
Romantic poets had insisted upon the power of nature as a power

for good, a moral force, and seen in it the power not only to invig-
orate but also to restore. It is in the spirit of the Romantics that the
children establish a connection between the spiritual world of self-
discovery and the physical world of the garden, between, in Colin's
words, magic and science.

Something as simple as a skipping rope, Susan Sowerby's inspirational idea, purchased for Mary out of Martha's meager earnings,
turns out to be Mary's salvation: "The skipping-rope was a wonderful thing. She counted and skipped, and skipped and counted, until
her cheeks were quite red, and she was more interested than she had
ever been since she was born" (73). But this wonderful thing was not
something she knew about in India, clear proof in Martha's mind, of
the inferiority of black people, for all their elephants and tigers and
camels. The correlation between physical exertion and character is
so clearly established that what emerges is practically a creed, a
creed that served well the colonial agenda. Burnett sees the English
climate as not only physically invigorating but mentally and
morally invigorating as well.

The Englishman must exert himself if he is to be superior to the
emasculated Indian, enervated by his climate. And the English-
woman must be robust as well if she is to serve as his consort. Francis G. Hutchins's study of British imperialism in India entitled *The
Illusion of Permanence* (1967) is well worth consideration in this regard. Hutchins indicates that for the Victorians climate was considered crucial in molding Indian character. "Alleged Indian languor,
sensitivity, fatalism, constitutional feebleness, preference for
despotic institutions, and sexuality, were all depicted at various
times as necessary results of India's 'constant vapor bath'" (61). Naturally, therefore, the Victorians were apprehensive about the effects
the Indian climate might have on their own health and physical
make-up. Quoting *Parliamentary Papers* from 1857–1858, Hutchins
discusses the concern that "the European constitution cannot survive the third generation" (61).

This concern is certainly reflected in Burnett's repeated references to Mary's lethargy and inactivity in India. As an English girl,
Mary is always superior to the natives, but in England she is often
identified as being "Indian." Her English self cannot bloom and
blossom any more than the flowers in the neglected garden until she
is in a true English environment. There could be no better personal

embodiment of this national product than Susan Sowerby, "the comfortable, wonderful mother creature" (Burnett 1912, 251) whose prescription for Colin is "Let him go playing', an' workin' in th' garden an' eatin' hearty an' drinkin' plenty o' good sweet milk an' there'll not be a finer pair [of legs] i' Yorkshire, thank God for it" (275). Susan Sowerby may be of modest means, but she has produced a collection of sturdy, healthy, and likeable children with round, red-cheeked faces and friendly grins. Indeed they are practically poster children for the salubrious and energizing effects of the British climate. Bixler comments, "The folk wisdom of the Sowerbys and their special concern for the manor children can evoke the complacent stereotype of the rural working class as happy naturals chiefly concerned with the welfare of their betters" (1996, 76). Similarly, when the British in India wanted to find "real Indians" or those they considered as such, it was to rural India that they turned.

We see this clearly identifiable association of environment and character in other writing as well. In *An Experience of India* (1971), Ruth Jhabvala, an expatriate English writer of Polish descent living in India, writes of seeing "wind and rain in the fresh complexions of visitors from abroad" and hearing "the wind stirring in English trees or a mild brook murmuring through a summer wood in their voices" (15–17). If temperament is destiny, then temperament needs the right climate and care to grow, just as the roses in the secret garden do. As Colin sees it, it is a combination of magic and science.

Might one consider the secret garden a metaphor for the colony that lies waiting to be discovered, ripe for exploration and in need of governance? M. Daphne Kutzer attempts such a reading in *Empire's Children*, stating that "Mary's behavior in the garden echoes that of colonial explorers in India and elsewhere" (2000, 59). Kutzer argues that in the end Mary herself is colonized by the garden and what it stands for: "sacrificial womanhood" (59). A garden is traditionally a woman's domain, after all, and it symbolizes her capacity to nurture. Bixler also remarks on the disappointment felt by many female readers (and females constitute the primary readership for this book) that once Colin arrives on the scene, Mary fades into the background (1996, 18). I would argue that while Mary is certainly subsumed in service of Colin, Mary becomes to Colin what the ideal women of the Empire were to their men: active and adventurous partners, but in a supporting role, perhaps, but as cohorts, never as stewards. In the final analysis, Mary remains a colonizer, for vigorous womanhood was as much a part of that endeavor as virile manhood. As she explores and tends the garden, she conjoins nurturance with a spirit of adventure, casting her as an ideal woman for the empire. It is through the type of hard physical work that the Victorians considered healthful, not only for the constitution but also for the character, that the garden is revived, or colonized, so to speak.

The transformation of the garden becomes a parable for the ordering of the lands bound by the Pax Britannica. While Mary is still in India, children chant the old nursery rhyme "Mistress Mary, quite contrary / How does your garden grow?" to tease her. At the end of the book, Mary might have answered "With silver bells, and cockle shells / And marigolds all in a row." Although the flowers in the secret garden are not quite all in a row and the transformation the children effect is not quite one of disorder to order, the garden is now cared for and cultivated. The flowers may grow profusely and in seeming disarray, but they are tended. Mary's transgression in entering the garden, which of course recalls Eve's transgression in the Garden of Eden, is replaced by accord. This corner of Yorkshire becomes iconic, suggesting the possibilities of empire and its potential. Empire effects such restoration and regeneration as Mary, Colin, and Dickon have brought to the garden. Empire builders cultivate the colonies with just this combination of rigor and nurturance. Generations of British colonizers tried to figure out where home really was. When they were in India, it was always in Britain, but when they went back for good, it suddenly seemed to be in India. At one point, Mary, on being told that she is to be sent home, asks: "Where is home?" (Burnett 1912, 9). In Burnett's book, Yorkshire is simultaneously a physical as well as a mental geography, a microcosm of the nation, of England, and ultimately of the Empire. It is also antonymic: the Edenic garden to India's barrenness. One of the most importunate metonyms of appropriation concerns the use of land, whether it is conceived of as clearing the wilderness, as in the American West, or making the desert bloom, as in the creation of the state of Israel. Where their own works were not present, settlers and colonizers saw only nothingness, and the transformation they sought became their justification for appropriation.

The Secret Garden is a narrative of nation in which nation becomes more denotative than connotative. Nation is inextricably
attached to location. It is a state of mind, but beyond that, it is a
state of being. Although it is also an impetus, a cultural entity, a
social force, and a signifying system, it is, above all, a place. It is
rooted in a particular soil, cultivated in a particular climate and,
in that sense, not portable. Ultimately, as visualized in this novel,
nation is not an "imagined community" but a physical as well as
a metaphysical one. It calls out to Colin's father, Archibald
Craven, in the Austrian Tyrol, and he returns home to discover the
magic that his native land has wrought, the transformation of his
son into a "laughable, lovable, healthy young human thing" (Burnett 1912, 296).

The final scene of the novel depicts Archibald Craven, the master of Misselthwaite, walking across the lawn with his son, as strong
and steady as any boy in Yorkshire. As Hutchins points out, "The
Victorians emphasized the ideal of dominant masculinity, admiring
a man who was physically strong, fond of vigorous sports, and capable of vast amounts of work" (1967, 54). The condition in which
Colin had existed prior to his rehabilitation was one that was more
akin to their standard conception of the Bengali: "The physical organization of the Bengalee is feeble even to effeminacy. He lives in a
constant vapor bath. His pursuits are sedentary, his limbs delicate,
his movements languid" (see Hutchins 1967, 67). Colin's social position and race vest him with power, but that power is impotent without action. When Colin becomes active, he reasserts his position in
the hierarchy, in the natural order, displacing Mary as the center of
the novel.

Other "theorists" of Indian character sought alternative explanations. James Mill ascribed the characteristic feebleness of the Indian
physique to diet. Charles Grant saw their religion with its proclivity
toward fatalism as the root cause of their perceived indolence. The
Baron de Montesquieu, with his insistence on a radical doctrine of
human equality, had postulated that within the space of one generation, Englishmen would be exactly like Indians if they grew up in India (Hutchins 1967, 67). The Victorians, however, preferred to see the
corrosive effects of climate as a more gradual though unrelenting
process. The reason why Colin's self-imposed invalid status, its re-

sultant indolence, his hypochondria, effeminate aspect, and fear of physical exertion would be perceived as undesirable, even repellent, becomes evident in the context of Mill's scathing study of the Indian character in his landmark *History of India*:

> The love of repose reigns in India. . . . "It is more happy to be seated than to walk; it is more happy to sleep than to be awake; but the happiest of all is death." Such is one of the favourite sayings, most frequently in the mouths of this listless tribe, and most descriptive of their habitual propensities. Phlegmatic indolence pervades the nation. Few pains, to the mind of the Hindu, are equal to that of bodily exertion; the pleasure must be intense which he prefers to that of its total cessation. (1840–1848, 64)

We see the enervating effects of the Indian climate on Mary, and Colin's sickroom replicates those effects. But once they experience the magic of the Yorkshire outdoors, they grow sturdy and intrepid, strong and merry, fit to be future adventurers or explorers.

Temperament is destiny, but temperament grows best in the northern lands where geography and climate combine to coax out the traits that will equip the child for success in the great enterprise of empire. Colin seeks the place where magic and science merge. He finds it in the secret garden, a virtual hothouse that nurtures him so that he can undergo a metamorphosis into the true British lad he is destined to become. This is clear from his pronouncement that "Magic works best when you work yourself" (Burnett 1912, 277). Colin learns that being proactive rather than resigned is being British.

The British absorption in adventure is evident in the other novel for young readers for which Burnett is still well known, *A Little Princess* (1906). It is a reworking of an earlier story published in 1887 as *Sara Crewe*. As *A Little Princess*, the tale was first published six years before *The Secret Garden*. Both books maintain the importance of character and share a similar emphasis on the value of grit, determination, industry, and forbearance. But whereas Mary's adventures are mostly outdoors or at least in the labyrinthine corridors of Misselthwaite Manor, Sara's are mostly in the mind, in a world of fantasy that she spins for her own and others' entertainment. In her impoverished and oppressed state, "the dreams she dreamed—the visions she saw—the imaginings which were her joy and comfort" (Burnett 1906, 214) are the only hospitality she has left to offer her friends. Sara uses her mind to effect change, whereas Mary uses her hands. But action and adventure are where her mind takes her, and her friends with her, as she spins tales of the French Revolution, or of castles and clarions, knights and ladies, pillaged lands and brave chatelaines.

Sara is a princess when she has every luxury and amenity, when she is dressed in a frock the color of a rose, with a wreath to wear on her black locks, when enjoyment and exercise bring a brilliant glow into her face (Burnett 1906, 57). And she is a princess still when she is so cold, hungry, and tired that her face is pinched, muddy water squelches through her broken shoes, and the wind penetrates her thin jacket as she walks through the streets on yet another errand. After her father dies she is left a pauper, dependant on the reluctant charity of her erstwhile headmistress. Finding a fourpenny piece in the gutter, she uses it to buy buns, but when she spots someone hungrier and more ragged and pathetic than herself, she gives the other all except one of the buns. That's part of being a princess, she reminds herself. And, as the author tells us, "If Nature had made you for a giver your hands are born open, and so is your heart; and though there may be times when your hands are empty, your heart is always full, and you can give things out of that—warm things, kind things, sweet things—help and comfort and laughter—and sometimes gay, kind laughter is the best help of all" (74). Above all, Sara is a princess inside. It is easy, she knows, to be a princess when you are dressed in cloth of gold, "but it is a great deal more of a triumph to be one all the time when no one knows it" (164).

Sara is in some ways the antithesis of Mary. Whereas Mary is at first petulant, peevish, and bratty, Sara is always gracious, compassionate, and generous. Until the downturn in her fortunes, others spoil her, but she is never spoilt and does not become the unpleasant child that Mary becomes. Mary helps Colin by being bossy and peremptory, which is, of course, just what he needs. Sara uses empathy and kindness instead and reaches out to the underdog. She practically personifies the benevolence that was such an integral aspect of the colonizers' self-image—that unshakable conviction that they were in the colonies to help those who had not the fortune of their birth, the privilege of their race. Sara is a true bearer of the White Man's burden: "Send forth the best ye breed," exhorts Kipling and she is the best, superior by virtue of character, not by virtue of position.

Whereas another child, Isobel Grange, had been the beauty of their fathers' regiment in India, with her fairy tale princess looks—long golden hair, dimples, rose-colored cheeks—Sara has short black hair, green eyes, and a thin physique. In fact, her appearance is practically a reversal of the fairy-tale princess look. But her charisma and charm afford her a power that is beyond physical beauty. None of the other girls is her peer in that regard. The girls she adopts as her protégés—Ermengarde, Lottie, and Becky—are ostracized by the others. Ermengarde is not intelligent, Lottie is much younger and also motherless, and Becky is a penniless drudge. Sara provides them with the protection of her special presence and, when she falls from grace because of the downturn in her fortunes, they reward her with loyalty and support worthy of the most devoted colonial subject.

While Mary matures and develops in character through the progress of the tale, Sara is simply proven. Even her adverse and dire circumstances cannot thwart the essential goodness of her nature. As Becky puts it, "Whats'ever 'appens to you—whats'ever—you'd be a princess all the same—an' nothin' couldn't make you nothin' different" (106). For Sara is not just a princess, she is a soldier. She embodies the essence of British stiff upper lip stoicism. To her credit, Burnett permits both the princess and the soldier to be important facets of the female. In fact, she allows Sara to appropriate "masculine" qualities. Being a girl, however, Sara must internalize those qualities. Her father used to say, "If Sara had been a boy and lived a few centuries ago . . . she would have gone about the country with her sword drawn, rescuing and defending every one in distress. She always wants to fight when she sees people in trouble" (26).

In Sara, Burnett projects all the qualities the British held most dear in their self-concept. Her courage and resilience, her determination and diligence, her grace under fire make her a shining example of the attributes they considered the endowment of race:

> Sara never made any mischief herself, or interfered with anyone. She worked like a drudge; she tramped through the wet streets,

carrying parcels and baskets; she laboured with the childish inattention of the little ones' French lessons; as she became shabbier and more forlorn-looking, she was told that she had better take her meals downstairs; she was treated as if she was nobody's concern, and her heart grew proud and sore, but she never told anyone what she felt. (112)

Sara reminds herself through clenched teeth that soldiers don't complain, that she is fighting a war. She tells Ermengarde how she promised her father all those years ago that she would bear their separation and now she must endure this final parting. "You have to bear things," she tells Ermengarde. "Think what soldiers bear! Papa is a soldier. If there was a war he would have to bear marching and thirstiness, and, perhaps, deep wounds. And he would never say a word—not one word" (34).

Naturally, not all English children or all English people are shining representatives of their race. Ermengarde is weak and lazy, Lavinia is spiteful and selfish, Lottie is often hysterical, and Jessie is silly. These are the counterfoils that better highlight Sara's ideal character. While in *The Secret Garden* the stage for the unfolding drama of character is outdoors and rural, in *A Little Princess* it is indoors and urban. In fact, one of the arenas where Sara's character is tried is her dark, dreary, rat-infested attic room. Such is Sara's resolve, however, and such is her compassion, that her response is to befriend the rat family and feed them crumbs whenever she can scrape them up. In *The Secret Garden* we experience the transforming power of nature; here, we experience the transforming power of the imagination. Sara invests rats and grand neighbors alike with outlandish names and pretends that she is a prisoner in the Bastille. And whereas in both stories there are regular references to India, the connection between character and climate is not insisted upon as assiduously here. We are simply told, once, in the beginning of the book, that "The climate of India was very bad for children, and as soon as possible they were sent away from it—generally to England and to school" (Burnett 1906, 3).

A Little Princess does, however, introduce an Indian character that is more fully realized than any in the later novel. Unlike the sketchy, entirely voiceless Indians of *The Secret Garden*, Ram Dass has a presence, actually takes up some space, and he has a voice. From his obsequious manner, Sara can gauge his familiarity with European children. Although his is a stereotypical Orientalist portrait, with his "picturesque white-swathed form and dark-faced, gleaming-eyed, white-turbaned head" (Burnett 1906, 158), Ram Dass does become an agent of Sara's rescue, although a secondary one. Sara, in fact, comments that "Without the help of an agile, soft-footed Oriental like Ram Dass, however, it could not have been done" (264). She is referring to his nimbleness and suppleness, which allows him to clamber up roofs. So it is the peculiar qualities of Oriental character that effect her rescue. They are important qualities, but place the Oriental firmly on a lower rung of the evolutionary ladder than the white man. Indeed, the primary agent of Sara's rescue, the one who is awarded most of the credit, is the one known as the "Indian gentleman," although he is really an Englishman who has resided in India for many years. Within that phrase alone is compressed the hegemony of empire. As in *The Secret Garden*, the hierarchy of race and class is asserted. Sara is now only a drudge herself, someone the cook feels free to insult and order around. But she is still European and, in recognition of that fact, Burnett has Ram Dass salaaming her. It is an acknowledgment of the fact that her race awards her superior status no matter what her social position might be. It might also be an acknowledgment of the princess inside.

Miss Minchin is now in the dominant position, but Sara can still inwardly dismiss her as "a poor, stupid, unkind, vulgar old thing" (165). Sara claims that she can sometimes imagine being wicked, but never vulgar (209). In the same way, she points out that being kind is better than being clever (210). Sara is both. She represents the best of British character. She is brave in the face of abandonment and terrible adversity and industrious in the face of exploitation. Although she has never needed to raise a hand for herself prior to this, her first instinct when Miss Minchin informs her that she is a beggar, an orphan, and homeless to boot, and must work for her living like Becky, is relief. A faint gleam of light comes into her eyes to Miss Minchin's surprise. "Can I work?" she asks, "If I can work it will not matter so much. What can I do?" (102). And work her Miss Minchin does, with a vengeance. She uses Sara to teach the younger children as well as to fetch and carry in the kitchen and the schoolroom. Miss Minchin had earlier betrayed her mercilessness when, in reference to Becky, she commented that scullery maids were not really little girls (81). The capacity for work is, after all, one of the key qualities that distinguishes the Christian from the savage, for the savage, as missionaries were wont to emphasize, had a propensity for idleness.

The connection between character and nationality is implied rather than stated in *A Little Princess*. In *The Secret Garden*, it is more directly articulated as we are shown the imbrication of environmental and moral factors. An English garden provides the fertile and matchless conditions for the growth of character. Still, even in *A Little Princess*, we never lose sight of the fact that Sara is English and that her triumph is a peculiarly English triumph, the triumph of character. Cedric, in the earlier *Little Lord Fauntleroy* (1886), is a male version of Sara. This had been one of Burnett's most popular novels but is now somewhat neglected in comparison to *A Little Princess* and *The Secret Garden*. Bixler and other critics have dismissed the little boy who is its central character as effeminate and sissy-like. In fact, Little Lord Fauntleroy has become a symbol of a feminine boy. But a close reading compels a very different interpretation. Little Lord Fauntleroy is, on the contrary, a testimony to the qualities of character that define the ideal English child. Far from being a sissy, he is "a little man" (Burnett 1886, 8). Little Cedric replicates his father's characteristics. Captain Cedric Errol is described in these terms: "But it so happened that Nature had given to the younger son gifts which she had not bestowed upon his elder brothers. He had a beautiful face and a fine, strong, graceful figure; he had a bright smile and a sweet, gay voice; he was brave and generous, and had the kindest heart in the world, and seemed to have the power to make everyone love him" (3).

Cedric is also, however, like his mother, sweet tempered and charming (6). In spite of his mass of soft, fine golden hair, his ringlets, and his big brown eyes framed by long lashes, and his "darling little face" (6), Cedric is still the archetypal English boy for, in addition to being handsome and kind, he is strong with "splendid sturdy legs" (6) and a "fearless" manner (7). He may have "charming love-locks on his shoulders" and "pretty manners," but he also has a "graceful strong little body" (9), "fearless eyes," and a "manly little face" (29). And he is a "very boyish little boy" (30).

Cedric may be affectionate and demonstrative in a stereotypically feminine way, referring to his mother as "Dearest" throughout, but his "warm, faithful nature" is combined with "a true heart" (26). Cedric's golden curls become a signifier of race while his courage becomes a signifier of nationality. Elsewhere Cedric's character traits are clearly gendered as "boy nature" (106). Over and over again the author points out that he is brave, determined, tough, manly, and strong, that he has determination and grit. With equal frequency we are told that he is kind, for kindness is just as important as strength in idealized British manhood. Cedric combines both "beauty and bravery" (157). In a telling passage, race, class, character, and appearance are all closely linked: "If Cedric had been a less handsome little fellow the old man might have taken so strong a dislike to the boy that he would not have given himself the chance to see his grandson's finer qualities. But he chose to think that Cedric's beauty and fearless spirit were the results of Dorincourt blood and a credit to the Dorincourt rank" (140). Cedric's grandfather, the Earl of Dorincourt, makes it a point to distinguish British manners from American, which he describes as "beastly, impudent, bad manners" (68). He had been convinced that his grandson, having been brought up in America, would turn out to be "a clownish fellow" (84).

Nation is embedded in the English boy, whose essential Englishness has remained incorruptible despite his American mother and his early years in America. Cedric's grandfather is concerned that his "American blood" (67) will tell. But his lawyer reassures him, saying, "I do not think it has injured him, my lord" (67). Cedric's essential Englishness is located in character. The servants at his grandfather's castle worry about the difficulties facing the little boy in his transition to another country, another lifestyle, and life with his gouty, bad-tempered grandfather. "But they did not know," the author tells us, "what sort of a little lord had come among them; they did not quite understand the *character* [my emphasis] of the next Earl of Dorincourt." Little Lord Fauntleroy is no fop but a strong little boy who strides "with a manly, sturdy little tramp" (59) and is seen "trotting manfully" (143) his very first time on a horse, much to the approbation of his grandfather who comments, "Not much afraid, is he?" (143). Cedric may be gentle, but he is no sissy; he is, in fact, a real English boy, who shows no fear of horses, huge dogs, or gruff old grandfathers. Nor is he afraid to be compassionate, dismounting from his horse in order to allow a village boy who is lame and tired to ride home on his pony (144). As the future Earl of Dorincourt he will be powerful but, like Sara, he has a strong sense of *noblesse oblige* as he both dispenses and remembers kindnesses.

Little Lord Fauntleroy may be a somewhat vapid rags-to-riches tale, but it is also a classic narrative of character, English character. While Cedric's grandfather "has always especially disliked America and Americans" (25), the author allows us to see Cedric's American friends as warm and faithful and his mother as an entirely laudable representative of her land. English and American are demarcated in terms of character, but they are part of the same race. Americans may not be as refined, but they are not uncivilized. We are allowed to contrast them, by implication, to the people Cedric hears about from a sailor who befriends him on his voyage across the Atlantic: the Wopslemumpkies and Parromachaweekins, who take turns scalping each other.

Marco, in *The Lost Prince* (1914), on the other hand, is clearly not English. This now obscure tale by Burnett concerns an imaginary European country, clearly Baltic in character, whose people have for centuries cherished the hope that a much-beloved prince who had to flee the cruelties of his father's reign will reappear through a descendant. The novel moves inexorably to its inevitable ending: Marco is that lost prince. Watching him pass by, while still obliged to live in relative poverty, two workmen observe his regal bearing: a fine, big lad with thick, black hair. They agree that he is clearly not English but Turk or Russian. Yet Burnett affords Marco all the qualities of an idealized English boy. The faithful family retainer recalls that even as a small child he was "strong and silent and sturdy" and traveled with them "as if he were not a child at all—never crying when he was tired or not properly fed" (289). Marco is faithful, trustworthy, and tractable. His calm bearing is foregrounded against the frenzied Samavians. Even the landlady, who dismisses Samavia as "one of these little foreign countries you can scarcely see on a map—and not a decent Englishtown in it!" (308), recognizes that Marco can be trusted.

Marco has been trained carefully by his father to develop these traits of character, to be disciplined, discreet, and self-reliant. An in-

digent English boy, nicknamed "The Rat" on the street and infor-
mally adopted by Marco's father, also shows the strength of his character by overcoming his handicap. He is a natural in terms of
soldiering and strategy and he offers Marco and his father his
unswerving allegiance. "You are a faithful friend and you have always obeyed orders!" Marco tells him (320). Burnett obviously
cooked up the whole Samavian scheme for the sake of a story, but
Marco is a thinly disguised British boy, who stands apart in nature
from his excitable and emotional people. The references to "the
game" recall Kipling's *Kim*. But *The Lost Prince* is primarily a narrative of character rather than of events.

Other tales by Burnett are seldom read and all but unavailable
now. *The White People* is a tale of a young girl, Ysobel, who lives in
her feudal castle in the "savage land" of wild and remote Scotland.
She is seen as an "inoffensive little barbarian," knowing no tongue
but her own, by "civilized" children from London or the South of
England when they are brought by their relatives to visit her. Ysobel
has the power to see the dead and, in this book, as in *The Secret Garden*, the moors become a sentient presence, practically a character in
themselves.

The Hunchback Zia is the tale of a little deformed Syrian boy
beaten and despised by the crone in whose care he has been since
birth. She sends him out to beg because his mesmerizing eyes induce people to take pity on him. When he develops leprosy, she ex-
pels him, whereupon he finds himself with travelers on the road to
Bethlehem where the grace of the infant Jesus cures him of both his
affliction and his handicap. He becomes straight and strong without
a blemish or a spot.

The correlation between nation and character is expressed un-
ambiguously in another classic of British childhood, one written
much earlier. Thomas Hughes' *Tom Brown's Schooldays* was published in 1857. It remains the great exposition of English character
and, like *The Secret Garden*, it has never been out of print. Jeffrey
Richards writes:

> *Tom Brown* is the most famous school story ever written, an auto-
> biographical account of schooldays whose influence lay in its re-
> flection, mythification and propagation of what was to become the
> dominant image of the public school, a place to train character and

produce Christian gentlemen. It highlighted three classic themes: the socialisation of the schoolboy, the inculcation of manliness and the religious awakening. Over the years the third of these themes, so characteristic of the mid-Victorian period, was to diminish, but the other two were to remain constant factors of the boys' school story. (Butts 1992, 3)

Tom Brown's Schooldays (1857) is about one of England's great institutions, the public school, Rugby in particular, and it is set during the period when Dr. Thomas Arnold was headmaster. Thomas Hughes himself attended Rugby between 1833 and 1842, the last years of Dr. Arnold's term there. Dr. Arnold's mission was focused on character building, because "on the eve of the Victorian period the atmosphere in most of the public schools had degenerated into an evil combination of somnolence, brutality, and anarchy" (Altick 1973, 253).

Moral training, Altick tells us, was executed chiefly through organized games, which took precedence even over academics: "In time, the main vehicle of moral training was agreed to be organized games, and during the latter half of the century the public schools were more concerned with prowess on the playing field and with shaping the morality of prospective Christian gentlemen than with brainwork" (1973, 253). This is borne out in the following pronouncement by the narrator in *Tom Brown's Schooldays*: "Let who will hear the boys their lessons, but let me live with them when they are at play and rest" (Hughes 1857, 49). We also learn that Brooke would rather win two schoolhouse matches running than get the Baillol scholarship any day, a pronouncement greeted with frantic cheers. Nowhere is the cult of character building more clearly propounded than in Hughes' novel. He envisages it as a mission statement for education itself: "The object of all schools is not to ram Latin and Greek into boys, but to make them good English boys, good future citizens" (49). The public schools sought to turn English boys into prospective Christian gentleman. Regimentation was part of that scheme, and its consequence was conformity. There was one mission and one mold. As Tom is being introduced to public school life, his newfound mentor warns him that "a great deal depends on how a fellow cuts up at first. If he's got nothing odd about him, and answers straightforward and holds his head up, he gets on" (71).

Tom's father, the squire, defines the public school mission succinctly as he ruminates on the eve of Tom's departure for Rugby:

> I won't tell him to read his Bible and love and serve God; if he don't do that for his mother's sake and teaching, he won't for mine. Shall I go into the sort of temptations he'll meet with? No, I can't do that. Never do for an old fellow to go into such things with a boy. He won't understand me. Do him more harm than good, ten to one. Shall I tell him to mind his work, and say he's sent to school to make himself a good scholar? Well, but he isn't sent to school for that—at any rate, not for that mainly. I don't care a straw for Greek particles, or the digamma, no more does his mother. What is he sent to school for? Well, partly because he wanted so to go. If he'll turn out a brave, helpful, truth-telling Englishman, and a gentleman, and a Christian, that's all I want. (Hughes 1857, 57)

Hughes cannot allude to qualities of character without referring to nation in the very same breath. In relating what it felt like to ride atop the "Tally-ho," a particular type of carriage, he describes the discomforts of numbing cold in the dark of early morning without rugs or plaids. Then he delineates its pleasures, among them "the consciousness of silent endurance, so dear to every Englishman—of standing out against something, and not giving in" (59).

We are told how almost all English boys love danger, how they can so easily be drawn into playing a game or climbing a tree or swimming a stream when there's a possibility of breaking a limb or getting drowned. It is only the exception who would prefer to stay on level ground, or in his depth, or play quoits or bowls. Words such as "bravery," "pluck," "strong," "straight," or "plain" abound. The cherished English taboo against tale-telling is maintained, but bullying is also disparaged. This was, of course, one of the great reforms instituted by Dr. Arnold at Rugby. Bullying in the period during which he was headmaster became associated with cowardice. In an impassioned speech, Brooke, a senior boy much respected and admired by his peers and juniors, defends the headmaster's reforms, which have evidently met with some resistance. He points out that Dr. Arnold isn't about to abolish cricket, football, bathing, or sparring or any of the time-honored sports but rather encourages them greatly. But he has gone after customs that were gratuitously mean-spirited like "taking the linch pins out of the farmers' and bagmen's gigs at the fairs, and a cowardly blackguard custom it was" (97). He also rid the school of hound racing and the patronization of public houses. The Doctor, as he was universally known, preserved the customs that were sound and sensible and the school was beginning to learn that he meant business, that what he said had to be done, and no mistake about it:

> And this was beginning to be pretty clearly understood; the boys felt that there was a strong man over them, who would have things his own way; and hadn't yet learned that he was a wise and loving man also. His personal character and influence had not had time to make itself felt, except by a very few of the bigger boys, with whom he came more directly in contact; and he was looked upon with great fear and dislike by the great majority even of his own house. For he had found school, and schoolhouse, in a state of monstrous license and misrule, and was still employed in the necessary but unpopular work of setting up order with a strong hand. (100)

Tom Brown's Schooldays virtually defines the English creed of character; it is exemplified especially by Tom and East in the Rugby of Dr. Arnold's stewardship. In *Empire and the English Character*, Kathryn Tidrick says that Tom Brown and Allan Quatermain "were virtual archetypes of the Victorian world view" (1990, 57). Of course, it is Dr. Arnold's enlightened example that becomes the beacon for them all. The creed of character was part of the Victorian worldview, the worldview of the empire, part of England's sense of itself. Thoughtlessness can be forgiven, but not meanness. Animal good spirits or high jinks are acceptable but not cruelty. East and Tom Brown are fair specimens of British youth (Hughes 1857, 127). They are active, adventurous, boisterous boys who don't balk at risks: "It never occurred to them to consider why such and such rules were laid down; the reason was nothing to them; and they only looked upon rules as a sort of challenge from the rule makers, which it would be rather bad pluck in them not to accept" (Hughes 1857, 147–48).

Like Burnett, Hughes shows us that there is more than one type of courage. Tom takes under his wing someone who is in need of his protection, as does Sara in Burnett's *A Little Princess*. But whereas Sara does so on her own initiative, Tom is invited to assume this role by Dr. Arnold. A young student called George Arthur, whose father has just died, is somewhat delicate in constitution and the headmaster has determined that what he needs is some Rugby air, long walks, and cricket—a prescription for the outdoors and exercise that recalls Susan Sowerby's in *The Secret Garden*. Tom glances over at Arthur, with his pale complexion, fair hair, big blue eyes, and his shy shrinking manner, and sees "at a glance that the little stranger was just the boy whose first half-year at a public school would be misery to himself if he were left alone, or constant anxiety to any one who meant to see him through his troubles" (Hughes 1857, 170). Of course, Dr. Arnold has realized this and that's why he, at the matron's prompting, puts Arthur in Tom's care. Arthur is to share Tom's study and is assigned the bed next to his.

In his early days at the school, Arthur demonstrates that there is a difference between physical frailty and moral cowardice. Arthur does what even Tom in his early days had not been able to do and that is to say his prayers publicly. Eventually, Dr. Arnold demonstrated at Rugby the nature of "manly piety" (177) but it had not taken hold yet, and when Arthur kneels by his bedside to say his prayers before retiring, as he had done every day from his childhood, some of the boys laugh and sneer at him and one "big brutal fellow" (176) hurls his slipper at him, calling him "a sniveling young shaver" (176). Tom hurls the item back at the bully's head and warns the others, "If any fellow wants the other boot, he knows how to get it" (176). But when Tom is in bed, Arthur's spiritual fidelity brings back to Tom his own promise to his mother never to forget to kneel by his bedside and give himself up to his Father before going to bed because he may never rise from it again, and he breaks down in tears. He has not kept this promise and this, he realizes, shows a lack of moral courage of the sort even the meek Arthur had been capable of: "Poor Tom! The first and bitterest feeling which was like to break his heart was the sense of his own cowardice. The vice of all others which he loathed was brought in and burned in on his own soul. He had lied to his mother, to his conscience, to his God. How could he bear it? And then the poor little weak boy, whom he had pitied and almost scorned for his weakness, had done that which he, braggart as he was, dared not do" (178).

The next morning Tom, with some hesitation and trepidation, hearing in his head his old friends calling him "Saint" and "Squaretoes," kneels beside his bed to say his prayers. From then on he says his prayers regularly, and for a few nights there is some sneering but this passes, partly because every boy knows that Tom could have thrashed any of them in the room except the monitor and would at any rate try upon the least provocation. None of them chooses to risk a fight because Tom Brown had taken it into his head to say his prayers. But more and more boys follow his and Arthur's example and before they graduate, bedtime prayers had become the regular custom and "the old heathen state of things" had disappeared (179). It teaches Tom an extremely important lesson: "the lesson that he who has conquered his own coward spirit has conquered the whole outward world" (179).

Arthur teaches Tom that the true nature of courage comprises moral as well as physical courage. But by mentoring Arthur Tom learns another important lesson, one that was critical to the colonial mission: a sense of responsibility and, although he has not consciously articulated or reasoned this out, or even clarified it to himself, "yet somehow he knew that this responsibility, this trust which he had taken on him without thinking about it, head-over-heels in fact, was the center and turning point of his school life, that which was to make him or mar him, his appointed work and trial for the time being" (199). For after all, the English public school was intrinsic to the great civilizing mission in which the nation was involved.

When William Delafield Arnold, one of Dr. Arnold's sons and the younger brother of the famous poet Mathew Arnold set out to India, he set out with the earnest attitude and moral principles inculcated by the father he so closely resembled in character. Dr. Arnold had denounced sensuality, lying, bullying, and disobedience at Rugby; these were all traits William Arnold ascribed to Indians and abhorred. But, as his novel *Oakfield; or, Fellowship in the East* testifies, he discovers that "the magnificent work of civilising Asia through British influence" is "Humbug in practice, and it has grieved many generous hearts before now to find it so" (Arnold 1854, 159). The character who pronounces these words, Middleton, also prescribes a program for the improvement of the moral temper of the British in India, for it was their low and corrupt conduct that led to this assessment and the disillusionment of the main character of the novel, Edward Oakfield, a thinly disguised version of Arnold. Middleton advocates "physical improvement first, then intellectual, then spiritual, that seems the natural order of things" (179), an order that most British would have endorsed in that age and one which is generally taken to reflect Dr. Arnold's philosophy. However, Jeffrey Richards tells us that Hughes' portrayal is not quite accurate. Dr. Arnold was certainly interested in both Christianity and education, and opposed to fighting, but he was not very interested in games— whereas Hughes was more interested in sport than in learning and believed in fighting when necessary (Butts 1992, 3). Richards says,

> Aspects of Hughes' message fed into the games mania and Empire-worship of the later nineteenth century, eclipsing the pronounced religious element of the second half of the book which had been Hughes' avowed object in writing it in the first place. So just as he had given second place to the intellectual commitment of his old headmaster, Hughes' own religious priorities were downgraded by a later generation of readers in favour of sport and character-building. (Butts 1992, 4)

Manly sport was coupled with manly behavior; the active life was privileged over the contemplative life. Thus, Middleton believes that to preach Christianity to the natives of India is to begin at the end. While the British in India are lacking in moral energy, the natives of India lack "manly energy," without which intellectual and spiritual development cannot take place. It is spiritual development that is W. D. Arnold's focus. He departs for India to "try once more to realise his theory of bringing religion into daily life, without the necessity of denying it at every turn in obedience to some fashion or dogma of society; and then, as to his work in life, was not every European in India engaged in the grand work of civilising Asia?" (Arnold 1854, 16). In *Tom Brown's Schooldays*, Thomas Hughes wrote, "In all the new-fangled comprehensive plans which I see, this is all left out [athletic sports], and the consequence is, that your great Mechanics' Institutes end in intellectual priggism, and your Christian Young Men's societies in religious Pharisaism" (1857, 33).

Soon after the publication of the fifth edition of *Tom Brown's Schooldays*, Hughes received a letter from a friend that he resolved to include should another edition come out. The author of the letter ("F. D.") states, "It was some comfort to be under the delusion that fear and nervousness can be cured by violence, and that knocking about will turn a timid boy into a bold one. But now we know well enough that is not true. Gradually training a timid child to do bold acts would be most desirable; but *frightening* him and ill-treating him will not make him courageous" (Wolff 1985, 356). F. D.'s prescription is, predictably, "*healthy exercise* and *games* and *sports*" but proportionate to the boy's strength and capacity. F. D. is concerned that boys in boarding schools are left to herd together with no law but that of force or cunning and sees no reason that the laws of civilization should be suspended for schools. "What would become of society if it were constituted on the same principles?" asks F. D. and answers his own question: "It would be plunged into anarchy in a week" (357).

F. D. favors increased supervision but acknowledges that this is not a satisfactory solution. His remedy is to divide the school into geographically separate localities by age group with boys between nine and twelve, twelve and fifteen, and above fifteen, living apart, a division preferable to one which, according to him, divides boys into despots and slaves (358). Hughes counters that bullies often rely on size rather than age and advocates instead self-respect and respect for each other, "*dynamics* rather than *mechanics*" (358). Further on he comments on Dr. Arnold's "unwearied zeal in creating 'moral thoughtfulness' in every boy with whom he came into personal contact" (360). Dr. Arnold taught them, says Hughes, and "thank God for it—that we could not cut our life into slices and say, 'In this slice your actions are indifferent, and you needn't trouble your heads about them one way or another; but in this slice mind what you are about, for they are important'" (360).

Hughes makes his didactic purpose in writing *Tom Brown's Schooldays* very clear: "My sole object in writing was to preach to boys: if ever I write again, it will be to preach to some other age. I can't see that a man has any business to write at all unless he has something which he thoroughly believes and wants to preach about" (1857, 359). In a sense then, writing was a moral duty, a service to the nation as well as to the individual. Indeed, Kipling, in urging Americans to "take up the White Man's burden," was reminding them of what he saw as British moral success. There was a strong streak of patriotism in service to the empire. It was more than a job, it was duty. One was serving not simply an immediate superior, but king, country, empire, indeed the race itself. The racial reference in Kipling's lines make that very clear. The impetus to work hard and to succeed was not driven simply by profit but by moral purpose. But as *Oakfield* indicates, practice often belied principle, and worldly values spiritual or patriotic ones. This became Arnold's central dilemma. How could a people lay claim to a civilizing mission if they were corrupt themselves? Of course, the corruption that troubled him was moral and spiritual in nature, not political or economic in any systemic sense.

When the element of Christianity is introduced to this civilizing mission, it extends it still further, beyond the cause of empire or of European civilization. It becomes a struggle of eschatological proportions, the struggle between good and evil as Dr. Arnold propounds it:

> In no place in the world has individual character more weight than at a public school. Remember this, I beseech you, all you boys who are getting into the upper forms. Now is the time in all your lives probably when you may have more wide influence for good or evil on the society you live in than you ever can have again. Quit yourselves like men, then; speak up, and strike out if necessary for whatsoever is true, and manly, and lovely, and of good report; never try to be popular, but only to do your duty and help others to do theirs, and you may leave the tone of feeling in the school higher than you found it, and so be doing good, which no living soul can measure, to generations of your countrymen yet unborn. For boys follow one another in herds like sheep, for good or evil; they hate thinking, and have rarely any settled principles. Every school, indeed, has its own traditionary standard of right and wrong, which cannot be transgressed with impunity, marking certain things as low and blackguard, and certain others as lawful and right. This standard is ever varying, though it changes only slowly, and little by little; and, subject only to such standard, it is the leading boys for the time being who give the tone to all the rest, and make the School either a noble institution for the training of Christian Englishmen, or a place where a young boy will get more evil than he would if he were turned out to make his way in London streets, or anything between these two extremes. (Hughes 1857, 131–32)

The school, then, is a microcosm of the colony. It allows a moral choice between good and evil, a choice with significance and ramifications not only for the individual but also for the public weal. And the perfect place to learn that lesson is the playing field, especially in a game like cricket, "the birthright of British boys, old and young, as *habeas corpus* and trial by jury are of British men" (Hughes 1857, 278). For cricket teaches discipline and reliance on one another. "It merges the individual in the eleven; he doesn't play that he may win, but that his side may" (278).

There is another important lesson to be had in public schools such as Rugby. It is "the lesson of obeying" (285). It is a crucial lesson for those who will serve in the far-flung reaches of the empire. There is no doubt that many of the boys of Rugby and their counterparts in other public schools were intended for colonial service, for "We are a vagabond nation now" (15), Hughes tells us early in the story. There are frequent references in the book to working and bearing the load "under the Indian sun" or in Australian towns and clearings (172). East himself proceeds from Rugby straight to India to join his regiment and "no fellow could handle boys better," predicts Tom of him, "and I suppose soldiers are very like boys. And he'll never tell them to go where he won't go himself" (284). Hughes is being only partly facetious when he tell us at the beginning of the book that the Browns are dispersed through the British Empire "on which the sun never sets" and that helps to account for its stability (4). Kathryn Tidrick points out that Frederick Courtenay Selous, an adventurer who was part of Rhodes's secret brotherhood in South Africa, entered Rugby seven years after *Tom Brown's Schooldays* was published, and his experience there so nearly resembled Tom's that the influence is unmistakable (1990, 56). Hodson of Hodson's Horse was another old Rugbeian.

Bertrand Russell, in fact, sees Dr. Arnold as a deliberate and purposeful empire builder, claiming that he was responsible for the creation of the modern empire builder, a man who, because he was "energetic, stoical, physically fit, possessed of certain unalterable beliefs," imbued with "high standards of rectitude, and convinced that [he] . . . had an important mission in the world," was adapted to exert authority at home and in the empire. His mission was to reform the benighted heathen (Mack 1973, 276).

It is no wonder then, according to Russell, that "the pupils of Arnold's disciples . . . believe in flogging natives of India when they are deficient in 'humbleness of mind.'"

"It is tragic," observes Russell, to think "of the generations of cruelty that he put into the world by creating an atmosphere of abhorrence of 'moral evil'" (Mack 1973, 276). Arnold, Russell claims, sacrificed intelligence to "virtue." The battle of Waterloo may have been won, he says sarcastically, on the playing-fields of Eton, but the British Empire is being lost there. "The modern world needs a different type," states Russell, someone "with more imaginative sympathy, more intellectual suppleness, less belief in bulldog courage and more belief in technical knowledge" (Mack 1973, 286). One might recall E. M. Forster's exhortation in *A Passage to India* that "one touch of regret" would have made his character, the colonial administrator Ronny Heaslop, a better person and the British Empire in India a better institution. One might also recall the high moral certitude of Oakfield, a thinly disguised version of W. D. Arnold, Dr. Arnold's son, and his vilification of the character of the natives of India.

It comes as no surprise that the fifth chapter of Hughes' novel is entitled "The Fight" and that it is a paean to fighting itself: "After all, what would life be without fighting, I should like to know? From the cradle to the grave, fighting rightly understood, is the business, the real, highest, honestest business of every son of man" (1857, 221). Hughes goes so far as to say that although he regrets it when folk fight the wrong people and the wrong things, it is preferable to having no fight in them (221). Hughes goes further. He distinctly identifies fighting with fists as the natural and *English* way for *English* [my italics] boys to settle their quarrels (236). "Learn to box, then," he advises boys, "as you learn to play cricket and football. Not one of you will be the worse, but very much the better for learning to box well" (236). He advises boys to avoid fighting if they can, if their reasons are sound and stem "from true Christian motives" or from "a simple aversion to physical pain and danger" (236) and not from that cardinal sin of character lapse: cowardice. The Browns themselves are a fighting family; they never hesitate to enter the fray: "they are a square-headed and snake-necked generation, broad in the shoulder, deep in the chest, and thin in the flank, carrying no lumber" (3). Richard Altick comments,

Team sports involved regimentation, discipline; and so the public schools joined the factories and the people's elementary schools in suppressing originality, devoting themselves instead to producing a standardized product at a luxury price. A favorable specimen of the system's operation would emerge from the sixth form (senior class) as an exemplar of self-control, honesty, responsibility, self-reliance, and leadership. He might well go on to distinguish himself in Empire service or in the socially exclusive upper echelons of the British Army, but little in the education that entitled him to wear the old school tie would have made him a gentleman of wide humanistic culture. (1973, 253)

Physical prowess, athleticism, a sense of adventure, risk taking, daring—these are not simply desirable masculinities; they equip a lad for service in the rugged outposts of the Empire. But there is a flip side, one just as important when a sense of noblesse oblige is required, and that is compassion. We witness Tom's compassionate and tender side when Arthur lies seriously sick. Tom is proud of his record as one who never bullied a little boy or turned his back on a big one. But Arthur wants more out of him. He wants Tom to give up using cribs and vulgus books. And, just as earlier Tom was shamed into keeping his promise to his mother to say his prayers by Arthur's intrepid example, he resolves to seek this new level of honesty that Arthur solicits from him. Arthur, in fact, presents a viable alternative portrait of English boyhood, one defined more by moral courage than by physical prowess. The essential traits remain intact, however, for Arthur is frail but not weak, sensitive but not cowardly. Besides, how many English schoolboys would identify with Arthur over Tom or East, especially in a book that George Orwell describes as "heavy with homosexual feeling, though no doubt the authors were not fully aware of it" (Orwell and Angus 2000, 465).

East is probably the toughest, most reckless, and resolute of them all, a boy who is absolutely true to himself with a strong inborn sense of right, yet who resists anything that is being urged on him for his own good. But we see a softer and more vulnerable side of East when he confesses to the Doctor that he had not been confirmed but would like to take the sacrament nevertheless. East breaks down weeping and is both comforted and uplifted by the doctor who asks him to come to the communion, as East is to be confirmed in the holidays. The Christian underpinnings of character development are made clear in this connection: "It cuts both ways somehow, being confirmed and taking the Sacrament" says Tom. "It makes you feel on the side of all the good and all the bad too, of everybody in the world. Only there's some great dark strong power, which is crushing you and everybody else. That's what Christ conquered, and we've got to fight" (Hughes 1857, 263).

The dean of Westminster, A. P. Stanley, and the bishop of Durham, B. F. Wescott, both old Rugbeians, protested that Arnold's work had been wholly misrepresented and that paradoxically the novel that defined Dr. Arnold's teachings for future generations and the school he strove to mold in accordance with his ideals actually misrepresents his values. "But of course it remains a rousing and delightful and realistic story of schoolboy life, the best of its kind" they admit (Wolff 1985, 355). The influence of English school stories extends not only to English children but also to the children of the British Empire. Public schools in India, Kenya, Nigeria, and other parts of the empire were patterned after the British model and it is to school stories as well as adventure stories that children all over the empire turned for heroes and heroines. An interesting footnote is *The Flashman Papers* by George MacDonald Fraser, published in the last decade, which (fictitiously, of course) purports to be the memoirs of Sir Harry Flashman, "the notorious Victorian soldier and scoundrel," and none other than the bully from *Tom Brown's Schooldays*!

Frederic W. Farrar's *Eric; or, Little by Little: A Tale of Roslyn School* (1858) was published only a year after *Tom Brown's Schooldays* and had been even more popular, although it is now quite forgotten and very difficult to find. This somewhat slushy school story concerns a boy who begins life in India where his father was a civilian but, as was the custom, is sent to England at an early age to be schooled. When he leaves the home of his loving relatives to enter a public school, Roslyn, based on the evangelical King William's College on the Isle of Man, he falls little by little from grace, getting into some serious scrapes, but never committing the cardinal sins of lying, stealing, or sneaking, although he is unjustly accused of theft. The preface to the twenty-fourth edition makes clear the didactic purpose of the book and its concern with character: "The story of 'Eric' was written with but one single object—the vivid inculcation of inward purity and moral purpose, by the history of a boy who, in spite of the inherent nobleness of his disposition, falls into all folly and wickedness, until he has learnt to seek help from above" (1985, 7). For all his transgressions and recklessness, Eric remains the idealized English boy because he bears the punishment he deserves in a manly and penitent way, endeavors to do his duty, pledges himself to strict obedience, and promotes school spirit. The book is even more "heavy with homosexual feeling" than *Tom Brown's Schooldays*, and it is more extreme in its depiction of bullying, sadistic beatings, cheating, and drinking. *Eric; or, Little by Little: A Tale of Roslyn School* betrays the peculiar combination of caring and cruelty that was the hallmark of many Victorian schoolmasters. It also reveals the redemptive power of male friendships, which were characterized not only by loyalty but also by love.

That the authors of children's stories, like other Britons of the time, saw their nation as engaged in a larger moral battle becomes clear in writing after writing. In this conception, colonialism was not so much about national conquest or expanding the empire as it was about it was about asserting the forces of reason and order over those of irrationality and chaos, of the Judeo-Christian tradition over the degeneracy of 'heathen' traditions and, in the final analysis, of right over wrong, good over evil. Embarkation on adventure in service of the Empire was not simply a physical challenge; it was a moral quest. The children's "classics" studied here indicate the central role played by character in that quest. The right character traits are critical to successful empire building. And the environment where they may be husbanded is an English environment, whether it is the Yorkshire moors, an English public school, or the testing grounds of adversity and urban poverty that Sara Crewe must endure. An English environment is necessary for the development of English traits, the schooling of English character. If, as Martin Green points out in *The Robinson Crusoe Story* (1990), "Humane and scientific enlightenment versus bloodshed and battle smoke" is how the English saw their own methods of empire building in contrast to others', then the role of character becomes especially crucial.

Two seminal works of the period, works that were contemporaneous with the zenith of the British Empire—James Barrie's *Peter Pan* and Robert Louis Stevenson's *Treasure Island*—contributed heavily to what Henry James termed an "apology for boyhood" in the cultural imagination. Kipling and the less famous but more popular writers of empire, such as G. A. Henty and Captain Marryat, would couple the cult of boyhood to dreams of empire in a manner that would keep them forever wedded. Across the Atlantic, Mark Twain would immortalize boys in the literary imagination. Boyhood culls (or, in the case of Peter Pan, crystallizes) the purer, more "innocent" masculine traits: strength and courage, physical pleasure and prowess, the yearning for adventure and for that which lies afar. But with manhood also comes the weight of the burden. Such qualities cannot simply be inculcated for their own sake but must be used in service of the Empire. Peter Pan is, of course, the boy who wouldn't grow up—not couldn't, but wouldn't, who wanted to remain trapped in adventurous fantasies rather than exchange them for the responsible missions of manhood. For with the latter, of course, comes responsibility.

We must, however, go further back in time to find the story that has remained the most potent cultural legend in England: *Robinson Crusoe* (1719), as Martin Green indicates in his comprehensive examination of the genesis of the Crusoe story (1990, 153). Its influence peaked as the empire peaked, in the last part of the nineteenth century. *Robinson Crusoe* is one of the great cultural repositories of the imagery of empire. Green calls it one of the culture's "founding myths" (195). One might even describe it as a creation story of empire. It is the consummate adventure tale but one within the bounds of possibility. It is fiction, but not fantasy, especially in the age of exploration in which it was written, when shipwrecks were fairly common occurrences. The historical role of the adventure story is clearly elucidated by Green:

> For adventure in this sense was the literary reflection (and to some extent the inspiration, intensification, communication) of the expansive imperialist thrust of the white race, the nations of Europe, which started around 1600 and which has not ended yet. That imperialism has been more than a matter of overseas colonies and conquests. It has involved technological invention, economic expansion, religious change, and political institutions. Adventure has been the main form within literature (and literature was in these two hundred and fifty years unusually powerful within culture) that inspired that thrust—inspired nationalism and imperialism and cultural chauvinism. Adventure has also, or therefore, been the liturgy—the series of cultic texts of masculinism. This word I use to mean that intensification of male pride that began in the seventeenth century, along with modern science and capitalism, and other great sources of contemporary culture. (1990, 2)

While G. A. Henty and Captain Marryat chronicled the triumphs and trials of the establishment of Britain's vast empire for scores of young aspiring empire builders, Robinson Crusoe is far more archetypal in nature. In some ways it could be considered an allegory of colonialism itself. Robinson Crusoe is a white man who discovers by chance an apparently unpeopled island of which he becomes ruler and conqueror, not by force and not just by expediency, but by his own wits and by moral right. For when he does discover human visitors to the island, he is appalled by their actions and takes it on himself to bring about their restitution. *Robinson Crusoe* deals not with any specific victory or any specific conquest but with something far more general, far more abstract:

> Thus the Crusoe story is a continental, not a national, one. Its versions reflected (to some degree inspired) the conquest by one continent, Europe, of the four others, Asia, Africa, America, and Australasia. It was easy and exciting—by the testimony of many writers—for Danes, Swiss, Frenchmen, perhaps above all, Germans, to take part in the great adventure, both literally and literarily, whether the flag flown from the fort was their own or British. It mattered, at least at first, that all those on the winning side should be Christian, preferably Protestant, but doctrine was rarely important. What mattered most—at first it seemed a mere common denominator, but it proved to be of tragic importance—was that all should have white skins. (Green 1990, 15)

Robinson Crusoe is white. His man, Friday, is black. Crusoe is civilized, Friday is a savage. Crusoe is resourceful and independent, Friday relatively helpless and dependent. Crusoe has technology on his side, Friday does not. Above all, Crusoe is Christian, Friday is a cannibal—and that in itself asserts the hierarchy, justifies its rightness, and positions Crusoe as the moral as well as physical ruler. This is acknowledged by Friday himself when he places Crusoe's foot upon his neck. Green comments that *Robinson Crusoe* can also be read as an anti-imperialist story, one that supports self-help rather than hierarchy, and glorifies the adventurous individual rather than official authority. But this is exactly what conquest by character constitutes. Crusoe is the antithesis of the cruel Spanish with their greed for gold and silver and their Inquisition, as Green indicates (23). Green states that Crusoe "clearly speaks for cultural forces (such as

the Protestant conscience and the democracy of labor) that powerfully opposed empire" and "for entrepreneurial hard work" (1990,
24). It is precisely such traits, however, that afford him his superiority. More perhaps than any other colonizer, with the possible exception of the French, the British premised their empire not so much on
physical power as on moral power, not so much on their needs as
their abilities, not so much on their external strengths as their internal ones, and not so much on their might as on their character.

Their greatest internal strength was perceived as character and
character was regarded as a product of nationality, as we have seen,
but it was also connected in a wider sense to race. Although the
qualities and skills that Crusoe exhibits as a survivor would have
been seen as recognizably English to the English, other Europeans
would have been permitted some claim to similar traits. This is illustrated when Crusoe rescues one of the cannibals' European prisoners. Although he is Spanish and Catholic, and Crusoe is English
and Protestant, the man's Latin greeting, "Christianus" establishes
their shared heritage as they combine forces against the natives.

Crusoe's references to himself as "Majesty the Prince and Lord
of the whole Island" are ironic. Crusoe knows that he controls and
commands the lives of his subjects, that he can award and withdraw
liberty at will, and that his subjects do not include any rebels. But
then his subjects are his dog, two cats, and a parrot! When Friday
lays his head upon the ground before Crusoe, kissing the ground
and setting Crusoe's foot upon his head, he is doing more than
thanking him for saving his life, he is acknowledging Crusoe's innate superiority. Of course, the fact that Crusoe's gun allows him to
kill an "Indian" from far off is a factor in Friday's awe.

In describing Friday, Crusoe's referents are all European. It is
himself and his race that he norms:

> He was a comely handsome Fellow, perfectly well made; with
> straight strong Limbs, not too large; tall and well shap'd, and as I
> reckon, about twenty six Years of Age. He had a very good Coun-
> tenance, not a fierce and surly Aspect; but seem'd to have some-
> thing very manly in his Face, and yet he had all the Sweetness and
> Softness of an *European* in his Countenance too, especially when he
> smil'd. His hair was long and black, not curl'd like Wool; his Fore-
> head very high, and large, and a great Vivacity and sparkling
> Sharpness in his Eyes. The Colour of his Skin was not quite black,

> but very tawny; and yet not of an ugly yellow nauseous tawny, as the *Brasilians*, and *Virginians*, and other Natives of *America* are; but of a bright kind of a dun olive Colour, that had in it something very agreeable, tho' not very easy to describe. His Face was round, and plumb; his Nose small, not flat like the Negroes, a very good Mouth, thin Lips, and his fine Teeth well set, and white as Ivory. (Defoe 1719a, 205–6)

The assumption of the aesthetic superiority of the Caucasian is unmistakable in this passage and looks forward to the theories of Knox, Gobineau, and others. Friday repeatedly signals to Crusoe his subjection and servitude, but Crusoe has already assumed it. In a supremely proprietary act, Crusoe names him Friday, because that was the day he saved his life, and teaches him to say *Master*. In return, he feeds and clothes Friday. Crusoe, in fact, becomes the consummate colonizer. He has the power to name, or rather to rename, as the early European explorers renamed islands, places, and peoples in the Americas. He assumes the power to provide and protect and expect perfect servitude in return. And Friday is the consummate colonized, "without Passions, Sullenness or Designs, perfectly oblig'd and engag'd; his very Affections were ty'd to me, like those of a Child to a Father" (209). It is the devaluation and abasement of the colonized that Albert Memmi described in his classic *The Colonizer and the Colonized* (1965) three centuries later. Reading *Robinson Crusoe*, one is tempted to ask of Crusoe, as Memmi does of the colonizer: "Why should he leave the only place in the world where, without being the founder of a city or a great captain, it is still possible to change the names of villages and to bequeath one's name to geography? Without even fearing the simple ridicule or anger of the inhabitants, for their opinion means nothing; where daily one experiences euphorically his power and importance?" (1965, 61).

Always entwined with Crusoe's awareness of Friday's natural inferiority is his acknowledgment of his innate virtues. God, he decides, employs his creatures for the best uses "to which their Faculties and the Powers of their Souls are adapted" (Defoe 1719a, 209) but he has also bestowed upon them "the same Powers, the same Reason, the same Affections the same Sentiments of Kindness and Obligation, the same Passions and Resentments of Wrongs, the same Sense of Gratitude, Sincerity, Fidelity, and all the Capacities of doing Good, and receiving Good, that he has given to us" (209). And when

God offers these folk the opportunity and occasion to use these faculties, they are ready to employ them appropriately, more so than Europeans to whom have been afforded the powers of instruction, the spirit of God and the knowledge of his word (209–10). Crusoe wonders why it has pleased God to hide this knowledge from so many millions of souls, who, judging from Friday, would make much better use of it.

It is certainly interesting that Crusoe attributes to the likes of Friday the possibility of reason, even on an occasional basis, because part of "Enlightenment" thinking was to see reason as an exclusively European faculty. For Crusoe the crucial distinction between Friday and himself is knowledge, specifically, of course, Christian knowledge. But he does recognize the advantage afforded by his gun, as when he comments on seeing through his glass a group of savages banqueting on humane [sic] Bodies, "for as they were naked, unarm'd Wretches, 'tis certain I was superior to them" (Defoe 1719a, 232). Crusoe sets out to teach Friday everything that would make him useful and helpful and also teaches him to communicate. Above all, Crusoe sets out to instill in Friday an abhorrence for cannibalism. Friday, of course, is the archetypal noble savage: simple, sincere, and content. The qualities Crusoe values in Friday are all consistent with those attributed to the noble savage: "unfeign'd Honesty" (213), his childlike affection, his unwavering loyalty: "Me die, when you bid die, Master" (231). Crusoe in declaring his love for "the Creature" believes also that Friday had come to love him more than it was possible for him ever to have loved anything before (213). Such knowledge as Friday possesses is rudimentary. For instance, he is a skilled paddler but knows nothing about sails or rudders, which also symbolizes his perceived inability to take control.

Friday is no Caliban, turning on the one who gave him language and using it to curse. Defoe is no Shakespeare. Absent here is all the complexity and density that the latter understood must be intrinsic to any relationship between colonizer and colonized. Long before Friday became his "slave," Crusoe feared the savages into whose hands he might fall, feared them far worse than the Lions and Tigers of Africa. He had heard that the people of the Caribbean coast were Canibals [sic] or man-eaters. His relationship with Friday indicates to him that they were not unremitting savages, that they had many redemptive qualities. But what he seems to cherish above all is Friday's selfless and deep devotion to himself: "I believe, if I would have let him, he would have worshipp'd me and my Gun" (212), Crusoe declares.

For all his affection for Friday and for all his admiration of his qualities, Crusoe can never acknowledge him as an equal, for ultimately he is a "blinded, ignorant Pagan" and his people "the most brutish and barbarous Savages" (217). But the possibility of conversion exists, and it is Friday who urges what Crusoe claims had not occurred to him. "You do great deal much good," Friday assures him, "you teach wild Mans be good sober tame Mans; you tell them know God, pray God, and live new Life" (226). Of course, the Christianity that Crusoe advocates is Reformation Christianity, and he does not hesitate to take a hit at the Roman Catholics, comparing Friday's accounts of the religious intermediaries of his people to the Catholic veneration of the clergy. The cryptic descriptions of his own religious practices that Friday provides is dismissed as religious knowledge of an inferior variety, and Crusoe sets out to instruct him in the knowledge of the true God (216).

Before Friday, however, there was Xury, a fellow captive in the service of a Turk who had disabled Crusoe's ship and taken him prisoner. Xury was just a boy but Crusoe, having escaped with him out of bondage, endeavors to make him his faithful follower and they sail southward "to the truly Barbarian coast." Crusoe, in spite of never having set foot there before, is still quite clear that "whole Nations of Negroes were sure to surround us with their Canoes, and destroy us" and, if they ventured ashore they "would be devour'd by savage Beasts, or more merciless Savages of humane kind" (23). So it is clear that his understanding of the people of these lands is based not on experience but on what was at the time commonly held beliefs about their savagery.

That these beliefs were not necessarily based on fact becomes clear when we study Columbus's journals, where he acknowledges the kind and generous nature of the peoples he encountered in the Caribbean. Of course, their munificence did not protect them from being massacred. Crusoe decides a priori that these "wild Mans," a term used by both Xury and Friday, were no better than beasts, and he describes "the horrible Noises, and hideous Cryes and Howlings" (25) that they heard. Throughout the story, savages and wild beasts are spoken of in the same breath, another indication that they were linked in the perception of sailors like Crusoe and explorers from Europe. There are frequent and fearful references to being devoured by wild beasts or savages. These are the brutish "other," in contrast to whom Europeans became convinced of their superiority and thus justified their conquest. That we are persistently reminded that they are black and stark naked establishes a long association between color and savagery that is still difficult to dislodge. This is the age of the slave trade and Crusoe makes reference to how easy it is to obtain gold dust, Guinea grains, elephants' teeth, and Negroes for the *Brasils* in exchange for trifles. Crusoe sells his boat and Xury to the captain who rescues them, and extracts from the latter a promise to set Xury free in ten years, if he converts to Christianity. Liberty for "savages" such as Xury is contingent on the civilizing influence of Christianity.

It becomes clear as Crusoe ponders his own actions in his journals, that he sees them as based on reason, although in moments of despair he had mourned his lack of rationality in venturing forth on abortive voyages and not heeding his father's advice. Reason is considered the final distinguishing factor between civilized man and savage. Reason is what allows Crusoe his enterprise and endurance. This is of course in tune with contemporary Enlightenment thinking. He lays it out plainly:

> So I went to work; and here I must needs observe, that as Reason is the Substance and Original of the Mathematicks, so by stating and squaring every thing by Reason, and by making the most rational Judgment of things, every Man may be in time Master of every mechanick Art. I had never handled a Tool in my Life, and yet in time by Labour, Application, and Contrivance, I found at last that I wanted nothing but I could have made it, especially if I had had Tools; however I made abundance of things, even without Tools, and some with no more Tools than an Adze and a Hatchet. (Defoe 1719a, 68)

Crusoe finds himself in the most dire of circumstances, without food, dwelling, clothes, weapons, or refuge, in despair of relief with nothing but death before him and the prospect that he would either be devoured by wild beasts or murdered by savages or else simply starve (70). It is his own resourcefulness that rescues and relieves him. He makes several forays to the shipwreck to bring on shore all the supplies he could salvage. He finds game to kill and builds himself a rudimentary dwelling and fence. Creatures that he cannot eat he skins to sew some clothes. He constructs tools and sets away stores. He domesticates some animals and plants seed. All these activities take not only "inexpressible Labour" (76) but also inventiveness and initiative. When Crusoe finds, to his astonishment, some barley growing, English barley at that, he can only attribute it to divine providence. Similarly, when he survives an earthquake (which almost undid all his hard work) and violent rain storms, he at last comes to the belief that the hand of God is at work, something to which he had not previously given thought but had "acted like a meer Brute from the Principles of Nature, and by the Dictates of common Sense only, and indeed hardly that" (88).

The English viewed character, along with Christianity, as one of the cornerstones of their civilization. And it is character that is the main theme of *Robinson Crusoe*. Most studies have attributed the durability and adaptability of this tale to its accent on adventure. But when one actually reads the text in its original version, there is very little action, adventure, or suspense in it. Instead, it is a painstaking and rather laborious account of Crusoe's careful and meticulous planning, provisioning, and survival skills. Sometimes his accounts amount to little more than lists:

> I had three Encouragements, 1. A smooth calm Sea, 2. The Tide rising and setting in to the Shore, 3. What little Wind there was blew towards the Land; and thus, having found two or three broken Oars belonging to the Boat, and besides the Tools which were in the Chest, I found two Saws, an Axe, and a Hammer, and with this Cargo I put to Sea; For a Mile, or thereabouts, my Raft went very well, only that I found it drive a little distant from the Place where I had landed before, by which I perceiv'd that there was some Indraft of the Water, and consequently I hop'd to find some Creek or River there, which I might make use of as a Port to get to Land with my Cargo. (Defoe 1719a, 50)

Or he lists for reader the provisions with which he fills his chest: "Bread, Rice, three Dutch Cheeses, five pieces of dry'd Goat's Flesh, which we liv'd much upon, and a little Remainder of European Corn" (50). What these descriptions do is expose his industry and energy, his diligence and determination, his enterprise and courage, his skills and resourcefulness. Furthermore, they reveal strength of character, resilience, and the exercise of reason. The lengthy and laborious descriptions then serve an extremely important purpose. They tell the reader how an Englishman functions in adverse circumstances. They tell the reader how an Englishman takes charge. In fact, they tell the reader exactly what it means to be an Englishman.

It is precisely for this, the fact of his nationality, that Crusoe thanks God when he comes upon the physical evidence of cannibalism, "Thanks that had cast my first Lot in a Part of the World, where I was distinguish'd from such dreadful Creatures as these" (165). We might infer that "a part of the World" refers to Europe as a whole as opposed to only England. But it is clear that Crusoe does distinguish among various European nationalities even while celebrating their commonality in opposition to the "other," the poor benighted people who had "no other Guide but that of their own abominable and vitiated Passions" (170) and thus were capable of such horrific acts. Again, reason becomes the chief distinguishing factor. Crusoe is so repelled by the evidence of cannibalism that he resorts to fantasies of revenge and plots to ambush and massacre twenty or thirty of them as retribution. But then he catches himself short "with cooler and calmer Thoughts" (170) and offers us a wonderful exposition of moral relativism. He asks himself by what authority he has the right to judge these men or execute them when Heaven has allowed them to carry out its judgment upon each other. He asks if they had ever offended him and whether he could know how God himself judges in such situations. He also acknowledges that their cannibalism is not committed as a crime, in defiance of their consciences or divine justice. "They think it no more a Crime to kill a Captive taken in War, than we do to kill an Ox; nor to eat humane Flesh, than we do to eat Mutton" (171).

Crusoe then goes on to make a key point. Just as it would be wrong for him to harm these people when they had not harmed him—in fact, did not even know of his existence—the utter barbarity of the Spaniards' actions against them was abhorrent, considering that they had not done the Spaniards any direct harm:

> That this would justify the Conduct of the *Spaniards* in all their Barbarities practis'd in *America*, and where they destroy'd Millions of

> these People, who however they were Idolaters and Barbarians, and had several bloody and barbarous Rites in their Customs, such as sacrificing human Bodies to their Idols, were yet, as to the *Spaniards*, very innocent People; and that the rooting them out of the Country, is spoken of with the utmost Abhorrence and Detestation, by even the *Spaniards* themselves, at this Time; and by all other Christian Nations of *Europe*, as a mere Butchery, a bloody and unnatural Piece for which the very Name of a *Spaniard* is reckon'd to be frightful and terrible to all People of Humanity, or of Christian Compassion: As if the Kingdom of *Spain* were particularly Eminent for the Product of a Race of Men, who were without Principles of Tenderness, or the common Bowels of Pity to the Miserable, which is reckon'd to be a Mark of generous Temper in the Mind. (Defoe 1719a, 171–72)

But while he recognizes the extent of the Spaniards' brutality, he never once refers to the Spaniards themselves as barbarians or savages, only to their barbarity or savagery, while the "natives" are consistently referred to as savages, a priori. In fact, it is specifically for this reason that they are not to blame for their actions, their barbarous customs "being in them a Token indeed of God's having left them, with the other Nations of that Part of the World, to such Stupidity, and to such inhumane Courses" (232).

Even Friday, whose noble nature Crusoe often acknowledges and for whom he claims a great affection, remains a savage in his estimation, *his* savage: "my Savage, *for so I call him* now" (204). Crusoe can also see the distinction between cannibalism and murder, just as he distinguishes between murder and the execution of prisoners of war. Friday tells him that only those captured in battle were eaten: "They no eat Mans but when make the War fight" (223). So their deeds were not different in kind from those of Christians "who often put to Death the Prisoners taken in Battle; or more frequently, [who] upon many Occasions, put whole Troops of Men to the Sword, without giving Quarter, though they threw down their Arms and submitted" (171). In the final estimation, however, it remains clear that Friday and his people are considered savages not specifically on account of their actions, although the alleged cannibalism is a factor, or on account of their appearance, although there are frequent references to their nakedness, but on account of who they are—their race, their very gestures and figures seen as barbarous (201).

The clearest indication we have in the book that character is connected to race comes when Crusoe has been watching through his spyglass another group of cannibals preparing for a banquet of human bodies, "a barbarous feast" (231) he calls it. Once again, he resolves, in what he describes as a "Fit of Fury" (231) to kill them all and once again he pulls back, asking himself how it was his call, his occasion, his necessity to attack people who had not wronged him, however barbarous their customs may be. It might be justifiable for Friday to do so, he acknowledges, because his people were at war with them, but not for him. Crusoe reminds himself that when God wishes to do so, God "would take the Cause into his own Hands, and by national Vengeance punish them as a People, for national Crimes; but that in the mean time, it was none of my Business" (232). The use of the word *national* is part of the lexicon of his perception; it is a coded word. When Crusoe finds a white man, with his hands and feet bound, primed to become part of the savages' feast, he is identified first by race: "a white Man," next by ethnography: "an European," then by religion: "the poor Christian" and finally by nationality: "Espagniole" (233–35).

Along with the Spaniard, another of the captives turns out to be Friday's own father, and it is an ecstatic reunion. Now Crusoe can pronounce with a great deal of self-satisfaction and only a hint of irony:

My island was now peopled, and I thought my self very rich in Subjects; and it was a merry Reflection which I frequently made, How like a King I look'd. First of all, the whole Country was my own meer Property; so that I had an undoubted Right of Dominion. 2dly, My People were perfectly subjected: I was absolute Lord and Law-giver; they all owed their Lives to me, and were ready to lay down their Lives, *if there had been Occasion of it*, for me. It was remarkable too, we had but three Subjects, and they were of three different Religions. My Man *Friday* was a Protestant, his Father was a *Pagan* and a *Cannibal*, and the *Spaniard* was a Papist: However, I allow'd Liberty of conscience throughout my Dominions: But this is by the Way. (Defoe 1719a, 241)

His dominion complete, Crusoe manages to escape with the help of an English captain whom he has rescued from mutineers. The mutineers are left behind on the island as a reprieve from the death sentence they would have faced in England. When, many years later, Crusoe returns to the island, he finds the remaining Spanish captives along with the villains he left behind. It is final proof of his colonization of the island that he feels free to divide it and share it with them, reserving to himself "the Property of the whole" (305).

Crusoe's survival is not simply his triumph, it is a testament to the endurance, resourcefulness, courage, and determination of the Englishman. The story is also a parable of colonialism as Crusoe finds, conquers, cultivates, and appropriates a territory, then establishes his right of dominion not by force of firearms alone, but by force of character. *Robinson Crusoe* is important to a study of character in children's stories because, as Martin Green testifies, it has known unprecedented popularity and has had numerous retellings in various versions, establishing thereby a remarkable continuity. It has been read in the original, in abridged versions, and in simplified picture book form. It is indeed something of a national narrative, setting forth an Englishman against savages, but also against nature itself. This is borne out by comparison to Robert Louis Stevenson's *Treasure Island*, which lacks the national self-consciousness of *Robinson Crusoe* and which is, to a far greater extent, a tale of pure adventure with no other apparent or significant agenda and follows what Dennis Butts calls "the familiar structure of the folk-tale": hero, quest, struggle, and homecoming (1992, 74). Whereas *Treasure Island* is predicated on a moral "other," *Robinson Crusoe* is, in the main, predicated on a racial other.

Mark Green, in *Seven Types of Adventure Tale* (1991), indicates:

> The Robinson story was also linked to ideas of work and value and property, to the "science" of economics in general—or political economy, as it was first called. The doctrines called mercantilism in England, and associated with Adam Smith there and with the Physiocrats in France, were held to derive at least their inspiration from the *Robinsonade*. That story was thought to demonstrate the way an entrepreneur *created* value—out of inert raw materials and the mindless labor he employed. Consequently, the opponents of mercantilism or physiocracy, like Marx, also referred to the Robinson story in attacking them. (60)

The Huguenots in France and the Protestants in Holland and Germany appropriated the Crusoe story. In addition, there is a link to the *philosophe* movement and to evangelical Christianity, the rise of which led to a revival of the story with Protestant missionary martyrs appearing in it (Green 1991, 59).

In 1974, a book entitled simply *My Journals and Sketchbooks* appeared that purports to be a possible discovery of the actual journal and sketchbooks of someone who was really called Robinson Crusoe. "A Remarkable Find?" is how Andre Deutsch, the well-known publisher, tells the story of its publication (Politzer 1974). On a dull winter day in 1966, he says, a stranger appeared in his office and placed an incredible manuscript on his desk. Thinking him "a simple dreamer," he tried to politely show him out, but the man, whose name was Michel Politzer, persuaded him of the import of his find. As he opened his case, a sour smell, the odor of he-goat mixed with mildew, emerged. Politzer lay out on his desk stiff scraps of goatskin and claimed that they were the authentic drawings of Robinson Crusoe, made on his island. Reminded that Robinson Crusoe was but a fictional figure, Politzer replied that he too believed that, just like every one else, until his wife inherited an old manor in Scotland from a great-grand-uncle. There, at the bottom of a chest in the attic, they found "a large and carefully wrapped parcel" that contained the drawings and manuscript he now showed Deutsch.

Michel Politzer claimed that, being an artist, he was immediately concerned about the restoration of the drawings, while his wife set out to transcribe the manuscript. He offered Deutsch his photographs of the drawings, which had been processed by using special film and filters. No other publisher would touch it, convinced that Politzer was delusional. But Deutsch admitted that he was "a little stirred" and that the adventures of the Robinson Crusoe of his youth passed before his eyes. Politzer confessed to being enchanted and enthralled by the story and persuaded Deutsch to publish his find. Deutsch ends his foreword with these words:

> It must be acknowledged that the drawings are remarkable, sometimes most affecting; they tell as never before the story of a man alone, living happily in the midst of wild nature.
>
> And after all, dear readers, is it necessary before publishing a story to be persuaded of its truth? Is it not better, if the story is a fine one, to let oneself be convinced, and to believe, even for a moment, that Robinson Crusoe really existed?

Such is the hold of Robinson Crusoe on the Western imagination. The book itself is a reproduction of the black-and-white line drawings, accompanied by text from the journals. The dust jacket offers the book as "a testament to the ability and ingenuity of man . . . by making use of the resources he has at hand—and within himself." In whichever form it is reproduced, this classic story is, however, really a testament to the ability and ingenuity of the *white* man. There are no drawings of Friday in this particular version, but the references to "shouting savages," "horrifying masks and feathers," "horrible" acts, (Politzer 1974, 76) or "cannibal tribesmen" (77) make amply clear the racial differences.

Few children of any age read *Robinson Crusoe* in its original, unabridged form. Indeed, few adults do. Most children read abridged or adapted versions. Many read it as a picture book. However, while the details and depth are lost, the essential point and purpose of the story and the main theme remain unaltered. To take one of many possible examples, *Robinson Crusoe*, abridged for young readers and published by D. K. Publishing, claims in the introduction:

> This *Eyewitness Classic* edition sensitively abridges the original text, simplifying difficult or archaic words and phrases, and including all the book's best known incidents.
>
> At the same time, the story is firmly set in its historical context. Information pages and fact and picture columns reveal Defoe's turbulent times, explain where he found inspiration for his central character, and help to chart Robinson's journeys. They also explore some of the book's fascinating background themes, such as the opening up of the New World by Europeans, and the hazardous life of a 17th century sailor. There is also a unique, specially researched map of Crusoe's exotic desert island, based on Defoe's own descriptions.
>
> As a wild and selfish young man with few skills and less sense, he runs away from his father's humdrum world and finds religious faith and qualities of patience, courage, and endurance he never dreamed he possessed. Turn the pages and become his companion on a thrilling, inspirational, never-to-be-forgotten journey. (Defoe 1719b, n.p.)

From this statement, it is obvious that children are meant to receive a message about character from this tale and that the message is intended as both moral and covertly racial.

As the annotations continue, we are told, "In the story, Robinson Crusoe becomes involved in the profitable, but very cruel, slave trade, and makes a fortune easily from investing in a sugar plantation. In the 1600s Brazil was emerging as an economically strong country, and it was a good life for the owners of the slaves and the plantations" (Defoe 1719b, n.p.). Since Defoe's novel does not refer at all to the cruelty of slavery, it is easy to slur over it in the annotations. A child is not expected to dwell on this point. Nor is a child expected to try to resolve the contrarieties of someone who is supposedly religious, patient, and courageous being involved in a cruel trade.

Crusoe's lengthy reflections on relative morality are abridged or eliminated, as are all references to the cruelty of the Spanish in their conquest of the Americas. Cannibalism is compared to eating animals. In the illustrations, Friday comes across as utterly barbarous, somewhat resembling a Neanderthal, whereas Crusoe, despite his overgrown beard and hair and improvised get-up has a certain nobility and dignity to his countenance. The historical context claimed by the introduction remains sketchy, and it skips over the profit motive as it does over exploitation and racial hegemony.

A brief consideration of one of the *Robinsonades* written primarily for children is warranted here. Robinsonades are *Robinson Crusoe* spin-off tales, such as *Swiss Family Robinson*. One of the most popular of them is *The Coral Island* (1858). It is perhaps the most interesting of the genre because it illustrates the "Manichean opposition" more starkly than almost any other. The story is related by a young English boy called Ralph, who is fifteen and apprenticed to a merchant captain on a voyage to the South Seas. On board ship, Ralph, a boy of eighteen called Jack, and a boy of fourteen called Peterkin become fast friends. When the ship is wrecked and sinks, all the crewmen perish except for the three boys who had separated themselves from the men, piling into a small boat in an attempt to survive. By making a deliberate decision to go their own way and take their chances, the boys are already engaged in a Darwinian struggle for survival. The boys exemplify both natural selection and adaptation to their environment. They wash up on a beautiful coral island. When Ralph mourns that they are lost, Peterkin retorts:

> "Do you know what conclusion *I* have come to?" said Peterkin. "I have made up my mind that it's capital—first rate—the best thing

that ever happened to us, and the most splendid prospect that ever lay before three jolly young tars. We've got an island all to ourselves. We'll take possession in the name of the king; we'll go and enter the service of its black inhabitants. Of course we'll rise, naturally, to the top of affairs. White men always do in savage countries. You shall be king, Jack; Ralph, prime minister, and I shall be—" (Ballantyne 1858, 23)

This is more than playacting or the bravado of young people. The premises assumed and the privileges claimed reek of imperialism and Social Darwinism. Daphne Kutzer notes that "Ballantyne was influenced by Victorian theories of race and evolution, ideas that were in the air even before publication of Darwin's *The Origin of Species*" (2000, 6), which followed a year after *The Coral Island*.

Underlying Peterkin's words is an awareness of what it means to bear the white man's burden, even though the book was published in 1858, well before Rudyard Kipling's famous poem of 1899. Peterkin talks of serving the black inhabitants of the island. Kipling exhorts taking up the burden "To serve your captives' need." When Peterkin is asked what would happen if there are no natives, he switches easily from a colonizing mode to a settler mode: "Then we'll build a charming villa, and plant a lovely garden round it, stuck all full of the most splendiferous tropical flowers, and we'll farm the land, plant, sow, reap, eat, sleep, and be merry" (Ballantyne 1858, 23). Whereas white men rise naturally to the top by virtue of their place on the evolutionary ladder, the inhabitants of the islands that they come across are "thoroughgoing out-and-out cannibals, whose principal law is: Might is right, and the weakest goes to the wall" (202). In describing them as such, Jack seems to completely miss the irony of his own actions or of the Social Darwinist view of things that Peterkin had earlier propounded.

In a passage reminiscent of *Robinson Crusoe*, the youths methodically catalogue the resources that remain to them. In fact, Jack, Ralph, and Peterkin become the prototypical English youngsters whose progeny we will meet in the next chapter in the works of Enid Blyton. They are strong, resilient, resourceful, and ingenious. They reconnoiter the land, set up supplies, think through situations, and act rapidly and responsibly. Jack is the natural leader and that acknowledgment from the other boys, and their acceptance of his leadership role, facilitate their own survival. The ability to acquiesce, to obey, becomes important in a social structure that depends on hierarchy. "I say, Jack, you're a Briton," Peterkin tells him, "the best fellow I ever met in my life" (29). Individual character and national character are fused in this dependable young lad.

It is important not only that they are in an island paradise, but also that they know how to master their environment, and Jack provides the key that unlocks that mastery: knowledge. Again, we are reminded of Crusoe. Jack is the wisest and boldest among them, and he has read about things. "So you see, lads, that we have no lack of material here to make us comfortable," he tells his companions, "if we are only clever enough to use it" (41). The exhilaration of cold bathing that the boys experience echoes the "Take a cold tub, Sir" philosophy of the boys' papers. "My readers will forgive me for asking whether they are in the habit of bathing thus every morning; and if they answer 'No,' they will pardon me for recommending them to begin at once," says the narrator (73). But the boys' experience on the coral island is not simply about survival or endurance. These are English boys and thus, in opposition to the "savages" they later encounter, they are rational beings. Ralph conducts little scientific experiments, preparing a tank with seawater and sea creatures as a sort of laboratory. He spends much of his time in observation and examination with the burning-glass. When the boys come across a pale green object just under the surface of the water slowly moving to and fro what appears to be a tail, they try to spear it. When the spear passes through and comes up untarnished, Jack and Ralph decide that it must be a phosphoric light. Jack and Ralph converse seriously about tides and ponder the formation of the large coral islands, while Peterkin plays the role of jester and acts as a foil for their serious scientific nature. This is one of the main differences between the English and the savages: rationality. The boys do not simply respond to their environment, they act on it; they attempt to master it by understanding it scientifically. Through Ralph, Ballantyne seldom misses an opportunity to afford his young readers a short lesson, whether on penguins, waterspouts, or monster waves.

The difference between the boys and the islanders is highlighted when they encounter cannibals whose barbaric behavior disgusts them. Jack's reaction, however, goes beyond disgust to righteous anger. While there is an acknowledgment that pirates are "white savages" (141) and their behavior reprehensible, it is not as bizarre or horrific as that of the islanders. But the pirates are considered more blameworthy because they know better. Bloody Bill, the crusty old seaman who befriends Ralph when he is borne away in a pirate schooner, tells him that the soft-hearted people in England would rather not know the shocking details of what he has witnessed, shutting their ears in disbelief to protect their sensitivities. But Bill assures Ralph that he knows for certain, as do many captains of the British and American navies, "that the Feejee islanders eat not only their enemies but one another; and they do it not for spite, but pleasure. It's a *fact* that they prefer human flesh to any other" (160). But there is a marvelous transformation when the natives take up Christianity, for then they give up their bloody ways and are safe to be trusted. "I never cared for Christianity myself," Bloody Bill admits, "and I don't well know what it means; but a man with half an eye can see what it does for these black critters" (161). When Ralph notes that he has not seen a reptile of any kind since he came to that part of the world, Bill replies, "No more there are any . . . if ye except the niggers, themselves" (166).

The notion that the natives, whether of India or various African clans or the South Sea islands, have no regard for human life, including their own, is so prevalent in writing about the empire that it has become something of a trope, and it appears in *The Coral Island* as well. In contrast, the boys care so much for their own lives and each other's that they fight for their survival and sacrifice their own safety for the sake of their companions. Their emotions on reuniting with Ralph reveal the strong bond they share. Once reunited, the boys determine to leave the coral island and set out to rescue a young Samoan woman who is being forced into marriage by the chief who had abducted her from her people. The young woman, Avatea, belongs to one of the Samoan Islands where Christianity had been introduced long before she was captured by the heathens of a neighboring island. In fact, the day after her capture she was to have joined the church that had been planted there "by that excellent body, the London Missionary Society" (204). The boys are welcomed into the Christian settlement, where they bear witness to the benefits of civilization.

The opposition between the anarchy of the heathen village and the order of the Christian village is obvious:

> The village was about a mile in length, and perfectly straight, with a wide road down the middle, on either side of which were rows of the tufted-topped ti tree, whose delicate and beautiful blossoms, handing beneath their plume-crested tops, added richness to the scene. The cottages of the natives were built beneath these trees, and were kept in the most excellent order, each having a little garden in front, tastefully laid out and planted, while the walks were covered with black and white pebbles. (Ballantyne 1858, 204)

Ralph cannot help contrasting it with "the wretched village of Emo" where he had witnessed so many frightful scenes, and he cannot help exclaiming, "What a convincing proof that Christianity is of God!" (205). If they need further proof, it is in the fact that, once converted, the natives are (magically) quite knowledgeable: "Indeed, Peterkin very truly remarked that 'they seemed to know a considerable deal more than Jack himself!'" (207). The same is certainly not true of the heathens. When the natives are first converted, the teacher, a native himself, shows them how to reduce coral to a fine soft white powder. They then rub their faces and bodies all over with it, symbolically taking on white characteristics, or at least those that people of their race are allowed to assume.

Along with the boys, we witness "sanguinary conflict" (213): the melee of heathen warfare; the terrible customs of the "savages"; the victors braining their victims on the field where they lie; their frantic dancing and wild gesticulating; their "hideous aspect"; the black, red, and yellow paints with which they daub their faces and naked bodies; and humans beings carried on planks to the sacrifice. But ultimately what saves the boys from captivity by these savages is not their pluck and strength, but Christianity itself. Tararo, the chief, whom they had originally helped during a battle on the coral island, but who had cancelled his debt to them when they attempted to rescue Avatea, converts to Christianity and releases them, allowing them to reclaim their schooner and set sail at last for England. The light of Christianity has been brought by an English missionary, tall thin, balding, with thin gray hair and a "clear grey eye" that "beamed with a look that was frank, fearless, loving, and truthful" (235). As the false gods of the island of Mango are reduced to ashes,

Avatea's lover pays tribute to Jack's qualities of character, qualities that he realizes are a result of being a Christian man:

> Young friend, you have seen few years, but your head is old. Your heart also is large and very brave. I and Avatea are your debtors, and we wish, in the midst of this assembly, to acknowledge our debt, and to say that it is one which we can never repay. You have risked your life for one who was known to you only for a few days. But she was a woman in distress, and that was enough to secure to her the aid of a Christian man. We, who live in these islands of the sea, know that the true Christians always act thus. Their religion is one of love and kindness. We thank God that so many Christians have been sent here—we hope many more will come. Remember that I and Avatea will think of you and pray for you and your brave comrades when you are far away. (237)

Although in this instance attributed to Christianity, the traits celebrated in this speech are those habitually considered apposite to the Englishman.

Typically, Ballantyne finds it necessary to debase the island natives to the furthest extent possible in order to contrast the character, demeanor, and behavior of the English boys. The "savages" do little else but kill and eat each other throughout the book. They are redeemed only when converted to Christianity, whereupon they act in a far more civilized fashion. Frederick Marryat's treatment of an African native in *Mr. Midshipman Easy* (1836) is much more benign in comparison. Marryat wrote about twenty novels for adults and children, most of them naval adventures. *Mr. Midshipman Easy* is the only one never to go out of print, and it remains the best known. Mesty's account of his warrior days is told in his own voice. No one speaks for him. We seldom hear the natives' voices in *The Coral Island*, except of Christianized ones. When Mesty describes how he kills a panther without assistance for the first time and becomes a mighty warrior, feared and respected, and then adds "Now, I boil the kettle for the young gentlemen!" (Marryat 1836, 112), his humiliation is evident. For the author allows us to first see him as he saw himself, powerful and dignified, then witness his mortification at his fallen status. Mesty, although a prince, is sold into slavery by those seeking to avenge his hasty actions and then escapes from it by concealing himself aboard an English merchant vessel. Even though he talks of the skulls and slaves he acquired in battle, and even though in his warrior days he wore the plume of eagle and ostrich feathers and had multiple wives, he and Jack develop a deep friendship, although it is not a friendship of equals. That this was not the norm is indicated by the barbs Jack has to bear about consorting with niggers. Yet, as Louis J. Parascandola states in his introduction, Marryat believed in distinctions between the races and the classes. In this respect he participated in the Social Darwinist thinking that underlay so many stories for children produced in this era. The persistent debunking of the principles of equality, social justice, and the rights of man that Nicodemus Easy, Jack's father, indulges in, can be extrapolated as a defense of colonialism.

While *Robinson Crusoe* was one of the earliest works to describe and depict the starkly perceived differences between physiognomy and character based on race, the famed tales of Rudyard Kipling are among the latest. By the time Kipling was writing, the superiority of white people was much more than a claim, much more even than a belief. It was considered a fact, a fact borne out by the triumphs of the empire, triumphs that the British, especially, repeatedly coupled to character. *The Jungle Books* lay down the law of the jungle: each species has its special character and its particular characteristics. In the law of the jungle, the merit and success of the individual and the merit and success of the group are tightly entwined: "For the strength of the Pack is the Wolf, and the strength of the Wolf is the Pack" (Kipling 1894, vol. 1, 91).

Throughout the stories, white men are distinguished from others, almost as though they are a separate species altogether, and assigned their own characteristics. For example, Rikki the mongoose is told what to do should he ever come across white men (Kipling 1894, vol. 2, 6). The connection between authority and ability is clearly established when Purun Bhagat considers that "if any one wished to get on in the world he must stand well with the English, and imitate all that the English believed to be good" (vol. 2, 56). For this is what it comes down to:

> You can work it out by Fractions or by simple Rule of Three,
> But the way of Tweedle-dum is not the way of Tweedle-dee.
> You can twist it, you can turn it, you can plait it till you drop,
> But the way of Pilly-Winky's not the way of Winkie Pop! (vol. 2, 177).

Even animals know that. When, in the story entitled *Her Majesty's Servants*, the little dog warns the camel that "My man's very angry" because the camel upset the tent, the bullocks immediately discern he must be white, whereupon the dog replies "Of course he is. . . . Do you suppose I'm looked after by a black bullock-driver?" (vol. 2, 192).

The animals know that the law of the jungle never orders anything without a reason and forbids beasts to eat man except to demonstrate killing techniques to their young, for then they must hunt outside the pack's hunting grounds. "The real reason for this is that man-killing means, sooner or later, the arrival of *white men* [my emphasis] on elephants" (vol. 1, 6). What it all comes down to is a plan. Each species has its order, each its degree, each person has his place. The law of the jungle can be reduced to one word: "Obey."

Beasts must and do obey just the same as men. Mules, horses, elephants, and bullocks must obey their driver, the driver his sergeant, the sergeant his lieutenant, the lieutenant his captain, the captain his major, the major his colonel, the colonel his brigadier, and the brigadier his general. The general, in his turn, obeys the viceroy who is the servant of the empress. "Thus it is done" (vol. 2, 197). In *Her Majesty's Servants*, this explanation is provided to an old Central Asian chief who has accompanied the Amir of Afghanistan as he witnesses a parade and cavalry charge of British troops. The chief, awed by the spectacle he has just observed, and the flawless discipline and order with which it was accomplished, asks a native officer how this wonderful thing was achieved. The officer answers: "There was an order, and they obeyed" (vol. 1, 197). To keep the law of the jungle is to prosper. To break it is to die. When the chief rues that this is not the case in Afghanistan where they obey only their own wills (vol. 1, 197), the native officer answers that it is for that reason that their Amir, whom they do not obey, "must come here and take orders from our Viceroy" (vol. 1, 197). This is the hierarchy; this is the degree. This is what maintains the order of the empire and ensures its success, and it is all ascribed to nature, to innate characteristics honed by evolution in the best traditions of Social Darwinism.

It all goes back earlier, of course, back to the Renaissance and the great chain of being where all degrees of perfection from the highest and fullest to the lowest and least are represented. The beings in the middle of the chain are dependent or contingent while, as one moves higher up, one finds further degrees of independence and self-sufficiency up to the absolute degree achieved by God. It must follow then that interdependence is an essential aspect of the chain. Human beings are placed between the beasts and the angels, but in Social Darwinism human beings themselves are graded. Since every existing thing in the universe has its place in a hierarchical order, which is divinely planned, it would be a logical next step to accommodate this scheme to a colonial structure.

The proportion of spirit to matter determines degree in the great chain of being. The idea of "correspondences" determines that reason should rule emotions just as the parent should rule a child or a king his subjects or the sun should govern the planets. According to Knox, Gobineau, and other specious theorists of race, nonwhite people are ruled by emotions while white people are ruled by reason. In the former, matter or physicality is emphasized, while in the latter it is spirit: mental and spiritual capacities. The racial biases of colonialism could quite easily conform to a more finely tuned version of the chain. This idea is certainly operative in Kipling's *Jungle Books*, where there is recurrent emphasis on the importance of keeping the law of the jungle, on maintaining the order. To do otherwise would be to leave one's proper place in the hierarchy, which, in turn, would mean to deceive one's nature. This was a relatively simple, streamlined, and effective system of internalizing authority in its strictest sense. It provided a rationale for colonialism that integrated the philosophical and the political.

Kipling's series of stories *Stalky & Co.* portrays the workings of degree within the intricate jungle of the British public school. The school in this story is not quite a public school but a school that prepares boys for military service, based on the United Services College that Kipling himself attended. "We're a limited liability company payin' four per cent," says one of the boys (1980, 639). Eighty percent of the boys in the school had been born abroad, in camp, cantonment, or upon the high seas, and 75 percent were the sons of officers in one or the other of the services. Some expected to obtain a queen's commission. *Stalky & Co.* is one of Kipling's most interesting and perhaps his most complex and sophisticated work. In the final analysis, it remains morally ambiguous. Its three protagonists—M'Turk, Beetle, and Stalky—are contemptible bullies, battle-hardened hooligans, and callous youths. But they are also entirely successful in the struggle for survival. They are the fittest in this struggle not only because they are ruthless but also because they are crafty and clever. They constantly adapt to their circumstances. They are not simply street smart, they are also intellectual, each in his own way, Stalky excelling in mathematics, Beetle in English and French, and M'Turk in Latin. M'Turk, in fact, reads Ruskin for his amusement. They mock the misspelling of the word "indifference" in a note they receive from other boys in their house.

The stratum of school society reflects the social structure of the country as a whole, where class speaks to class, and there is a fine balance based on mutual understanding. It is this understanding that M'Turk exploits to save their skins when they have been trespassing on the grounds of a local landowner. He plays the part of an indignant squire: "It was the landed man speaking to his equal—deep calling to deep—and the old gentleman acknowledged the cry" (1980, 569). The school is the Darwinian world of tooth and claw. In a wry statement that would seem to belie his jingoistic pontifications elsewhere, Kipling says "They were learning, at the expense of a fellow-countryman, the lesson of their race, which is to put away all emotion and entrap the alien at the proper time" (576). The three hark back to the bullies in *Tom Brown's Schooldays*; they are unlike Tom and his friends who, for all their frivolities, are well intended and participate heartily in school spirit, though there is something of East in Stalky. They are also antithetical to the idealized schoolboys we find in the boys' papers or in the adventure stories of Enid Blyton, whom we will meet in the next chapter.

As school stories go, they are in fact, antiheroes. They bear none of the traits of character prized by the British and claimed as peculiar to their constitution, or at least not overtly. They are cunning rather than resourceful, tough rather than strong, aggressive rather than courageous, and wily rather than ingenious. They are not the types of boys the housemaster understands, boys who attend house matches and can be accounted for at any given moment. He has heard M'Turk openly deride cricket—even house matches—and Beetle has no regard for the honor of the house. The boys scoff at the ideal school type: "If we attended the matches an' yelled, 'Well hit, sir,' an' stood on one leg an' grinned every time Heffy [the headmaster] said, 'So ho, my sons. Is it thus?' an' said, 'Yes, sir,' an' 'No, sir' an' 'Oh, sir,' an' 'Please, sir,' like a lot o' filthy fa-ags, Heffy 'ud think no end of us," says M'Turk with a sneer (572). We are not meant to like these boys or to approve of their behavior, but we are meant to appreciate their skill as they maneuver and manipulate the system. Only Foxy, the sergeant, recognizes their abilities, telling the boys "I wish I'd ha' had you in my company, young gentlemen" (578).

The boys mock the one thing on which social order most depends: obedience. It is the law of the jungle, and they break it with impunity. They deride "the flannelled crowd," (594) a reference to cricketers. Cricket is a game that has come to symbolize all that is best in British character. It is, above all, a team sport; the word itself has become a metaphor for fairness. We might recall the central role cricket plays in *Tom Brown's Schooldays,* which ends with an account of Tom's last cricket match. When Beetle complains that a comment from King, a teacher who is the bête-noir of the boys, is not fair, Stalky replies "My Hat! You've been here six years, and you expect fairness. Well, you *are* a dithering idiot" (595). They mock idealism and innocence, telling another boy, Orrin, with great sarcasm, "There's something about your pure, high, young forehead, full of the dreams of innocent boyhood, that's no end fetchin'. It is, indeed" (600). The time-honored traditions to which their housemaster refers "of steps and measures, of tone and loyalty in the house and to the house" mean nothing to them. The house is a microcosm of the school, which, in turn, is a microcosm of the system.

Connections are frequently established between this layered, hierarchical, and tyrannical world and that of the empire. For example, reference is made to the sergeant having served in the mutiny. When he wishes that the boys had been in his company, his implication is that young men such as these brutal boys would have been good fighters for the empire. There is, in fact, a direct tie between the school and India. It is preparing the boys for service to the empire. Many of its old boys have served in India and have either died in the fighting or returned to the school to tell their stories. It is India where Stalky ends up, after attending Sandhurst. M'Turk is bound for Cooper's Hill, the engineering college that trained engineers for the empire. We see clearly how their escapades in school become training for Stalky's daring exploits in India. When the masters deliberately overlook the terrible hazing that two senior but relatively new boys suffer at the hands of Stalky and company, as revenge for their own bullying of another boy, the Reverend John tells them "Boys educate each other, they say, more than we can or dare" (635).

The discipline of the masters is selective and erratic, their justice arbitrary. In this world, immorality is less of a sin than impudence (647). By the time the three boys leave the school, although they were not trusted enough to become prefects, they have earned a grudging respect from the head and most of the masters. In return, they respect the head for his courage in saving, at risk to his own life, the life of a boy dying of diphtheria by sucking out his mucous.

While Stalky and company are far from being model English boys, they are, in the end, all successful—Stalky in military service, M'Turk in engineering, and Beetle in journalism. Their success is based not on the sterling qualities so celebrated in most of the books we are dealing with here, but on a perversion of those qualities. The complexity of the story lies in the connection between the school and the empire in India. Kipling's telling of this story is not valoristic but utterly realistic. He is not celebrating the boys' character so much as establishing the connection between their character and their subsequent success. One of the most quizzical of the stories is "The Flag of Their Country." During defaulters' drill, which the sergeant conducts for those who have earned black marks for various offences, an old gentleman enters. It turns out that he is General Collinson, K.C.B., a member of the College Board of Council. The general has no idea that the drill is a form of punishment, mistaking it for a cadet-corps. He singles Stalky out as "the kind of boy you should cultivate" (650). On the general's recommendation, an attempt is made to establish an actual corps but as yet their drills are not public.

The general, delighted that his recommendation has been acted upon, spreads the word among his friends. A friend of a friend, a conservative Member of Parliament, decides to address an assembly of the boys on "patriotism." Stalky and company scoff at what they perceive as his "giddy patriotism" (658). The speaker drones on about how the boys of today will make the men of tomorrow and upon the men of tomorrow "the fair fame of their glorious native land depended" (659). Some of them, he expects, will look forward "to leading their men against the bullets of England's foes; to confronting the stricken field in all the pride of their youthful manhood" (659). As he rambles on about honor and glory and the deeds of their ancestors, the boys feel that they are being outraged by a fat man who considers marbles a game, a reference to his injunction that life was not all games, not all marbles. Finally, the M.P. reaches for a cloth-wrapped stick: "This—this was the concrete symbol of their land—worthy of all honour and reverence! Let no boy look on this flag who did not purpose to worthily add to its imperishable lustre. He shook it before them—a large calico Union Jack, staring in all three colours, and waited for the thunder of applause that should crown his effort" (660). But the applause never comes. Instead, there is silence. The head saves the situation by swiftly rising to propose a vote of thanks and the school applauds furiously, not out of appreciation but out of relief.

The flag lies unrolled on the desk as the boys line up against the wall. Only the sergeant is moved by it. A prefect takes it, rolls it up rapidly and tosses it into a locker. This is greeted by "quick-volleyed hand-clapping" (660). The sergeant expects the flag and the speech to stimulate the boys to drill. The M.P. had said before he left that the corps may adopt it as its own. Instead, the volunteer cadet-corps disbands: "dead—putrid—corrupt—stinkin,'" says Stalky. He has been crying and tries to cover it up as pretence. It's not that the boys did not recognize the flag, but it was not displayed at the college and "it was no part of the scheme of their lives" (660). It is a complex, multifarious, and rather bizarre scene, especially when one considers that it was written by the same person who wrote the poem "Take up the White Man's Burden." In it patriotism becomes problematic, or at least the brand of patriotism the M.P. preaches and practices, which is nothing short of jingoism.

Ultimately, however, *Stalky & Co.* fails as a critique of empire although it does problematize two key issues: preparation for service in the empire and the character necessary for this service. The best preparation is not flimsy moralism, false patriotism, or empty academic exercises, but being subjected to a cruel, callous, and cold-blooded world where dog may eat dog and live to tell the tale. And the best character is the one who can undertake this and survive, best not in a moral sense but in an adaptive sense. Whereas Henty's heroes have a sense of rightness, of moral certitude, Stalky and the other two boys have a sense of power, of might. So is this too a story of natural selection and adaptation? Is Kipling saying that the work of colonizing is and must be cruel, callous, and cold-blooded, and cricket is not the best preparation for it? In his biography, *The Strange Ride of Rudyard Kipling: His Life and Works*, Angus Wilson writes,

> To the mindless insubordination of the Americans, as he saw it, and the complacent attachment to petty codes and regulations of contemporary England, he proposed his own way of life. It is a code that seeks to give the fullest rein to individual skills, energies and cunning for the evasion of minor rules and the outwitting of lesser authorities, while always upholding a strong sense of the overall need for a higher law or social cohesion to which the individual must submit himself in total self-discipline and responsibility. In *Stalky & Co.* he conveniently brought home the lesson, by constantly overriding the prevailing English public-school ethics, which derived ultimately from the great influence of Thomas Arnold's reforms at Rugby School in the early years of Victoria's reign. (1978, 48)

The head symbolizes that law in *Stalky & Co.* The boys respect him, although grudgingly, and accept his punishment even when it is not entirely fair because they know that it is necessary to the preservation of the social order. And that is where the story may be said to fail as a critique of empire. Unlike E. M. Forster's *A Passage to India*, it is not a critique of the behavior of empire. Unlike George Orwell's *Burmese Days*, it is not a critique of the principles of empire. It is rather a critique of the training for empire, but in the final analysis it upholds it. Stalky's emotional collapse after the flag incident betrays the depth of his feelings for what the flag stands for. It is not something to be trivialized. It is only "poor little street-bred people" (like the M.P. and the sergeant perhaps) "who yelp at the English Flag!" These words are from Kipling's poem "The English Flag," which ends with the question "What is the Flag of England?" and calls upon the "Winds of the World," a reference evidently to the British Empire, to declare.

Sometimes, however, I am not sure. There is still room, I believe, for interpreting the story as an exposé of the way in which the empire really works and of its heroes as nothing but a bunch of louts. In the last story of the series, however, Stalky graduates from lout to hero, although an insubordinate hero who accepts orders only when they suit his book (683). The setting is a baronial estate that belongs to one of the old boys who is sitting around a fire with other old boys reminiscing about schooldays and service in India. Many of them are home on leave. M'Turk is there, and Beetle, who narrates the story, but Stalky is still in India. "Stalky is the great man of his Century" announces one of them, while another agrees "Adequate chap. Infernally adequate" (676). They recount some of Stalky's exploits, which are audacious, highly risky, and not entirely legitimate, in fact, very similar to his school escapades.

In one, Stalky is holed up in an old stone fort in Afghanistan with his Sikhs. Only four days worth of supplies remain. His subaltern lies dead in the watchtower in a foot of drifted snow. They recount how the snow lay all white on his eyebrows and when Stalky moved the lamp it looked as if he were alive. But what produces a shudder is their recollection of "the beastly look on Stalky's face . . . with his nostrils all blown out, same as he used to look when he was bullyin' a fag" (678). This correspondence establishes a direct connection between Stalky the schoolboy and Stalky the soldier. The comment made by Stalky's senior native officer that Stalky "was an invulnerable *Guru* of sorts" is borne out when Stalky disappears and reappears after a severe snowstorm, coated with claret-colored ice. "Do you know what that maniac had done?" asks one of the men assembled around the fire, someone who had been present on the occasion. He then proceeds to tell them. Stalky had dropped over the edge of a ditch in darkness and a howling snowstorm and made his way down to the bottom of the gorge, forded the stream which was half-frozen, climbed up on the other side along a track he'd discovered, and emerged on the right flank of one of the warring parties. What he does next is a daring act of strategy that essentially confuses the two factions warring against them. Their allegiance is broken as they mistake Stalky's acts for those of the other faction.

The Sikhs and the Pathans, famed fighters, both want to adopt Stalky as their own. "Stalky stalked," says one of the men around the fire. "That's all there is to it" (680). Stalky can speak the native languages and crack bawdy jokes with his men, among whom he is clearly admired and much respected. As his former schoolmates continue their narration of Stalky's daring feats, they tell how he sends a message by getting a bugle player to play a tune, popular in their schooldays, from one of their theatricals. At that point the men around the fire interrupt the story by singing the old song, five times through. The song, played by a native bugler, is a signal sent by Stalky so that his message might be delivered to the right man.

The test is whether the intended recipient of the message knows the end of the song. The man relating this account tells how he finished the tune on the bugle, whereupon he was given Stalky's message. Stalky frequently acts on his own authority, again, as he did in school. One of the men tells how he was instructed to send Stalky an official telegram chastising him, but followed it up with an unofficial telegram containing another song from their school theatricals. Stalky would understand that this countermanded the official telegram.

Called up by the viceroy for his transgressions, Stalky behaves exactly as he did when called up by the head. Officially disgraced, relieved of his command, but completely unrepentant, he was last seen lording it in the village of his native officer, where he is treated like a king. The group then realizes that what Stalky has done is to duplicate an old school trick. "There's nobody like Stalky," pronounces one of them. Beetle, who narrates this story, replies, "That's just where you make the mistake. . . . India's full of Stalkies—Cheltenham and Haileybury and Marlborough chaps—that we don't know anything about, and the surprises will begin when there is really a big row on" (685). This is a reference to the First World War and to those who have no idea what war is all about, "who go to the front in first-class carriages" (685).

The reference to school songs and tricks establishes a clear correspondence between school and Empire in this final story of the series and indicates that from school to Empire is not so much a graduation but a continuum. Stalky remains something of a renegade, belying the lines from the poem that precede the story:

> This we learned from famous men,
> Teaching in our borders,
> Who declared it was best,
> Safest, easiest, and best—
> Expeditious, wise, and best—
> To obey your orders.

The title of the story itself, *Slaves of the Lamp*, offers some interesting possibilities. Is the lamp the Empire? Who are its slaves? What does the word suggest? Stalky is ultimately a T. E. Lawrence–like character of whom Graham Dawson writes:

Lawrence's own narrative derives its psychic intensity from its yoking together of extreme opposites. Indeed, it constitutes a locus of virtually all the unconscious phantasies of power and desire through which, according to psychoanalytic thinking, sexual identity is constructed. The story incorporates the ambivalent desires to give and take life, to create and destroy, kill and save, rescue and punish. It deals with hope and betrayal, victory and defeat, prohibition and transgression, reward and punishment. Lawrence fluctuates between an omnipotent, messianic (or Satanic?) sense of personal power, and humiliating, denigrating experiences of absolute powerlessness; between narcissistic self-love and self-hatred; strength and vulnerability; being the leader and the led; actively doing, yet passively done to; in control and yet controlled; concealing, yet revealing; giving in and holding out; triumphant victor, yet abject failure; courageous yet fearful; pure, yet guilty; aggressor, yet victim. (1994, 209–10)

The moral ambiguity of *Stalky & Co.* is further illustrated by George Orwell's contention that the book has had an immense influence on boys' literature, often by reputation, even among people who have never even seen a copy of it. Orwell goes so far as to say that the main origin of the school stories of the boys' papers is *Stalky & Co.* More than once, he says, he has come across a reference to the story in which the word was spelt "Storky" (Orwell and Angus 2000, 466). The stories in the boys' papers are, however, far more sentimental.

Kipling's most famous work, *Kim*, is a very different sort of book. In *Kim*, racial boundaries become somewhat blurry and the hierarchical order is therefore, on occasion, disturbed, though it rights itself in the end, of course. In *Kim*, three of the characters cross the boundaries of racial identity. Kim, of course, is an Irish lad whose father, a young color-sergeant of the Mavericks, an Irish regiment, stayed on in India to take a post on the railway while his regiment returned without him. He lost his wife to cholera and began drifting and loafing, the three-year-old Kim in tow. Finally he fell victim to opium, learning the taste from a woman who, after his death, takes care of Kim. The woman wants Kim to wear European clothes, but he finds it easier to slip into Hindu or Mohammedan garb when engaged in certain business. Similarly, he slips in and out of identities, more at home in a wedding procession or eating with his native friends than with the members of his own race. When he finally falls into the hands of his father's regiment, his respect for the colonel is based on the fact that "No man could be a fool who knew the language so intimately, who moved so gently and silently, and whose eyes were so different from the dull fat eyes of other Sahibs" (Kipling 1901, 100).

Released temporarily from the boarding school in which he has been placed, he convinces some women of ill repute to stain his skin brown and heads for a cookshop "where he feasted in extravagance and greasy luxury" (108). He reverts to native speech with exultation and, able to participate once more in native life, "In all India that night was no human being so joyful as Kim" (108). On another damp night, as he follows his friend, the horse dealer Mahbub, he beds down under the wheels of a horse-truck with a borrowed blanket to cover him, amid brickbats and ballast-refuge, between overcrowded horses and grubby Baltis, not a situation to appeal to most white boys, as the author tells us, "but Kim was utterly happy" (116). Sometimes he dreams in "Hindustanee" with never an English word.

As we are continually reminded, however, Kim is a sahib and the son of a sahib, although, as his friend the lama observes, no white man knows the land and the customs of the land as he does. Sometimes his white side lies utterly dormant as when he vehemently resists the suggestion that he'd like to be a soldier: "There was nothing in his composition to which drill and routine appealed" (79). An English boy would be expected to take naturally to drill and routine. Kim's life prior to the boarding school in which he had been enrolled, St. Xavier's, had been without restrictions. He was unfettered, untroubled, and unregulated. "He much disapproved of the present aspect of affairs, for this was the very school and discipline he had spent two-thirds of his young life in avoiding" (84). It would seem that his very sensibility was more in tune with India than with his own race. At the school he is positively depressed, finding the food unappetizing and the company uncongenial: "The indifference of native crowds he was used to; but this strong loneliness among white men preyed on him" (87). But the way of Tweedle-dum is not the way of Tweedle-dee. Order will assert itself: "each in his degree" (Kipling 1894–1895, vol. 2, 201).

Slowly Kim's true nature begins to assert itself and he thrives again, donning his white identity as he does the white drill suit and rejoicing in the newfound bodily comforts and the opportunity to use his sharpened mind over the tasks they set him. As Mahbub is wont to remind Kim, "Once a Sahib, always a Sahib," (Kipling 1901, 91). And, as he is reminded at the school, "One must never forget that one is a Sahib, and that some day, when examinations are passed, one will command natives" (106). Kim makes a note of this, for he begins to understand where examinations lead. When the lama tells him that it is well to abstain from action, Kim reminds him that he has been taught at the school that to abstain from action is unbefitting a sahib. And he is a sahib, he adds (181). Father Victor assures him that at St. Xavier's they will make a man of him, a white man and (he hopes) a good man. It is perhaps the closest we come to seeing how conscious and carefully crafted was this construct of character.

Kim does, however, frequently question his identity, wondering who exactly he is, asking who is Kim and sometimes reclaiming his individuality:

> I go from one place to another as it might be a kick-ball. It is my kismet. No man can escape his kismet. But I am to pray to Bibi Miriam and I am a Sahib—and he looked at his boots ruefully. No; I am Kim. This is the great world, and I am only Kim. Who is Kim? He considered his own identity, a thing he had never done before, till his head swam. He was one insignificant person in all this roaring whirl of India, going southward to he knew not what fate. (Kipling 1901, 100)

That he is a sahib is something he often has to remind himself. He knows instinctively, however, that his identity is more complex than that and so he settles repeatedly on "I am Kim" as his answer, sensing that to be Kim is to be a sahib who has incorporated India, who has assumed some of its myriad identities, while retaining at the core his whiteness. Kim is actually Irish, not English; M. Daphne Kutzer points out that "Kim has a number of traits Victorians would have seen as quintessentially Irish: he is acquisitive, crafty, quick and witty with his tongue, and 'Friend to All the World,' a charmer" (2000, 20). However, in a colonial context the fact that he is a sahib—in other words, that he is white—supercedes national distinctions. These might be brought to play internally, but externally, in opposition to the "other," differences dissolve, are whited out, so to speak. Lurgan Sahib, who introduces him to the Great Game, is a kindred spirit. He wears English clothes but speaks Urdu like a native: "Sweetest of all—he treated Kim as an equal on the Asiatic side" (Kipling 1901, 129). Like Kim he can shed and assume identities with the ease of a costume change. In *Nation and Narrative*, Ernest Renan declares, "A nation is a soul, a spiritual principle. Two things, which in truth are but one, constitute this soul or spiritual principle. One lies in the past, one in the present. One is the possession in common of a rich legacy of memories; the other is present-day consent, the desire to live together, the will to perpetuate the value of the heritage that one has received in an undivided form" (Bhabha 1990, 19). Kim cannot quite share the nationhood that is derived from the past and dependant, according to Renan, on sacrifice. But he can participate in the nationhood that exists in the present, which is contingent on consent but, more importantly, on racial legacy.

Mahbub Ali supplies information about explorers of nationalities other than English. Kim is similarly an explorer of identities. But whereas Kim is a synthesis of identities (English, Irish, and Indian), Hurree Babu is merely a hybrid. He attempts to appropriate British speech and dress, but combined with his Bengali idiom and native garments he ends up a polychromatic and rather absurd mongrel: "He represents in petto India in transition—the monstrous hybridism of East and West," comments the Russian, one of two foreigners for whom Hurree Babu is serving as a guide. The other foreigner, the Frenchman, replies, "He has lost his own country and has not acquired any other" (Kipling 1901, 204). Both Hurree Babu and Kim, however, each in his own way, have attempted to cross the boundaries of race and nation, Hurree Babu in a comical fashion and Kim in a somewhat whimsical fashion. That Hurree Babu is not allowed to successfully cross over, and Kim is, asserts the colonial order. Being a sahib, Kim has the prerogative to take on Indian identities but for Hurree Babu to attempt to assume any type of British identity is transgressive; for Kim, it is transformative. The lama introduces a spiritual angle to the theme of transformation, reminding Kim that "the flesh takes a thousand thousand shapes, desirable or detestable as men reckon, but in truth of no account either way" (Kipling 1901, 181). We are all souls seeking escape, he points out, but in the end Kim seeks not to escape his identity but to reconcile its multiplicities.

Kutzer says that ultimately the racial typing in *Kim* does not undercut the theme of transformation (2000, 20). But one could claim that it does just that precisely because, as she points out, "Both Kim and the lama end up as their true selves, back where they belong in the world: Kim as a member of the ruling British class, the lama back in his beloved northern mountains, wiser if not successful through his attempts to escape the Wheel of Life." It is undercut because character traits are so precisely assigned to the races; they are presented as fixed rather than fluid. We are told about "the terrible, bubbling, meaningless yell of the Asiatic" (Kipling 1901, 117). Hurree Babu confesses that he is "unfortunately Asiatic, which is serious detriment in some respects" (Kipling 1901, 191). The Russians claim that "Decidedly it is we who can deal with Orientals!" (213). We are informed that "Kissing is practically unknown among Asiatics" (227), and a passing reference is made to "some mysterious Asiatic equivalent to the still-room" (235). Kim is able to store an entire trove about his body "as only Orientals can" (238). Hurree Babu lies "like a Bengali." Asiatic and Oriental are used as general amorphous terms to denote Asians, while English or sahibs or white are used as general amorphous terms to denote the British. It is not clear, for instance, how the Russians, who are the enemy in this case, would have been categorized, but they are certainly distinguished from the English. The English, we are told, "do eternally tell the truth" (119), the "Sahibs never grow old" and are a "strong-backed breed" (186). Reference is made to British pride, and when Kim reviews a situation with his natural-born authority, he does so "from a Sahib's point of view" (216).

In other passages, the behavior of the Englishman is distinguished from that of a Russian, especially in terms of how he relates to the natives. For instance, while the Englishman does not presume familiarity with the Asiatic, he is not gratuitously cruel to him either. The Englishman always travels with a retinue, unlike the Russians, ignorant sahibs who are foolish enough to follow a Bengali's advice. By the time Kipling was writing, notions of character, race, and nation were so intricately entwined that such truisms would have been accepted with little or no resistance. Kim's testing ground of character is the antithesis of Mary's in *The Secret Garden*. While she needed the good earth and the bracing climate of the English countryside to fully develop her national traits, Kim finds himself amidst the commotion and confusion of the Indian urban landscape. Although his Indian identity is celebrated, it is ultimately superceded by his superior lineage, and the character traits that prevail are the ones Kipling and all these other writers claim for the white race: honesty, strength, endurance, courage, and, in the end, the ability to accept discipline. In Kim as in Colin, reason and magic merge in *The Secret Garden*, but reason prevails.

Perhaps it was G. A. Henty, more than Kipling or any of the other authors whose names are inextricably associated with British imperialism, who was responsible for inculcating in young minds the notion that character constitutes destiny. Henty (1832–1902) was born and died roughly thirty years earlier than Kipling (1865–1936). In Henty's adventure stories for boys, the personal story and the historical story are always imbricated. He was hugely popular. Sales of his books were estimated at 150,000 every year with cumulative sales in the worldwide market (including the United States, where he was widely read) totaling 25 million by 1952 (Butts 1992, 69). His readers accompany the young heroes of his books as they accompany the great generals and leaders of their times in daring exploits and decisive battles, English boys learned how their empire was won and preserved. They learned the names, the dates, the strategies, and the statistics of battles and sieges. They learned the names of storied regiments and of infamous foes. They learned about cavalry charges, native horsemen, and infantry soldiers. But above all, they learned what it was to be an Englishman. Empire becomes the birthright of the brave. "How brave you English boys are," the Ranee tells Ned and Dick in *In Times of Peril*, "No wonder your men have conquered India" (141). And in *With Clive in India* (1884), the hero, Charlie, notes, "it is astonishing what brave men can do" (123). Henty immediately affords authorial sanction to this statement: "In the after wars which England waged in India, the truth of what Charlie said was over and over again proved. Numerous fortresses, supposed by the natives to be absolutely impregnable, and far exceeding in strength that just described, have been carried by assault by the dash and daring of English troops" (123).

Time and again, English prowess in battle is proven. European skills are superior to that of the native troops, of course. But this is not just about racial superiority. It is about national superiority. In Southern India, in the early days of company rule, national superiority had to be established because at first the French held the advantage. But the British, under the leadership of Robert Clive, eventually established their dominance. The Empire depends on men of character, as the history lesson that Charlie and his companion get from a veteran doctor in the service of the company indicates:

> This, lads, was a memorable battle; it is the first time that European and Indian soldiers have come into contest, and it shows how immense is the superiority of Europeans. What Paradis did then, opens all sorts of possibilities for the future, and it may be that either we or the French are destined to rise from mere trading companies to be rulers of Indian states. Such, I know, is the opinion of young Clive, who is a very longheaded and ambitious young fellow. I remember his saying to me one night when we were with difficulty holding our own in the trenches, that if we had but a man of energy and intelligence at the head of our affairs in Southern India, we might ere many years passed be masters of the Carnatic. I own that it appears to me more likely that the French will be in that position, and that we shall not have a single establishment left there; but time will show. (Henty 1884, 28–29)

The lesson is driven home to young boys in Henty's books: British success is a result not simply of superiority in battle, or of arms, supplies, and other means, but of character: "The conquest of these vast tracts of country had been achieved by mere handfuls of men, and by a display of heroic valour and constancy scarce to be rivalled in the history of the world" (1884, 338).

Although Henty is unabashedly triumphal in his accounts of British derring-do, he is not entirely one-dimensional. We do see instances of cowardice, of poor planning and organization, and of individuals who do not uphold the prized British qualities. Charlie, in *With Clive in India*, finds out that the condition of Madras was far worse before the French occupation. Whereas the British chiefs think of nothing but trade, caring little about squalor and misery, the French have larger ideas. They improved fortifications, built wide roads and an esplanade, several new houses, and cleared rubbish and offal on the beach (44). The recent history of the British in the Carnatic is related to Charlie and another young man, Peters, by an older resident: "It's a history of defeat, loss of prestige and position," he tells them. "We have been out-fought and out-diplomatized, and have made a mess of everything we put our hand to" (57). Robert Clive himself, to whom credit is usually given for the British ascendancy over the

French in India, is represented by Henty as a complex character, though a hero nonetheless. We hear about his coolness, confidence, and courage (75), but also that he is "a queer, restless sort of chap," "straightforward and manly" but also "often gloomy and discontented" (47). In *With Clive in India* we also see Englishmen behaving in an utterly cowardly fashion. But it is clearly established that such behavior is out of character. In this, Henty is firmly in keeping with other British novelists of India, Maud Diver, for instance. When Mr. Drake refuses to send his ships so that the besieged garrison in the fort in Calcutta can embark, Charlie retorts furiously "And you call yourself . . . a British sailor! You talk of danger, and would desert a thousand men, women, and children, including two hundred of your own countrymen, and leave them at the mercy of an enemy!" (203). The account is historical. Stanley Wolpert in *A New History of India* refers to "The stampede of able-bodied men who abandoned Fort William that wretched June day," forcing many women and children to remain behind, "for the boats were not large enough to carry everyone to safety down river" (179). Rather than acknowledge that the British are not always brave, Henty depicts them as acting out of character.

Service in the East India Company's small army was not popular and not always a path to gain and glory. But Charlie arrives in time to participate in the decisive sieges of Arcot, Ambur, and Seringam, and in the Battle of Plassey, and experiences the infamous "Black Hole of Calcutta." When he set out from England in the service of the company, he was a boy of sixteen. When he returns to England ten years later, he is wealthy and has been promoted to the rank of lieutenant colonel. In the meantime, this young lad, fresh out of school and with no prior military training, is able to prove himself on the battlefield and entrusted with more and more responsibility. He is even assigned to a rajah friendly to the British who wishes his troops to be trained in the English manner. Charlie is able to effect great victories for this rajah and is richly rewarded in return. English drill and discipline bring about a tremendous transformation in the native troops, of which Charlie is made commander.

Indians are portrayed as indifferent to whichever group rules over them—Muslim, English or French—and as a people who respond with "apathetic resignation" to their circumstances (1884, 164), an attitude in clear contrast with the spirit of survival and resistance displayed by the English. It is a common notion in British writing about India. The artistry of the Indians is admired, but their fighting spirit deplored. "They are wonderfully clever and ingenious," Charlie observes as he admires the delicate and intricate work a man in the bazaar is turning out with rough tools. "If these fellows could but fight as well as they work, and were but united among themselves, not only should we be unable to set a foot in India, but the emperor, with the enormous armies which he would be able to raise, would be able to threaten Europe" (Henty 1884, 101). But then Charlie wonders how it is that the Sepoys, after only a few weeks' training, fight almost as well as their own men, and how it is that when they are commanded by their own countrymen they fail to fight well (101). Elsewhere, his friend and fellow officer, Peters, observes, "It is singular that, contemptible as are these natives of India when officered by men of their own race and religion, they will fight to the death when led by us" (325).

Little attempt is made to provide anywhere near the degree of detail about the lives, locale, culture, and customs of the Indians who are referred to generically as natives, savages, or even (by some characters) as "haythen niggers" (Henty 1884, 166). Tim, Charlie's devoted Irish attendant who uses this term, does, however, come to an understanding and even "toleration" of Islam as he observes the devotion of Hossein, Charlie's other retainer:

> He had come to the conclusion that a man who at stated times in the day would leave his employment, whatever it might be, spread his carpet, and be for some minutes lost in prayer, could not be altogether a hathen [sic], especially when he learned from Charlie that the Mahommedans, like ourselves, worship one God. For the sake of his friend, then, he now generally excluded the Mahommedans from the general designation of heathen, which he still applied to the Hindoos. (220–21)

The language of the region, which Charlie studies with an Indian "moonshee" or teacher is never named, but referred to in vague and generic terms as "the native language" (114). When an Indian displays impressive courage, it is almost always because of his devotion, loyalty, and commitment to an Englishman, as with Hossein in *With Clive in India*, who saves Charlie's life a couple of times in return for the fact that Charlie once spared his. In giving him a second chance, Charlie's measured justice is contrasted with the hasty and impetuous sentencing of the rajah who orders him executed. Similarly, in battle, English order and discipline are contrasted with poor organization and proclivity for chaos on the part of the natives. Indians, it is noted by Charlie, are better at offence than at defense. Insistently, we hear about instances of British bravery in the battlefield, in every single story.

In *For Name and Fame; or, Through Afghan Passes* (1886), the cool and steady conduct of the British is measured against the "slight resistance" of the Afghans whose "one thought was to effect their escape." Even when British forces are outnumbered, they triumph over the Afghans by sheer grit. We see the Afghan armies awed by what they have witnessed of British fighting forces:

> Detached bodies, indeed, often crept up near the walls and kept up a musketry fire at any troops showing themselves there. But no attempts were made to batter down the walls or to make anything like a resolute assault. Ayoub's army had indeed greatly lost heart. If 1500 British soldiers attacked under circumstances of the greatest disadvantage, had killed 6000 or 7000 of their assailants, what might not be the slaughter which a greatly superior force would inflict when sheltered behind stone walls? (Henty 1886, 220)

The hero of the story, William Gale, knows that, if led well, a British force could be trusted to take any position held by the Afghans, if not by direct attack, then by flank movements.

Henty does not entirely falsify history in this work but he certainly manipulates it. A comparison of his account of the "Black Hole of Calcutta" to that of Stanley Wolpert, a well-respected historian of India, indicates that Henty's facts are more or less accurate. Wolpert refers to a careful study by Brijen Kishore Gupta that suggests that Sira-ud-daula had not personally ordered or been informed of the situation. Henty acknowledges this indirectly by stating that an attempt had been made by "some native officers" to find a building to confine the prisoners, but they were unable to obtain one. The officer in command then ordered the prisoners into the small room, which became known as the notorious black hole. Henty describes it as eighteen feet square, while Wolpert tells us that it measured fourteen by eighteen feet (Wolpert 2000, 179). Henty is correct in depicting only one female prisoner, who, in his imaginary account, goes on to marry his hero, Charlie. In his description of the room "heaped high with the dead," Henty is probably following the account by J. Z. Holwell, who was commander of the remaining garrison of English soldiers. Professor Gupta suggests a smaller number confined and twenty-one survivors (Wolpert 2000, 179). Henty's use of the pronoun "our" as in "our troops" or "our authority" makes it clear that his books are addressed to an English audience, an audience that at the time would have read or received similar accounts and that, in any case, would have been, because of distance or patriotism, disinclined to doubt that events unfolded as Henty said they did. Even in this day and age, PrestonSpeed Publications upon the reissue of some of Henty's titles makes this claim: "His [Henty's] ability to bring his readers action-packed adventure in an accurate historical setting makes the study of history exciting, and removes the drudgery often associated with such study" (n.p.). Certainly Henty offers his young readers a plethora of logistical detail that adds a sense of authenticity. The following paragraph from *For Name and Fame* is a typical example:

> The force selected to march from Cabul to the relief of Candahar under the command of General Roberts consisted of the 92d Highlanders, 23d Pioneers, 24th and 25th Punjaub Infantry, the 2d, 4th, and 5th Ghoorkas, the 72d Highlanders, 2d battalion of the 60th, the Norfolk Rangers, the 2d, 3d, and 15th Sikhs. There were three batteries of artillery and four cavalry regiments, the 9th Lancers, the 3d Bengal Cavalry, the 3d Punjaub Cavalry, and the Central India Horse. This gave a total of about 10,000 fighting men. There were, in addition, 8000 followers to feed, 7000 horses, and some 8000 transport and artillery mules and ponies. (1886, 220)

True to the tradition of British writing about India, the so-called fighting races are celebrated—the "Ghoorkas," the Sikhs, and the "Punjaubees"—the "Ghoorkas" (Gurkhas) as small, active mountaineering men to whom war is a passion, the Sikhs and the "Punjaubees" (Punjabis) as "tall stately men, proud of the historical fighting powers of their race. They had fought with extreme bravery against the English, but once conquered they became true and faithful subjects of the English crown, and it was their fidelity and bravery which saved England in the dark days of the mutiny" (1886, 224). So the favored groups are seen as a reflection of the English themselves.

A sense of nation is ubiquitous. As Will is convalescing from his wounds, his best medicine is the English voices he hears around him and the kindness he receives (Henty 1886, 136). Class-consciousness is also present. The good, simple folk who find Will when, as a baby, he had been kidnapped and then abandoned, are convinced that he comes from good blood, a conviction borne by others who meet him as well. His fellow commissioned officers are puzzled by his lack of knowledge of cricket and a classical education. But he is well accepted all the same, because character is more important, and Will is pleasant and gentlemanly. Above all, he is plucky and daring and shares his fellow officers' feelings that they would much rather be in the fighting than out of it. Will is modest about his successes, another quality much prized and respected. This is what the colonel says to him:

> I have heard from Major Harrison what you had told Captain Mayhew concerning your birth; and certainly your appearance and manner go far to sustain the belief that the tramp who left you was not your mother, and that your parents were of gentle birth. I do not say that a man's birth makes much difference to him; still, it does go for something, and in nine cases out of ten the difference both in face and figure is unmistakable. Unless I am very wrong, your father was a gentleman. However, that is not to the point: it is your quickness and activity, your coolness in danger, and the adventures which you have gone through which interest us in you. (1886, 84)

Will's promotions and successes are the result of his character, not his class, and his character reflects the best of the British. Like Henty's other young heroes, he is more a composite of characteristics than a fully developed or complex character: characteristics such as bravery, determination, resourcefulness, intelligence, diligence, and dedication. His role in this novel and the role of the other heroes is primarily as exemplar, to enable boys to identify with him and to aspire to emulate him someday. It is advice about character that he receives from the kindly porter's wife who practically raised him. She tells him to "act right and straight and honourable," to work hard at his books, to never tell a lie or use bad language, to always speak "manful and straight, no matter what comes of it" (17).

Much before his exploits in India, Will is apprenticed to a smack or fishing vessel. When he is shipwrecked, along with a Dutch boy

he had befriended on the voyage, they establish themselves as saviors within a community of Malay villagers by helping them successfully strategize their battles against their enemies. Both Will and
Hans are shown as superior to the Malay, but Hans accedes to the
British boy when it comes to leadership, invariably grunting an assent to his suggestions. When Will asks "What do you say, Hans?"
in soliciting a response to his plan, Hans replies "I don't zay noding.
. . . I don't have no obinion at all; if you dink zat is ze best plan, let
us do it" (52). The author tells us that "Will's superior activity and
energy astonished the Dutch lad, whose movements were slow and
heavy; while Will, on his part, was surprised at the strength which
Hans could exert when he chose" (40). Will finds it curious that the
Malays, "who have no hesitation in attacking English ships and
murdering their crews, have yet a sort of superstitious dread of us"
(65). In a rare display of relativist thinking, Henty allows Will to use
an analogy to the days of persecution of witches. Left to themselves,
witches could cast deadly spells, it was believed. In spite of that fear
there was no hesitation in putting them to death (65).

In contrast to the strong patriotic feelings of the British, the
Afghans are portrayed as lacking in this quality to the point that they
will fight with the British against their countrymen and co-religionists.
Henty does have an understanding of the region. The following description still holds true of the Afghanistan of today: "It must be remembered that Afghanistan has for centuries been rather a
geographical expression than a country. Its population is composed of
a great number of tribes without any common feelings or interest, and
often engaged in desperate wars and conflicts with each other" (156).
But to offer Henty's books as an aid to parents in the education of their
children, as does the Lost Classics Book Company, another company
that has reissued some of Henty's titles, is another matter. One can only
extrapolate from their statement that the ideological bent of the education expected from Henty's books is part of the publisher's agenda.
The phrasing: "Recognizing the need to return to more traditional
principles in education" is certainly coded language. Anticipating that
readers might remonstrate that the "education" is avowedly imperialistic and does not shy away from descriptions of subject peoples as
savages or heathen niggers, the publisher offers this mild disclaimer:
"Some of the quotes and expressions in the book reflect the attitudes of
their time and do not necessarily reflect today's attitudes" (n.p.).

The publisher's objectives are openly espoused on the website of the Lost Classics Book Company:

> We believe that building children's character should go hand in hand with their education. With this aim we are bringing you great books from the late 19th and early 20th centuries that teach and entertain while encouraging virtues like love of country, service to others, self-discipline, honesty, and honor. In a world that worships the new, we are resurrecting the values of an earlier, more enduring America, free from the modern trappings of "political correctness" and "revisionism." Our mission is to republish the finest textbooks, readers and historical novels of the past. (www.lostclassicsbooks.com)

If proof were needed that character education is part of an agenda that still prevails, this is it. In addition to six Henty titles, Lost Classics has reissued titles by Edward Stratemeyer, Jame Otis, Oliver Optic, a biography of Kit Carson, and the histories of Edward Eggleston. There are also books on grammar and a "lexile measure" to match students to books on their level of reading ability, based on test scores.

PrestonSpeed Publications also participates in this agenda. Their website recounts how in the early days of their reintroduction of Henty's works they received blank stares or, more typically, the response: "Henty? I've never heard of this Henty!" "Well, we loved the books," they declare, "and wanted to see Mr. Henty's stories enjoyed by a whole new generation of readers." PrestonSpeed has rereleased thirty Henty titles. In addition, they are putting out a Makers of World History Series, the first release being Alexander the Great, and a Makers of American History Series, with *John Smith: Gentleman Adventurer* as the first release. The Disney cartoon of Pocahontas is termed a caricature, apparently because it does not celebrate Smith sufficiently, whereas their version "unveils a man who was a hero in his time, so that he can once again be a hero in ours" (www.prestonspeed.com).

From the boys' papers to the curricula of contemporary Christian homeschoolers, Henty has been highly regarded by those seeking to train character as well as minds. "The Henty books have helped reflect the thinking of Western civilization," says Michael Farris, president of the Home School Legal Defense Association

(*Washington Times*, May 16, 1998). People hungry for old-style heroes who model masculinity and muscular Christianity for boys and for old-style morality, unambiguous and uncompromising, are snapping up Henty's books by the thousands every month. "A growing number of Americans are turning in frustration to a children's writer of a decidedly different kidney, a man who fought in the Crimean war, published its earliest work in *Union Jack* magazine, and spent his life celebrating the twin virtues of British imperialism and Victorian manliness: G. A. Henty," says Adrian Wooldridge in an article entitled "Henty's Heroes" in *The Economist* (December 11–17, 1999).

George Grant, writing in *World Magazine*, reminisces about the excitement with which he would check out a new Henty book in his local library, rush home and read it, sometimes in one sitting. Grant also refers to Henty's "fiercely accurate narratives" that "range across the whole spectrum of human achievement, highlighting the greatest characters and the most decisive moments in history."

In the book for which this note was included, *In the Heart of the Rockies*, Henty uses almost every stock image in his portrayal of "Redskins." They are shown shooting the buffalo gratuitously even when they have plenty of meat, "just for the sake of his tongue" (1894, 83). This is hardly "fiercely accurate," since it was the white settlers who killed buffalo for sport and who were responsible for the virtual extinction of buffalo herds. Native Americans were known instead for using every part of the animal and for only killing what they could use. Bison tongue became in fact a delicacy among white settlers and rotting carcasses without tongues were left littered across the prairie. It is the consensus of many respected historians of the American West that the slaughter of the buffalo ended the civilization of the Plains Indians. Young homeschoolers devouring Henty's tales for character education and Christian values will learn, in direct opposition to historical fact, that "There are a few of the Indian tribes whose word can be taken, but, as a rule, words mean nothing with them, and if we had put ourselves in their power they would have tomahawked us instantly, or else taken us down and tortured us at their villages, which would have been a deal worse" (1894, 116). Historian Dee Brown, on the other hand, indicates that the southern Cheyennes knew "they could never again trust in the word of any white man or in his treaties or scraps of paper" (1994, 107).

These inconsistencies are but a small sample of the imperial perspective that informs Henty's stories, a perspective the dust jacket of *In the Heart of the Rockies* describes as "Christian." Given the particular warp of this tale, the assessment offered by the dust jacket bears an especially poignant irony:

> Young people across America are rediscovering G. A. Henty, the 19th-century literary genius whose historical adventures inspire boys to honesty, courage, diligence, and duty. Writing from a Christian perspective, Henty weaves the adventures of a fictional boy hero together with real-life events. His stories are as accurate as they are exciting, so children get important lessons in history which they remember long afterward. Just as important, these lessons come without the immoral overtones of modern novels.

The point is this: Not all the "classics" are lost. Many are being revived in the great push for books that build character, or, one might note, character in a very definite mold. Many "classics" still circulate widely in schoolrooms, libraries, and children's collections. They are recommended by parents, publishers, librarians, and teachers. Kutzer notes that these books remain in print "not because children are clamoring for them . . . but because adult teachers, parents, scholars, and historians deem them worthy" (2000, 11). She adds that because these books have remained in print and are still read, they have influenced attitudes to empire in the children's books that have followed them, well into the 1980s.

To return briefly to Herbert Kohl's question, "Should we burn Babar?" the answer remains a resounding "No!" Nor should we prevent or even discourage children from reading any of the books mentioned in this chapter. But, aside from any specific agenda, to allow them to be framed as classics and leave it at that is to honor them and thus inevitably, if not always inentionally, to affirm the values, notions, perspectives, and prejudices they put forth. Character building was an essential aspect of training empire builders. As Kutzer comments, "Empire and its effects were a part of everyday British life, and appear matter-of-factly in fiction for children. Like most imaginative literature, these classic children's texts do not set out consciously to propagandize for nation and empire, but they do nonetheless" (2000, 10). Kohl attempts to formulate "a radical story" as an antidote. However, Henty's stories would conform to many of his criteria if not to his ideological intentions. There can be no formula, only questioning, and the label "classic" immediately forecloses questioning. The answer is guided reading. Read in context, followed by fair and open discussion, against and along with other accounts, other experiences, such books are valuable, not simply as tools but as conduits. To encourage and facilitate such reading is not asking too much of the child, but it asking a lot of the adult.

4

The Blyton Books

Quite apart from my millions of English-speaking readers, I have to consider entirely different children—children of many other races who have my books in their own language. I am, perforce, bringing to them the ideas and ideals of a race of children alien to them, the British. I am the purveyor of those ideals all over the world, and am perhaps planting a few seeds here and there that may bear good fruit; in particular, I hope with the German children, who, oddly enough, are perhaps more taken with my books than any other foreign race (and this applies to the German adults too!). These things, of course, are the real reward of any children's writer, not the illusions of fame, or name or money.

—Enid Blyton, foreword to
A Complete List of Books: Enid Blyton

Her journey towards woman hood is not likely to be very easy, but from her parents she will learn what the Crown of England really means and she will learn from them why our monarchy stands so firm. The British Crown has come to stand as an epitome of the best qualities of our race—stability, tolerance, integrity, a sense of duty to God and country. She is being well trained to bear the heavy responsibilities that will one day fall to her lot.

—*The Girl's Own Annual* (circa 1939, vol. 61, p. 292)

When, in 1833, Lord Macaulay, in his famous Minute on Education, proclaimed the exemption "from all natural causes of decay" of "the imperishable empire of our arts and our morals, our literature and our laws" (July 10, 1833), Enid Blyton, a phenomenon of children's publishing, had not even been born. Yet Blyton's books have borne out this prophecy to a greater extent than perhaps those of any other British writer. The author of hundreds of titles for children ranging from primary to early secondary school students, titles that have sold in the billions, Blyton publishing would appear to be an imperishable empire in itself. Like Disney movies, her books spawn souvenirs and products that position children as consumers, though her fans also create clubs and contribute to charities. Enid Blyton is one of the most widely translated authors of all times. Blyton books, sometimes in sanitized or updated versions, are still selling in large numbers, not only in Britain but also throughout its former empire.

I recall, years ago, sitting around the dinner table at Mount Holyoke College in Massachusetts with a group of students, both American and foreign. Most of the foreign students there that evening came from the countries of the British Commonwealth. As the conversation turned to favorite childhood authors, Enid Blyton's name popped right up. Our American contemporaries at the table were both amazed and amused by our excitement and enthusiasm as we compared characters and recalled plots. None of them had heard of this writer, so familiar to young readers in the Indian subcontinent, Australia and New Zealand, and former British colonies in Africa and the West Indies. Enid Blyton has been translated into 128 languages, according to her biographer Barbara Stoney. It is important to emphasize that Blyton is still widely read in Britain's former colonies, and the concept of ideal character she propounds still propagated, even to children who would not be expected to participate in it because they lack the right racial pedigree.

This point is underscored in Rohinton Mistry's novel, *Family Matters*, where a nine-year-old boy, Jehangir, growing up in a Parsi family in Bombay, continually frustrates his father by his love for Enid Blyton's adventure stories, especially the Famous Five. His father regards them as "rubbish" and wonders why the school library still retains such books. "But Enid Blyton is fun for children," his wife, Roxana, remonstrates. "It doesn't do any harm" (84). Yezad disagrees, saying it did them immense harm. It encouraged children "to grow up without attachment to the place where they belonged, made them hate themselves for being who they were, created confusion about their identity" (84). Yezad had read the same books when he was small, and they had, he said, "made him yearn to become a little Englishman of a type that even England did not have" (84). When Jehangir and his brother Murad fantasize about the food they read about in their Enid Blyton books, Yezad informs them that if they ever tasted that "insipid foreign stuff," instead of merely reading about it in "those blighted Blyton books," they would appreciate their mother's tasty Indian cooking. What they need, he tells them is "an Indian Blyton, to fascinate them with their own reality" (101).

References to Enid Blyton in a number of postcolonial literary works indicate just how ubiquitous her stories were and still are in the countries of the Commonweatlth. Nyasha, in Tsitsi Dangarembga's *Nervous Conditions*, tells us, "I read everything from Enid Blyton to the Brontë sisters, and responded to them all" (93). While Lucy, in Jamaica Kincaid's novel of the same name, in searching for an alternate name tries out Emily, Charlotte, and Jane, after Emily and Charlotte Brontë and Jane Austen, writers whose books she loved, but finally settles on Enid "after the authoress Enid Blyton" (149).

Blyton was by no means the first or the only trendy writer of boarding school stories, but she is certainly one of the most prolific and popular. She is also perhaps the only one whose books are readily available and widely read all over the British Commonwealth, which is why I focus on her in this chapter. After all, in importing her books, the countries of the Commonwealth are importing not just a commodity but also an ideology. The first author to write school stories for girls was probably Sarah Fielding, whose book *The Governess; or, Little Female Academy* appeared in 1749. L. T. Meade (1854–1914) is said to have established the girls' school story with her enormously popular *A World of Girls* (1886). Other popular writers of such stories include Angela Brazil, whose influential first work, "A Terrible Tomboy," was published in 1904; Elinor M. Brent-Dyer, who wrote between 1924 and 1968; Elsie Jeanette Oxenham who wrote eighty-seven books and many short stories for girls between 1907 and 1959; and Dorita Fairlie Bruce (1885–1970), whose school stories for girls were written during the period between the two world wars. Angela Brazil is considered the first author of girls' books to write her stories from the characters' points of view—and the first to write entertaining rather than moralistic stories. It was her conscious intention to write amusing and enjoyable tales in which the characters acted like normal human beings. Her books were aimed at the ever-more-emancipated girls emerging in the early part of the twentieth century, and it is their perspectives and points of view that she sought to represent. Like Blyton's schoolgirl heroines, Brazil's were often androgynous. In an article published in the May 1990 issue of *Book and Magazine Collector*, Katharine Gunn says of Brazil's books, "The stiff upper lip is as prevalent as in boys' stories: girls are always being exhorted to 'brace up and be sporty' and 'turn off the waterworks.' And as a reward for all this bracing up, there were sweet treats galore, cheesecake being a particularly sought-after favourite among the girls" (Gunn 1990).

Similarly, in his chapter on "Social Class and Educational Adventures: Jan Needle and the Biography of a Value," Fred Inglis points out that Enid Blyton "keeps in vigorous circulation the great myths of boyish manliness, of the efficacy of individual action, of the great solidarities of friendship, of the joys of spontaneous freedoms innocent of all authority except a silent moral law" (Butts 1992, 85). Blyton clearly owes a great deal to the earlier school stories that were her equal in terms of popularity—the Greyfriars school stories in the *Magnet* and St. Jim's in the *Gem*; these were periodicals primarily intended for boys but also read by girls and, indeed, by adults. Her very title, "The Famous Five" is lifted from the Greyfriars group comprising Harry Wharton & Co. Fatty, in the *Five Find-Outers* series, is clearly based on one of the most famous schoolboys of all time, Billy Bunter, "the fat Owl" of St. Jim's. Blyton's tautology as well as her character concepts owe a great deal to these earlier models. In his essay on the boys' weeklies, George Orwell writes,

> A constantly recurring story is one in which a boy is accused of some misdeed committed by another and is too much of a sportsman to reveal the truth. The "good" boys are "good" in the clean-

living Englishman tradition—they keep in hard training, wash behind their ears, never hit below the belt, etc etc—and by way of
contrast there is a series of "bad" boys, Racke, Crooke, Loder and
others, whose badness consists in betting, smoking cigarettes and
frequenting public houses. (Orwell and Angus 2000, 464–65)

Anyone interested in the English concept of character, in terms
of an idealized sense of self, would find Blyton's books highly in-
structive. In Maud Diver's *Desmond's Daughter* (1916) General Wyndham explains, "The military virtues are the bed-rock virtues." The
military virtues were also the bedrock of Blyton's conception of
character. From the Boy Scout movement to the legendary regiments
of its vast empire, the British cherished the qualities that were bred
in battle, celebrated their prevalence in peacetime, and championed
their instillation in their young. Courage, cooperation, discipline, a
strong sense of duty, endurance, responsibility, resolve, resourcefulness, and a vast reserve of energy are among these qualities. Add to
that a sense of purpose, a determination to do one's duty and to
maintain an esprit de corps. From time to time Diver liked to have
her characters proclaim the old Heroclitus saying, referred to earlier,
"Temperament is destiny." One is not necessarily born with the right
type of temperament, although, of course, one must have the genetic
predisposition that an Anglo-Saxon lineage guarantees. From there
on it must be cultivated, and Blyton's books reveal this careful
process as it occurs through childhood. In spite of the contemporary
characters and situations of her books, she is actually writing in the
tradition of the Victorians in this respect, for one of their favorite
themes was the schooling of character. But although the Blyton stories are carrying on a tradition, there is an important difference.
They are devoid of the persistent Christian references of the earlier
stories: *Tom Brown's Schooldays*, for instance, or the evangelical and
maudlin *Eric; or, Little by Little: A Tale of Roslyn School*. Character, in
her books, is built up through entirely secular means and methods.
    One of Blyton's best-known series, "The Famous Five," concerns
a band of intrepid children who range between the ages of ten and
twelve, and their dog. They include two brothers, Julian and Dick,
aged twelve and eleven, respectively; their sister, Anne, aged ten;
their cousin, Georgina, or George, as she much prefers to be called,
aged eleven, and her rambunctious but loving dog, Timmy. Julian,

as the oldest, is responsible for the rest when they are out on their own, appointed by his father to be in complete charge. His father adds that the other children *must* realize that Julian is in charge, and they *must* do as he says. Julian's response to his father is terse and dutiful, worthy of a subaltern being handed an assignment by his senior officer: "'Yes, sir,' said Julian, feeling proud. 'I'll see to things all right'" (*Caravan* 1946, 22). In turn, the other children accept his authority without question. In fact, Julian consistently assumes the demeanor and claims the skills of someone on a military mission. He reconnoiters the terrain, reads maps, prides himself on picking excellent camping sites, speaks or issues orders with calm determination, and even appears with field glasses swinging on the end of their straps. The entire group gets ready for a camping trip with all the panache of military men setting out on an expedition, reminding each other not to forget sweaters, swimsuits, torches, candles and matches, portable radios, and even sweets.

Julian's brother, Dick, is not being entirely facetious when he addresses him as "Captain." And, as among military men, there is a strict hierarchy of rank, in this case determined by age, gender, and domain. Anne, who greatly enjoys keeping house, claims that their bunks would not be made, their meals would not be cooked, and their caravans would not be kept clean if it weren't for her. So although Julian thinks he's in charge of them, she really is. And although the highest compliment any one could pay George is to tell her that she is as good as a boy, it is Julian who is told to "take care of the girls" (*Billycock Hill* 1957) or, in his absence, Dick, who is appointed to "Look after the girls" (*Caravan* 1946, 107). Cowardice is the worst thing a boy can be accused of, so when Julian considers taking the party out of the hills and camping somewhere else to avoid danger, because he bears responsibility for their safety, he is pounced upon by the others who tell him not to be a coward. And he is only half-hearted about his proposition anyway. As the leader of the group by virtue of his age and character, Julian's instinct is to act prudently but he fears, at the same time, any hint of cowardly behavior.

In *Five Go to Billycock Hill* (1957), when the children hear a high-pitched and shrill whistling sound within a cave, a sound that fills their eardrums until they feel like bursting, they race out of there and stand panting outside, discussing the strange and horrible noise. In the safety of their tent they agree that it was most unusual and weird, but that doesn't stop Julian's recriminations: "'All the same, we were a bit cowardly,' says Julian, now feeling rather ashamed of himself" (124). When the chimpanzee, Pongo, in *Five Go Off in a Caravan* (1946), beats Julian to the draw in rescuing the circus boy, Nobby, the latter tells him, "You're a real friend, you are. Good as Pongo, here" (*Caravan*, 120). In comparing his courage to that of the chimpanzee, Nobby pays him the highest compliment. Julian's polite manner and clear, pleasant voice never fail to reassure people in authority, people like the RAF guard in *Five Go to Billycock Hill*, or to unnerve those who are up to no good. Even Aily, the little Welsh waif in *Five Get into a Fix* (1958), senses that Julian is "good and kind and strong, and his arms were very comforting" (159).

Courage is so intrinsic and cherished a component of English character that it is valued in girls as well as boys. Further, even girls who are unabashedly feminine like Anne are allowed this quality, so highly appreciated is it. In *The Famous Five and the Knight's Treasure*, which is one of the "reconstituted" Blyton books ("a new adventure of the characters created by Enid Blyton" [1986]), Anne falls off her bike. The author feels obliged to excuse her tears, even though she had fallen into a ditch of stinging nettles, received some nasty grazes, and sprained her ankle, enough to make most of us cry. In *Five Get into Trouble*, we are told that Anne, being the smallest, tires the most easily on long walks and bike rides, yet kept up with the others "valiantly" (25). As for George, who prides herself on being like a boy, breaking down is anathema. In *Five Get into a Fix*, some huge farm dogs attack her beloved dog, Timmy. It turns out to be just a skin wound but at first George is shaken: "She stalked off with Timmy at her heels, her head well up, bitterly ashamed of two more tears that suddenly ran down her cheeks. It wasn't like old George to cry! But she was still not quite herself after being ill" (48). "For it is not that the Englishman can't feel," E. M. Forster assures us in "Notes on English Character," "it is that he is afraid to feel. He has been taught at his public school that feeling is bad form. . . . He must bottle up his emotions, or let them out only on a very special occasion" (1936, 5).

Crying must be excused or explained. In *The Secret of Moon Castle* (1953), which belongs to another adventure series, Blyton feels obliged to make a scene as scary as possible but at the same time excuse Jack's startled reaction to it. The portrait of Lord Moon comes alive, complete with eyes that glow and flash angrily and a horrible hiss. As Jack backs away, Blyton feels constrained to offer this explanation: "He was not a timid boy, and had plenty of courage—but this was very unexpected, and very eerie too, in that dim room, with the musical-box playing its tinkling music all the time" (92). In *Five Go to Billycock Hill*, when Toby, the boys' school friend, receives the news that his cousin, an RAF pilot whom he adores and the five have come to admire, may be a traitor, he becomes pale. "To everyone's horror Toby's face crumpled up and tears poured down his cheeks. He made no attempt to wipe them away; indeed, he hardly seemed to know that they were there." No one knows what to do except Timmy, who licks Toby's wet face, whining as he does so. Later Toby mops his cheeks with his hanky and is surprised to find it damp. "Gosh, I'm a sissy to go on like this!" he apologizes. Of course it turns out his cousin was no traitor after all, but a hero whose plane had been stolen by foreign spies.

Courage was clearly one of the imperial qualities that were so prized and privileged. Just as the British recognized and respected any display of courage in their colonial subjects, the Famous Five are willing to do so in a child from the lower classes or even in gypsies. They acknowledge, for instance, the "spunk" of a feisty young tomboy of a girl who is frequently described as a "ragamuffin" (*Five Fall into Adventure* 1950, 22). The redemptive quality of courage is plainly illustrated in this comment by Julian: "She's dirty, she's probably very good at telling lies and thieving, but she's got pluck" (*Adventure*, 41–42). Later, when Jo saves George from the villains' clutches, George turns to Julian and Dick and says, "She's wonderful. She's the bravest girl I ever knew. And she did it all even though she doesn't like me" (*Adventure*, 153). It is Julian who defines for us the meaning of cowardice, simultaneously affirming the value of courage: "Cowardice is just thinking of your own miserable skin instead of somebody else's," he points out to the rich kid, Richard, in *Five Get into Trouble* (109). Richard later redeems himself by hiding in the boot of the crook's car and thus escaping to summon help for all the trapped children. But earlier he had proved himself to be a coward, even by his own admission. Julian reminds him that Anne, little as she is, couldn't be a coward even if she tried, because she is more worried about others than about herself.

Blyton's concept of ideal character does not simply reflect her own preferences, values, or inclinations. Nor does it arise out of a social vacuum. It is, instead, part of a coherent construction that comprises various elements of the ideology of an entire nation. It is reflected in contemporary writers and in the writers who preceded her. It is reflected in the expressions of the populace, in letters and journals and jottings. It is reflected in public statements and in private sentiments. And nowhere is it more clearly reflected or more cogently stated than in the ideology of the Scout movement and the writings and speeches of its founder, Lord Baden-Powell, as Michael Rosenthal's seminal study *The Character Factory* (1984) indicates. C. W. Saleeby, who wrote extensively on the subject of eugenics, asserted that nurture was equally as important as nature in shaping the character of an imperial race, and nurture, of course, results from instruction and schooling. In Saleeby's estimation, the Scout movement was "the greatest step towards the progress of eugenics since 1909" (Rosenthal 1984, 159).

The constitution of British character is as complex in Blyton's books as it is in the context of muscular colonialism. Certainly not all Britons are deemed worthy of its highest ideals. Distinction is consistently made between those who are of the right sort and those who aren't. When the children in the Famous Five series go to a farm to ask for food to purchase, the farmer's wife undercharges them and will not hear of taking any more money for her goods. "It'll be a pleasure to see your bonny faces at my door!" she says. "That'll be part of my payment, see? I can tell you're well-brought up children by your nice manners and ways. You'll not be doing any damage or foolishness on the farm, I know" (*Caravan*, 67). Similarly, Mr. Gringle in *Five Go to Billycock Hill* decides that the cousins look like a very nice lot, not the type who would leave litter about or start fires in the lovely countryside. "We shouldn't dream of it," confirms George (51). They are sensible children, Mrs. Jones, the farmer's wife in *Five Get into a Fix*, observes when she sees them clad in heavy coats, scarves, and woolen hats to go out on a snowy winter's day. Nobby the circus boy needs no one to tell him that he is not of their sort, and his cruel uncle scornfully refers to his friends as posh folk.

More important than being the right sort, however, is being a *good* sort. Thus the farmer's wife is a good sort, simple as she is, because she looks out for the children and keeps them well supplied.

Nobby is a good sort, although he is somewhat dirty and speaks with his mouth full, because he is sincere and loyal, solid and helpful, all qualities that are cherished components of the English conception of ideal character. Joan (the spelling varies in some books), the cook who works for George's family, addresses the children as Master and Miss, thus betraying her inferior social status; nevertheless, her smiling, good-tempered, and generous nature makes her a good sort. Country folk, whether they are farmers or domestic workers, are considered solid and wholesome because they possess the approved traits. Above all, they are decent, a quality that Cecil Rhodes claimed repeatedly for the Anglo-Saxon race, even while pursuing the most indecent tactics in his quest for power and riches (see Tidrick 1990, 49).

Character can therefore trump class, even, at times, race. Being of the wrong sort or the wrong type is more significant than being from a socially or economically inferior background, but often they overlap. The wrong types in Blyton's books all stand out in terms of appearance. They are often described as scruffy, mean, or foreign looking, with straggly moustaches or small eyes, dark and thin or, alternatively, tall and broad, bad tempered, often with a physical or mental defect such as a limp or a slouch or a slow manner. They always constitute the "other," often an "other" of amorphous foreign descent or of unspecified but alien nationality. In these characters, some feature always sticks out, deviates from the norm, whether it is a stoop or a too long nose or too thick lips or long untidy hair or even a beard. The following description from *Five Fall into Adventure* is typical: "The man looked even worse. He slouched as he came, and dragged one foot. He had a straggly moustache and mean, clever little eyes that raked the beach up and down" (20). The unsavory characters may be raggedly dressed or give off "an unpleasant, unwashed kind of smell" (20). Often the bad guys are dark as opposed to being simply sunburnt, as the children often get from their love of the outdoors. Mr. Gringle, the butterfly collector in *Five Go to Billycock Hill*, is not a bad guy as such but clearly an ornery one. As soon as he is introduced, he is marked by his "peculiar figure," "untidy" appearance, and "hair much too long" (51). One of the villains, a foreign spy, is described in signature fashion as "small and thin, with a pinched-looking face, and dark glasses" (96). The villains of the piece are often foreigners, as in *Five Get into a Fix*, where they intend to mine the uranium that lies beneath a Welsh estate to produce bombs with the complicity of the estate owner who has virtually imprisoned his own mother to further his nefarious scheme.

At times, however, the association between being from the "wrong" race or the "wrong" class and being of the "wrong" character is quite blatant. In most of Blyton's stories, the villains are quite clearly from an underclass: often gypsies or circus folk. Racial references appear as well. In *Five Fall Into Adventure* the face at the window, which had "nasty gleaming eyes," is described by Anne as very dark, "perhaps . . . a black man's face." (*Adventure*, 30). This is highly reminiscent of "the dark face" of Ram Dass (Burnett 1906, 198) in *A Little Princess* "pressed against the glass and peering in" (231). In a book from another adventure series, *The Secret of Moon Castle* (1953), we have this description of the villain: "A man came into the room. He stopped short at once when he saw the children, and gazed at them, astounded. He was short, burly and very dark. His eyes seemed almost black, and his big nose and thin-lipped mouth made him very ugly" (33). This man is English, but his seditious activities clearly establish him as being of the wrong type. His black eyes and dark complexion become signifiers, establishing a plain if spurious connection between race and character.

Worst of all, such types always treat animals badly; they kick dogs or offer them poisoned meat. Perhaps nothing is a more telling giveaway of the lack of proper temperament. In the colonies, certainly, there is ample evidence to suggest that the British valued proper treatment of animals more than the proper treatment of natives. Lord Baden-Powell reminisces about the dog in Africa who, thirsty and hungry, took his bowl in his mouth and went to find the local magistrate, knowing that, as an Englishman, he would take care of an animal (Rosenthal 1984, 258). The ruler of the native state of Alwar in Rajasthan was exiled by the British for dousing his polo pony with petrol and setting it on fire when it had misbehaved, while his transgressions against his human subjects were more easily forgiven. Beating a coolie on a British plantation would most likely have resulted in less outrage than beating a horse or a dog. In *Five Get into Trouble* we are told about an awful bodyguard that Richard's father had who used to "kick the dogs around terribly." "*Oh!* What a beast!" responds George (31). Hurting animals is not decent, nor is hitting girls, as the hapless boy who strikes out at

George, mistaking her for one of his own sex, is reminded, or as when Richard agrees in *Five Get into Trouble* that "No decent boy hits a girl" (33).

Decency, however, is constituted primarily through the medium of character, not class. Although class can have a formative effect on character, economic and social obstacles can be overcome by disposition. We are told, of Jo in *Five Fall into Adventure*, that she'd be all right cleaned up—her external appearance is not then a fixed feature of who she is but rather the result of her circumstances—something that can be changed by a hairbrush and some soap and water, for she can't help being dirty (40, 42). In many of the Famous Five adventures, one character, usually a child, crosses over to the side of good, joining forces with the five and sometimes saving them by showing them a way out of one of their scrapes. Nobby in *Caravan* and Jo in *Adventure* are examples. "You think I'm mean and thieving and not worth a penny," Jo says, "and I expect you're right. But I can do some things you can't, and if you want this thing, I'll do it for you" (143).

There is also some fluidity where gender roles are concerned. Gender roles are strictly defined, yet consistently crossed, though only from female to male—never in the other direction. George, one of Blyton's most famous and best-loved characters, is far more than a tomboy. She prefers to be called by the masculine version of her name, dresses like a boy, and nothing lifts her spirits so much as being mistaken for a boy. George can outswim most boys and is "as brave as a lion" (*Fix*, 46). In *Five Go to Demon's Rocks* (1961), Tinker, the son of her father's friend, sums her up: "Never mind—you *look* like a boy, and you're often as *rude* as a boy, and you haven't an awful lot of manners" (67). When, in *Five Fall into Adventure*, Dick gets into a fight with a "gypsy" girl, misled by her boyish appearance, which is similar to George's, he is mortified at learning that he has actually hit a girl. "It's the first time I've ever hit a girl, and I hope it'll be the last" (*Adventure*, 23). In the same story, George is told that she can't keep thinking that she's as good as a boy, because she has to deal with the realization that "Girls can't go about fighting" (23). The highest compliment that George can pay another girl is to tell her that she is as good as a boy.

In her firm insistence on freedom and flexibility in the assignment of gender roles and identity, George offers young girls a role model that was nothing short of avant-garde at the time of her creation. In an interview with Marjorie Anderson for the BBC on January 13, 1963, Blyton revealed that George was her favourite character. Although as a rule her characters were imaginary, she said, George was based on a real girl she once knew who also had a dog. Asked why George was her favorite, Blyton replied, "Because she was a very strong personality and made an impression on me and because she was a kind, good, generous brave child whom I thought would be a splendid character for any child's book" (www.bbc.co.uk/ bbcfour/audiointerviews/profilepages/blytone1.shtml).

The spirit of adventure and the ability to be assertive are, however, clearly identified as masculine traits in Blyton's books. What George is doing is appropriating these traits, rather than owning them. This is less radical than degendering traits of character. This point is further illustrated in *Five Go to Demon's Rocks* when Julian assures his aunt that "We will help with the housework and we'll do any odd jobs too. You've no idea how fine I look with an apron round my waist, and a broom in my hand!" (17). And even George smiled at the prospect of Julian in an apron. When a boy takes on the female role, it is only in jest. In *Five Go to Billycock Hill*, the girls are asked to help with the tea while the boys talk to Toby's cousin Jeff, asking him eager questions about planes and flying. While both Anne and George listen to Jeff speak so intently that they don't even notice Toby's trick of offering sifted sugar to go with the radishes and salt to go with the strawberries, it is only the boys who can aspire to be pilots like Jeff. In *Five Get into a Fix* we see that George would much rather carry in things than make up the beds (85) and, in *Five Get into Trouble*, we are told that she can't even boil an egg successfully. The assumption, of course, is that as a girl she should be able to do so.

What George embodies is not so much the neutering of traits traditionally considered male but their reassignment. Such traits comprise determination, boldness, the ability to assert one's wishes, and the quest for adventure among others. The ideal English male would, of course, be born with these traits, but the ideal English female would be allowed to assume them in conjunction with her assigned domestic role. Thus Anne, who enjoys nothing more than setting out cherry buns and steaming cups of tea for everyone, also refuses to be left behind or to forgo an adventure. After all, as the author tells us, if there is any adventure about, the five are bound to be right in the middle of it. Further, Anne issues a friendly warning to Dick in *Five Get into Trouble* not to take her for granted when he gently teases her about her domestic propensity: "Look, she's got the food all ready. You're fantastic, Anne. I bet if we stayed here for more than one night Anne would have made some kind of larder, and have arranged a good place to wash everything—and be looking for somewhere to keep her dusters and broom!" (23). Anne reminds him that she does this because she enjoys it, leaving unsaid the reminder that it is not because she has a natural instinct for it.

While all the children are involved in adventures, it is usually the boys who implement action, while the girls facilitate it. The boys ask the girls to get supper ready while they prepare the camp. The boys go to investigate funny goings-on in *Five Go to Billycock Hill* while the girls must stay behind in the camp. Toby is immediately allowed to accompany Julian and Dick when he asks, but George and Anne are not—yet it is they who rescue the boys by dispatching Timmy when they don't return by midnight. This pattern is repeated in other stories as well. In *Five Get into a Fix*, Anne and George remain in the mountain chalet while the boys go down the winding mountain path, "still white with snow," to report the strange goings-on that they had witnessed the previous night (140). It is interesting to note that within the ideal concept of character, propounded by Blyton and other English writers within the colonial era, almost all the traits traditionally assigned to males (with the possible exception of aggression) can be assumed by females, but almost none of the traits traditionally associated with females can be assumed by males with impunity. The only possible exception is that of kindness. Julian and Dick are kind, although they are tough. But, in spite of George's insistent transgression, it is they who assume the leadership roles for the most part and accept them as their birthright. For the most part, the boys remain the enforcers, the girls the enablers.

A striking characteristic of the children in the Famous Five series is the autonomy that they are allowed, an autonomy that allows them to satisfy their thirst for adventure. The children order and pay for their own supplies as they set out to the lighthouse. They are allowed to convalesce on their own at a Welsh farmhouse, where they beg to be permitted to stay at the mountain hut because "It's so *much* nicer to be quite on our own and independent!" (*Fix*, 56). Yet adults have the final authority, even license to deal out stern discipline when necessary. In *Five Fall into Adventure*, when the five are left on their own with only the cook, Joan, to keep an eye on them, it is Julian who makes all the important decisions in regard to their safety or their course of action. Julian and Dick are the ones who hatch the plan that puts them on the kidnapper's trail. Only once does Joan intercede, saying "I tell you, if they [George and Timmy] don't turn up soon I'll take matters into my own hands" (124).

As George's parents leave for their vacation, her mother reassures her father that Julian is almost grown and can cope with anything that turns up. So the household is put in charge of Julian, rather than Joan, who is an adult. Julian, by virtue of gender and class, is invested with this authority in spite of being a youngster. In *Five Get into Trouble*, Julian is left in charge because Joan is ill, and "if *Julian* can't look after the others, he must be a pretty feeble specimen," his uncle remonstrates when his aunt has doubts (9). Timmy, George's dog, is routinely appointed to a guardianship role. "Good old Tim," George tells him. "If it wasn't for you we'd never be allowed to go off so much on our own, *I* bet!" (*Billycock Hill*, 7). Freedom is based on trust and, although the children are subject to adult authority, if they don't abuse that trust, they may be freed from it. David Rudd indicates that this concept reflects "Blyton's Froebel philosophy that children should be left to their own devices as much as possible, and should be given a rich, natural environment; then they will grow 'straight'" (Rudd 2000, 98). This harks back to *The Secret Garden* and Burnett's philosophy, articulated especially by Susan Sowerby. Blyton also sees rural England "as the perfect nursery in which the Five can flex their moral and mental muscle" (Rudd 2000, 98). Nurturing responsibility—or, in the words of John Buchan, "the gift of responsibility" (1928, 264)—assumes special significance in the British colonial context where the relationship between the colonizer and the colonized was seen as one of stewardship.

Throughout Blyton's books we are insidiously reminded of the connection between individual character and national character. Acts of courage or fortitude, which seem to come naturally to the children, are reflective not only of their individual character or their upbringing, but also of their very Englishness. This is effected by using foreigners or people on the margins of English society as contrastive agents. They are ill-defined "others" whose characteristics or features are vaguely foreign even if they are not. What Blyton values above all is a normative standard and the maintenance of hierarchical structures. Conformity merges with obedience in her conception. The child should act in conformance with familial, legal, societal, class, and gender expectations. Only allowable autonomy or deviations are permitted. For example, transgressions are clearly identified as such and may either be tolerated, as in the case of George, or disallowed, as in the case of Nobby. English children must also act in conformance with national character and when they do not (as with Richard), they must be taken to task.

Foreigners have long been seen by the insular people of an island as not only invasive but corruptive, polluting both physical purity and moral or spiritual stability, as the goals of the National Council of Public Morals indicate (Rosenthal 1984, 144). Nationality is a prerequisite but not a guarantee of proper character development. In the context of Blyton's books, nationality is specifically English as opposed to British. She is quite capable of casting aspersion on the Irish and the Welsh. Julian wonders if Jo is Welsh, based on her appearance. Patrick in *The Six Bad Boys* (1988) is identified as a wild Irish boy. Often it is poor rather than rich children who are depicted as plucky and honest. In *Five Get into Trouble*, the little rich boy, Richard, whose dissembling gets them into hot water, shrinks silently into his corner when chided. "He was very miserable. Nobody liked him, nobody trusted him. Richard felt very, very small indeed" (83). We have already seen that people of the working class are usually presented as solid if sometimes simple-minded citizens. Their reliability, loyalty, diligence, and honesty all contribute to the fact that they are an inalienable part of English society, even if not of the upper echelons.

Characters such as Joan/Joanna, the cook, or the sundry farmers and their wives who keep the children endlessly supplied with picnic foods (hardboiled eggs, cold meats, fresh fruits and vegetables, and the ubiquitous pies and tarts or new rolls and bread) are not, however, prototypes for the colonial adventurer. They are yeomen, too rooted, too stolid for that—the true people of the soil. Tidrick tells us that evangelicalism's political legacy was the concept of a society where obedience by the lower classes toward the ruling classes was based not simply on duty but on love (1990, 4). Food functions metonymically in Blyton's adventure stories and is part of that love. A "whopping great tea" typically consists of a large ham;

crusty loaves of new bread; boiled eggs; crisp, cool lettuce; red radishes; an enormous cake; scones; honey; homemade jam; slabs of butter; and jugs of icy-cold, creamy farm milk from the dairy or, alternatively, hot cocoa or tea in a brown teapot. The fresh, wholesome, home-grown or produced food is associated with the essence of England, her soil, her climate, her labor. Blyton's plump, jolly, and eminently sensible farm wives recall Susan Sowerby in *The Secret Garden*. The geographical landscape is often indeterminate in these stories—we seldom know where exactly in the British Isles the various coves and caves, farms and hills, are situated. Kirrin Island, Kirrin Castle, and Kirrin Cottage are across a bay, but Blyton does not get more specific than that. We know that it is an English landscape: gorse, heather, purplish hills, rocky shelves, rushes, green and golden countryside, the green of the growing corn and grass and the gold of the buttercups, silver streams, "dark green patches that are woods" (*Billycock Hill*, 37).

Like the landscape, the children are clearly English, their nationality expressed primarily through their character. All are well outfitted to be empire builders. Julian in particular is upright and reliable to the point where he is consistently put in charge of the others. Of course, he is the eldest, but he is also perhaps the steadiest and most sensible and yet he is not so stodgy as to duck a mystery or adventure that comes his way. Julian is capable: he can read maps, use a compass, or summon cabs and porters with equal equanimity. He is eminently rational; it is to him that the other children turn when a sound decision must be made or leadership sought in the midst of a crisis. Anne is the youngest and somewhat tentative, George is too impetuous, and Dick too much of a risk taker. Yet those qualities complement Julian's and together the children, especially with the added component of Timmy's boundless energy and exuberance, present a composite of the ideal candidate for colonial ventures.

The five stick together. Their loyalty to each other is fierce and unrelenting; for one of them to betray or abandon another, or even to let him or her down, is unthinkable. We see here as ideal a representation of the "firm and brotherly" league as one can hope to get. In *Empire and the English Character*, Kathryn Tidrick writes:

Evangelicalism, as Eric Stokes showed nearly thirty years ago, opened English eyes to India's existence as a vast field for social and spiritual reform: it showed the English what work they could do. But it also, and equally importantly, supplied a conception of authority which, because it happened to take root in India under conditions which were highly mythogenic, was of immense importance in defining the ideal to which men of empire thereafter aspired. This conception of authority was rooted in the evangelical cult of personal example. (1990, 3)

All the children collectively, but most particularly Julian, set a personal example by their actions and behavior. Nor would it be too preposterous to see Timmy's discipline, obedience, and loving fidelity to the four children, most particularly to his mistress, as exemplary as well.

Tidrick points out that belief in the power of the personal example amounted to little more than the ratification of the age-old aristocratic claim to leadership. Thus it lent itself easily for export to the Empire. Those in power were eminently qualified to rule, while those who were subjugated were eminently eligible to be ruled (4). Thus it is that Julian, Dick, George, or Anne is always setting an example for those who become (usually inadvertently) involved in their adventures. They teach Nobby to be better mannered, Jo to be cleaner and tamer, Richard to be courageous, Tinker to be less annoying, and so on. And they teach them not just by telling them but also by the power of personal example. In Blyton's other adventure series as well, the Secret Seven or the Five Find-Outers with their incorrigible and somewhat humoristic leader Fatty, the children display similar qualities. They are curious, adventurous, sometimes mischievous, but always decent. Even in the Secret Seven series where Jack's sister, Susie, is excluded from the group, the members act the way they do because Susie goes out of her way to be a pest, not because they are mean-spirited.

That Blyton meant the children she portrayed in her prodigious output of stories to model English character is borne out in her own statements:

Quite apart from my millions of English-speaking readers, I have to consider entirely different children—children of many other races who have my books in their own language. I am, perforce, bringing to them the ideas and ideals of a race of children alien to them, the British. I am the purveyor of those ideals all over the world, and am perhaps planting a few seeds here and there that may bear good fruit; in particular, I hope with the German children, who, oddly enough, are perhaps more taken with my books than any other foreign race (and this applies to the German adults too!). These things, of course, are the real reward of any children's writer, not the illusions of fame, or name or money. (Blyton n.d., 3)

That British ideals are desirable, that British children should be emulated, Blyton clearly takes for granted. It is also clear that she uses a child's natural proclivity to identify with young protagonists to facilitate imitation.

The Lawrence brothers, John and Henry, who served in India in the middle part of the nineteenth century, embodied the value of personal example. Tidrick tells us that John and Henry Lawrence came from exactly the sort of background "where evangelical enthusiasm was most likely to express itself in an impulse towards the leadership of men" (1990, 6). Neither man condoned the gratuitous use of force, yet they found for it a moral justification in the exercise of legitimate punishment, which would then preclude the need for illegitimate oppression (12). It was John Lawrence who curtailed the indiscriminate killing and looting that followed in the wake of the rebellion of 1857. Had the rampage not been stopped, he said, the English would have ranked with the earlier and (in their mind) less legitimate conquerors of India. They would not have been able to boast that they had conquered and held India by different methods and for different purposes than their predecessors. And they would not have been able to flatter themselves that their practices and aim was "to preserve, to humanise, to elevate, not to persecute, to pillage or to destroy" (28).

Says Tidrick, it was a strange irony that it was John Lawrence, even though he championed the calculated use of force, who taught the British public that all that really mattered was a few good men. "Find them, he seemed to be saying, give them responsibility, and all would be well" (29). That is just what the children of the Famous Five series are: a few good "men." And they certainly have the gift of responsibility; it is, in fact, vested in them (Julian in particular) each time they set out on their own. It is responsibility that affords them their amazing and unusual autonomy. Analogous to the autonomy granted to the group in Blyton's series, is the responsibility awarded to Indian officers who were expected to be able to take charge when necessary without the direct supervision of English officers. Personal qualities were an indispensable prerequisite for the men who ruled India and the other colonies. It was, however, India that was considered the premier service, and so it was in India that they were most emphasized. Finding a few good men among the natives conformed to the policy of stimulating loyalty by bestowing trust, a policy explicitly set forth by John Jacob (Tidrick 1990, 31).

Trust, responsibility, and scrupulous fairness, combined with courage, resolve, decisiveness, determination, and physical prowess, were the idealized traits of the empire builders, and we see these qualities at their inception in Blyton's children. Perhaps no one mapped this character as meticulously as the person whose very name is synonymous with empire building: Cecil Rhodes. His premise was simple. The Anglo-Saxon race is the finest race in the world, "the best the most human, most honourable race the world possesses" (Tidrick 1990, 50), so the more of it they inhabit, the better it will be for the human race. It is the ultimate irony that this concept emerged from one of the most cruel, ruthless, cunning, and greedy of all the empire builders. To Rhodes, the grab for land was mitigated by the conviction that the British Empire was morally justified because it was uplifting to the colonized. The origin of the Rhodes scholarships was the dream of a secret society "with but one object—the furtherance of the British Empire and the bringing of the whole uncivilised world under British rule for the recovery of the United States for the making the Anglo-Saxon race but one Empire" (Tidrick 1990, 50). In this context, one cannot help but see as an incipient cohort of this nature the secret society in Blyton's Secret Seven adventure series.

For Rhodes and his recruit, Frederick Courtenay Selous, the word *adventurer* was free of the taint it had assumed: "'One hears the gentlemen who have got concessions to exploit the Matabele and Mashuna countries stigmatised as adventurers. . . . Adventurers!' Yes, and not, after all, a term of reproach to an Englishman, for surely Clive and Warren Hastings were adventurers, and adventurers have made the British Empire what it is" (Tidrick 1990, 66).

Blyton's adventure tales instill in imaginative youngsters an appetite, even a yearning, for adventure similar to the exploits of the characters they come to identify with. That this may even be Blyton's intent is indicated when, in *The Secret of Moon Castle* (1953),

Nora declares "We really ought to have a book written about *our* adventures. . . . They would make most exciting books." Paul agrees, "And everyone would wish they knew us and could share our adventure" (*Moon Castle*, 47). Blyton's adventure stories then become both affirmative and inspirational in terms of stimulating the spirit of adventure in children.

None of the five, even little and somewhat reticent Anne, can resist an adventure. When Anne notes in *Five Get into a Fix* that they always seem to run into trouble, Dick immediately responds, "Give it a better name, Anne, old thing. . . . Adventure! *That's* what we're always running into. Some people do, you know—they just can't help it. And we're those sort of people. Jolly good thing too—it makes life exciting!" (152–53). And although the five often find themselves in some pretty dangerous situations, trapped in caves with a rising tide, pinned down by evil foreigners who are mining uranium for bombs, or barricaded by bad characters, they use their wits and resourcefulness to extricate themselves. The promise of a hidden treasure or the lure of a mystery usually draws them into such adventures. But it is the process they value, not the material rewards. When they discover treasure, as in *The Famous Five: And the Knight's Treasure* (1986), they make sure it is restored to the financially strapped farming folk on whose land it was found. The powers of observation and deduction that are developed during such escapades are expressly referenced by Baden-Powell as an essential building block of character: "When once observation and deduction have been made habitual in the boy, a great step in the development of 'character' has been gained" (Rosenthal 1984, 166).

In fact, it would not be entirely far-fetched to read the Famous Five series as something of an unintentional parable. Colonial explorers sought wealth and fame, but also sought to satisfy their thirst for adventure in itself. Sometimes the latter was allowed to obfuscate, quite deliberately, the former. Further obfuscation occurred by offering moral or ideological justification for the enterprise of empire and the control of the material resources that was its primary, if covert, purpose. Blyton's children have a well-defined sense of what is principled and proper in terms of their behavior, actions, or even their mission. There are frequent injunctions, usually from Julian to those outside the group, in this regard. For instance, in *Five Go to Demon's Rocks*, he admonishes Tinker: "That's enough. We don't tell tales about our parents in public" (43). Jo, in *Five Fall into Adventure*, is often chided by the others about her lying and thieving ways, while Richard in *Five Get into Trouble* is reprimanded for his irresponsibility. Conversely, Julian, as we have seen, is admired by Nobby for his courage, while Jo becomes devoted to Dick because of his kindness. In *The Secret of Killimooin* (1943), we are told, "All the children thought the world of their promises and never broke one" (70). Jack might participate in a certain amount of dissembling in order not to break his promise, but he maintains it in form if not fully in spirit.

"Imperial nations," declared Robert Cust, "must have Imperial instincts; the highest self-control, an entire absence of greed and lust for gold, a pity for the wounded and slain" (Tidrick 1990, 77). Earlier we saw how even Anne, the youngest of the four, was possessed of the highest self-control, giving way to tears only when circumstances overwhelmed her. In *The Knight's Treasure*, the five find themselves caught in a dark cave, with water coming up to their chests. "How were they ever to keep afloat in this stormy sea as it filled the cave and rose higher and higher?" the author asks (112). But even in such dire circumstances, the children maintain their self-control and stay calm, although anxious and even desperate, and rely on their inner resources to rescue them. In *The Secret of Killimooin* the children's father succinctly sketches the character of the prototypical British child, the sort of child (not coincidentally) well suited to setting forth on adventures in far-flung places: "It doesn't do to coddle children too much and shelter them. . . . We don't want children like that—we want boys and girls of spirit and courage, who can stand on their feet and are not afraid of what may happen to them. *We want them to grow adventurous and strong, of some real use in the world!* [my emphasis]. So we must not say no when a chance comes along to help them to be plucky and independent!" (*Killimooin*, 11).

The absence of greed is illustrated in *The Famous Five and the Knight's Treasure*: "The children told the Sergeant that even if any of the treasure-trove belonged to them, they didn't want it—they wanted all of it to go to the Loftings, so that the hard-working farmer could pay back the money he owed, and Mrs. Lofting needn't serve cream teas any more" (126). And as far as the third imperial instinct is concerned, that of pity, we have innumerable examples of the compassion the children extend to those less fortunate than themselves. Nobby is consistently included in their picnics and tea parties. They act almost like surrogate parents to the little Welsh waif in *Five Get into a Fix*. When Jo's father abandons her and leaves her to the mercy of a "queer and horrible" man called Jake, she confesses that she is hungry. Dick immediately puts his hand into their shopping basket and pulls out a packet of chocolate and some biscuits. "Tuck into these," he tells her. "And if you'd like to go to the kitchen door some time today and ask Joan, our cook, for a meal, she'll give you one. I'll tell her about you" (*Adventure*, 64). Acts such as these abound and indicate the children's kindliness even to those on the outside, even when at first (as with Jo) they don't much like or approve of them.

Although the five celebrate adventure for its own sake, adventure also has a higher purpose, namely the assertion of moral authority and the righting of moral order. There is a clear, if crude, sense of bearing a burden, the burden that is a complex of character, class, and race. M. Daphne Kutzer in *Empire's Children* shows us that there is a continuum between colonial expansionism and heroic exploration. When Robert Falcon Scott's expedition to the South Pole failed and he was upstaged by the Norwegian Roald Amundsen by only a month, he wrote to a British public that had made him a hero: "We are setting a good example to our countrymen, if not by getting into a tight place, by facing it like men when we were there" (Kutzer 2000, xx). The association between character and nationality is relentless.

Even something as simple as the children's loyalty to each other and to those they love and trust takes on a different aspect when viewed in the context of empire. Children in a group tend to stick together; there is nothing portentous about that. But the cohesion of the Famous Five or of the Secret Seven goes beyond the pulling together of children or even the sort of gang loyalty we witness in groups like the Greasers and the Socs in S. E. Hinton's *The Outsiders* (1967). There it is forged by survival instincts, the need for surrogate families and similar factors. The children in Blyton's groups are middle to upper-middle class and from safe, secure backgrounds. Their allegiance has an ethical aspect to it. It is based on higher principles, on a moral code. Where it will lead becomes clear in the following passage from Stanley Wolpert's *A New History of India* (2000). Commenting on the role of regional greed and mutual mistrust in Indian diplomacy, Wolpert says,

> The British, by contrast, for all their interpresidency rivalry and squabbling, were paragons of united action and national loyalty. More than military tactics, mercantile enterprise, or technological advantage, it was this capacity of the British to sublimate individual desires, greed, and dislike of other Englishmen to the imperative of working together toward a national (or company) goal and obeying orders accordingly, that helps explain the paramount position the Company Raj came to hold over all of India. (199)

The British conviction of their strength of character was unshakable except in a few doubting dissenters. The British were confident in their possession of the imperial qualities. Of course, the qualities Cust describes as such were more a part of an imperial myth than an imperial reality. There was a crass cruelty that prevailed in many aspects of colonial and settler life, and there was also a niggling pettiness. Tidrick brings our attention to books such as *The Land That Never Was* by the wife of a settler in East Africa who declares, "The unwritten law of helpfulness in exiled places that one read about in pre-war novels existed only in story-books!" (Tidrick 1990, 150). For a full exposé, based on personal experience, of the more distasteful side of British colonials, one needs only to read George Orwell's *Burmese Days* (1949). But Blyton reserves traits such as cruelty or pettiness for her "villains" and for her less likeable characters. The children who are her heroes and heroines might sometimes be impatient or impulsive, hasty or hotheaded, but they are never mean or petty or deceitful. For, as Blyton frequently reminds us, "They are that kind of children" (*Killimooin*, 140).

There are three other parallels that bear mentioning. In many, if not most of the Famous Five adventures, there is a contestation for space that parallels the contestation for land: the tussle between the children and the circus folk for camping grounds in *Five Go Off in a Caravan*, for instance, or the competition for the lost treasure in *The Famous Five and the Knight's Treasure*. Selous was blatant and arrogant enough to inform the members of the Royal Colonial Institute that this was actually a proud British characteristic: "to take possession of any country we think is worth having, and this piratical or Viking instinct is . . . a hereditary virtue that has come down to us in the blood of our northern ancestors. All other nations would like to do the same, and do so when they can; but we have been more enterprising than they, and, so far, have had the lion's share" (Tidrick 1990, 76). It would be difficult to miss the note of entitlement in Julian's voice when he informs the men from the circus, "We shall stay here as long as we want to" (80), though he does, somewhat condescendingly, acknowledge that they (the circus folk) too have a right to be there. Similarly, the children claim superior rights to the knight's treasure, if only on behalf of the struggling farm folk on whose land it is discovered.

The British recognized and respected in people of "lesser races" the qualities they considered intrinsic to their own character: courage, loyalty, steadfastness, the capacity for hard work, athletic prowess, stoicism, and so on. Those who shared such qualities—groups such as the Masai, the Sikhs, or the Gurkhas—were held in higher esteem and favor than their fellow countrymen. In India, the British distinguished between the virile races and more effeminate ones, "their spurious theories about "martial races" and "nonmartial races," Wolpert terms it (2000, 241); athleticism and sheer grit were vital qualifications for the former. As Tidrick comments, "The British have always been prepared to give a measure of recognition to the imperial qualities of other races, especially when these races have been absorbed into their own dominions; for obvious reasons of self-esteem, conquerors especially enjoy the subjection of those who were formerly paramount" (1990, 174). Similarly, in the Famous Five adventures, recognition is given to those of questionable backgrounds if their character is redeemable. Jo and Nobby are examples. Although they are not of the right sort, socially speaking, their pluck and resolve are recognized and respected.

Leadership is another quality that is celebrated in the literature of the Empire, whether it be historical essays, legends and myths, or literary output. The integrity and success of an empire depends on its leaders. Leaders loom large in the lore of the British Empire: John and Henry Lawrence, Rajah James Brooke, General Gordon, Cecil Rhodes, Frederick Courtenay Selous, Hugh Clifford, Lord Delamere, Lord Mountbatten, and so on. Leadership was a quality that was important to the British self-concept as well as to their colonial enterprise. Consummate leaders are Blyton's favored children. The boys are permitted to lead more than the girls, but George can often be found lending direction to the others. In *The Secret of . . .* series, Peggy and Nora are as active in adventure as their brothers and since Blyton's school stories, which we will come to later, concern all-female schools, girls like Daryl and Sally are, inevitably, in leadership roles. It is not a very long journey from being a leader to being a ruler; the British saw themselves as the ultimate ruling race and claimed their moral authority accordingly.

In his review of *Ornamentalism: How the British Saw their Empire*, Richard Gott writes, "When they [the British] saw their Empire, they did not really know, or they chose not to know what was being done in their name" (Gott 2001). What was being done in their name were sometimes some pretty dastardly deeds, and their illustrious leaders were not exempt. It is no wonder then that they liked to imagine their leaders at the lonely outposts of empire as capable of incredible kindness rather than the incredible barbarity of the type that Conrad sculpted into our imagination in the form of Mr. Kurtz, a character based as much on historical antecedent as on the extravagances of his imagination. These mythical Titans "were the men who burnt themselves out with work in the districts, riding all day and writing their reports through the night, charting revenue maps, planning canals and digging wells, maintaining jails, building roads, bearing their White Man's Burden without a whisper of complaint or regret" (Wolpert 2000, 224).

The ideal of leadership connects all the Blyton books, most especially those of the various adventure series. That the capacity for leadership is linked to nationality is made most clear in *The Secret of . . .* series. There, the group consists of four siblings: Jack is the oldest, an orphan adopted by the family, golden-haired Peggy comes next, and the twins, Mike and Nora follow, with their dark curls. But accompanying them on all their adventures is young Paul, who is the youngest of the five. Paul is heir apparent to the throne of Baronia, a made-up country but ostensibly East European in flavor. By making the prince the youngest, Blyton avoids being too blatant in awarding the leadership roles to the two English boys, but the intention is clear nevertheless. Paul has his moments of bravado, as when he insists on following his captured bodyguards into the caves, saying, "I am going to rescue them. . . . I am a Baronian prince, and I will not leave my men in danger. I go now to find them!" (*Killimooin*, 73). But bravado is distinguished from bravery when Mike chides him, telling him not to be an idiot. The boys know that when Paul gets these types of ideas into his head there is no stopping him, and he is again referred to as an idiot.

Paul runs impetuously into the moonlight with Jack and Mike tearing after him, yelling, "You're going the wrong way, and adding, "You really are an idiot. You'd be lost in the mountains if we hadn't come after you" (74). Clearly, it takes the level-headed courage of the English boys, not the burst of bravado that Paul displays, to successfully rescue the men. Paul might think big: 'I'm going to see,' said the little prince, who seemed that night to be more than a small boy. "He was a prince, he was growing up to be King, he was lord of Baronia, he was going to take command and give orders!" (77). But it takes Jack's good sense to prevent him from falling into a trap; he pulls him back as he is about to go down into a dark hole. Jack always goes first, both by virtue of age and by virtue of character. He is clearly of the same mold as Julian, adventurous but sensible, daring but reliable.

There is no doubt that Paul is plucky. In spite of being smaller and younger than the other two, he manages to keep up with them. But the two British boys are clearly privileged in terms of leadership skills and level-headedness. Jack and Mike immediately want to explore some abandoned mines, but Paul has to be teased into it. "Do *you* want to come, Paul?" they ask him, "or would you like to stay and look after the girls?" (102). Occasionally, Jack and Mike participate in nocturnal adventures from which Paul is excluded, as are their sisters because they are all sleeping. When an English child is scared, even a girl, Blyton feels obliged to explain and justify that fear, as we have seen with Anne. But when Paul is scared—for instance, when he lets out a loud cry at the hiss that is mysteriously emitted from time to time in Moon Castle—Blyton does not feel compelled to offer her usual aside. After all, Paul is not English and so his fear does not need to be excused or justified.

The introduction of Paul and Baronia into these adventures permits Blyton some unabashedly jingoistic moments, using her characters as mouthpieces, as when Paul's mother, the queen, exclaims in *The Secret of Moon Castle* what a wonderful country England is (41). When Paul admits that much as he likes England, he still prefers his native Baronia and perhaps they will too when they visit, Mike exclaims, "Rubbish. . . . As if any country could be nicer than our own!"

(*Killimooin*, 15). Baronia is allowed superior aircraft design and chocolate, but it is clear that it is a somewhat backward country and lurking danger belies its beautiful surfaces, "smiling under the summer sun. . . . It was not 'tamed' like their own country—it was still wild, and parts of it quite unknown" (20). And, she might well have added, ripe for exploration and conquest! Michael Rosenthal indicates that the journal *Scouting for Boys* blurred the thin line between creating a healthy pride in the genuine achievement of one's country and inducing instead a smug sense of the superiority of the true Briton. It is a blurring that the great public schools of Baden-Powell's time fostered, and it is not surprising that a movement that is as "explicitly a product of the public school system as Scouting should share not only the ideals of that system but also its prejudices" (Rosenthal 1984, 179).

In Blyton's adventure books there is, however, considerable confusion about specific cultural identities. Being British is obviously superior, but the Baronians are Europeans, so their alien aspect is somewhat tempered. Besides, Paul is part of the children's group. Like Jack and Mike and Peggy and Nora, he is being educated in an English public school. The bad guys in these books are not Baronian, but a shady Englishman who employs unidentified foreigners who mutter and yell in strange tongues, or robbers who lurk in the depths of the Baronian forests and don't quite belong anywhere, "men without a home" the goatherd calls them (*Killimooin*, 50). In fact, the children's housekeeper feels obliged to defend Baronian servants when the castle's caretaker, Mrs. Brimming, scornfully predicts that those foreign servants will turn everything to rack and ruin (*Moon Castle*, 61–62). Blyton frequently succumbs to metonymic tropes as in her reference to the "hordes" of Baronian servants or her probably inadvertent use of the pronoun "it" to refer to Paul's baby brother.

In one of the Five Find-Outers books, foreigners are used to provide comic diversion. Fatty disguises himself as a woman and then goes "all foreign," flapping about with his hands, moving his shoulders up and down and saying "Ackle-eeta-oomi-poggy-wo?" (*The Mystery of Holly Lane* 1953, 30). "It was so easy to talk gibberish," he muses later (*Holly Lane*, 30). The author also pokes gentle fun at the accent of a French couple, the French being frequent targets of Blyton's teasing humor. But the couple is otherwise portrayed respectfully and certainly presented as far more astute and agreeable than the local policeman, Fatty's nemesis, Goon. Of course, at the time Blyton was writing, a period that followed two devastating world wars, xenophobia was acceptable, even respectable to an extent (see Rudd 2000, 133). A different point is being made here: it is not simply that the foreigner is the "other," but that the foreigner, as "other," provides the dissimilarity against which the English could define and describe themselves.

In one of Blyton's school stories, *Claudine at St. Clare's* (1944), Claudine, a French girl who is rather liked by the others for her sprightly manner and amusing habits, is also set apart by her "very un-English ways" (*Claudine*, 17). Claudine copies from others' homework but does not consider it cheating, because she does so openly. She also borrows without permission and forgets to return things. She does so without malice and, when told by Hilary that she might at least ask before she borrows things, Claudine replies with a sigh "Oh, you English! Well, I will be good, and always I will say 'Dear Hilary, please, please lend me your so-beautiful silver pencil'" (*Claudine*, 19). The other girls laugh as she rolls her expressive black eyes around and uses her hands in the same way her aunt, Mam'zelle, the school's French teacher, does. They realize that "After all, she hadn't been in England very long—she would learn English ways before the term was over!" (*Claudine*, 19). In clear contrast is Carlotta, who, despite belonging to a circus family, possesses prized English instincts. She was "absolutely honest, truthful and straight" (*Claudine*, 17).

The Mam'zelles in Blyton's school stories are the quintessential French caricatures—mostly jolly and forgiving, although there is one dour Mam'zelle in Malory Towers. But Mam'zelle Dupont in the Malory Towers series and the Mam'zelle in the St. Clare series are amiable, entirely gullible, and somewhat silly, the frequent target of the girls' "*treeks*," as they call them. Blyton pokes fun at the French through them and, although it is all in good jest and even loving to some extent, the French teachers with their emotional and excitable ways, incredulity, impetuousness, and volatility provide a foil for the far more rational, ordered, stable, and steady English mistresses. Similarly, the penchant of French girls, such as Claudine, to avoid all physical activity, especially swimming, is in sharp contrast to the hardy English girls who, for the most part, favor it. Claudine sums up the difference thus: "You English girls are clumsy with your needles. You can bang all kinds of silly balls about, but you cannot make a beautiful darn!" (*Claudine*, 24).

Blyton's school stories project a world of women. In fact, aside from the odd handyman who makes a cameo appearance or the odd male teacher who does not figure prominently, there are no male characters in these books. When the group of girls we follow through the forms are close to completing their careers at Malory Towers, they discuss their future. One wants to go to a Swiss finishing school, much to the chagrin of her father, but quite a few are continuing their education at the college level; one wants to be a nurse, while others will pursue their talents in art, music, and singing, and two horse-crazy girls have plans to start their own riding school. Not one mentions any marriage plans! Clearly, these are women who are ready to take a leadership role in life and to pursue independent careers. In fact, the girls of Blyton's school stories are being readied as more than mere consorts for empire builders, though they would be ideally fitted for rugged frontier lives. In many ways, the qualities being inculcated in them are the qualities of empire builders themselves, or as close as females can get.

In Blyton's school stories, more than in any of her other books, we are provided with a pithy portrait of the best of British character, as it was popularly perceived. We see it in the stern, strict, but kindly and fair teachers. These are calm, efficient, and consistent women, possessed of a sense of humor. Miss Grayling, the headmistress, who is both loved and feared and held in the highest awe and admiration, addresses the new girls at the start of every term. She speaks the same words every time, words that amount to a creed:

> One day you will leave school and go out into the world as young women. You should take with you eager minds, kind hearts, and a will to help. You should take with you a good understanding of many things, and a willingness to accept responsibility and show yourselves as women to be loved and trusted. All these things you will be able to learn at Malory Towers—if you *will*. I do not count as our successes those who have won scholarships and passed exams, though these are good things to do. I count as our successes those who learn to be good-hearted and kind, sensible and trustable, good, sound women the world can lean on. Our failures

are those who do not learn these things in the years they are here. (*First Term* 1946, 20)

The wording may vary slightly from year to year, but the message does not: "You will all get a lot out of your years at Malory Towers. See that you give a lot back! Be just and responsible, kind and hard-working. I count as our successes those who leave here as young women good-hearted and kind, sensible and trustable, good sound people that the world can lean on. Our failures are those who do not learn these things in the years they are here" (*Second Form* 1947, 16).

In every version, there is reference to the world, indicating that these young women are expected to pursue a mission and exert an influence that extends well beyond the domestic sphere and well beyond national boundaries. When the first Malory Towers book was written, the year was 1946. In only one year, Britain would lose India, the crown jewel of her Empire, and that loss would precipitate the ultimate demise of the Empire. But the imperial impetus and worldview had been part of Britain's very being for so long, it would continue to prevail. In Miss Grayling's customary speech to her young charges, there is an unmistakable exhortation to serve the Empire, subtle or subliminal though it may be. When Miss Grayling addresses a girl who finds herself in a spot of trouble, she reminds her sternly that Malory Towers is a school with "traditions of service for others, for justice, kindliness and truthfulness" (*Second Form*, 138). It is a school that, as Darrell points out, "makes you stand on your own feet, rubs off your corners, teaches you common-sense, makes you accept responsibility" (*In the Fifth at Malory Towers* 1950, 101). The young women who attend what they believe is the finest school in the kingdom are expected to fulfill a destiny. And character is the path through which that destiny is pursued.

Let us examine more closely, in the context of Blyton's school stories, the qualities this ideal character comprises. The students of Malory Towers come from comfortable if not always affluent families. Most, like Darrell Rivers, who is one of the main characters, belong to the upper-middle class. Darrell's father is a surgeon. They have a cook and a gardener and a nice home. But some girls are there on scholarship and, as long as they "fit in" where their work ethic and behavior are concerned, they are in no way shunned. On the other hand, it does not do to be too rich or aristocratic and, if one is, it certainly does not do to advertise the fact. Braggers are among the outcasts in British schoolgirl society, and those whose bragging is based on lies fare even worse. Daphne, at Malory Towers, makes up rich parents, parties aboard yachts lit up with little lights, frilly frocks with pearls all over, and a prince who sits next to her. When she is exposed, Miss Grayling tells her that the only way she can salvage herself is by confessing to her classmates and allowing the good in her cancel out the bad. Because of a heroic deed in saving another girl's life, Daphne is forgiven and, chastened, admits her true status.

Class certainly matters in the world of school stories, but class is not necessarily an adjunct to wealth. In one of the *Malory Towers* books we meet Jo, whose father is extremely rich but also extremely coarse and crude. He encourages Jo to disregard the rules and follow in his own footsteps, his nickname in school having been Cheeky Charlie. Jo is portrayed as "bumptious and brazen" (*Last Term at Malory Towers* 1951, 33) and she ends up being expelled, her great wealth of no use to her in this world where character counts above everything else. Nor do good looks provide salvation for someone who lacks the right qualities. One of Blyton's most memorable schoolgirl characters is Gwendolyn Mary in Malory Towers. She is pretty in storybook-princess fashion: golden hair and pale blue eyes, and she is from a well-heeled family. But except for a glimmer of hope and a touch of regret at the end, Gwen remains irascible. She has been thoroughly spoilt by her mother and governess and is petulant and snobbish.

Gwen is neither a good student nor a good athlete. In fact, she abhors physical activity, especially swimming, and her wimpy ways add to the disfavor in which she is continually held. Sally sums her up thus: "You can't play tennis, you can't swim, you squeal when your toe touches the cold water, you don't even know all your twelve times table, baby! And then you talk of it not being worthwhile to show what you can do! You can't do a thing and never will, whilst you have such a wonderful opinion of yourself!" (*First Term*, 43). Throughout the series, Gwen is the target of the other girls' sometimes cruel teasing, but they tease her with impunity. Blyton allows her to remain an unsympathetic character until almost the very end, because her personality is of the wrong type and does not radically change.

Who then is the right type? Perhaps no one signifies this more completely than Darrell Rivers, who comes close to being the series' heroine. Darrell is smart, a good student, particularly at writing. She plays a marvelous game of tennis, and she is a powerful swimmer. She is as strong as Gwen is weak, as plucky as Gwen is cowardly. She keeps her word and never sneaks, another deadly sin in the British schoolgirl handbook, and one that Gwen is quite capable of committing. Unlike Gwen, Darrell understands teamwork and has a sure sense of sportsmanship.

Darrell's best friend, Sally, also shares these qualities. Alicia, another member of the core group, shares many of them, but Alicia does not have a sense of responsibility, which Sally clearly has, and that's why it is Sally who is chosen as head of the form. Accompanying a capacity for leadership must be a sense of responsibility, and along with that must go kindness. But Alicia, although popular and fun-loving, brilliant and athletically talented, can also be "rather hard," as Sally says. "She wouldn't bother to help people if they were in trouble, she wouldn't bother herself to be kind, she'd just be head-of-the-form and give orders, and see that they were kept" (*Second Form*, 3). More is asked of a head-girl. Darrell is not chosen at first because she has one flaw, a hot and sudden temper. But she also repents rapidly and apologizes graciously and, once she has learnt to bring it under control, she too has a turn as head of the form.

Some faults are, however, more forgivable than others. And so Darrell's temper, Sally's somewhat stolid personality, Mary-Lou's timidity (which is different from cowardice), Irene's and Belinda's absentmindedness, and Bill's and Clarissa's single-minded preoccupation with horses are allowable faults. But deceit and malice, conceit and cowardice, snobbery and selfishness, disloyalty and a lack of love for the outdoors cannot be forgiven. Nor can snitching or bragging. Again, it is Miss Grayling who enumerates, in her annual address to new students, the traits so integral to this idealized conception of British character at its best: eager minds, kind hearts, a willingness to help and to accept responsibility, a good understanding of many things, a good heart, being kind, being sensible and trustable, and being good, sound women the world can lean on. "All these things you will be able to learn at Malory Towers," she tells them, "if you *will*" (*Last Term*, 21–22). These qualities then could be taught and could be learned. Miss Grayling counts as her successes those who have schooled themselves in these traits of character while at Malory Towers and as her failures those who have not. The right nationality is a prerequisite for preferred character traits, but without volition and a suitable environment they may not be borne to fruition.

That this portrait of British character was not painted in isolation, a product of Blyton's own idealism, that it was an archetype ingrained in the national consciousness, is indicated by its repeated appearance in the literature of the empire. In extolling the virtues desirable in the ideal Englishman for India, Maud Diver mentions vigorous action, scrupulous fairness, strong leadership, a pioneering and proselytizing spirit (Singh 1988, 166). These are the very qualities that Miss Grayling advocates for her girls at Malory Towers— even the proselytizing, which is expressed as school spirit. Maud Diver, as was mentioned earlier, was one of the most prolific authors of grown-up adventure stories during the heyday of the British Empire in India. Like her counterparts, Mrs. Flora Annie Steel, Alice Perrin, B. M. Croker, and E. W. Savi, Maud Diver wrote in the first decades of the last century about Anglo-Indian lives and loves. The term *Anglo-Indian* formerly denoted the English person who dwelled in India. The Anglo-Indian reader of such novels, usually female, could easily identify with the heroines, while the reader in England could find interest in all the stock elements of popular romances or adventure stories, enhanced by the exotic settings.

Stories of action and adventure abounded in this era, stories about the various campaigns and wars that the British fought in India. Henty has already been mentioned. In an article entitled "G. A. Henty's Idea of India" published in *Victorian Studies*, Mark Naidis comments on the effectiveness of Henty's stories in transmitting not only imperialist sentiment but also the conviction that the British had triumphed in India through their "courage, energy, and moral uprightness" (1964, 58). The same message emerges in Blyton's stories except that it is slightly more oblique and, of course, not directly concerned with India alone. Blyton's books are not ostensibly about the Empire at all. This renders them particularly interesting for my study, in addition to the fact that they are still so widely read in all the countries of the former British Empire. It would not be difficult to isolate the imperial message in the works of Henty or Buchan, but Blyton's stories are seemingly distant and detached from the context of empire. One would be hard put to find any mention of the Empire at all. Similarly, other authors of popular action and adventure series did not necessarily set out to fire youngsters with enthusiasm for the Empire or to instill in them the requisite qualities for becoming empire builders. But they were doing just that and, at some level, they probably knew it. Character building was an inviolable part of Britain's national destiny, practically an unwritten master plan. It was an essential element of the burden they felt compelled to bear by virtue of their superior moral fiber.

Diver spares no effort in extolling the virtues of race. "To England's great good fortune, there were usually men on the spot who could be relied on, in an emergency, to think and act and dare in accordance with the high tradition of their race" she assures us (Diver 1921, 321). And what were the requirements of that high tradition? Not very different from the requirements of a successful student at Malory Towers: physical prowess, gallantry, inner and outer strength, integrity, ability. What was being asked of those who served the Empire was exactly what Miss Grayling asked of her girls: work, service, and duty. In *Desmond's Daughter* (1916), Diver pronounces, "Their work isn't mere work just for themselves. It's service—duty" (222–23). The privileging of physical activity is another parallel. Girls who are afraid of the water or skittish about sports are held in high disdain. In fact, the British love for the outdoors is reiterated over and over again as a peculiarity of national character, a peculiarity that separates them from, say, the French. "That is another thing I do not understand about you so-jolly English girls," says Claudine, "this out-of-doors" (*Claudine*, 39). Later she bemoans, "Ah, life was very very hard at this so-sporting English school, with its love for the cold, cold water, and for striking at balls so many times a week, and for its detestable nature-walks, and . . ." (*Claudine*, 45).

Since a majority of the officers in the Indian civil and military services were products of public schools, the discipline, ethics, and codes of behavior of these schools directly influenced the governance of India. Sport and work were considered part of the same ethic. The one was a preparation for the other and, far from being mutually exclusive, they had, in fact, the same goal. "The idea that the exercise of power is in itself a good thing," writes Rene Maunier, "action, struggle, even sport itself, are proposed as ideals; the vision of the gentleman again! To strive, to play games, to win, that is the destined part for the perfect man to play; all expansion is sound and good, for it deploys the energy of the strong" (1949, vol. 1, 34).

Maud Diver commemorates the triumphs and achievements, the struggle and survival, of not only the men but also the women of the Empire, and it is in her portraits of the latter that we see most clearly how easily a Darrell Rivers can morph into a Honoraria Lawrence. An empire builder's wife would need to share the same qualities of fortitude and rectitude, resilience and resolve, as her husband, although her application of them would, of course, be circumscribed by gender and custom. Diver disliked flippant or frivolous women, not only because they were unsuited for life in India outside the social circles of large cities but because they did not make fit consorts for empire builders and gave the Empire a poor image. On the other hand, her ideal woman was not aggressive or domineering either. Honor Desmond, who is modeled on Honoraria Lawrence, can ride a horse as well as any man, but she can also tenderly nurse a sick person. While strong and brave, she can still offer herself to her husband "with that superb completeness of surrender which is the distinctive mark of a strong woman's love" (Diver 1907, 371). Honor Desmond is indeed a virtual composite of Darrell, Sally, Bill, and Mary-Lou.

If Honor Desmond is the right type, there is, of necessity, a wrong type of woman for this role as well, and Diver offers us a sketch in the form of Honor's predecessor, the first wife of Sir Theo Desmond. Later in the novel *Captain Desmond, V.C.* (1907), Diver has this first wife killed off by "a Mahomedan fanatic" so as to allow her hero to find the perfect woman to take her place. Evelyn, unlike Honor, is a complete misfit for the rugged life of the frontier and is therefore utterly unsuitable as a partner for such a splendid specimen of Anglo-Indian manhood as her husband, Desmond. She loves life in Lahore with its rounds of parties and polo, but she dislikes intensely the border area where, she complains, the regiment seems to take precedence over everything else and the men are always in uniform. Evelyn is not bad so much as wrong for the role she is expected to play. She lacks courage, endurance, and strength, and she is weak willed. She is Gwendolyn all grown up. Honor Desmond's antithesis is also illustrated in a host of minor characters, such as the cowardly Mrs. Elton in *Far to Seek* (Diver, 1921) whose "mountain of

flesh hid a mouse of a soul" and who is terrified by the "least unusual uproar at a railway station or holiday excitement in the
bazaar" or Mrs. Hunter-Raynard in the same novel who claims that
natives give her "the creeps." In *Far to Seek* Diver succinctly sums up
such women thus: "All their values were social—pay, promotion,
prestige" (308).

Clearly, Blyton cherishes, respects, and values the very same
qualities and traits of character as do Diver and hosts of contemporaneous novelists of empire. Darrell and Sally especially, as well as
other members of their form, would meet Diver's criteria admirably
for successful service at the Empire's outposts. The first two can be
considered embryonic frontier wives with their understanding of
the difference between what Miss Grayling calls the coward's way
and the hero's way (*Last Term*, 114). Girls such as these understand
the importance of standing up for themselves. They know that it
does not do to be too sensitive. When a new girl tells Darrell of her
sensitive nature, the latter brusquely advises her to get over it, for
"In her experience people who went round saying that they were
sensitive wanted a good shaking up, and, if they were lower school,
needed to be laughed out of it" (*In the Fifth*, 21). When Darrell is
head of fifth-form games and Sally is nominated to assist her, Darrell daydreams about training some of the younger players and
making them "first class," resolving not to stand any nonsense from
them as she licks them into shape and makes sure they understand
that they will have to "toe the line" now (*In the Fifth*, 27).

It is interesting to note here how persistently Lord Baden-Powell,
founder of the Boy Scout movement, linked skills acquired in sports
with skills practiced in war: "The army *fights* for the good of its country as the team *plays* for the honour of its school. Regiments assist each
other as players do when they *shove together* or *pass the ball* from one
to other; exceptionally gallant *charges* and heroic *defences* corresponding to brilliant *runs* and fine *tackling*" (Rosenthal 1984, 96). Aside
from fostering skills, sports also serve to nourish the concept of teamwork, so essential to success on the playing field, the battlefield, and
the larger arena of empire. Blyton would most likely agree. Her heroines are tough, rugged, no-nonsense girls who will grow into women
perfectly suited for the tough, rugged, no-nonsense lifestyle of the
frontiers of empire, where those who cannot withstand its rigors must
be licked into shape or sent back home, and toeing the line becomes a

useful skill. But Darrell does acknowledge that "it took all sorts to make a world, and there was a place for the Moiras and Gwens and Maureens . . . and for the Sallies and Irenes and Belindas as well" (*In the Fifth*, 30). The place for "pet-lambs" like Gwen or like Diver's Evelyn is certainly not doing "thankless work" under "trying conditions" in the "scattered villages" of India where a "few civilians stand for the Government and the King Emperor, for virtually the whole British race" (Diver 1931, 127). British individuals in India did not simply represent themselves. They represented a nation, a system, and an entire race! What is needed for places such as India, or the African colonies are, in Miss Grayling's words, "good-hearted and kind, sensible and trustable, good, sound women the world can lean on" (*Third Year*, 20–21), the sort of women that the Darrells and the Sallies and the Irenes and the Belindas will grow into. That Miss Grayling sees them as serving the world and not simply their own country is certainly significant.

By introducing the odd American as well as the odd French girl, Blyton finds a way to remind her reader that the girls represent their nations as well as their race. Like the French, the American girls— Zerelda at Malory Towers and Sadie at St. Clare's—establish alterity. They enable us to see just how steady and solid English girls such as Darrell and Sally are, as opposed to the somewhat vain and affected Americans whose only interest seem to be movie stars! Zerelda's long, beautifully polished nails and well-kept hands provide a clear contrast to the "tough little English girls" (*Third Year*, 43). "You're a queer person, Zerelda," scolds Darrell, looking at her earnestly. "You're missing all the nicest years of your life—I mean, you just won't let yourself enjoy the things most English girls of your age enjoy. You spend hours over your hair and your face and your nails, when you could be having fun at lacrosse, or going for walks, or even messing about in the gym" (*Third Year*, 37). Similarly, Sadie is described as "an American girl with no ideas in her head at all beyond clothes and the cinema" (*Second Form*, 5).

That the girls in Blyton's school stories represent not only themselves but also their nation and race is further illustrated by the fact that Zerelda worries she is letting America down when she allows "these English girls to be so much better at everything" (*Third Year*, 44). When Miss Grayling admonishes her not to slide down any further in her work, she also reminds her, "You belong to a great country, and you are her only representative here. Be a good one if you can. And I think you can" (*Third Year*, 47). This was the one thing that could touch Zerelda, the author tells us, "Gee. She stood for America" (*Third Year*, 47). Later she urges herself to remain strong: "Keep your chin up, Zerelda! You're American. Fly the Stars and Stripes! Make out you don't mind a bit" (*Third Year*, 54).

That the British temperament is considered the most beneficial is signaled by the teachers' approval of "jolly good long walks" (*Second Form*, 53) and muddy ones at that. Whereas the French mistresses favor girls who are artistic or clever with a needle, the English ones prefer girls who are sporty as well as trustworthy and hardworking, even if not talented. They value the solid student and the superb athlete. Above all, they value a wholehearted approach. As Miss Potts advises Darrell, "when you choose something worthwhile [*sic*] like doctoring—or teaching—or writing or painting, it is best to be whole-hearted about it. It doesn't so much matter for a second-rate or third-rate person and you mean to choose a first-rate job when you grow up, then you must learn to be whole-hearted when you are young" (*First Term*). Cowardice is one of the most despised traits of all, as is weakness or feebleness or being a ninny (*First Term*, 106, 128). What else counts? Strength of character and determination, fairness and kindness, generosity, courage of course, decency, obedience, hardiness, honesty and straightness, loyalty, being "sensible and sturdy and stolid" (*In the Fifth*, 139). These are the cardinal virtues for a British schoolchild.

A sense of honor is claimed as an almost exclusively English trait. Alison explicitly appropriates it as "our sense of honour" (*Claudine*, 80). Claudine repeatedly reminds the others that she does not have the funny and rather uncomfortable English sense of honor to worry her. When she locks the mean matron in a room to prevent her from finding out about their midnight feast, she confesses to the headmistress, "I suppose it is not a thing that any English girl would have done, with their so-fine sense of honour, but I am French" (*Claudine*, 115). That Malory Towers and St. Clare's are schools for character as well as for scholastics and sports is patent. Miss Grayling makes it clear, "the girls didn't come to Malory Towers only to learn lessons in class—they came to learn other things too. . . . Perhaps those things were even more important than the lessons!" (*Third Year*, 48). And Miss Roberts at St. Clare's reminds

Mam'zelle that "There are other things as important as lessons. . . . We are not out to cram facts and knowledge into the girls' heads all day long, but to help them to form strong and kindly characters too" (*Second Form*, 96). Darrell recites a litany of advantages provided by a good English education. "Shows what Malory Towers does to you!" she says as they marvel at Mary-Lou taking the principal part in the pantomime when she had started out at the school "scared even of her own shadow." "Still," continues Darrell, "I suppose any good boarding-school does the same things—makes you stand on your own feet, rubs off your corners, teaches you common-sense, makes you accept responsibility" (*In the Fifth*, 101).

Neither the teachers nor the girls appreciate "silliness and boringness and conceitedness and boastfulness" (*In the Fifth*, 72). Obsequious forms of help, flattery, and self-effacement are not appreciated, nor is "saintly" behavior, being a doormat, or a "suckup," a snob, a sneak, or someone who runs down her parents in public (*Last Term*, 10). Surely this smashing, super "wizard" world was a breeding ground for leaders and surely, with such training, the British produced a righteous coterie of them. They liked to think so, of course, but the reality indicates otherwise. If one turns away from the apologists or the celebrants of the Empire to more cynical writers like E. M. Forster or George Orwell, one finds far more of Blyton's wrong type featured among the British in India than her right type. Diver distinguished between noble, generous, kindhearted, and compassionate Englishmen and gratuitously cruel or petty-minded ones and acknowledged that both existed. But in her mind the former far outnumbered the latter. Most of those who served the Empire would tend to agree with her perception. But Orwell and Forster show that people who could be snobbish handled the daily business of empire: petty-minded, cruel, and distinctly unfair people who set the British self-image on its head.

Miss Theobald's admonition to a student in *Claudine at St. Clare's* that we must never judge people by what they have but by what they are, that kindness and friendship are earned and not bought (147), reiterates the British conviction that they held their empire by moral and not physical force, by superiority of character, not superiority of means. And when silly, superficial Angela at St. Clare's is caught firmly by the arms by two girls who sit her down violently, "almost jerking the breath out of her body" (*Claudine*, 126) as they tell her that she is going to have to listen to them whether or not she wants to, we sense that sometimes force may be used righteously in the employment of a higher purpose. To read these scenes as small parables, predictive of the patterns of empire, is not as far-fetched as might at first seem. After all, the British public school was and is well acknowledged as a breeding place for empire builders. To do so is simply to recognize how deeply and insidiously the ethos of empire pervaded the British consciousness. As Gott (2001) argues, "When they [the British] saw their Empire, they did not really know, or they chose not to know what was being done in their name."

"Empire was the vehicle for the extension of British social structures—to the ends of the world," writes Gott in his review of David Cannadine's work *Ornamentalism: How the British Saw Their Empire*. Gott continues, "We now know that the British Empire was essentially a Hitlerian project on a grand scale, involving military conquest and dictatorship, extermination and genocide, martial law and 'special courts,' slavery and forced labour, concentration camps and the transoceanic migration of peoples. Whatever way we now look at Empire, this vision must remain dominant" (2001, 15). It is, however, a vision that Maud Diver and other romanticists of empire would vigorously deny. So would Enid Blyton, who would perhaps argue that the British are racially incapable of that sort of behavior.

The ordinary servants of the Empire were expected to voice their support and promise their obedience, but not to think about it or question it. Doing so, George Orwell confessed, made them feel guilty. In *The Road to Wigan Pier* (1937), he recalls sharing a train compartment with a member of the Educational Service, a stranger:

> Half an hour's cautious questioning decided each of us that the other was "safe"; and then for hours, while the train jolted slowly through the pitch-black night, sitting up in our bunks with bottles of beer handy, we damned the British Empire—damned it from the inside, intelligently and intimately. It did us both good. But we had been speaking forbidden things, and in the haggard morning light when the train crawled into Mandalay, we parted as guiltily as any adulterous couple. (146–47)

At Malory Towers, such behavior would be considered bad form, disloyal and treacherous. The British public schools trained their students to do their jobs to the best of their abilities and to obey orders, not to question or to protest. Self must be subsumed in the service of society, the latter strictly defined, constricted, and identified with the national interests. As Orwell indicates in the passage quoted above, such activities as questioning, criticizing, even thinking were suspect and seditious. The law of the jungle is, after all, "Obey!"

Blyton's school stories reveal how dearly the British cherished and how deeply they valued personal relations. Indeed, congenial personal relations are often considered compensatory for strained political ones. Even Orwell, despite exposing the underside of empire in *Burmese Days,* concedes that it is still possible to be an imperialist and a gentleman (see Raskin 1971, 48). Personal decency matters more than public policy in this scheme of things. And, if anything, Malory Towers is a school for personal decency. By illustrating to the reader what constitutes character, and by indicating that character, except in the most extreme cases, such as Gwen's, can be taught, Blyton reiterates the strong sense of moral rectitude that the British claimed as their birthright.

Tidrick refers to this ingrained notion that the Empire can be run on character. She points to the actions of Sir Ralph Furse, who was in complete charge of recruitment for the Colonial Service between 1919 and 1948. For Furse, the public schools were the best breeding grounds for the service. He was a product of Eton and Oxford himself. The qualities he looked for in the men at the outposts were "integrity, fairness, firmness, and likeableness" (Tidrick 1990, 216), all qualities Miss Grayling looks for in her girls. Tidrick points to the essential contradiction "that for a hundred years, from the middle of the nineteenth century to the middle of the twentieth, the British governing classes were educated in an atmosphere which combined the toleration of a merciless brutality with perpetual exhortations to be good" (1990, 216). Perhaps this is the reason that Blyton tacitly approves of girls like Gwen being criticized and even teased, sometimes cruelly it would seem to us. Blyton lends narrative approval, allowing her readers to accept it as Gwen's just deserts.

Malory Towers is, of course, a very different sort of place from the Rugby of *Tom Brown's Schooldays,* even the reformed institution, for the latter is still a world where only the strongest survive. Strength must be tempered by kindness and understanding. It is the lack thereof that costs Alicia her headgirlship in the *Malory Towers* series. And it is the lack thereof that led E. M. Forster to comment of his character Ronny Heaslop in *A Passage to India*, "One touch of regret—not the canny substitute but the true regret from the heart—would have made him a different man, and the British Empire a different institution" (Forster 1924, 51). Again, this correspondence in perception between children's and adult writing is no coincidence; it is born out of a common consciousness.

"The schools were aware of the importance of the gerontocratic process and called it 'learning to command and obey,'" states Tidrick (1990, 218). She goes on to claim that they also served to instill an appreciation of power and an awareness of what it would be like not to have it. In his comprehensive and fascinating study of the genesis of the Boy Scout movement, Michael Rosenthal comments that a major impetus for its founding was Baden-Powell's dream that it would enable boys of a poorer class to resemble their upper-class brothers. Baden-Powell understood that the upper-class boys did not need scout training for themselves, as the public schools they could afford to attend imparted "the spirit of self-negation, self-discipline, sense of honour, responsibility, helpfulness to others, loyalty and patriotism which go to make 'character'" (Rosenthal 1984, 90). The Boy Scout movement was therefore a sort of character factory for the lower classes in the same way that the public schools were for the upper classes. To that extent Baden-Powell exhorted the latter to take up scouting, not for their own needs but to serve the former in a spirit of noblesse oblige (Rosenthal 1984, 91).

That character must be cultivated and then harnessed in the service of country, that it was imbricated with nationality, was widely believed. It went even further than that. The esprit de corps must be employed for Britain's global interests as well:

> Whatever else they might have sought to achieve, most late Victorian public schools aspired to produce one overriding trait in their boys: an all-consuming loyalty—to side, to institution, to class, to country. This was the message they preached, the reflex they attempted to engender. As an institution committed to the perpetuation of the privileged classes who had access to it, the public schools emphasized those conservative virtues of conformity and obedience that would best guarantee the continuation of the *status quo*. (Rosenthal 1984, 91)

And the status quo meant not only preserving the hierarchy of British society but the hierarchy of Britain's empire. Rosenthal indicates that in an international report on moral instruction in schools published in 1908, H. Bompas Smith, headmaster of King Edward VII School in Lytham, goes so far as to say that the public schools aim at training their students "to become worthy members of the social group of which the function is the *control and guidance of the work and thought of others* [my emphasis]" (Rosenthal 1984, 91).

Along with loyalty, leadership skills were held in high esteem and there is no doubt as to the reason for this. Tidrick comments,

> The avowed purpose of the public schools was to produce leaders, and if we are to understand by leaders rulers capable of extracting the voluntary compliance of the ruled, we must concede that they produced them. Whether the capacity for leadership extended beyond the special circumstance of school is another question. The fact that it was assumed to do so had its own importance.
>
> The school, indeed, produced an over-supply of leaders. Some of them were absorbed by the empire, where they constructed an administrative system remarkable for the degree of local autonomy exercised within it, and where they pursued, amid uncomprehending but generally unresisting natives, dreams of winning the trust and loyalty of their charges by their integrity, fairness, firmness and likeableness. (220)

Almost word for word, these are the very qualities that Miss Grayling exhorts her charges to pursue in her traditional address to the new students on the second day of school at Malory Towers. Again, the similarity is no accident. Blyton did not produce this conception of character out of a vacuum, but out of her participation in the national consciousness and her belief in a national character, however disingenuous it may have seemed to those on the outside. The children in Blyton's books are being equipped with character traits that will enable them to serve their country and their empire, and will prepare them for exploration and dominion. Nor is Blyton singular in her insistence on such qualities. M. Daphne Kutzer indicates a similar preoccupation in the books of R. M. Ballantyne, who she says, presents the reader in *The Coral Island* with a number of tropes that will return repeatedly in children's books, tropes that propose the benevolence of empire, for it breeds "resourcefulness, leadership, pluck, moral virtue, and chivalry" (Kutzer 2000, 10), all qualities cherished by Blyton as well.

As Kutzer points out, "The omnipresence of empire and its images in popular juvenile fiction is no surprise" (2000, 10). Empire was as much a part of the national consciousness for the British as the frontier was for the Americans. Both empire and frontier were schools for character where virtues instilled in childhood could be developed and honed and perfected. For the readers of the Famous Five, the Secret Seven, the Five Find-Outers, The Secret of . . . series, and others, these fictitious childhood adventures evoke the possibility of real life ones in the far flung corners of the Empire. The hunt for stolen or lost treasure simulates the search for and subsequent exploitation of natural resources, of gold and diamonds, rubber and ivory. The villains thwarted and outsmarted by these children suggest those who attempted to thwart the British in the countries they colonized.

Readers of Frank Richards's Greyfriars school stories, "the apotheosis of public school mythification," according to Jeffrey Richards (Butts 1972, 9), will recognize in Blyton's the same admiration for "guts, integrity, tradition," the derision for the glutton, the sneak and the thief, and the mockery of the American and the French (Butts 1972, 13). Blyton is clearly an emissary of empire, but in a changing context of newly emergent nations, she is forced to be less valoristic in her approach while still upholding its ethos. Considering that even as she was still writing, her books were being read by children of many different countries, cultures, races, and ethnicities, it is astonishing that there are practically no children from the British Commonwealth represented in her stories. Even the Greyfriars school stories included a prominent Indian character, Ram Singh. The Empire does not emerge as a corporeal presence in Blyton's books as it does in Ballantyne's, Henty's, or Kipling's; there are no clearly identifiable connections with the colonies, as in the works of E. Nesbit or Frances Hodgson Burnett. Yet the children in her stories are infused with a sense of responsibility and resourcefulness that leaves little doubt that they are being bred as future leaders. In this context, qualities of leadership are not only a matter of instinct or cultivation but also a matter of volition, of destiny, a matter of honor and a matter of right. A nation that believed so completely in its own moral superiority could hardly doubt a destiny afforded by the force of character.

5

Across the Atlantic

If a race is weak, if it is lacking in the physical and moral traits which go to the makeup of a conquering people, it cannot succeed.

—Theodore Roosevelt

There were more men in the new communities than in the old who saw, however imperfectly, the grandeur of the opportunity and of the race-destiny; but there were always very many who did their share in working out their destiny grudgingly and under protest. The race as a whole, in its old homes and its new, learns the lesson with such difficulty that it can scarcely be said to be learnt at all until success or failure has done away with the need of learning it. But in the case of our own people, it has fortunately happened that the concurrence of the interests of the individual and of the whole organism has been normal throughout most of its history.

—Theodore Roosevelt

By all the unwritten laws of savage warfare it is always the redskin who attacks, and with the wiliness of his race

> he does it just before the dawn, at which time he knows
> the courage of the whites to be at its lowest ebb.
>
> —James Barrie, *Peter Pan*

A sense of adventure and the yearning for an active and energetic way of life, a spirit of endurance and resilience, raw courage and fortitude, loyalty and trustworthiness, qualities so prized by the British, and so valued as intrinsic to their national character, were embraced on the other side of the Atlantic as well, where they pooled to form the frontier spirit. The character components that were a necessary part of the equipment of the frontiersman or woman differ hardly at all from those of the empire builder. While the historical situations differ in the details, they also reveal a remarkable similarity. Both demanded the drive and the desire to explore, the capacity to endure all sorts of trials and tribulations, the will to conquer and dominate, and the determination to overcome any resistance or break down any barriers that stand in the way—peacefully if possible, ruthlessly if necessary. But while the means were much alike, the ends were not. Colonization was satisfied with control and did not necessitate or preclude settlement, whereas settlement was part of the plan for the frontier, and the idea of homesteading afforded it a more rosy and romantic aspect.

In *The Frontier Spirit and Progress*, Frank Tucker writes, "Frontiers and *utopias* are viewed similarly in some ways. New frontiers have often been idealized, and new lands acquired an idyllic quality in the popular imagination. Being remote and little known, their defects went unnoticed" (1980, 21). The British colonial enterprise and the American westward expansion were propelled by many of the same objectives and motives. They demanded many of the same forces from both within and without. Tucker indicates the prominence of the frontier spirit in many of the science fiction stories popular at the time and tells us that some of the characters in these tales speak in a style identical to that used by imperialists in the nineteenth and twentieth centuries. As an example, he provides this excerpt from Joseph P. Martino's science fiction story, *Zero Sum*, one of many that exemplify the frontier spirit: "Expansion and colonization are essential to the survival of humanity. The day we lack the courage to expand, we will have taken the first step towards extinction. . . . Our expansion should be peaceful as long as this is possible. . . . . But we must never hesitate to fight for what is rightfully ours, or we shall take our place in history alongside the Terran dinosaurs and elephants, while the stars go to more vigorous races" (Tucker 1980, 24). The more vigorous races are those with courage, with energy, with fight. Tucker makes an interesting and significant point in discussing serial stories of adventure for young people. He points out that the plot is quite interchangeably applied to all frontier-type situations.

A common theme cuts across the adventure stories of G. A. Henty as well, if not a common plot. Tucker observes the titles advertised in an early Horatio Alger book. They comprise adventure stories about African exploration, South American travels, sea adventures, the American West, and British colonial exploits in Asia as well as a story of the Maori war and a tale of the Crimea. What's startling about Tucker's observation is that all these far-flung tales of adventure are on a single list of ninety-one books for boys then sold by A. L. Burt Company Publishers in New York. Tucker tells us,

> In an *Analog* editorial of 1971, the famous science fiction writer John W. Campbell said that the dominant life form on any planet must have a profound competitiveness, a "tendency to attack and conquer frontiers." The frontiers will be geographical, intellectual, and industrial, he said, but only "frontier-crossers" could achieve ownership of their own planets. This generalized type of "frontiersman," as Campbell sees him, is rigidly disciplined, especially in the sense of self-discipline. He has been exposed to harsh realities, and so he is pragmatic, unable to indulge in irrational fanaticism. (24)

This is a character type that flourished not only in the pages of boys' adventure stories but on the remote settlements and stations of both the American frontier and the British Empire. Tucker makes a pertinent observation when he suggests that the very titles of American schoolbooks, which often incorporate the words *discovery* and *exploration*, "show a kind of frontier interest, an emphasis on the 'growing edge' of man's aspirations, discoveries, and enterprises" (32).

Frontier-oriented pages in the Ginn Basic Reading Program Junior High School series (comprising *Discovery through Reading*, *Exploration through Reading*, and *Achievement through Reading*), along with recommended books, constitute one-fourth of the overall reading for the set (Tucker 1980, 35). This set enjoyed wide popularity in the United States between the years 1938 and 1960 without any radical alteration of their concept or content. Tucker includes in his study extensive tables and charts that indicate the attention to and emphasis on discovery and exploration, colonial history, territorial expansion, and inventions, particularly in texts after 1915 (1980, 35–41). He also demonstrates the attitudes to other peoples that emerge from some of these texts, widely used throughout the school system in the United States. For instance, Augustus S. Mitchell's *A System of Modern Geography* (1840) states categorically that the European or Caucasian is "the most noble of the five races of man" and attributes to them the "most valuable institutions of society" (Tucker 1980, 39–40). Jedidiah Morse, in a book published in 1800, described Islam as a "contagion" and called Mohammed a "deceitful hypocrite," while D. M. Warren terms him a "false prophet," in his work published in 1872. Nathaniel Dwight in 1806 used the description "a pack of thieves" to refer to the Arabs (Tucker 1980, 40). Almost two centuries later, Pat Robertson and Jerry Falwell continue in this tradition, accusing the prophet of being a pedophile (because of the pubescence of one of his wives) and a terrorist. Lt. Gen. William G. Boykin, as we saw earlier, likened Islam to idol worship and, on another occasion, said that the U.S. war on terror was a fight "with Satan." The more things change, the more they remain the same. Much more recent studies of textbooks offer ample evidence that such recidivist thinking still exists, and a disastrous event, such as that of September 11, 2001, pushes many of us back to the ignorant characterizations of earlier times.

Even in newer, more enlightened textbooks, European nations and the United States are generally credited with almost all major inventions and discoveries, while the contributions of other cultures are relegated to prehistory or the ancient cultures section, if they are mentioned at all. Is it any wonder, then, that "primitive," "barbaric," and "savage" are words consistently chosen to describe the actions of those with whom the United States may be in opposition at any given time? When the historical figures of American history are set forth as natural-born leaders: rugged, enterprising, valorous, determined, but the same qualities in the leaders of other nations are differently interpreted as bloodthirsty or cruel, is it any wonder that the founding of the American state has developed into something of a creation myth? Historians Joyce Appleby, Lynn Hunt, and Margaret Jacob write in *Telling the Truth about History*:

> At the center, then, of American history was an undersocialized, individualistic concept of human nature set in an overdetermined story of progress. Deeply etched into the collective imagination, this history distributed social merit and public attention—and through them political authority. Shoring up the frail unity of thirteen rebelling colonies, it assumed the absolutist character of a mythic tale of origins for a mighty industrial nation. (125)

People in other countries often identify the characteristics of the American West with the characteristics of the United States as a whole and fuse the persona of the cowboy with that of the American in general. Many years ago, my father returned from an extended trip to the United States where the Indian government, for which he worked, had sent him. He brought back cowboy outfits for my two brothers and, for me, a cowgirl outfit. No one had to tell us, all below the age of ten at the time and living on the other side of the world in the tropical city of Madras, about Roy Rogers and Dale Evans. For us they signified the United States in much the same way as a snake charmer would have signified India for American children. We donned these outfits at the next costume party, or fancy dress party as we called it. The pictures survive in my album to this day.

The American West and the rich progeny of African American culture—spirituals, soul, gospel, blues, jazz, hip-hop, and so forth—have differentiated the United States from its cultural mother continent of Europe. American writers first disseminated the stories of the American West and embedded them in the popular imagination, but it was Hollywood filmmakers who spread those stories throughout the world:

> American writers made the settler families of the land west of the Appalachian Mountains the carriers of a new and vibrantly democratic civilization. They were never depicted as invaders even though blood was always spilled in violent contestation with the Indians before any territory was opened up for settler occupation. The iconography and literature of the westward movement instead evoked a peaceful tableau in which the sunburned and hardy pioneer father

walked beside his Conestoga wagon, Bible in his hand, his rifle at the ready should any hostile force attempt to repel his "castle on wheels." The history of these migrations served both American democracy and American nationalism, the former by celebrating the courage and fortitude of ordinary white citizens and the latter by justifying the seizure of territory long occupied by native Americans. (Appleby, Hunt, and Jacob 1994, 115)

It is exactly this—the courage and fortitude of ordinary people—that is celebrated in the novels of Maud Diver, Flora Annie Steel, Ethel M. Dell, Rudyard Kipling, and other writers of the British Empire.

American adventure stories stem from this tradition, the tradition of boys' reading, a tradition that comprises some of the best-loved classics of English literature, among them *Robinson Crusoe, The Pilgrim's Progress, Gulliver's Travels, Treasure Island*, and others. The stories studied in this chapter are, however, more in the tradition of R. M. Ballantyne and G. A. Henty, in intention if not in style. As Martin Green points out in *Seven Types of Adventure Tale*, adventure stories prepared boys for the life of men just as romances prepared girls for the life of women (1991, 42). It is no accident that adventure stories "follow the flag," their popularity flanking the progress of empire builders or pioneers. Though adventure stories can be disguised or dressed up as biography or climbing narratives, explorer books, war stories, and so on, as Green points out (1991, 38), the adventure stories written primarily for boys are unabashedly jingoistic in tone and didactic in purpose. Their primary purpose is to promote the pioneering spirit or empire-building spirit, as the case may be. In that sense, they are all about character.

The American West caught the imagination of the writers and readers of American adventure stories in much the same way as the North West Frontier region of the Indian subcontinent or the Arabian Desert did for their British counterparts. In "Domesticating the Frontier: Gender, Empire and Adventure Landscapes in British Cinema 1945–59," Wendy Webster quotes Jeffrey Richards, who notes that in "Lives of a Bengal Lancer" (1935) Gary Cooper replaced an English actor who was the original choice and was advised to think of the film as a western set in India (2003, 97). Similarly, in the film *North West Frontier*, the train replaces the stagecoach as hordes of "Indians" descend to attack it and are warded off. The director was an Englishman who moved to Hollywood in the early 1960s. At times, the pull of the West was irresistible. Martin Green comments that James Fenimore Cooper, one of America's most accomplished practitioners of this genre, would have preferred to see the United States turn its attention to the east, toward the ocean and Europe, rather than to the west, toward continental empire because "the drive west meant both the slaughtering of Indians and releasing the antinomian forces in American society. Both those ideas were repugnant to Cooper. But the public welcomed his Natty Bumpoo stories with such enthusiasm that he was induced to write more of them, and so help fuel the drive to empire" (1991, 114).

Appleby, Hunt, and Jacob see the idea of "*Homo faber*, man the doer, whose activities in the world are enlarged by a generous nature" as a new model of human behavior (1994, 111). But it was more an adapted model than a new one. The British perfected the art of mitigating the more egregious aspects of empire through moralizing, through insisting upon what the above historians call "the productive ideal, investing the unceasing doing and making of things with transcendent value" (Appleby, Hunt, and Jacob 1994, 111). But whereas land, as Appleby et al. point out, became the means for this achievement for the pioneers, it was not the land itself but the control of the land that mattered most for the empire builders.

The similarity in values or self-concept on both sides of the Atlantic should come as no surprise for, as Appleby et al. point out, "the new American nation was an alien European outpost perched on the Atlantic shelf of a vast continent, its legal link to Great Britain severed by rebellion" (1994, 95). Rather than a radically different self-image, Americans developed a modified one, molded to their own unique circumstances: "Those who were liberated from America's traditional orientation to Europe were the ordinary men and women who sought affirmation of their tastes and values in the celebration of what was distinctively American: its institutional permissiveness, its pervasive practicality, its reforming zeal, above all its expanded scope for action for ordinary people" (Appleby, Hunt, and Jacob 1994, 99).

One has only to look around to see how pervasive the West still is in American life and lore. From films to children's games, team mascots to theme parks, cuisine to clothes, an arcane image of the American West still prevails despite revisions and updates. Tucker provides us with an exhaustive survey of Western culture: dramas, novels (including the famous dime novels), melodrama theater, Western shows (the most famous being Buffalo Bill's own Wild West Show), magazines, songs, serialized radio adventure programs, all of which perpetuated the glamour and the glory of the American West. Most significant, for this study, are the many serializations for young people. Not all were concerned with the West, but almost all sent a character westward in one or more volumes (Tucker 1980, 50). Here, too, there is a similarity with novels of empire, where characters were often sent out to the colonies. In more modern times, Zane Grey's and Larry McMurtry's Western novels, Hollywood westerns with icons such as John Wayne and Clint Eastwood, and TV shows such as *Gunsmoke*, *Bonanza*, and *Wyatt Earp* are still influential. Not all perpetuated the stereotypes or told only one part of the story. Tucker cites James Daugherty's *Daniel Boone*, for instance, as relating both the joyous and the grim aspects of frontier life and not downplaying the conflict with the Indians. The Clint Eastwood Westerns are not the morality tales that constitute most of the John Wayne films. The former reveal the underside of the Western myth and project its protagonist as an antihero. Samir Singh, a scholar of film and history, comments that Eastwood was in fact "inverting the traditional and romantic conceptions of heroism, morality, and existence" and "shattering and critiquing heroic conventions and expectations" (e-mail to the author, October 10, 2003). Most Westerns, however, tell a heroic story and at the center of all heroic stories is a hero or a heroic event, usually historical. Kit Carson, Billy the Kid, Wild Bill Hickok, and George Custer are the most celebrated, and they are celebrated not only for their deeds but also for their character, which, as a composite, became a virtual template for young boys.

In this chapter, I focus on a selection of adventure stories written in the 1940s and 1950s, intended for boys but quite likely read by girls as well. These are the types of books that Americans, including many leaders, who are now middle-aged or older, will have read as children in much the same way as so many well-known personalities on both sides of the Atlantic acknowledge reading and being greatly influenced by Henty's writings. In fact, as I read these books I was struck by their similarity to the works of Henty, Marryat, and other chroniclers of the heroic deeds of empire. They may lack their panache, many are quite pedestrian, but out of them all emerges an ideal of character that is quite evidently a received standard. This

There is little to distinguish one hero from another in terms of individual characteristics. We are meant to perceive character in this sense as a product of Western civilization, appropriated in the service of its expansion. It is a conception that owes a lot to Social Darwinism:

> Although Darwin referred to pigeons and not people when he used the word "race" in his title, others used his work to explain why Europeans colonized other parts of the world (they were the superior race), why war was good (the death of the loser was "natural"), and why Anglo-Saxons should form their own organizations to rule the world. Eighty years later, Nazi ideologists would construct a rationale for genocide out of the same themes. (Appleby, Hunt, and Jacob 1994, 69)

When people derive their ideas, their images, and their information from similar (if not the same) sources, they read or hear or tell the same stories, so they are likely to develop a sense of themselves and their communities that is based not so much on what they are but on who they are. Who they are then becomes a monolithic conception that does not reflect the diverse constitution of the community. The stories all become essentially the same story. Many of the stories are about deeds but deeds develop from character. Character then becomes one more construction, one more story that is based on perception and contingent upon the teller. Appleby, Hunt, and Jacob comment,

> When Americans began self-consciously constructing a national identity, they emphasized those American practices and values which distinguished their society from the mores and institutions of old-regime Europe. In doing so, they became partisans in the raging battles between the defenders of hierarchical tradition and the champions of radical reform. Since the Enlightenment ideals which Americans called upon were themselves the objects of a long and contentious struggle over the nature of truth, Americans found themselves locked into a way of seeing themselves which was strongly derivative of European cultural wars. (Appleby, Hunt, and Jacob 1994, 102)

It was a way for Americans to see themselves that was also strongly derivative of the European (specifically English) self-image, and boy's book after boy's book reveals this. It is a construction based on race, specifically on what the historian Ronald Takaki terms the "racialization of savagery" (1993, 24). The various peoples of the American continent were homogenized as "Indians" just as the settlers united under the white umbrella even though, like the "Indians," they came from a number of nations. Colonialism and conquest are contingent on the social constructions of racial identity and racial difference. In the United States of America, national identity was established, paradoxically, by political separation from England but also by racial unity with England and disconnection from the people of the American continent. The deterministic view of racial character then becomes one of the primary rationales for colonial expansion. According to Takaki, the social constructions of the terms "civilization" and "savagery" were developing in three sites—Ireland, Virginia, and New England (1993, 26). Those characteristics that conformed to the image of Indians as savage were stressed over those that suggested otherwise. For instance, prowess in hunting was stressed over prowess in farming or cultivation of crops. Takaki makes a crucial point when he indicates, "This social construction of race occurred within the economic context of competition over land. The colonists argued that entitlement to land required its utilization. Native men, they claimed, pursued 'no kind of labour but hunting, fishing and fowling.' Indians were not producers" (39). The nature of the encounter was not uniform, Takaki tells us. In Virginia, cultural causes were ascribed to what was perceived as Indian savagery, while in New England it was racialized, Indians signifying a demonic race who "personified the Devil and everything the Puritans feared—the body, sexuality, laziness, sin, and the loss of self-control" (43).

In *Daniel Boone: Boy Hunter* (1943) by Augusta Stevenson, the young Daniel befriends an Indian boy about his age, a boy called Wolf, who is described as tall, slender, and handsome. Wolf is friendly and they sport together. That evening Daniel talks excitedly about Wolf to his parents. In fact, he cannot talk about anything else but how smart and friendly Wolf is. Mr. Boone points out that it is not surprising that he would be friendly since he belongs to the Delaware tribe, a tribe that had always treated the white settlers well. When his brother offers to take Daniel to Wolf's village, his mother remonstrates that Daniel does not yet know Wolf well enough to visit. "Why, I know him now, Mother," Daniel protests. "He's just like Henry and the other boys I play with. I can't see a bit of difference." But his mother's reply is swift and sure: "There is a difference and thee will find it out in time" (65).

When Daniel claims to like the Indians' color, his family chuckles good humoredly and when he says "I wouldn't care if I were red," his brother teases him "You'll turn into an Indian if you don't watch out," while his sister adds "Seems to me his skin is a little red now" (102). Of course, friendly tribes such as the Delaware are portrayed in a much more benign fashion than "strange Indians," but the racial difference remains ineffaceable, as Daniel's mother points out. Sure enough, Wolf's true colors emerge when he loses a foot race to Daniel. Wolf's dark eyes glitter with hate and he shakes his tomahawk at him. On a subsequent occasion, Daniel has to let Wolf win a race before peace is restored. Daniel learns his lesson about Indians. When Pete McGuire, a member of his community who "understands" Indians, comments, "Well, you boys learned some more about Indians today," Daniel replies "I did. . . . I learned that I'd rather play with Henry and Ned and the other boys. They don't get jealous" (122). What Daniel learns is that character is racially determined.

Pete offers the reader a glimpse into the Indians' psyche, pointing out that they could hardly enjoy the sight of hundreds of white men in their forests, or looking at clearings and farms and cabins where they once hunted. "Do you think they love us when they have to trudge twenty miles or more to find a deer?" he asks. Indians who come to save them from an attack are "splendid Indians" (85). Those who attack are "fierce savages" (84). But even the splendid Indians are patronized, with Mr. McGuire assuring his community that nothing would please the Indians more than a feast (85). Much later in the novel, the governor of Virginia warns that he has bad news, that the Indians are rising up, determined to drive white men out of the country. Many tribes have united, even those that were bitter enemies, resulting in thousands of Indian warriors on the warpath, ready to attack.

The news goes out that a scout has been sent to warn the surveyors who are hard at work, since so many new settlers want to buy land along the Ohio. This scout is none other than Daniel Boone, for "no one knows the Indians better" (176). Daniel, we are told, "knows all their tricks" and has a few of his own (176). Later Daniel tells the governor that he has studied Indians for more than thirty years, learning their language and hunting, fishing, and trapping with them. He has been a prisoner in a Cherokee village, he informs the governor, and has had Indians for friends. Not one has ever been disloyal to him, he claims. Whereupon the governor replies, "Why, you surprise me, Mr. Boone. . . . You seem to think well of them" (183). The governor then comments that he is sorry that Boone does not hate Indians because he was hoping that he would join the army that is being sent against them. In a display of disloyalty to a people who, by his own admission, have never been disloyal to him, Stevenson has Boone reply, "I have never said I would not fight them, Governor, for I would. They must be conquered. They must be driven out of this land" (183).

In *Lies My Teacher Told Me* (1995), James Loewen indicates that policymakers in the early nineteenth century used as "a rationale for removal" the notion that Native Americans stood in the way of progress (129). Boone echoes this sentiment in Stevenson's story when he adds, "If we do not conquer them, they will conquer us. America will again become a wilderness. There won't be a farm or a settlement anywhere" (Stevenson 1943, 183). This pronouncement is met with much approval from the group. Yet, a little later we are told that Daniel felt crowded when too many settlers moved near. He said he couldn't breathe close to towns and settlements. The contradiction is left unresolved. At the very end of the book, we see a somewhat domesticated Daniel in "a homemade suit of cotton, leather shoes and his new broad-brimmed hat of black felt" and are told that he was very neat and trim. A preacher tells a crowd waiting to see him that Daniel Boone "helped to make America a great and strong country. . . . He, and he alone, opened the door to these rich valleys and plains beyond the mountains. He led the way. Thousands followed him" (192).

Of course, the frontier did not fall far to the west at that point in time. The farm where Daniel Boone grew up was on the edge of the Pennsylvania wilderness in the little settlement of Exeter. But it was a lonely situation with no other cabin within a mile or any other farm or clearing near it (Stevenson 1943, 27). Buffalo Bill was born on the frontier in Iowa and moved to a town on the Missouri River on the Missouri side. As Loewen points out, "Calling the area beyond secure European control 'frontier' or 'wilderness' makes it subtly alien. Such a viewpoint is intrinsically Eurocentric and marginalizes the actions of non-urban people, both Native and non-Native" (1995, 108). But what came to be described as the frontier spirit was already rising in Daniel and his brothers. "It would take more than a dark forest to frighten those strong frontier boys" (Stevenson 1943, 27–28). Farming, hunting, trapping, and fighting are among the activities the boys participate in, activities that make them hardy and brave. A boy cannot go after the cows until he knows his directions, for if he should get lost he might never see his home again unless found by a search party. Daniel is taught to point to the north after being blindfolded and turned around three times. Hunting is another activity that demands courage, but although frontier boys consider it fun to hunt they never hunt for fun (146).

Frontier boys have to know how to hide from savages, for while they may be at peace with the Indians today, no one knows what will happen the next day (38). When Daniel's mother expresses her concern about Daniel's spelling, his father, who is the squire, scoffs at her, retorting, "He's not going to live in some safe little settlement. . . . He's going to be out in the woods with wildcats, wolves and bears. He's learning ways to protect his life. And spelling isn't one of them" (158). Daniel may not read his schoolbooks very well but he can read books that many a college professor cannot. "Listen to the names of them," his father exhorts. "Tracking. Sounds. Signs. Calls. Directions. Winds. Clouds. Hiding. Throwing. Aiming. Sighting. Shooting. Range. Plants. Poisons. Medicine. Indians. Animals and a dozen others" (159). Daniel knows them by heart. As in English school stories, we see the privileging of physical prowess over book learning. The squire resolves that the girls should do the spelling, but Daniel will do the hunting.

We get but a glimpse of native cultures in this book—Wolf is briefly humanized as Daniel's playmate but then dismissed as untrustworthy. References are made throughout to savage Indians, bearing out Loewen's point that when white Americans were dispossessing the Indians of their land, they justified their actions shrilly, denouncing native cultures as primitive, savage, and nomadic. Stereotypes of their stealth, their cunning, their acuity, and their capacity for cruelty had been exported across the Atlantic, as we see from this description in *Peter Pan*: "On the trail of the pirates, stealing noiselessly down the war-path, which is not visible to inexperienced eyes, come the redskins, every one of them with his eyes peeled. They carry tomahawks and knives, and their naked bodies gleam with paint and oil. Strung around them are scalps, of boys as well as of pirates, for these are the Piccaninny tribe, and not to be confused with the softer-hearted Delawares or the Hurons" (Barrie 1928, 985).

Writers often invoked the blessings of God, who was reputed to favor those who "did more" with the land, Loewen tells us. In the essay "Indians" referred to in the prologue, Jane Tompkins writes,

> My research began with Perry Miller. Early in the preface to *Errand into the Wilderness*, while explaining how he came to write his history of the New England mind, Miller writes a sentence that stopped me dead. He says that what fascinated him as a young man about his country's history was "the massive narrative of the movement of European culture into the vacant wilderness of America." "Vacant?" Miller, writing in 1956, doesn't pause over the word "vacant," but to people who read his preface thirty years later, the word is shocking. In what circumstances could someone proposing to write a history of colonial New England *not* take account of the Indian presence there? (Gates 1985, 61)

In the foreword to his book *Buffalo Bill*, written in 1943, Frank Lee Beals, who was (significantly enough) the assistant superintendent of the Chicago schools, states,

> The story of the winning of the West is one of the most thrilling chapters in the history of our country. It is a story of the plains, filled with the courageous deeds of gallant men and women. One of the colorful figures among those who helped push our civilization westward over the plains was William Frederick Cody, better known and loved as "Buffalo Bill." This story of his adventurous life was written to give young Americans some idea of how much they owe to those who helped lay the foundations of this great country of ours. It is also hoped that it will serve to keep alive the name and fame of "the last of the great scouts." (Beals 1943b, n.p.)

Bill Cody, as Beals portrays him, shares many traits with the Daniel Boone of Stevenson's portrayal. They share an eagerness for adventure and an enjoyment of the outdoors. Both become loyal, steadfast, and courageous scouts. Beals sums it up thus: "Buffalo Bill, the last of the great scouts, is at rest in the West that he loves so well. His spirit looks out over the trails he once rode and over the plains he helped make safe for the settlers of a growing nation. He had the courage of a scout, the vision of a pioneer, and the faith of a loyal American" (1943b, 251).

Buffalo Bill's love of the West is referenced frequently. He is described as "the young hero of a sturdy, growing nation" (211) who wants to do his share in building the West. Thus, the actions and adventures of these western heroes are always contextualized as part of the process of nation building and the cause of progress. Buffalo Bill's courage is contrasted with the cowardice of the Indians that the reader witnesses right in the opening pages of the book. As young Billy begs his uncle to give him a job with a wagon train and his uncle, Alec Majors, finally agrees, the door to his office bursts open and a scout rushes into the room, buckskin clothes torn and stained with blood. Majors jumps to his feet and asks what happened. "Indians!" the scout replies. "Surprise attack—no chance to defend ourselves—all the men were killed—wagons burned—animals driven off. Our outfit was completely wiped out" (6). The animals and wagons can be replaced, Majors mourns, "but we cannot replace such men" and he acknowledges the good fight that the scout assures him they put up (7).

The men of the wagon train sing a song about "the savage to affright" (22). Indians are frequently yelling, racing, or sweeping down in these books. To be fair to Beals, we are occasionally given snapshots of the Indian side of things: "White man shoot our buffalo, take our land, and kill our people," says Yellow Hand, one of their great warriors and chiefs. Elsewhere in the story, Buffalo Bill acknowledges, "I know how dearly they love their tribal lands, and I understand their bitter feeling against the white men who would take those lands away from them" (214). Augusta Stevenson in *Buffalo Bill: Boy of the Plains* (1948) also offers sympathetic portraits of Indians, showing us friendly young braves who have a sense of humor, caring boys who show a deep concern for Bill's health when he is down with the measles, and families who "act just as white people do when they are at home," as Bill tells Kit Carson, somewhat surprised. Bill adds, "The chief plays with Wren just as my father played with me. He jokes, too" (Stevenson 1948, 141). Elsewhere, Bill comments on the good manners of his young Indian friends, for

"Bill had learned a good deal about Indian politeness" (81), having accepted his friends' hospitality from time to time. We learn that Indians don't hunt for fun, only when they need food (50).

Stevenson also depicts outlaws, horse thieves, aggressive homesteaders, and other white men who are "just as bad as Indians" (122). In fact, Bill's father remarks that he'd rather trust the Kickapoos than his malicious neighbor and his crowd (20). When, in Beals' account, an army officer tells him that they need more troops in the West to keep the Indians quiet, because they seem to be forgetting the treaty they made with the white men, Bill immediately remonstrates "The white men are the ones who are breaking the treaty. . . . It must be stopped at once. If it is not, we cannot blame the Indians for going on the warpath this time" (Beals 1943b, 226). The officer asks Bill if he is defending the Indians, and Bill replies: "I am sorry for them. . . . They are determined to hold what little land they can still call their own. They must be protected from the greedy settlers who are slipping into their reservation and grabbing their land. If we can't stop the land-grabbers we are in for a great deal of trouble" (227).

In yet another account of Buffalo Bill's life, *The Story of Buffalo Bill* (1952) by Edmund Collier, we are told very specifically why the advent of settlers in greater and greater numbers troubled the Indians. We are told that the coming of the white men meant the end of the buffalo, which provided the red men with almost everything they used: meat, robes, blankets, tepees and bows. Collier adds,

> Without the buffalo, the age-old Indian way of life would end. Some of the Indians had tried to be peaceful. But some of the white men had broken treaties and raided Indian villages, killing all the braves, squaws, and papooses.
> At last even the peaceful Indians had begun to fight back. They had attacked wagon trains. They had killed men working on the railroads. They had raided settlements. (Collier 1952, 147)

Collier also depicts Issac Cody, Bill's father, as angry that a family with many slaves had bought land near his and aimed to use slave labor to farm it, all because men from Missouri rode across and voted even though they had no right to do so. They used guns and a cannon to back their actions. He tells his wife, "This is supposed to be a democracy. But if men can back up their votes with guns and cannon, we don't have democracy" (91).

The overall perception of white people as civilized, ordered, progressive, and generally good in spite of greedy elements among them ensures that such asides don't make much of a dent. For example, later in the book, Collier completely neutralizes the effect of his little lesson on the justice of Indian retaliation when he tells us that the frontier "was tamed." The railroads had been built across the country, the buffalo were almost all exterminated. The fact that Buffalo Bill Cody earned his name by personally eliminating, on his own count, 4,280 buffalo goes unmentioned (Brown 1994, 273). The Indians could no longer be considered a threat (164). The Indian was, however, differentiated from the Negro in one very important respect: his love of freedom and relationship to nature. It was well understood that he abhorred forced servitude whereas the Negro was often considered a natural servant who was happy serving a white Christian master. As long as the master treated him kindly and fairly, he was assured of the Negro's loyalty and obedience (see Davis 1966, 176). Similarly, early accounts of the people of the New World veered between noble savages and ferocious cannibals.

In any story, point of view is what establishes the perspective, and we are always told about the Indians from the white person's point of view, in the white person's voice. We are not allowed to identify with them as people or as individuals, enter their homes or participate in their family lives as we do with the pioneers or settlers. The average American reader will feel estranged from even the "good Indians" by the frequent references to war drums, smoke signals, painted faces, whoops and bonnets, scalping, shadowy presences, surprise attacks, and savagery. Even books for very young readers, books that are just beyond picture books, carry references to "red rascals" as in *Jerry and the Pony Express* by Sanford Tousey, published in 1936. Jerry's horse, Bolivar, "had smelled Indians before, and did not like them." Even when they seem friendly enough, Jerry is cautious and takes no chances as he "had seen the damage their arrows could do to a rider." In Collier's book, Bill points out Plum Creek as the place where he killed his first Indian, much as people point out where they killed their first deer or shot their first duck. Indian communication consists mostly of ughs, grunts, hisses, signals, and "Hows." Stevenson lumps all Indian vernaculars together in a generic "Indian language" (1943, 52). References to "Indian trouble" or Indians as horse thieves or categorizing Indians with outlaws and blizzards as among the dangers of the road further alienate the reader and preclude identification. The risk of alienation is even greater when the reader is a young child.

At the end of each chapter, Beals includes a set of questions. Almost all concern white people, or if the question is about an Indian, it is only in reference to his relationship with white people. For example, "Who was the Indian chief who spared Bill's life?" (1943b, 99). It is the Indians who begin the wars, and it is the Indians who, when their power has been broken, beg for peace (245). Beals tells of the signing of a peace treaty awarding the Indians a large tract of land in what is now the state of South Dakota and the right to hunt on land farther west. One of the provisions of the treaty is that no white people will be allowed to enter the lands given to the Indians. Of course, we are not told about the quality of the lands or the losses of the Indians. The treaty is made to sound generous and benevolent. But although the Indian war drums were now silent, "the people who lived in the west knew that danger was not gone from the plains. They knew that the Indians still hated the whites and that roving bands of braves would quickly take advantage of any opportunity to steal or to kill" (223). Indians pose the threat, not those who denied them their rights or appropriated their lands.

Almost every book claims that Indians are untrustworthy and impede progress. Augusta Stevenson recounts how Chief Rain-in-the-Face, whose son, Little Wren, Bill has saved from drowning, does not seem to recognize Bill or to remember his own promise never to forget Bill's act. Bill then remembers Kit Carson's words in regard to Indians: "Your friends will become your enemies" (1948, 158). At the end of the book, we see a large crowd awaiting the train from the east and the transport of the mail to the far west by Pony Express riders. They joke about the Plains tribes' resistance to the Pony Express. Perhaps they expect whites also to communicate through smoke signals. But then a fur trader puts a brake on their hilarity with this serious explanation of the Indians' resistance: "I can tell you why they are angry. They don't want iron tracks across their grazing land. Nor iron horses rushing through their forests and scaring the game away." The teacher adds, "Nor do they want schoolhouses and colleges. . . . Indians must change their ideas." The minister concurs, "They must become farmers and raise their meat instead of hunting it." The fur trader concludes, "Well, they haven't changed their ideas yet. . . . They will make it hot for those Pony Express riders. I'd hate to be one of them" (Stevenson 1948, 167).

The picture that we are left with following the flight of Sitting Bull and his followers to Canada is one of progress: "The next few years brought many changes to the West. Cities and towns sprung up where once Indian villages had stood. Fields of grain grew on the old Indian hunting grounds. Railroads carried the freight once hauled by the wagon trains. Old stagecoaches no longer rattled over the trails and only a few herds of buffalo were left from the millions of buffalo that once roamed the plains" (Stevenson 1948, 246). Brown's historical account offers us the same picture but from a different perspective: "Most of the buffalo in the southland had already disappeared, and in the north they were fast becoming silent heaps for the bone wagons. There was no new place to go. The Black Hills were taken away, the last hunting grounds were a pathway for the new iron road. The Grandmother Land, Canada, whence Sitting Bull had fled, was poor refuge" (Brown 1994, 237).

The physical feature that Beals emphasizes in Buffalo Bill is his curly golden hair. This is a telling detail that reveals the lack of historicity in Beals' portrait and perhaps the internalized racial intent. According to noted Western historian, Richard Slotkin:

> He [Cody] had begun to "cultivate a resemblance to Custer, doffing his famous *vacquero* suit for fringed buckskins, high boots, and a broad-brimmed hat, like those worn by Custer in popular illustrations of the battle. He trimmed his long hair, beard, and mustache to resemble Custer's. The difference between his dark hair and Custer's famous "Long Yellow Hair" was not at all jarring in an age of black-and-white illustration and as Cody's hair became gray with age the difference disappeared. (1992, 77)

The golden curls that Beals emphasizes then becomes a signifier that permits the direct association of racial characteristics and character traits. This is akin to Enid Blyton's portrayal of villains as foreign looking and dark. In Augusta Stevenson's book, however, we find a more accurate representation when an Indian brave describes Bill as handsome, tall like an Indian, and with brown hair and brown eyes (1948, 33).

Billy, with his "quiet determined spirit" (Beals 1943b, 20) or his resolve to take good care of his mother and sisters, builds up our esteem for the character of white people as a whole. In Augusta Stevenson's portrait we see the young Bill as strong for his age, industrious, and capable. He has keen eyes and good manners, keeps his word, and is fair. He is patriotic. He has a way with horses, accurate aim, and a quick trigger finger (Stevenson 1948, 76–77). He is always vigilant, never off guard (76). "He's got the makings of a good plainsman," a soldier comments (59). His cousin Horace, who is teaching him to hunt and trap, sees him as another Kit Carson (63) and determines that he can ride like a Sioux Indian (78). His endurance and courage are unmatched. Even as a boy of fourteen, he makes the longest continuous horseback ride in history. He is a boy who is determined that he will not fail (Beals 1943b, 143). Over and over again, Stevenson applies the word "brave" to him and relates anecdotes that illustrate that bravery: Bill saving his father's life by warning him of an Indian attack or rescuing an Indian boy from the rapids.

When a woman wonders in regard to Bill how a boy of fourteen can be one of the Express Riders, a hunter answers "A boy that age is a man out here on the frontier. . . . You don't need to worry about Bill Cody. . . . He grew up on the trails to the Far West" (Stevenson 1948, 168). The future of the West depend upon such men, men like Bill and his Uncle Alec, who taught him how important it is for each man to do his share in this great work. Bill resolves he will continue to do his part. Such men are men of "courage, faith, and honor" (162). Temperament is indeed destiny. Bill Cody's Wild West Show was the spectacle that testified to that fact. It was to be the story of the dangers and hardships faced by the pioneers in their struggle against the Indians of the plains. It was to be the story of the "winning of the West" and "what the men of the West did to help build a nation" (Beals 1943b, 249). According to Beals' book, Bill gets the idea while reliving the old days on the plains. He recalls the long weary miles, the wonderful fellowship of the men, the songs and jokes, dangers and hardships, the stagecoach holdups (248). "Once again," Beals relates, "he saw the Indians hiding in ambush along the trails, the burning wagon trains, the buffalo stampedes, and outlaws lying in wait to hold up the 'Boys of the Pony'" (248–49). As he watches a stagecoach arrive rattling, with its galloping horses and sees the passengers alighting, he notices the driver throw the reins to the station agent. The driver steps down from his high seat and strides into the station followed by a group of excited boys. "The old

West," says Bill to himself, "The old wild West!" (249). Then he gets his idea, laughing to himself as he realizes that this is how he can help both the West and the East: "I'll take the West—my old wild West—to the East. I'll show the people in the East what the men of the West did to help build the nation" (249).

What Cody actually showed, according to Richard Slotkin, was both a pictorial and a moral truth. While he sought accuracy, he also sought a good show. His reenactment of "Custer's Last Fight," Slotkin tells us, was intended to suggest that he might have saved Custer had he arrived in time, thereby boosting his own status as a hero. The only trouble was, Cody was not involved with that battle-field and was not concerned with Custer's column until later (Slotkin 1992, 76). The "moral truth" of Cody's Wild West production, Slotkin states, was "its exemplification of the principle that violence and savage war were the necessary instruments of American progress" (77). Slotkin does note, however, "the care and considera-tion with which Cody treated his Indian performers and the wild animals used in the Wild West" (77).

Slotkin also notes that the "Custer's Last Fight" reenactment in the Wild West Show both looked back to the past nostalgically "as an elegy for the *entire* period of American pioneering" and to the fu-ture by presenting a parade of the "Congress of the Rough Riders of the World," with Native American tribesmen recently conquered by the imperial powers riding beside each American or European unit and Buffalo Bill at the head of the entire congress, signifying not only his personal preeminence, but that of the United States as well (79–80). The scene is described in Collier's account, and we can imagine young boys thrilling to it: "Then a single figure on a tall white horse came through the entrance. His long hair flowed over his shoulders. Mustache and goatee pointed up his face. He rode tall and straight, with the easy swing of a man who lives in the saddle. He guided the spirited horse to the center of the arena without ef-fort" (Collier 1952, 181).

Stevenson tells us "Mr. Cody made a wonderful picture when he led the parade riding his great white horse. The people went wild" (1948, 182). They also went wild when they saw him shoot, we are told. People wanted to know all about him (183). And, also according to Stevenson, everyone in London wanted to see the show. Queen Victoria saw it twice, the second time taking some three hundred guests comprising kings, queens, princes, or dukes and their families with her. General Sherman wrote to Colonel Cody, who cut a fine figure on the way home as he stood on the captain's bridge to greet the large crowd that had gathered to welcome him. Stevenson quotes Sherman as saying, "You have shown an important phase in our country's history. Without this, the plains would still be too dangerous to cross" (189).

The publicity for the Wild West Show, especially in later years, stressed more and more vigorously its educational mission, advertising it as "AN OBJECT LESSON" and as "a living monument of historic and educational magnificence" (Slotkin 1992, 82). If we note the adjectives that appear in this billboard, we find "brave," "noble," "bold," and "reckless," all requisite components of heroic character. Slotkin makes an extremely important point when he indicates the conflation of the frontier myth and the new ideology of imperialism. This was fully achieved in 1899 when "Custer's Last Fight" was replaced by the "Battle of San Juan Hill," celebrating the heroism of Theodore Roosevelt, whose First Volunteer Cavalry Regiment was, significantly enough, nicknamed "The Rough Riders" (Slotkin 1992, 82). "By incorporating Roosevelt into the Wild West," Slotkin states, "Cody would seem to have conferred the very honor Roosevelt sought through his energetic hunting, soldiering, and writing about the west: a place in the pantheon of frontier heroes whose founder is Daniel Boone and whose latest demigod is Buffalo Bill" (83).

The conflation, however, is not only with the new ideology of imperialism but clearly with the old one as well. The very same qualities of character that were celebrated on the American frontier were also celebrated on the frontiers of the British Empire, especially the "Wild West" of that region, the North West Frontier of the Indian subcontinent. Both were perceived as regions of rugged landscapes, continual skirmishes, intricate codes, and arcane cultures. Above all, both British colonizers and American settlers viewed themselves as engaged in a clash of civilizations. Kit Carson expounds on this in unambiguous terms in Beals' book: "We whites belong to another civilization. We are builders. The Indians are content to live as they have always lived. They have tried time and again to stop our march of progress, but they cannot do it" (Beals 1943b, 214). The practice and principles of the American frontier and the British Empire are strikingly similar. It comes as no surprise then that they celebrated similar characteristics in their heroes.

It is obvious from the inconsistent accounts of these heroes that the writers took ample liberty with historical detail, embellishing and adapting it to suit their own needs. Some accounts overlap, such as those of Bill's excitement upon first learning to write or his broken leg or his chance meeting with his cousin, Horace, who helped to train him. Others differ wildly: Chief Rain-in-the-Face's son is called Little Wren in Stevenson's book and Red Hawk in Beals'. Bill's sisters are variously named. Stevenson has Bill's father die because he caught cold from hiding from the nightriders. Collier's account is different, in that a supporter of slavery stabs Bill's father because of his public advocacy against slavery in Kansas. Weakened by the wound, he died from a cold two years later. The authors choose different episodes in Bill's life to describe. The disparities indicate that these accounts are not entirely historical. What is important is that they are presented as though they are, for generations of little boys read them in that spirit. Collier's book ends with a description of the Wild West Show and the very last line, one that follows an account of Buffalo Bill's deep voice soaring over the grandstands, is "A boy's dream had come true" (1952, 182).

Certainly, the accounts of the advent of white people and their relationship to those who already lived on the land are sugarcoated and even sentimentalized in these adventure stories. It is important to look at such accounts in any study of character, for how people perceive themselves is how they project themselves. A more accurate and truthful accounting of the relations between white people and Indians would hardly have served as exemplar for boys and girls. Historian James Loewen writes in *Lies My Teacher Told Me*:

> Similarly, textbooks give readers no clue as to what the zone of contact was like from the Native side. They emphasize Native Americans such as Squanto and Pocahontas, who sided with the invaders. And they invert the terms, picturing white aggressors as "settlers" and often showing Native settlers as aggressors. "The United States Department of Interior had tried to give each tribe both land and money," says *The American Way*, describing the U.S. policy of forcing tribes to cede most of their land and retreat to reservations. Whites were baffled by Native ingratitude at being "offered" this land, *Way* claims: "White Americans could not understand the Indians. To

them, owning land was a dream come true." In reality, whites of the time were hardly baffled. Even Gen. Philip Sheridan—who is notorious for having said, "The only good Indian is a dead Indian"—understood. "We took away their country and their means of support, and it was for this and against this they made war," he wrote. "Could anyone expect less?" (1995, 115–16)

Loewen is right about Squanto and Pocahontas. Many of the boys' adventure stories feature Squanto, and Disney has made Pocahontas a legend, especially among little girls. In A. M. Anderson's *Squanto and the Pilgrims,* published in 1949, and part of the American Adventure Series, Squanto is used as a mouthpiece for the author's impression of his own people. As the young Squanto asks his father when they will go on the warpath again, they begin to talk about the coming of the white men. When Squanto comments that they are strange people, his father replies, "Yes, but they are good to us. They come to our village to trade with us. We give them our furs and they give us presents" (Anderson 1949, 46). Squanto agrees with his father's portrayal, replying, "I like the white men. We always have a good time when they come to trade with us. I wish they would come to our village more often" (46). We see the white men welcomed enthusiastically by the braves when their ship sails in, while the white men return the greeting with friendly waves and cheers. Some congenial trading ensues and everyone is left happy. Colonists' journals tell a different story, however, one that includes theft and plunder on the part of the Pilgrims (Loewen 1995, 91).

In *Squanto: Friend of the White Man* (1954) by Clyde Robert Bulla, we do see that Squanto's mother is somewhat suspicious, but Squanto meets with nothing but kindness and generosity from the white people who befriend him and, after taking him on their ships as they trade, return to England with him: "He was happy that the people in London were so kind to him. He was happy to be in the land of the white men" (42). In this version, Squanto learns that there are white men of evil intention, but he tells the other captives, "All white men are not like Captain Hunt. . . . Many white men are good. I know because I lived among them" (63). In books about Native American boys like Squanto, Indian boys are allowed some of the same qualities as white ones. As Squanto and other young braves make ready for war, an old man bids him, "Be bold" while another says, "Watch and take care" (52). Bringing honor to his tribe is as important to Squanto as safeguarding the interests of his people would be to Buffalo Bill. Here again, we see white men who behave dishonorably and betray Squanto—not English in this case, but Spaniards. But such actions are linked to individuals not nations or they become dissipated in the big picture, the picture of Native Americans as savages, noble or otherwise, and white men as civilized. In the big picture, noble savages are still savages: sometimes malevolent, often unreliable, and mostly childlike, as in the scene where Anderson shows them "wild with fear," begging the white men not to shoot them and promising to be good (125). Or in the scene where the Puritan governor admonishes Myles Standish for being too aggressive. "We will be firm. We will also be gentle," he tells him (105).

Native Americans, as represented in these stories, are the quintessential "half-devil and half-child" of Kipling fame. In many books it is implied that Indians would do anything or give up anything for beads. But they are also capable of extreme savagery, as when news comes of English settlers in Virginia killed in the hundreds by Indians. Squanto hears Captain Standish "say something about savages who kill women and children" (Anderson 1949, 149). Such images tend to stick in children's minds, especially when reinforced by popular myth and legend or by facile representations in mixed media. The eulogy to Squanto with which the book ends states, "The Indians of Squanto's tribe had been proud and strong. Their war chiefs had known no fear. Bold had been their warriors. Mighty had been their hunters. All but one young brave have been forgotten. Only Squanto is still remembered. He was the good, true friend of the Pilgrims" (155). It is our tendency to associate these qualities specifically with Squanto. James Loewen points out that textbooks give only individual characters such as Squanto and Sacagawea individuality and agency (1995, 80). After all, Indians were perceived as part of the wilderness that the pioneers were struggling to transform into civilization. They blended with the landscape.

The chapter "A Treaty of Peace" (Anderson 1949) describes the coming of the Plymouth pilgrims; Plymouth stands in the very same spot where Squanto's village once stood. It was wiped out by some unnamed disease, according to this version, leaving not a single survivor, the convenient vacancy filled then by the new village of the Pilgrims who, kindly enough, offer Squanto a home where his home once was. Considering he was the only survivor of his tribe, it is not surprising, as Loewen points out, that Squanto threw in his lot with the Pilgrims (1995, 92). In Anderson's book, it is the great chief, Massasoit, who relates what had happened to Squanto's people and his: "Many moons ago a great sickness came to the land of the Indians. In every village there was sorrow. Many, many Indians died" (1949, 92). Massasoit continues, "Once I had many villages. Once more than thirty thousand people belonged to my tribe. Now there are little more than a thousand left. In many villages all the people died. Now the villages are silent" (92). Anderson tells the boys and girls reading this book that "quick, hot tears filled Squanto's eyes" as he realizes that this is why his village is silent. His people are dead, and he is the last of them. What they all fail to mention is what Loewen calls "the plague story" (1995, 92) was the depopulation of whole towns and the deaths of hundreds from diseases, most especially smallpox, unfamiliar to the land (86).

Squanto makes a rapid conversion to Christianity, promising to worship the Pilgrims' God for the rest of his life. From the portrait painted here, the pilgrims would appear to be patient, kindly folks, sometimes a little suspicious but certainly generous and grateful as the chapter "The First Thanksgiving" indicates. Loewen calls such versions "our national origin myth" and points out that "the archetypes associated with Thanksgiving—God on our side, civilization wrested from wilderness, order from disorder, through hard work and good Pilgrim character traits—continue to radiate from our history textbooks" (1995, 93). In Bulla's book as well, the Pilgrims are depicted as brave and friendly, the relations between them and Massasoit's people entirely congenial: "The Indians and white people knew that they were to be friends. They began to nod and smile at one another. They shook one another's hands" (1954, 99). We see how industrious and resolute the Pilgrims were, trusting in God even in the most adverse circumstances and sharing their meager rations with new arrivals. Appleby, Hunt, and Jacob (1994) comment,

> The United States could serve as an ideal for humanity only if human aspirations were funneled into the vessel labeled "autonomous,

hardworking, self-reliant man." Here becomes apparent the troubling contradiction in a history which glorified freedom and went on to assert that the only thing people were free to do was engage in relentless self-improvement. Through all these years while schoolchildren learned to celebrate their country's undoubted achievements, they were also conditioned to accept unquestioningly the implicit values of individual responsibility and decision-making. They were also taught to think within a cultural frame of reference that was predominantly male in gender, white in color, and Protestant in religious orientation. Making, doing, building, increasing, growing—these were compulsory virtues. (125)

These virtues are exemplified in books such as *Squanto and the Pilgrims*. Any suggestion that the Pilgrims return to England is met with resolve not to give up their freedom of worship. Of course, while we hear how the Puritans lacked this freedom in England, we do not hear anything about their denial of this very freedom to other religious groups: "The self-conscious crafters of American identity took great pride in religious freedom, but the colonial groups like the Puritans of New England openly embraced orthodoxy—banishing dissidents, whipping Baptists, even executing four Quakers" (Appleby, Hunt, and Jacob 1994, 106).

The self-conscious crafters of American character took special care to omit such details in children's books, just as their English counterparts had done on behalf of the Empire. After all, such details simply did not gel with the character they were attempting to construct for children. One must acknowledge, however, the existence of books that pay tribute to the nobility of Native Americans in their own right, not only because of the assistance they offered the settlers. Frank Lee Beals' *Chief Black Hawk* (1943), also part of the American Adventure Series and published in 1943, is one of them. In the foreword he writes,

> The story of the American Indians is a record of a brave, proud people. Their struggle to preserve their own way of life against the advancing civilization of the white man is tragic, but it is filled with deeds of high courage and patriotism.
>
> One of the most famous of all Indians was Black Hawk, war chief of the Sauk nation. He was loved by his followers, feared, but respected by his enemies, and misunderstood by the white man.

> It is hoped that this story of Black Hawk will help to bring back something of our early pioneer life and a better understanding of our American Indians. (1943a)

In spite of the somewhat proprietary tone, Beals really does mean to pay tribute to the heroism of the American Indians. He offers numerous accounts of their strength, exceptional courage, and tribal loyalty—all qualities much appreciated by the white man in his own character. We also hear of their honesty, how very few Indians ever stole from a cache of food that was not theirs, for instance (24). We hear how they were required to be trustworthy and honorable, to obey orders, and accept punishment and we hear that "a Sauk never lies" (49).

Beals also makes a significant statement when he shows the Shawnee Chief Tecumseh telling Black Hawk about the Louisiana Purchase and warning him that their lands will soon be settled by the white man and he and his people will be pushed toward the west (46). Black Hawk resists, telling Tecumseh that he will not lead his braves to war unless his lands are threatened, because he promised his people peace, and doubting that the white people will make war or take land from peaceful Indians. We then hear from Tecumseh this important proclamation: "I want to unite all of the Indian tribes. We have always fought each other. We must forget the past. We have a new enemy—the white man" (46). A white scout called Kilbourn expresses his gratitude to Black Hawk for saving his life by not betraying him. Later he muses, "I already sense the great love and devotion Black Hawk feels for his people and their lands. He is as much a patriot as I am" (81–82).

Some of the questions at the end of the chapter are hard questions: "Who had the right to sell the Sauk lands?" asks the fifth; "Why did Kilbourn call Black Hawk a patriot?" asks the ninth. One wonders how the children answered them. We see Black Hawk trying to unite the Indians to fight in order to reclaim the homelands that had been taken from them. After the war dance, he addresses his braves, tomahawk held high: "Sauk braves," he says, "for more than a hundred years we were a powerful, happy, and united nation. We had our homelands and our hunting grounds. We were feared and respected by other Indian tribes. Now we are a divided nation. Much of our glory is gone. All this has happened because the white men have taken our lands. I want to lead you back to Saukenuk. Let us unite and become the powerful nation that we were not so very long ago" (166).

Another Sauk chief, Keokuk, has a different perspective on the situation, arguing that the Indians are outnumbered and will not receive support from any quarter. "Someone has lied to you, Black Hawk. I beg of you, lead your people to peace. Do not lead them to war" (168). But it is unmistakably Black Hawk toward whom the reader's sympathy is directed as we are presented his point of view even in the conflict with the U.S. Army, a rare occurrence in such adventure stories. For instance, he sends a message with Kilbourn, whose life he spares once again, even though Kilbourn now fights against his people. The message is this:

> "Many years ago when you were my son I promised you that a Sauk would never harm you. I do not break a promise. When you return to your white war chief I want you to tell him that Black Hawk wanted to be a friend of the white people. They would not let him be a friend. They, not Black Hawk and his people, dug up the tomahawk. And tell your white chief," continued Black Hawk, "that I meant no harm to the palefaces when I returned to my village. Tell him that the Sauk flag-bearers were on their way to ask for peace." (190)

Of course, we do get into the good Indian/bad Indian situation when we see the Sauk chiefs telling their braves that if they have killed any white women and children, they are not Sauks and the braves replying that they had not—but the Potawatamie had. In fact, the Sauks save the lives of two young white girls that they had captured. Black Hawk puts these girls in the care of his wife and sends them safely back to their people. Later, when Black Hawk asks the trader, Davenport, to "tell the white people that I did not make war against their women and children" (249), Davenport replies, "The people of America already know that. . . . While you fought the white soldiers, many women and children were killed. But your braves did not murder them. They were killed by Indians, but not by your Sauk braves" (249).

In the end, the book leaves us with mixed feelings. Beals tells us, "Black Hawk was more than a war chief to the Sauks. He was their leader and protector. He fought to defend the homes and the lands of his people. He was defeated and put in chains. But high in the list of famous patriots is the name of Black Hawk, Indian Chief" (250). It is especially important that Beals terms him a patriot, as much a hero to his people as Andrew Jackson, who ordered Black Hawk finally free after he had been kept prisoner with his two sons in ball and chains. Children reading this book would certainly grieve for the chief who had to endure a dreary prison after having lived his entire life in the wilds. They would flinch at the description of the braves, weak from fatigue and hunger, trying desperately to swim to safety across the Mississippi ahead of the advancing soldiers, or of squaws tying their papooses to their backs and trying to swim across while horses plunge into the river with children fighting to hold on to their backs. Or at this description: "The battleship 'Warrior' came nearer and nearer. Over the cries and shouts of the people the boom of the ship's cannon thundered. Many of the fleeing people were killed. The muddy Mississippi water flowed red" (229).

The prevailing impression is of a noble chief who fought bravely to defend and protect his people and to reclaim their lands, but whose time is over. Black Chief is urged by his white friends not to look back. "You and your people must look toward the future," Davenport tells him. And the future, as Beals reveals it at the end of the book, is positive and progressive. The orders of President Jackson, in regard to Black Hawk, his sons, and the two other Sauk chiefs who had been imprisoned, read "First take them to our cities in the East. After they see our country they will know we have many white men who will fight to protect their people. Then we can all live in peace" (243). His people are busy, Davenport informs him, and only awaiting his return to be happy. At last, Black Hawk accepts the changed times and prays to the Great Spirit to "teach the white men to love the old Sauk lands. Guide me and my people to a new life. Bring peace to all" (248).

A peaceful picture is indeed what we are left with: "Black Hawk and his followers brought their choicest furs to him each spring. The Sauk's cornfields were fertile. The people were no longer hungry and ragged. 'My people are happy," Black Hawk said to Davenport. 'We are as happy as we can be away from Saukenuk'" (249). In the end, then, Black Hawk articulates the white man's vision, which was to cultivate the land and domesticate the wilderness of which Black Hawk and his people were a part. "The colonizing imagination," comments David Spurr in *The Rhetoric of Empire*, "takes for granted that the land and its resources belong to those who are best able to exploit them according to the values of a Western commercial and industrial system" (1993, 31).

The importance of Beals' dignified and fair portrait should not be underrated. It was a rarity for its time. He pays this touching tribute toward the end of the book: "And this heritage of courage, pride, and dignity is found in the Indians of today. Their love and devotion to their past cannot be misunderstood. Their love and devotion to the ideals of freedom and democracy cannot be questioned" (251). But what we are ultimately left with is a tragedy of history—two peoples each wanting the same thing. Beals leaves us with a nice show of unity. He tells how only a short time back he heard that an old Indian chief called his braves to defend their country, which is in danger, and to rally around the flag they love, which calls for their help. "Go, my braves," Beals quotes him as saying, "and defend with your lives the freedom of our country. Fight beside your white brothers. Point your guns with theirs. Your flag—my flag—our flag will not come down. Go, my braves, and return victorious!" (251). Of course this show of patriotism is understandable in light of the fact that the book was published in the middle of the Second World War.

Augusta Stevenson's *Tecumseh: Shawnee Boy* (1955) also endeavors to tell a tale from the perspective of Native Americans but with far less conviction. Although we do come to know of Tecumseh's bravery, the book is really meant to showcase Daniel Boone rather than Tecumseh. According to this account, Tecumseh saves Daniel when the Shawnee take him captive. When he confides in his sister that he will not tell on Daniel, she retorts, "Why not? All white men are our enemies" (99). "He isn't," says Tecumseh in response, referring to Boone. "He is good and kind. All the boys like him. He likes us too" (99). Earlier, we're told that Daniel had hunted and trapped with three Shawnee hunters one winter and lived in the same hut with them like brothers. The hunters had taken a liking to him.

An entire chapter is devoted to the dissent within Tecumseh's tribe over what to do about the loss of their lands to the white folks, with some warriors advocating war and others peace, some advocating moving towards the Great Plains out to Missouri and others staying and fighting. The dialogue is somewhat stilted and devoid of emotional intensity. It is hard to feel moved and swayed by

"Brothers, we must fight the white men! . . . Shall we stand by like children while they take our land? Shall we let them push us out?" (126). But we see Tecumseh's strength and courage in retrieving a sacred doeskin shirt that his sister had been making for him and the treachery of the white traders who took it. We hear his father's pride when he declares "that boy has enough courage for three warriors" (162). Chief Black Fish commends Tecumseh with words very similar to those that have been used in reference to Daniel Boone, Buffalo Bill, and other frontier heroes. He praises the boy's courage in tracking the traders, his common sense in walking home instead of paddling upstream, his hunter's knowledge in finding ways to keep alive in the forest, his education for knowing which berries and plants were safe to eat, and his skill with his weapons. "You should become a great hunter when you have reached the age of manhood," the chief predicts. "You will bring much meat to your village. The same good judgment and common sense may in time make you a leader, even a chief. I am proud of you, little brother, and so is every Shawnee" (179).

The final chapter, "Tecumseh, Great Orator and Chief," offers a convincing if not compelling account of Tecumseh's attempt to unite the tribes and the failure of his efforts. In it we are told that, in 1809, the commander of the U.S. troops in Vincennes became alarmed because he feared an Indian uprising, an uprising not of one tribe alone but of all the tribes in the Northwest Territory. He sends two spies to listen to one of the long speeches Tecumseh is reputed to be making, speeches that excite the other chiefs. Stevenson records for us her version of one of these speeches and it is a dramatic one:

> Brothers, once there was not a white man in all this country. Then it all belonged to the red men. Then we were a happy people. But now all is different. White men came to our lands, a few at first, and our fathers treated them as friends. Then many came. Now they are like the leaves on a tree—they cannot be counted. Brothers, they have seized much of our land by trickery. They bought it from men who had no right to sell. All of the tribes' chiefs had not consented. And the white men knew it. They took advantage of our ignorance. They paid for our forests with beads! (1955, 183)

Some "angry mutterings" ensue and Tecumseh continues,

Brothers, they have driven us from the great salt water. They have forced us over the mountains. They will push us into these lakes unless we stop them. They are greedy for land. Brothers, we must stop them! But one tribe cannot do it. There are too many of these palefaces. It will take all the tribes of this Northwest Territory. And also the tribes beyond the Mississippi, even to the Gulf of Mexico. They must unite, for this will give them power. Then let the whites have their seventeen "states." We will have an Indian state. And it will be larger than all of theirs together. It will extend from the Great Lakes to the Gulf of Mexico. And from the Ohio to the Mississippi and beyond. We will make our own laws and lead our own lives. Then the white men cannot trouble us, for they will not enter our state. There will be no quarrels then over game and fish. The races will be separated by water. (183–84)

The book ends with Tecumseh's disappointment when only a few chiefs appear to support an Indian state. To Stevenson's credit, she doesn't end with any scenes of progress or jingoistic sentiments, but with Tecumseh's resolution to keep working for an Indian state until the day he dies (192).

Far more typical than Stevenson's fair account of Tecumseh's cause or Beals' sensitive and sympathetic portrait of Black Hawk, his people and cause, is *Jim Bridger: Mountain Boy* (1955) by Gertrude Hecker Winders. The inscription transcribed at the end of the book notes that Bridger was celebrated as a hunter, trapper, fur trader, and guide. He "discovered" a number of sites, including the Great Salt Lake and the South Pass in the Rockies. He was also in charge of the survey for the Union Pacific Railroad. The archetypal mountain man, the book describes his childhood and subsequent exploits as an adult. Our first introduction to Native Americans in this story, published in 1955, is to "Redskins" who are on the warpath. They are but part of the landscape, the flora and fauna of the West: "'The West!' Jim forgot all about the war. Living in the West would be a million times more fun than fighting. He thought of setting his traps in mountain streams full of beaver. He thought of ell, Indians, buffalo, strange rivers, new mountains—especially the mountains, so high that snow stayed on them even in summer. He was so excited he felt choked. All he could say was, 'The West!'" (60).

Indians are no more than caricatures here and are often referred to as savages. When Jim's father comments that he had heard that in

Cincinnati there had not been trouble with Indians on the river for twenty years, one of the settlers replies, "We'll never be safe from Indians" (81). Jim loves to listen to tales of life "in the savage lands" (96). Vague reference is made to peace agreements with the Indians but there is no elaboration of or commentary on the issues involved.

There are some exceptions, but they are not especially significant. When a boy says, "I thought all Indians wanted to kill white people," Jim replies, "There are many good Indians . . . and many wise ones. If I had not learned from the Indians how to love the mountains, I'd have been dead long ago" (165). At one point, as he spends the night on the prairie, he concedes, "I know why the Indians hate the whites" (100). He realizes that "We spoil all this. Our cabins, fields and fences ruin the hunting and the camping grounds" (100). Jim thinks of all the new houses being built in St. Louis and comes to the conclusion that that part of the country is getting too crowded. The other characters often remark that Jim walks like an Indian, with a quick light step and holds himself straight like an Indian. Over and over again Jim's bravery is extolled. He is extremely observant, noticing and remembering everything, and never afraid of anything. It is significant that no mention is made of similar qualities in his childhood companion, Dan, "a Negro boy" (13). At the very end of the book, a Boy Scout is driving through Kansas City with his parents on their way to a tour of the West when he informs them that Jim Bridger is buried there, and he must visit the site because he promised his troop he would. He asks his father to read off all it says on the monument so that he can write it down for his troop at home. As he closes his notebook, when he's done transcribing the words, his mother exclaims, "What a lot the country owes Jim Bridger!" She adds "What a brave man he must have been!" (187). "And patient and hard-working." The boy's father responds, "To dream is one thing; to carry out a dream takes patience and energy as well as courage." The Boy Scout sums it up: "He had them all" (187).

Jim Bridger: Mountain Boy is part of the Childhood of Famous Americans Series. So is Augusta Stevenson's book on Tecumseh. In the publisher's list of titles, I counted only three on Native Americans until that point; the other two were on Sacagawea and Pocahontas, both considered friendly to white people. Titles about colonial and frontier heroes abound. In terms of sheer numbers, the positive portraits of white people would easily have overwhelmed those of Native Americans. Both books were published in the same year, 1955, yet Winders offers no explanation of why Indians were considered or called savages. There are no single quotation marks or authorial asides to explain that she is simply reflecting the perspective of the times. Just as in *The Secret Garden*, this lack of intervention suggests a collusion between the author's and the character's points of view.

There is also the question of identification. Which white American boy could resist the picture of Wild Bill Hickok painted by Stewart H. Holbrook in his book *Wild Bill Hickok Tames the West*? (1952). It is a picture of a fearless man who let his bright yellow hair ("auburn," according to Dee Brown [1994, 199]) grow long the way the Indians did, who wore his trademark white shirts with pleated fronts, and who carried a pair of ivory-handled revolvers. Holbrook tells an exciting tale of Hickok's various exploits and adventures. He had a way of getting out of desperate situations when there seemed no way out. In one he recovered from terrible injuries sustained from being severely mauled by a great grizzly that was crazed by the injuries inflicted upon it. When Bill killed the bear, it lay upon him until a freight wagon driver found him, barely breathing, on the Santa Fe Trail. He was bleeding from multiple wounds and his scalp was hanging down over his face. In another he is surrounded by two hundred or more Indian braves, leaps up on one of their horses, kills the rider, and urges the horse out of the circle before the Indians even realize what had happened. In yet another tight situation, when he has been spying for the Union forces during the Civil War, he is imprisoned by the Confederate Army and awaits execution at dawn. A terrible thunderstorm ensues; in the gleams of lightening he finds a common case knife, uses it to slay the guard, dons his clothing, and takes off through the woods.

After the Civil War, "the new land of promise was believed to be in the American West" (77). There, Hickok works as a scout for the famed General Custer and later with Buffalo Bill Cody. But what brought him his fame was his ability to tame the wild towns of the frontier and put fear into criminals. "With the Indians under control, at least for a time, the greatest danger to human life and property in the west was to come from dishonest and criminal white adventurers. These people were flocking to the new towns and giving the region its deserved name of the 'wild and woolly' west. Wild Bill was ready to change his career to meet the new conditions" (94). He was a sure shot, faster on the draw than anyone else was, even picking off one criminal behind his back without turning around by using the mirror before him to take aim. Wild Bill Hickok is the archetypal figure of the Old West: dashing, dangerous, and extremely exciting. But the book also tells us about his family's sympathy for escaped slaves. In fact, the book begins in his childhood home, which was a stop on the Underground Railroad. We are also told of his fascination with and knowledge of Indian customs and lore.

Another legend of the Old West is immortalized in Quentin Reynolds' *Custer's Last Stand* (1951). In this work we are again exposed to the good Indian/bad Indian conundrum. "There were certainly some bad Indians," we are told, "but there were many good Indians, too. The United States government had made many peace treaties with the Indians. Yet if one small band of outlaw Indians attacked a stagecoach or a settlement, the treaty was forgotten and the whole tribe condemned to death" (101). But we are also told that Autie, as Custer was nicknamed, became a general to fight Indians and that even as a child he knew that it was the Indians who massacred the soldiers as he points his gun at imaginary Indians. We are told that Indians fight savagely, not like West Pointers (91). Of course, any savagery in the West Point fighting style is not observed or not remarked upon, even in the actions of the Seventh Cavalry who had learned to hate Indians, for they had lost many soldiers and blamed the Indians for these losses (93).

In reading this book, a little boy is certainly intended to thrill to the bravery of the cavalry: "The Indians? They took one look at the onrushing Seventh and ran" (119). However, in terms of the famous battle called Custer's Last Stand, the author does acknowledge, "They [the Indians] were brave men, fighting for their homes, fighting for their wives and children. The odds were against them, but no one surrendered and only the wounded were captured" (96). But the emphasis is on Custer's courage, which impresses even the Indian chief (109). Here again, the Indians stand in the way of progress: the Sioux resisted the railroad, they were not "content" (114). Of course, what chance have the Sioux to express themselves when the only language they are capable of is "Eeeeeee . . . ahhhhhh!" (142). However, Reynolds does not go so far as to justify the attack. "Everyone has to judge for himself who was right" is his evasion (115). He attempts to downplay Autie's involvement by saying that he was a soldier and his job was to obey orders (115). Dee Brown tells us, however, that George Armstrong Custer "came to the West with the cold-blooded intention of making a glorious career out of the business of slaying Indians" and that "he was irascible, cruel to his men, and completely barbarous in his relations with the Indians" (Brown 1994, 102).

In *Will Rogers: Young Cowboy* (1951) by Guersney Van Riper Jr., we hear young Willie's father lament that the country is getting too civilized for him. The year is 1885. Willie's sister Sallie tells him that the Indians were there long before the white people came from Europe and, somewhat surprisingly, adds, "Why, we're all descended from the very *first* Americans" (25). Willie's response, reflecting his immediate associations, is to ask why they don't live in wigwams and to talk about going on warpath. But his dream is to become a cowboy, and the book is replete with references to lassos, lariats, and ponies. We see Will befriend some Cherokee boys and get into trouble at school. But once again, the main point of the story is to showcase an active, athletic white boy for whom adventure and the outdoor life had an irresistible appeal.

Jim Bowie: Boy with a Hunting Knife (1953) tells essentially the same story, except it is about a hero of the Alamo: "Under General Houston the Texas army met the Mexicans in the battle of San Jacinto. 'Remember the Alamo!' shouted the Texans. That cry fired the Americans' courage. They defeated Santa Anna and won independence for Texas. Nine years later Texas joined the United States" (190). Bowie died on his cot in the Alamo. He died fighting, firing a pistol from each hand and then, with his famous knife, killing nine of the enemy until a Mexican sword pierced his heart. "Even the enemy saluted him as a brave man" (192). "America will never forget him," we are told. But the real story is not about the actions or achievements of Jim Bowie. Or of Davy Crockett or Daniel Boone or Buffalo Bill or Wild Bill Hickok or Kit Carson or George Custer. The real story is one of character. So one could go on and on, looking at book after book and still be hearing the same story. All these American heroes had aspirations as boys, all were adventurous, all were tough, all were fearless, all loved the outdoors, had sharp eyes and strong skills, all were unusually observant, all were loyal and loving toward their families, all were trustworthy and all served their countries.

The one exception is *Little House on the Prairie* (1935) and the other titles in that series. There the hero is not a little white boy but a little white girl. Laura shares the same qualities as the little boys in these other books. She is strong, brave, resilient, forthright, adventurous, and so on. In fact, she considers it shameful to cry and struggles to keep her tears from flowing. In that sense, the book is a departure. But although Laura's mother is resourceful and strong, it is the father's presence that reassures the girls and makes them feel safe. Its depictions of Native Americans as thin, fierce, and lugubrious men and of their terrible war cries, yelps, savage voices, and throbbing drums are, however, far more stereotypical than those of Beals, Stevenson, and others, perhaps because it predates them. The only good Indian is a dead Indian, say many of the settlers, and Laura's mother believes they should keep themselves to themselves. But Laura's father disagrees and describes Soldat du Chene, the Osage chief, as one good Indian.

Racial features—brown skin, straight black hair, black eyes—are constantly emphasized, as is the Indians' nakedness. Laura wishes briefly that she were a little Indian girl, but the author hastens to assure the reader that she didn't mean it and it was a naughty wish. She only wanted to be naked in the wind and sun, a noble savage, and covets an Indian baby that she sees as a tribe rides past their homestead, as though it were nothing more than a doll. In fact, she refers to the baby as "it," crying out "Oh, I want it! Oh, I want it!" She can offer no other explanation for her need than that the baby's eyes are so black. Although one can safely assume that this is not what the author intended, her desire for the baby can be read as symbolic of the appropriation of the Indians' land and rights by pioneer families, an appropriation that, aside from contingency, resulted from an assumed authority and an "Oh, I want it" attitude. In fact, once the long line of Indians disappears over the horizon, Laura sits on the doorstep and looks into the "empty west" where the Indians had gone. Ingalls' description of the land where Laura has just seen a long line of people enter as empty can be interpreted in two ways. It can be seen as a projection of Laura's own emptiness in not being able to get the baby. She senses a loss but is too young to comprehend its full import. Or it can be seen as the propensity of settlers to view land they wish to appropriate as unoccupied and unused by anyone else. Laura's father briefly explains that the Indians' resentment stems from being moved west so many times but concludes that they ought to have sense enough to know when they are licked. Of all the books mentioned in this chapter, it is only Laura Ingalls Wilder's that are still popular, yet the image of the Native American they project survives in a myriad other ways.

As the British did with the people of India, the early pioneers in the new nation of the United States of America used the Native Americans as a character foil to test, compare, contrast, and indulge their own self-concept. The result has been a character construct that has proven stubborn and resistant. Disseminated by popular literature and film, it is only now beginning to be dislodged. In *The Imperishable Empire: British Fiction on India,* I comment,

> No image about India was more treacherous than the British image of the Indian. Nowhere was it manifested more than in their writings on India. The Anglo-Indian writer did not create this chimera, but he recreated it consistently. To use Albert Memmi's words, "he takes up all the usual expressions, perfects them, and invents others" (80). The English concept of the Indian character was part of the writers' tradition—social as well as cultural—and they helped to make it part of a literary tradition as well, for they believed implicitly in the truth of that tradition. In order to indicate the degree of prejudice and prevarication in the portrayal of the Indian in their literature, it is not necessary to do much more than reproduce it. In depicting the Indian character, most writers were merely composing "an effective version of the pious tradition" (Auerbach 14). Their representations might vary in degree, but they never vary in kind and common traits can easily be discerned in almost all of them. (1988, 121)

The same holds true for the popular literature and visual representations of the American West as well.

As was previously mentioned, we see in British colonial literature admiration for the "virile races," those people whose qualities most closely reflected the qualities the British cherished in themselves. It is why they respected and even admired the Sikh or the Gurkha or the Masai. Similarly, in many adventure stories about the American West, a Black Hawk or a Tecumseh shares some of the same qualities as the pioneers, but that does not radically change the narrative. Native good guys were as much the exception as white bad guys: the horse thieves, the smugglers, the unscrupulous gold grabbers, or the rowdy lowlife of the frontier. What was especially appreciated in the former was their grit, their spirit, and their love of freedom. These qualities were considered key components of American national character. Authors of adventure tales about the American West can admire the nobility, courage, loyalty, lineage, and so forth of Native Americans. They can see these qualities as less refined versions of their own. Many western heroes came to respect and admire certain Native American chiefs. Identification with them was possible in a way it was not with African American leaders whose features and skin color were just too alien. Seldom do we find children's books of the time extolling the virtues of a Frederick Douglass or a Sojourner Truth in quite the same way. In the Childhood of Famous Americans series of the time, only one title is devoted to an African American and that is Booker T. Washington. That has since changed as the series has continued. Appleby, Hunt, and Jacob tell us "Despite the vigor of the abolitionist attack, slaves themselves were condemned by their blackness, the reigning assumption that darkness of skin color accompanied weakness of intellect being routinely inculcated in classroom teaching" (1994, 110).

The extent to which many Native Americans internalized the noble savage image of themselves can be seen from a memoir published in 1902 by Charles A. Eastman, entitled *Indian Boyhood*. Although written with evident nostalgia, not only for his own boyhood but also for a way of life fast disappearing, it is a generally romantic account, its idyllic descriptions occasionally mitigated by observations of difficulties or hardships or injustices. The piece was first published in a popular periodical for children called *St. Nicholas,* the circulation of which far exceeded the combined total for *Atlantic, Harper's, Century,* and *Scribner's* magazines (Dykema-Vanderark 2002, 12). Such periodicals had a tenuous hold on the cultural imagination of children in the United States (see Dykema-Vanderark 2002, 12). In many ways, although not all, they were the counterparts, across the Atlantic, of the British boys' papers. What is most striking about the piece is Eastman's easy acceptance of the dichotomy of civilized and savage that was such a fundamental part of the structural relations between white people and Native Americans.

Throughout the book, Eastman refers to his people and their ways as wild, primitive, or savage and the ways or perceptions of white people as civilized. Phrases such as "savage warfare" (56), "savage life" (63), "savage heart" (43), or "savage wealth" (182) abound and are set against phrases such as "to a civilized eye (107) or "civilized clothing" (288). Eastman reiterates many stock images of the Native American, referring to "the veil of Indian reticence" (155) or the "moccasined foot" that "fell like the velvet paw of a cat—noiselessly" (87). His elaborate explanations of their customs and habitat make it clear that he is writing primarily for a white audience. But he also challenges other stereotypes such as the alleged lack of a sense of humor and faculty for mirth in Native Americans. Clearly he has accepted the standard explanation of the time that knowledge among the Native Americans was not scientific but instinctual. Indian women, says Eastman, are astute students of nature "after their fashion" (23).

Differences in character were both connected to race and freed from it depending on the exigency of the situation or the constraint of the argument. Spurr points out that a paradox of colonial discourse is that "the desire to emphasize racial and cultural difference as a means of establishing superiority takes place alongside the desire to efface difference and to gather the colonized into the fold of an all-embracing civilization" (1993, 32). Another instance of paradox is the civilizing mission itself which, while it claimed to bring the benefits of a superior culture, scorned those among the colonized peoples who best succeeded in assuming that culture. To see yourself reflected is not the same as seeing yourself imitated. In what they described as the virile races, the British saw some of their qualities reflected as did the pioneers in the Native American nations they favored. In hybrids like Kipling's Hurree Babu or even in those who were perfectly assimilated and acculturated, they saw ludicrous or ominous imitation.

A major difference between Native American and white leaders, as they are represented in these books, is the degree to which they are able to master their environments, a marker of the civilized man in post-Enlightenment thinking. Yet it was the Native Americans who were indisputable masters of their physical environment, and it was they (Squanto, for example) who had to show the white people how to survive in this strange land, or how to scout with acuity. But the white man was considered master of his destiny as well, while the Indians were often seen as hopelessly bewildered, muddled, fatalistic, or just out of sync with the times. Temperament is destiny, but so is adaptation and advancement; in terms of scientific know how, reason, discipline, and order, the other races could not compete.

In his famous book *The Frontier in American History* (1920), Frederick Jackson Turner says that at first the wilderness masters the colonist for it finds him a European and turns him into an Indian. But little by little, the colonist transforms the wilderness, not into the old Europe, but into something new, something truly American. "And to study this advance, the men who grew up under these conditions, and the political, economic, and social results of it, is to study the really American part of our history" (Turner 1920, 4). To Turner, the frontier was the meeting point between savagery and civilization (3). The trader and the settler were the pathfinders of civilization; Turner sees the history of the development of the United States as social evolution, as a series of ever evolving political transformations (12).

All the books mentioned here were written in the forties and the fifties, except for *Little House on the Prairie*, which was first published in 1935. These were the decades when most of the contemporary politicians and presidents in the United States were children. It is no wonder that so many of them repeatedly use the frontier as a metaphor to express what is quintessentially American. It was Woodrow Wilson who said that the American spirit was bred in the wilderness (Tucker 1920, 9). Yet one has only to compare the adventure stories of British and American writers to realize that the American spirit is not as unique as myth would have it. And it is wrest not so much from the wilderness as from the confrontation between cultures.

One of the clearest indications that character was perceived as a facet not only of race but also of nationality can be seen in Canadian adventure stories about their western territories. To take one example, *The Queen's Cowboy: James Macleod of the Mounties* by Kerry Wood, published in Toronto, we see there a somewhat less enthusiastic appraisal of the frontier spirit, called here an "expansionist spirit." The author tells us, "An expansionist spirit was at that time stirring the Americans, who were opening up their own west and looking covetously northward across the boundary" (Wood 1960, 23). The Canadians are presented as far less wild, far more law abiding and civilized, than their American counterparts. Indians respect the

Canadians and the British redcoats more than they do the Americans, we are told. Americans are callously indifferent to Indian deaths, whereas in Canada, although murders of red men had occurred in the past, once police had arrived to protect the lives of both tribesmen and white settlers on British soil, there is law and order (49).

The traders knew that law enforcement had come to the Canadian West. In contrast, we hear about how American whiskey traders attacked a band of sleeping Canadian Indians, killing men, women, and children. Later, we see the Canadians defend the slain Indians against the Americans, among whom the dominant sentiment seemed to be "What did the lives of a few Indians matter?" (77). In a somewhat sardonic tone, the author describes the West on the other side of the border:

> The American wild west was in evidence that morning. Gun-toting cowboys, buckskin clad trappers followed by their dusky women, groups of stolid-faced Indians, riflemen busy organizing hunts to kill and skin a hundred buffalo a day, with all the riff-raff who prey upon workers. There were gambling dens, honky-tonks, saloons and pool-halls, a few false-fronted hotels, rough and ready cafes. Boisterous men were having a last spree before heading into the wilds to trap beaver during the coming winter. Others were traders, loading whiskey and other stock into Conestoga wagons and bull-carts. There were good natured shouts as friends parted, loud curses as fighters jostled outside saloons. A star-wearing sheriff stood on the board walk, but his presence did not prevent almost daily shootings. (45–46)

Indians are still referred to as "a thousand painted savages" (57) or as "red lords" (63) or pictured proffering their gratitude. In one scene, Macleod clasps the brown fingers of the Indian chief of the Blackfoot Confederacy, Crowfoot, as he tells the chief that he brings greetings from Queen Victoria "and her sincere thanks for keeping the peace between Indians and white men in his beautiful land" (63). Again, there's a little dig at the Americans when we are told that the friendship between these two men was to mean much to Canada, for it was one that prevented war in the lands to the north of the border. The Mounties were there to protect those who were obedient to the queen's laws and to punish those who broke them. They would always be fair and just, Macleod stressed; their motto was "Maintain the Right" (65).

We see the extent to which the Indians preferred the order that the Mounties brought to the anarchy and violence of the American whiskey traders. They could count on the Mounties to treat them fairly. The contrast is made even clearer when a drunk and abusive American trader yells that he will appeal to his friends in Washington and is told that since his offence was committed on British territory, he is subject to the queen's laws (68). In fact, it is claimed that Sitting Bull and the Sioux were migrating to Canada to save their lives. The Mounties had tamed the frontier, but their purpose was to make "further colonization safe and practical" (86), an aim put forth as commendable, of course. Indians are designated "ours" or "theirs" as though they were so much property. But here too we do get a sympathetic aside: "Yet Indians were not wholly to blame, for they were defending their very lives. There had been a series of broken promises, invasion of reservation grounds, corrupt Indian agents making huge profits at the expense of tribal welfare, abuses and harsh treatment that angered not only Sitting Bull but all chiefs of the Sioux Nation. Their homelands had been ruthlessly plundered by whites" (96).

Macleod himself, as depicted in this book, is the model empire builder or, in this case, dominion builder: strong, firm, compassionate, and fair, and the author clearly associates these qualities with his Canadian nationality and British antecedents. His men are disciplined and endure hardship, deprivation, and ordeals stoically. Elsewhere as well we see the Canadian in action when Walsh refuses to back down or be scared off by a threat from Indians he was accusing of being horse thieves. He remains firm and upholds his authority. Canadians have their own national story, and it is different from the American one. In *Sons of the Empire* (1993), Robert H. MacDonald tells us,

> In hundreds of popular fictions, the Mountie was described as a peculiarly imperial hero, a man whose character was moulded by the best of Anglo-Saxon virtue. He might be an English lord or a ne'er-do-well, a younger son from across the Atlantic or the hired man off an Ontario farm, but it was certain that he was only to be found in the best of company, a hardened veteran of a dozen trails or campaigns. With his fellow adventurers he had come from the ends of the earth to the Canadian prairies to prove his manhood. (47)

It is interesting that as the United States gained preeminence as a world power and began its era of expansion, children's literature became less focused on moral correction and more focused on ideological issues. Anne Scott Macleod, commenting on early children's literature in the United States in *A Moral Tale: Children's Fiction and American Culture, 1820–1860* (1975), states,

> Except for frequent and pious references to George Washington, the American past was largely ignored. The pioneer struggle against the wilderness, which was to provide material for hundreds of children's books in later times, was never the subject of these early tales. In fact, wilderness was hardly mentioned at all; it would have been impossible to discover from children's stories the enormous expansion to the West that took place in the period. The American Revolution, in its rare appearances, was not an occasion for adventure tales, but for close and earnest reasoning about the moral implications of war in general. (18)

Frederick Jackson Turner famously attributed to the conditions of frontier life specific and uniquely American characteristics and intellectual traits:

> That coarseness and strength combined with acuteness and inquisitiveness; that practical, inventive turn of mind, quick to find expedients; that masterful grasp of material things, lacking in the artistic but powerful to effect great ends; that restless, nervous energy, that dominant individualism, working for good and for evil, and withal that buoyancy and exuberance which comes with freedom—these are traits of the frontier, or traits called out elsewhere because of the existence of the frontier. (1920, 37)

This sense of energy and expansiveness does concur with the popular perception of Americans and with their self-image, but it could just as easily apply to, say, Australians and their self-image. Turner sees the frontier as a testing ground in much the same way as the British saw the frontiers of their empire. Turner's description does, however, reflect a people eager to fashion a distinct identity and self-conscious of their adolescence. Essentially, in setting reason against passion, impetuous or passive courage against a more deliberate sort of courage, instinctive freedom against intellectual thought, and careful cultivation of the land against atrophy, so-called theorists were only reiterating the old dichotomous values. As with other groups, Indians became the "other" against which the self, this new self that had to be distinguished from the old European one, could be established.

For Americans, after the revolution, Roy Harvey Pearce tells us, it became an urgent imperative to study the Indian and his nature. Not only was the Indian disappearing from America but he was idealized as *the* American. "It was, in fact, an American duty to clear up European misconceptions of the Indian and to give him his savage due" (Pearce 1988, 77). Clearly, this was one of Charles Eastman's intentions in his boyhood memoir. Pearce's book is entitled *Savagism and Civilization*, and it is a detailed and thorough study of Social Darwinism as applied to structural relations between settlers and indigenes in the United States. Referring to the famous speech by Chief Logan, said to have been addressed to Lord Dunmore in 1774, and celebrated in the version given in Jefferson's *Notes on the State of Virginia* (1784), Pearce comments, "Yet the speech, and the tradition which it marked, could not be for Americans evidence of the absolute nobility of the savage. Rather for them it marked the inferior kind of nobility of the savage, a nobility which achieved its ends by emotion rather than by reason, by action rather than by thought, by custom rather than by law" (79).

The similarity of perception between the British in their colonial empire (particularly India) and the white settlers of North America becomes evident. The concern, says Pearce, was to indicate both that the Indian was part of the ultimate unity of mankind and that he had fallen from his proper humanity (80). So, too, the "Aryan brother" in India was regarded by the British as distantly fraternal, yet descended from his former preeminence, a sort of prodigal brother at best. American understanding of the Indian depended on the idea of savagism, the structure of which derived from European sources. The major theoretical debt was to a group of eighteenth-century Scottish writers, one of whom wrote on the North American Indian. This was William Robertson in his work entitled *History of America* (1777). The intention of this group was to construct a sociology of progress, to theoretically explain social stability, regress, and progress: "The Scots held that it might be conjectured back from empirical evidence how God was revealing His Word to modern man slowly but surely, how modern man was thus slowly but surely progressing to high civilization, how he had left behind him forever his savage, primitive state. This was the grand Christian, civilized Idea of Progress" (Pearce 1988, 82).

Churchill's view of the Afghan tribes as opposed to both Buddhist civilization in the region and British colonial rule would fit right into it, as would the Christianizing and civilizing mission of colonial rule and institutions. Pearce points out that social, technical, and moral progress were regarded as identical, and living fully in society was man's highest aim (1988, 83). Since this was exactly what Native Americans did, their placement in this scheme of progress was determined not so much by how they lived as by the perception of how they lived. As Pearce comments:

> We simply have to remind ourselves, for example, how hard it is for us to find a place in our world for societies which achieve their ends in ways which seem to deny the fundamental moral, social, and political hypotheses of our society. Thus forewarned, perhaps, we can proceed to see how, in a nineteenth century milieu, the savage, as known in stern fact, could and did prove savagism, progress, and the manifest destiny of American civilization. (1988, 105–6)

Epilogue

We have seen that colonization materially kills the colonized. It must be added that it kills him spiritually. Colonization distorts relationships, destroys or petrifies institutions, and corrupts men, both colonizers and colonized. To live, the colonized needs to do away with colonization. To become a man, he must do away with the colonized being that he has become. . . . He must cease defining himself through the categories of colonizers.

—Albert Memmi, *The Colonizer and the Colonized*

The oppressed and the exploited of the earth maintain their defiance: liberty from theft. But the biggest weapon wielded and actually daily unleashed by imperialism against that collective defiance is the cultural bomb. The effect of a cultural bomb is to annihilate a people's belief in their names, in their languages, in their environment, in their heritage of struggle, in their unity, in their capacities and ultimately in themselves.

—Ngugi wa Thiong'o, *Decolonizing the Mind*

A total description draws all phenomena around a single center—a principle, a meaning, a spirit, a world-view, an

> overall shape; a general history, on the contrary, would
> deploy the space of a dispersion.
>
> —Michel Foucault, *The Archaeology of Knowledge*
> *and the Discourse on Language*

The promotion of muscular character continues—muscular in a moral sense and muscular in a physical sense. Good is still battling evil. Just read the comics and watch the cartoons, or watch Disney films. Even that publishing phenomenon, the Harry Potter series, is really just a recycled English school story and adventure story rolled into one with special effects. It is a kinder and gentler boarding school with updated coeducational policies, multicultural children with names like Cho Chang and Padma and Parvati Patil, who nevertheless blend into the boarding school background, and an updated finite, real-time scheme. Harry will eventually graduate from Hogwarts instead of remaining suspended in time like the characters in the school stories of yore. Each book occupies a school year. Harry Potter shares, however, the love of adventure and excitement of the young protagonists of those older stories. Like them, he upholds all that is best in British character. He is upright, kind, fair, resourceful, courageous, loyal, tough, curious. He helps those who are weaker and fights with all his might against those who are mean or evil. He will never go over to the dark side, he vows. J. K. Rowling gives good and evil a contemporary cast when she has Quirrell proclaim that there is no good and evil, only power and those who are too weak to see it. Harry Potter is yet another amazing white boy who is a born leader. This is not to decry the charm of the story, or its important role in getting children to read. It's simply to say that it reiterates what we've always known: you have to be white and (mostly) male to lead. Hermoine is smart and savvy but still plays a secondary role.

For an exhaustive and far-reaching study of comic books as cultural representation, I would direct readers to the superb work entitled *Comic Book Nation: The Transformation of Youth Culture in America* (2001) by Bradford W. Wright. Wright looks at the birth of the comic book industry between 1933 and 1941, how comics provided superheroes for the common man and how they served the needs of race, politics, and propaganda. He also considers comic books in conjunction with postwar America and comic books in conjunction with the culture of the Cold War. Wright examines the controversies surrounding comic books and their role in effecting cultural change. One of his most important and interesting chapters is "Great Power and Great Responsibility," where he takes up superheroes in a superpower. Spiderman's injunction that with great power comes great responsibility is, of course, directly in the tradition of the white man's burden.

Writing about the jungle comic books, which are usually set in Africa or Asia, sometimes in Latin America, Wright states that at the center of these adventures is a hero who is sometimes male and sometimes female but always white. This hero champions Western interests and sensibilities in the savage lands, bringing order into chaos and defending them from external threats. The hero is often a jungle "lord," if male, or a "queen" or even a "goddess," if female. Sometimes the hero is just an adventurer who is connected to the British or French Empires. But he is there to save the savage lands whose ways he understands better than even the natives do. The latter need the intervention of the hero because they are not able to govern themselves and are easy prey for evil agents of various sorts (36). This is how Wright sums up these early comic books: "Paternalistic, imperialistic, and racist, the jungle comics showed the reductionist comic book style at its ugliest. They posed justification for Western colonial domination and white supremacy enforced through violence" (36–37).

The continuing popularity of superheroes—Superman, Batman, Spiderman, and so on, and of series such as *Star Wars*—is testament to the timeless appeal of the morality play. These heroes may not always be on the side of the law, but they are always on the side of good. Wright shows us how responsive comic books were to the needs of the time, providing superheroes during the Depression years and patriotic defenders during the war years. Comic books became a potent symbol of cultural power, just as Saturday morning cartoons and video games are now. The new empire is that of globalism, which is the neocolonial vehicle of the *mission civilisatrice*. The qualities of character endorsed by comic and cartoon superheroes are the very qualities of character endorsed by the empire. Brawn must accompany brain, supreme strength and courage carry the day, the quest for good is untiring, and the fight against evil unending. We see both great strength and great kindness in the character of the hero. Might is right, but might is sustained by power, and power is sustained by responsibility.

The direct linkage of episodes to political positions and ideological stances is explored in detail in Wright's chapter on "Race, Politics, and Propaganda." That character is directly associated with race he makes quite clear. After the attack on Pearl Harbor, public perception of the Japanese was brutal and "comic books rendered the Japanese using the most vicious caricatures that artists could imagine" (45). One of the roles that comic book creators took upon themselves, says Wright, was to explain how a race that was supposed to be inferior could have built up such tremendous military power. One explanation was imitation. The Japanese could imitate but not invent, so they stole American secrets and technology (47). Thus, the racial superiority stayed intact. The contours become clearer when an enemy is racially distinct. Following the first Gulf War, the vehicle for vicious caricatures of Arabs, similar to the comic book caricatures of the Japanese Wright descibes, is the video game.

There have been numerous articles and editorials about the deleterious effects of such games and of Saturday morning action cartoons. There is no need to go into those shows in detail, for there is little detail or subtlety and little to distinguish them from each other. Instead, we see the same, basic good vs. evil plot reduced to its crudest level and then reconstructed with technological effects and embellishment. All one needs to do is to list the qualities of the Mighty Morphin Power Rangers or, going back further in time, of He-man and She-Ra, to see that they are the direct descendants of the jungle comic heroes and also share many characteristics with colonial adventurers in the novels of Buchan, Henty, and others. Perhaps the most raw of all the various media that explore the heroic quest are video games. The worst of these have degenerated to such a rude version of the good guy/bad guy story and have become so unprincipled in their indulgence in gore and guts violence that they make the colonial adventure tale seem complex in comparison. The Saturday morning action cartoons prime us for the eschatological pronouncements of politicians like George W. Bush and their penchant for reducing the complexities and subtleties of global politics to the struggle between good and evil. The virtual reality of video games prepare us to remain detached at the massive destruction of modern aerial bombardment. After all, our television screens show us only what we have already seen in the video games: a blip, a flash, and a puff of smoke.

In his essay on the boys' papers of the late nineteenth century, George Orwell refers to the fact that there is a common audience for school stories, stories of the Wild West, the Frozen North, the Foreign Legion, crime (from the detective's angle), the Great War (Air Force or Secret Service, not infantry, Orwell points out), the Tarzan motif in various forms, professional football, tropical exploration, historical romance, and scientific invention (Orwell and Angus 2000, 475). The intertextuality of Orwell's list is telling in itself. Old-fashioned adventure stories are still being written and still being read by youngsters. The *Dear America* series, intended for girls five and up, and the *My Name Is America series*, intended for boys of the same age group, are worth looking at. Published by Scholastic, these series aim for a realistic effect that is further enhanced by the provision of actual photographs on the cover and the back pages of each volume. When one looks back on the adventure stories of the past, one sees how far this series has come. Each volume is devoted to a particular time period or historical period embodied in the life of an individual child and written in the form of a journal kept by that child. One significant difference from the series of the past is that these books are not all about little white boys. The list includes a Revolutionary War patriot, a Chinese miner, a Finnish immigrant, a Civil War Union soldier, a black cowboy, a transcontinental railroad worker, a Pilgrim boy, a person on the Lewis and Clark expedition, a World War II soldier, and a Japanese boy in the internment camps. There is then the important difference of perspective. One must note, however, that most of the authors are white. For instance, *The Journal of Ben Uchida, Citizen 13559: Mirror Lake Internment Camp: California 1942* (1999) is written by Barry Denenberg who, one may make a fairly safe assumption, is not Japanese. "It would, I thought, be best to see it through their eyes," the author assures us and he attempts to do just that. One wonders, however, why the publisher could not have found a survivor of the internment camps to tell the story.

In the historical note that follows each story, we are told of the Chinese Exclusion Act of 1882 and other egregious incidences of discrimination against Asians. The note informs the reader of the rescinding of Executive Order 9066 by President Ford, who called for an honest reckoning of national mistakes as well as of national achievement (141).

But it ends with the signing of the Civil Liberties Act of 1988 by President Reagan, who said on that occasion, "Blood that has soaked into the sands of a beach is all of one color. America stands unique in the world, the only country not founded on race, but on a way—an ideal. Not in spite of, but because of our polyglot background, we have had all the strength in the world. That is the American way" (141). Would a Japanese writer who had actually experienced the internment camps have left unresolved the historical contradictions provoked by in these words?

Dissenting and even unorthodox views are allowed some airing in these stories, which don't shy away from dealing with racism. For instance, in the above volume, we hear the boy say,

> "Mrs. Watanabe thinks the whole thing is a 'disgrace.'"
> "Why are we being rounded up like we're criminals while the Germans and Italians come and go like nothing is happening?" she asks, and before Mama has a chance to open her mouth she answers, "Because we look different. The Germans and Italians are Caucasians and we are Orientals." (17)

In *A Journey to the New World: The Diary of Patience Whipple: Mayflower, 1620* (1996) by Kathryn Lasky, the historical note acknowledges that although the Pilgrims signed the Mayflower Compact calling for elections, the idea of religious freedom did not extend to anyone outside of their church, nor did it even allow a member to openly question the government or the religion (187). While Patience Whipple tells us that one of the Pilgrims has "a very powerful fear of these feathered men," she provides the reader with a different perspective through her own appreciation of the color and the feathers of the Indians and her disapproval of the governor's suspicions of them. Attitudes that indicate bias are credited to specific characters rather than offered as normative: "Mr. Wagor said we would be outnumbered and at the mercy of the savages. Sometimes I felt this way on Wooster Street because most of the people were from different parts of Italy from us and there were so many Irish and German families there too. But it did not keep me from playing outside" (89). This also disengages the word "savage" from the idea of race.

On the same lines, in *The Starving Time: Elizabeth's Jamestown Colony Diary* (2001) by Patricia Hermes, we see a progression in Elizabeth's perspective. At first she sees the Indians as alien and threat-

ening as she complains that they stare and do not know it is not polite to mind another's business (78). But when she is rescued by an
Indian man who picks her up when she swoons and lays her gently
down outside the gates of the settlement, along with food for days,
she regards them in an entirely different light: "Now I will tell you
a secret. I no longer feel so afraid to go out into the forest. I no longer
feel so afraid of the Indians. Many of them are good and kind. Although I know this: Papa will slay me if I should ever do that again"
(83). The distinction between her approach and her father's, and her
awareness of that distinction, adds a complexity not often present in
such stories. Also complex is Elizabeth's refusal to generalize and
her understanding that "Indians are like white folks in that some are
honest and kind, others are liars and thieves" (105).

The books also offer important historical, sociological, and
cultural perspectives. For example, in *A Journey to the New World*,
we are told that "Everyone says the Lakota Sioux are a warrior
tribe and very fierce" (Laskey 1996, 86), and in *West to a Land of
Plenty: The Diary of Teresa Angelina Viscardi: New York to Idaho Territory, 1883* (1998) by Jim Murphy, we are told that "There was still
what many people referred to as the 'Indian problem' out West
(though most Native American tribes had already been forced
onto reservations by this time)" (190). The qualifiers: "Everyone
says" or "many people" immediately contextualize such statements, or attribute them to specific viewpoints. In most of the
older accounts, on the other hand, they would have been served
up as the truth. Whereas in the older adventure stories—those by
Beals, Stevenson, and others—a critical voice is accommodated, it
is almost invariably the voice of a white man. Although it con-
demns some of the more egregious examples of wrongdoing during the time of western expansion, it also allows for qualification
or remorse, which adulterates the effect to some degree. It is, in
any case, a disembodied voice.

In *My Heart Is on the Ground: The Diary of Nannie Little Rose, a
Sioux Girl* (1990) by Ann Rinaldi, the voice of dissent is the voice of
the Sioux girl herself, and it is an impassioned one:

> In The-Time-That-Was-Before, our chiefs have made large mistake
> in giving over our lands. The whites swarm on them like locusts.
> They cut the trees, spoil the hunting, make us live on reservations,
> and pay us ann-u-itee for the land the chiefs sold. Then they make

us owe them money. Nine dollars for small bit of sugar, eighteen for bad pork, ten for sour lard, and more for bad meat, when in The-Time-That-Was-Before we got all these things from our mother the earth. And no ann-u-itee money is left. And we starve. Grandfather tells it that there is nothing on the reservation for the young people. His eyes are closed, but I think maybe so, he sees things others do not see. (5)

Little Rose is sent to a boarding school for Indian children, where she learns to keep some things to herself, such as the fact that whites have double meanings for words in their treaties. Not only does she understand fully the historical process that resulted in her situation, she also has a strong sense of identity and of place:

I come from the place called Dakota. My people belong to the Great Plains tribe. Our men are very brave and honorable. Our women are noble. At one time my people ruled much good land— all the Black Hills, which the whites give us in a treaty in the year They-Killed-One-Wearing-A-Striped-War-Bonnet, 1868. Then the white man finds gold in the Black Hills and the treaties are forgot. My people are put on reservation on the Missouri River. (12)

Little Rose makes important distinctions between her tribe and others, such as the Cheyenne and Sioux, a distinction that the white people who run the school often forget to make or deliberately attempt to obliterate, saying "You are all Indians" (15).

Little Rose's voice sometimes seems contrived because of the author's attempt to inject authenticity into it, as when she uses the appellation "Woman-Who-Screams-A-Lot" to describe a particularly nasty teacher. But she reverts to the voice of a child: "I hate Woman-Who-Screams-A-Lot. I saw a mouse in the kitchen today. I wish it would bite her" (80). Also somewhat contrived are the frequent asides about Indian customs, but at least they are contextualized and afforded dignity. And Little Rose takes direct aim at the historical actions of the white man when she says, "Oh, I did not know how hard it would be to keep a promise to a friend! But we Sioux always keep our word. It is part of our honor" (100). Her ethnic pride is an important antidote to the years of denigration: "The chiefs came today! Our school band played as they came over the wooden bridge and through the gate. Two young girls gave them flowers. Oh, they looked so fine in their blankets and turkey tails and hats full of feathers. I was so proud. How can our teachers see them and want to change us from what we are?"(101–2).

In *The Girl Who Chased Away Sorrow: The Diary of Sarah Nita, a Navajo Girl* (1999) by Ann Turner, the historical note is direct and relates what happened in her times without mincing words. It puts a very different spin on Kit Carson, hero of countless adventure stories for boys:

> Colonel Christopher "Kit" Carson was a known hunter, trapper, scout, and Indian fighter who was put in charge of Carleton's plan to conquer the Navajo people. Carson continued the policy of guerilla warfare—burning crops, taking prisoners, and capturing sheep and goats. During the summer and fall of 1863, his campaign was successful. In January 1864, he and his men even entered the Canyon de Chelly, *tseyi*—a place sacred to Navajos and a stronghold for them—marching through and capturing more Navajo prisoners. Without food, without animals, they could not live. (n.p.)

Elsewhere, the historical notes are often blandly factual (as the facts are conventionally perceived) and acknowledge but do not get embroiled in controversies. For example, in *The Journal of Joshua Loper: A Black Cowboy: The Chisholm Trail, 1871* (1999) by Walter Myers, we hear that Joshua's father, who fought on the Union side in the Civil War, was not welcome to live in the South and was shot at by the Ku Klux Klan. There are also numerous references to slavery. The historical note to *Across the Wide and Lonesome Prairie*, on the other hand, is far more uncompromising, even though the author, Kristiana Gregory, strives to remain neutral:

> In 1845, as newspaperman named John L. O'Sullivan used the phrase "manifest destiny" in an article he wrote about westward expansion. His theory was that since American democracy was so successful, Americans had a divine or God-given right to take over any land they desired, and even a duty to do so. Many citizens agreed with this philosophy, and were eager to establish homesteads on the newly acquired territories. The Indians who lived there were primarily semi-nomadic and believed that the land belonged to everyone. But because the pioneers had a very different

cultural concept of private ownership, they claimed the land as
their own, despite the fact that the Indian peoples had lived there
for over ten thousand years. (Gregory 1997, 144)

Additional and alternative voices and perspectives are a significant development in these children's stories, which have certainly
come a long way from the romantic, idealized, and ahistorical adventure stories of the past. Most significant for this study, however,
is the decreased emphasis on character. These accounts are not focused on temperament so much as on event or episode. They are
rich in detail and provide children with a lively account of smells,
sights, sounds, sicknesses and hurts, family matters, and experiences. Since the books in these series are written in a journal format,
the intention is to adopt a child's perspective. When character is addressed, there is often a reversal from the old conceptualizations, as
in this passage from *West to a Land of Plenty*:

> There were positive consequences to this type of travel, of course.
> Girls were often required to solve problems usually left to the men
> and boys. They did work they had never done before—such as drive
> a fully loaded wagon over rough terrain; they faced sickness and
> death, sometimes on a daily basis; they often lived and functioned
> on their own with little or no help. These things left girls with a
> stronger sense of self—they could do the work, they could overcome
> obstacles and fear, they could survive. (Murphy 1998, 191)

The historical note tells us frankly that females left their homes
proper young women in neat and decent clothes, with hair and nails
groomed, but soon became dishevelled in the close confines of a hot,
steamy train or because of the rigors of wagon travel or the effects of
frequent food poisoning. The boys' lives as depicted are more
rugged and physically challenging than the girls' but that is attributed to historical circumstance, not to innate personality differences.
There is far less overt masculinizing of traits, although we do get
lines such as "Your first trail is always a hard one, but you will come
back a stronger man for it" (10). There is certainly much less in the
way of jingoistic paeans to nation and race, although discreet connections are sometimes made, as in the reproduction of the Reagan
speech. Occasionally, traits are still associated with nationality, as in
this passage from *The Journal of Ben Uchida*: "Mama responds

'Shikatagani,' trying to convince Mrs. Watanabe to make the best of the situation. Mama's very Japanesey when it cones to things like this" (Denenberg 1997, 17). But the association between temperament and race is generally far more sparing and subtle than in the older adventure stories.

A third series put out by Scholastic is the Royal Diaries, which profiles famous queens around the world, among them Elizabeth I; Cleopatra; Nzingha, Warrior Queen of Matamba; Marie Antoinette; Isabel, Jewel of Castilla; Anastasia; and Lady of Ch'iao Kuo. These serial books are certainly not impervious to criticism, but they are a small sampling of how changing perceptions and readings of history allow for changing perspectives and more broad-based interpretations, without sacrificing readability and interest. The same holds true for fiction about other historical events. For instance, a recent picture book about westward journeys entitled *Sunsets of the West* by Tony Johnston presents Indians as saviors because they bring pioneer families food when they have none, but it does not get into the dispossession of land or other thorny issues. Some might argue that this redefinition itself represents a selective tradition. But the Scholastic serial books referred to here are far less didactic than those of old and leave space for reader response.

To find a class of texts for children that are as ideological as the thrilling adventure stories that celebrated colonial conquest, one would have to turn to Disney. Disney is to globalism what those texts were to colonialism, both participatory and celebratory. Of course, nowhere is Disney openly selling or promulgating globalism, even though Disney characters are recognized worldwide. The days of a Buchan or a Henty unabashedly glorifying empire are gone. Disney is far more disingenuous in its methods, putting forth its films as wholesome all-American entertainment, universal in appeal, and representing the best of American achievement and technology, while they promote old-fashioned values and family fun.

Ariel Dorfman and Armand Mattelart have written a devastating exposé of the methods, practices, intentions, and ideology of Disney (both the man and the empire), entitled *How to Read Donald Duck: Imperialist Ideology in the Disney Comic* (1984). In his introduction to the English edition, David Kunzle writes, "The man who ruthlessly pillaged and distorted the children's literature of the world is hailed (in the citation for the President's Medal of Freedom, awarded to Disney in 1964) as the 'creator of an American folklore'" (17). The authors point out that the Disney empire is looked upon as "a great bridge that allows human beings to communicate across national boundaries. And amidst so much sweetness and light, the registered trademark becomes invisible" (28).

Similarly, Henry Giroux's seminal study *The Mouse That Roared: Disney and the End of Innocence* (1999) extends the discourse about Disney from the level of meaning and critical analysis to the level of public discourse. Giroux examines the role played by Disney in shaping public memory, national identity, gender roles, and childhood values, in defining and determining who qualifies as an American, and the role played by consumerism in American life (10). Giroux asks us to consider what children learn from Disney within the context of larger questions, such as "What does it mean to make corporations accountable to the public? How do we link public pedagogy to a critical democratic view of citizenship? How do we develop forms of critical education that enable young people and adults to become aware of and interrogate the media as a major political, pedagogical, and social force?" (11).

A key issue that Giroux investigates is the issue of cultural power. It is the issue that my book contends with as well, for implicit in the promotion of a particular character type is cultural power.

> Pedagogy in the more critical sense illuminates the relationship among knowledge, authority, and power. It draws attention to questions concerning who has control over the conditions for the production of knowledge. Moreover, it delineates the ways in which the circuit of power works through the various processes through which knowledge, identities, and authority are constructed within particular sets of social relations. (Giroux 1999, 125)

Like Giroux and Dorfman, I see the culture of children as "an important site of contestation and struggle" (Giroux 1999, 91). In that sense, books and films for children can become a commodity, a commodity of culture produced for a consumer, unless they are countered or at least tempered by training in the type of critical pedagogy and critical education that Giroux advocates. Parents, teachers, and ultimately children must all participate in this effort, must understand the forces of cultural production. I will not attempt to duplicate Giroux's extensive analysis of Disney's animated films and how they "influence the way America's cultural landscape is imagined," although I have made many of the same observations. I will simply focus briefly on those aspects that in my observation pertain to a study of character.

When Disney gives life to legendary or fabled characters, such as Aladdin or Pocahontas, or makes movies on contemporary themes, it becomes apparent that there is a continuum in terms of character construction and context with children's stories of an earlier era. The same attributes of character that were privileged in colonial literature are being privileged in Disney movies: valor, daring, resolve, enterprise, and so on. These traits are now available to a wider variety of characters, characters such as Pocahontas and Mulan, who are bringing an external diversity to Disney. But they are valued less for themselves than for the degree to which they conform to the prevailing paradigm, the signifiers of which remain male and Western. Mulan, for instance, takes on traditionally male skills and qualities—prowess in battle, courage, resourcefulness, and so forth. What's new is to see these time-honored traits in a Chinese female. At the end of the film, however, she reverts to her traditional role as dutiful daughter and doting wife. "Rather than aligning herself against the patriarchal celebration of war, violence, and militarism," Giroux points out, "Mulan becomes a cross-dresser who proves that when it comes to war she can perform as well as any male" (1999, 102–3). We are reminded of inveterate female leaders such as Golda Meir, Indira Gandhi, and Madeleine Albright. Gender roles are exchanged but not transcended. Similarly, Mulan's Chinese identity becomes simply a sort of cultural cloak: "Mulan becomes an exoticized version of the All-American girl who manages to catch the most handsome boy on the block, square jaw and all" (103).

The same is true of Pocahontas, who is redeemable as a heroine chiefly because of the role she plays in saving a white man. Giroux points out that the film is a "Hollywood rewrite of history that bleaches colonialism of its genocidal legacy" (101) for we are never told about the disease, death, and destruction that John Smith's countrymen would bring to Pocahontas's people. Disney bleaches or simply excises the more seamy side of history: "In the Disney version of history, colonialism never happened, and the meeting between the old and new worlds is simply fodder for another 'love conquers all' narrative. One wonders how this film would have been viewed by the public if it had been about a Jewish woman who falls in love with a blond Aryan Nazi while ignoring any references to the Holocaust" (Giroux 1999, 102).

John Smith's treatment of Pocahontas is glossed over, his abuse of her intervention and subsequent abduction is simply subsumed under the heading of "love conquers all." Pocahontas herself is exoticized and sexualized, although she is only a girl, in much the same manner as Asian women have historically been treated by Hollywood. In contrast, Disney's Snow White, presumably about the same age, is presented as pure, innocent, and chaste. Snow White lacks entirely Pocahontas's seductive capabilities. Of course, Pocahontas is more proactive and even powerful. It is interesting that Disney films follow the established pattern of vesting some degree of power in women but not in men from other cultures. In British colonial fiction about India, relationships between Indian women and British men were sometimes portrayed but almost never the inverse. India was also seen metaphorically as the female partner and England as the male. Social structural relations ensure that power is less threatening when located in the female.

The Lion King was one of Disney's highest grossing films; the videocasette alone grossed sales of more than $20 million within a few weeks of release. The success of this film, which brought Disney a billion dollars in profits over the course of only two or three years, sent Disney stock soaring. The trailer for *The Lion King* promises to take us "deep into the wilds of Africa," into "a dazzling new world of adventure" where a "heroic young cub named Simba is destined to become King of the jungle." It would have been truer to nature to have made the female cub the hero instead. The words of the trailer summon forth all the metonymic associations of Africa with wilderness and primitivism, a place for adventure rather than cerebral pursuits. Of course, Giroux and many others have commented upon the racialization of the roles. Scar, the evil lion, has the darkest coat, the blackest and most scraggly mane. The other lions are noticeably lighter, running from cream to gold with rich brown manes. The racial and social associations are further defined by the accents: high-class British accents for the royal family, urban, black inner-city accents in the case of the hyenas. Disney relentlessly associates dark complexions with evil character, from Scar to Maleficent and her

dark-skinned, subhuman friends in *Sleeping Beauty*. The signification is hardly subtle: the good characters are generally lighter
skinned and wear lighter shades of clothing.

Perhaps the most blatant exploitation of metonymic associations
in Disney is the opening sequence of *Aladdin* with its soundscape of
Arabian nights music accompanying an image that suggests a sway-
ing woman or perhaps a snake superimposed on a background of
flames. In the next frame, a man rides a camel as he sings:

> Oh I come from a land
> From a faraway place
> Where the caravan camels roam.
> Where it's flat and immense
> And the heat is intense
> It's barbaric, but hey, it's home.
> Where the wind's from the East
> And the sun's from the West
> And the sand in the glass is bright
> Come on down
> Stop on by
> Hop a carpet and fly
> To another Arabian night.

The original version of the fourth line was "Where they cut off your
ear / If they don't like your face." Protest from Arab American
groups was at least partially responsible for the change. Jack Sha-
heen, who has written widely about the stereotyping of Arabs, and
radio personality Casey Kasem led a public relations campaign
protesting the anti-Arab themes in *Aladdin*. Disney ignored the
protest at first but eventually agreed to change that one line, although it remained unchanged on the CD. The outrageous sixth line
was also left in. "More important," says Giroux, "the mispronuncia-
tion of Arab names in the film, the racial coding of accents, and the
use of nonsensical scrawl as a substitute for an actual written Arabic
language were not removed" (Giroux 1999, 105).

Even more egregious is the next frame where the same obsequious little man with very dark skin, a huge orb of a turban, and an
accent that veers between South Asian and Middle Eastern tells us,
"It begins on a dark night, where a dark man waits with a dark purpose." Jafar's goons are short with rotund bellies and abundant

black beards. The concurrence of dark skin and evil intentions is not just suggested, it is stated. So the evil characters all have turbans, dark skins, and foreign accents along with sly, cunning demeanours, garnished with grins and leers. Aladdin and Jasmine who, presumably, are of the same ethnicity as the villains, have light complexions, slim figures, and American accents instead. Aladdin, except when he is in disguise, does not wear a turban or sport a beard. He has Caucasian features, having been spared the large hooked Semitic nose that his compatriots sport. The genie calls him Al. In other words, he becomes yet another white hero, fortified with the requisite qualities of courage as he rescues Jasmine, and compassion as he offers his delicious bread to children more needy than he and inspires his monkey to do the same. Aladdin is trustworthy—his question to Jasmine: "Do you trust me?" is answered in the affirmative. "Be yourself," he is constantly told—a diamond in the rough. Instead, he passes for white. Jasmine's father, the sultan, recognizes in the end Aladdin's unimpeachable moral character. Even his search for riches is redeemed by his transformation into a prince on the inside as well as the outside; Aladdin has proven his worth. In the end, the criterion for the princess's consort is not royal blood but "whoever she deems worthy." Character once again becomes the criterion.

So, Aladdin is not really from Agraba, a composite Middle Eastern country, but from America. He is Al, the boy next door. Why would Disney separate Aladdin and Jasmine from their compatriots? The answer is evident: they needed characters with whom children in America could identify. They also needed the good and evil bifurcation and, of course, the good characters had to be aligned with the home audience in America. Since the setting and storyline precluded any overt alignment, this was achieved through the blatant use—or rather, misuse—of race. The bad guys not only look barbaric but also act barbaric. When the princess has escaped from the palace and innocently picks an apple from a fruit stall, the shopkeeper seizes her wrist and asks, "Do you know what the penalty for stealing is?" Aladdin comes along to save her. When American troops were purportedly "liberating" Afghanistan from the Taliban, the public was frequently reminded of the barbaric and primitive social practices that the regime not only allowed but also revived. Iraq is a much more modern and progressive country, so its "liberation" could not be staged in quite the same manner. There, the focus is on the excesses of an undoubtedly brutal regime. The point is that the plot is familiar. Like Indian villagers who take pleasure from the familiarity of the Hindu epics that are recounted over and over again, the rescue of a people from themselves becomes the great American attack archetype.

Other scenes in *Aladdin* consolidate stock images and characters of indeterminate Eastern origin: the pushy salespeople, greedy shopkeepers, and a fakir on a bed of nails or traversing hot coals. The reaction from people of Arab descent was not purely academic. Like other victims of racial stereotyping, they probably saw it as a matter of survival because negative stereotypes have provoked attacks and abuse. Many Sikhs report that children have pointed to them in public places and called them Jafar. And, of course, every little Asian girl with long black hair down her back is exoticized as a Princess Jasmine. In the wake of September 11 and the second Gulf War, the misrepresentation of people from the Middle East and the emphasis on their barbarity, cruelty, and evil make the president's job easier as he prepares the American people to accept war. All he has to do is refer (in racially coded terms) to the enemy as primitive or barbarian. The groundwork will already have been done. People fed on a diet of Disney and similar image factories will fill in the blanks. It is easy to see how the clash of civilizations can originate in cultural production that in turn feeds political policy and economic power:

> The control, production, and distribution of such films [as Disney's] should be analyzed as part of a wider circuit of power. In this context, Disney's influence in the shaping of children's culture cannot be reduced to critically interpreting the ideas and values Disney promotes. Any viable analysis of Disney must also confront the institutional and political power Disney exercises through its massive control over diverse sectors of what Mark Crispin Miller calls the "national entertainment state." The availability, influence, and cultural power of Disney's children's films demand that they become part of a broader political discourse regarding who makes cultural policy. (Giroux 1999, 112)

While Giroux's book exposes the corporate abuse behind Mickey Mouse's smiling face, Dorfman and Mattelart expose another danger of Disney. "The threat," they say, "derives not so much from their embodiment of the 'American way of Life,' as that of the

'American Dream of Life.' It is the manner in which the U.S. dreams and redeems itself, and then imposes that dream upon others for its own salvation, which poses the danger for the dependent countries. It forces us Latin Americans to see ourselves as they see us" (1984, 95). Children's literature and film often tell a story of the survival of the fittest. How the fittest are determined and defined becomes significant in the context of child development and culture. In many Disney films, physical prowess, self-sacrifice, attractive athletic appearance, rationality, and forward-looking characters are set in opposition to the antimodern, the mendacious, or the mysterious and magical. This opposition is really the old Orientalist–Imperialist opposition. Even in its benign form, as in *Pocahontas*, it is recognizable. In that film, the link between nature and "noble savages' is expressed through Pocahontas's symbiotic relationship with a pet raccoon, a bird, and an old tree that acts in a motherly fashion and offers her advice. The spirituality and synchronicity with nature that was so striking in Native American cultures is thus trivialized. It is presented as mystical rather than rational, or based on a sophisticated understanding of ecology that contemporary society is only now beginning to acquire.

There is little question that each culture favors a different set of traits and characteristics. In a classroom where there is a conglomerate of cultural backgrounds, such as in contemporary America, the privileging of particular traits means that the fittest become those who most closely conform to a set mold of character or a preconceived style of leadership and success. Typically, athletic ability is privileged over artistic ability, assertiveness over diffidence, an adventurous nature over a timid one, an extrovert over an introvert, a fulsome personality over a taciturn one. The report cards my children would receive in the Amherst, Massachusetts school system in their elementary years included a category that somewhat baffled me. It was called "Ability to take risks" and the more the child took risks, the higher the mark he or she was given. Just the opposite would have been the case had one of my elementary school teachers in India been doing the grading, for risk taking implies the possibility of danger. Our teachers preferred us more cautious and compliant. Picture books such as *Shy Vi* treat shyness almost as a defect or a disability that needs treatment. In another, *Boo to a Goose*, the mother frets because her six-year-old son seems too timid. "You must face up to him sometime soon—you're almost as big as he is," she tells him. "A boy nearly six years old should be able to say boo to a goose." When Jimmy finally succeeds in yelling boo loudly to the goose, all the animals hail him as "Jimmy, the conqueror!" Success is thus associated with aggression, victory with dominance.

Our understanding of feminism is sometimes so shallow that we take it to mean the assumption of those qualities that have been conventionally allocated to men. The liberated woman is seen as the one who is most like a man. So, instead of probing the rubric of power itself, of dominance or aggression and ambition, of the value system that keeps some people in sway over others, we simply reassign traits. Instead of what Betty Friedan calls for, a paradigm shift, we simply accept the male model of ideal character. The "male model or its sexual obverse" is the oppositional choice that we are left with and this is what Friedan calls the impossible dilemmas of the old paradigm (Friedan 1997, 7). Bauer, in his study of the "New Man" in Soviet psychology, points out that emotionality is a highly valued trait of the Soviet man, so long as it can be controlled and does not rule the man (1952, 52). The privileging of particular personality traits and their attribution to national characteristics is an essentializing process that chooses to ignore the influences of history and politics.

In his impressive study of the specifically British model of masculinity, *Soldier Heroes: British Adventure, Empire and the Imagining of Masculinities* (1994), Graham Dawson states, "In the course of writing this book I have become increasingly persuaded that the history of Empire continues to maintain a determining influence over cultural and political life in modern Britain. The book will, I hope, contribute to the better understanding of that influence, and suggest some of the ways in which the national past may persist in the psychic lives of post-imperial generations" (8). In his introduction, Dawson brilliantly exposes the way in which the Falklands war betrayed the persistence of the national past. He writes,

> The Falklands-Malvinas War constitutes the context in which work
> for this book was first conceived and begun. Its original motive was
> a wish to understand how popular support for such a war was possible in post-imperial Britain, fuelled by my desire to see emerge a

politically effective refusal of the Britishness asserted and celebrated in this way. In Conservative thinking, British national identity was construed as an unchanging essence of qualities supposedly common to the British people. For this to be contested, an alternative account would need to emphasize instead those material processes, both cultural and political, through which a national collectivity comes to recognize itself as such and secures the affiliations of men and women. Integral to this analysis would be a theorization of national identity as a fundamentally gendered construct, and an exploration of how masculinities and femininities can be mobilized on behalf of the nation. (3)

The soldier as (in Dawson's terms) the "quintessential figure of masculinity" (1) is not unique to British narratives. Much of Dawson's analysis of the recapitulation of the imperial past that occurred during the Falklands-Malvinas war can be applied to the entirely different context of U.S. military action in Iraq. We have seen the similarities between imperial and Western narratives. What is significant is what Dawson describes as the "popular masculine pleasure-culture of war" and the question that he asks in his introduction: "Might there be a relation between the fantasies of boyhood, the reproduction of idealized forms of masculinity, and the purchase of nationalist politics?" (4). The children's literature included in my study provides the answer: a resounding "Yes."

Heroic narratives begin as early as picture books. Of course, independence, autonomy, and assertiveness often dissipate in adulthood and give way to the compliance and conformity cherished by the corporate world or to the political assent demanded in times of war. This is consent, not as it is understood in modern democratic ideology, but as Gramsci speaks of it, as a psychological state suggesting tacit acceptance of the sociopolitical order. The children's literature discussed here emerged out of "consent" in the specific sense that Gramsci uses the term (see Femia 1987, 35ff.). Consent transpires from a wide-ranging geographical, cultural, and critical spectrum. Gramsci's famous doctrine of hegemony extends the power base from economics alone to culture, morality, and ideology as well. Contemporary thinkers see increasingly clearly the relativist nature of our sense of morality—for instance, the extent to which it is influenced by religion, economics, gender, ethnicity, or social class. Similarly, notions of character are part of an "associated field" (to use Foucault's term) that involves nation, historical period, prevailing market forces, ideological interests, and so on. This is the externality of the internality of character.

Children's literature is not written by children but for children. It comes out of an adult world and only the most conscientiously crafted pieces or only the most vapid ones can be free from the "associated field." The relationship between children's literature and adult consciousness becomes the discursive practice, to use another of Foucault's epistemological terms. Foucault writes,

> Instead of exploring the consciousness/knowledge (*connaissance*)/science axis (which cannot escape subjectivity), archaeology explores the discursive proactive/knowledge (*savoir*)/science axis. And whereas the history of ideas finds the point of balance of its analysis in the element of *connaissance* (and is thus forced, against its will, to encounter the transcendental interrogation), archaeology finds the point of balance of its analysis in *savoir*—that is, in a domain in which the subject is necessarily situated and dependent, and can never figure as titular (either as a transcendental activity, or as empirical consciousness). (1972, 183)

In an essay entitled "The Other: Orientalism, Colonialism, and Children's Literature," Perry Nodelman draws an analogy between the colonial subject and the child. Reiterating Jacqueline Rose's premise that children's literature is a form of colonization, Nodelman attempts to explore "the parallels between Said's descriptions of Orientalism and our representations of childhood in both child psychology and children's literature" (1992, 29). Nodelman's analogy is muddled by the colonizers' proclivity to regard the colonial subject as a child anyway. But more problematic, in both practical and political terms, is Nodelman's implication that the silencing, oppression, and objectification of the child can be compared to that of the colonial subject. It amounts to a trivialization of colonial subjugation. "We adults . . . use our knowledge of 'childhood' to dominate children," he says, and provides an example from his children's classroom. Without denying the very real oppression of a manipulative or abusive teacher, this analogy falters on historical grounds. There is simply no comparison in scale or outcome between the authority asserted by adults over children *as a group*, especially through the medium of children's literature, and the political, economic, and cultural domination of entire countries for centuries. However, Nodelman does make a valid if not entirely original claim when he points out that, as with the "Oriental," children are used as a sort of synecdoche, allowing the part to stand for the whole and the whole for the part. He is also absolutely right to emphasize the disjunction between images of idyllic childhood innocence and the realities of modern children's lives (31).

Character is a product of various factors: genetic influences, internal impulses, familial expectations, and cultural and temporal norms among them. It is also the product of education. To quote Foucault again: "Every educational system is a political means of maintaining or modifying the appropriation of discourses, with the knowledge and power they bring with them" (1972, 46). If we think of character as one type of discourse, its connection to knowledge and power is evident. Character is also the product of experience—individual experience, collective or group experience, and national experience; the latter influence is often neglected. Nations are ideological as well as political and geographical entities, and ideology employs culture as its handmaiden. Character develops in cultural space. Jacques Derrida refers to "the organized field of speech," which subsumes the speaking subject. "The speaking subject discovers his irreducible secondarity, his origin that is always already eluded; for the origin is always eluded on the basis of an organized field of speech in which the speaking subject vainly seeks a place that is always missing" (1978, 178).

This organized field is, before it is anything else, a cultural and a historical field, according to Derrida. In a sense, stories written for children, perhaps more than any other type of stories, become *la parole soufflé* or speech that that is spirited away or stolen, as Jacques Derrida explains it. He says, "All speech fallen from the body, offering itself to understanding or reception, offering itself as a spectacle, immediately becomes stolen speech. Becomes a signification which I do not possess because it is a signification" (1978, 175). The theft of speech is not the same as any other theft because it forces us to confront the nature of theft itself. The minute we speak we, in a sense, lose ownership of our words. Inscribed speech or writing is always stolen. "Always stolen because it is always *open*. It never belongs to its author or to its addressee, and by nature it never follows the trajectory that leads from subject to subject" (178). The signifier then becomes autonomous and says more than the speaker intends, which makes possible the passivity of the speaker's intention.

Children's writing can be seen as the dispossession, the "purloined breath" (177) of children's writers and the possession instead of those who appropriate it on behalf of their own agenda, even if that is the nation. Of course, when the writer is participatory, it can hardly be called dispossession. In the conception of character put forth by the writers discussed in this study, the marked traits are significant not only for what they are, but for what they are not. They depend on a system of "othering" for demarcating between national and ideological character types. Demarcation is systematized not only by character type, however, but also by race and nationality. Nations have their metaphors, chosen from landscape or physiognomy. And nations have their narratives, told through myth and legend, literature and lore, ballads and oral transmission. The stories written for children can often be the truest telling of the national narrative. Authors write the nation into the narratives they put forth for children. They construct a child that both embodies and performs the nation. The child is the repository of myths, the embodiment of narratives of time and place, the persona, the guise, and the pretext. The nation is personified in the child. Children's literature can simply reflect prevailing ideologies or it can become an instrument for their implementation, an agent of institutional power in itself. For too long, its role in the totality of the Weltanschauung, in its genesis and in its diffusion, has been ignored or disregarded. It is time to pay attention to the earliest sources of our perceptions.

Bibliography

Primary Sources

Anderson, A. M. 1949. *Squanto and the Pilgrims*. Chicago: Wheeler Publishing.

Arnold, William Delafield. 1973. *Oakfield; or, Fellowship in the East*. New York: Humanities Press.

Atkins, Jeannine. 1995. *Aani and the Tree Huggers*. New York: Lee and Low Books.

Ballantyne, R. M. 1858. *The Coral Island*. London: Octopus Books, 1980.

Bannerman, Helen. 1899a. *The Story of Little Black Sambo*. New York: Lippincott, 1946.

———. 1899b. *The Story of Little Black Sambo*. New York: Platt & Munk: n.d.

———. 1996. *The Story of Little Babaji*. New York: HarperCollins.

Barrie, J. M. 1928. *Peter Pan*. New York: Viking, 1991.

Beals, Frank Lee. 1943a. *Chief Black Hawk*. Chicago: Wheeler Publishing.

———. 1943b. *Buffalo Bill*. Chicago: Wheeler Publishing.

Blyton, Enid. 1941. *The Twins at St. Clare's*. London: Methuen.

———. 1943. *The Secret of Killimooin*. London: Collins.

———. 1943. *Summer Term at St. Clare's*. London: Methuen.

———. 1944. *Claudine at St. Clare's*. London: Methuen.

———. 1944. *The Second Form at St. Clare's*. London: Methuen.

———. 1945. *Fifth Formers of St. Clare's*. London: Methuen.

———. 1946. *The Famous Five: Five Go Off in a Caravan*. Kent: Hodder and Stoughton, 1967.

———. 1946. *First Term at Malory Towers*. London: Methuen.

——. 1947. *Second Form at Malory Towers*. London: Methuen.

——. 1948. *Third Year at Malory Towers*. London: Methuen.

——. 1949. *The Famous Five: Five Get into Trouble*. Kent: Hodder and Stoughton, 1991.

——. 1950. *The Famous Five: Five Fall into Adventure*. Kent: Hodder and Stoughton, 1968.

——. 1950. *In the Fifth at Malory Towers*. London: Methuen.

——. 1950. *Secret Seven: Adventure*. Kent: Hodder and Stoughton.

——. 1951. *Last Term at Malory Towers*. London: Methuen.

——.1951. *Secret Seven: Well Done, Secret Seven*. Kent: Hodder and Stoughton.

——. 1953. *The Mystery of Holly Lane*. London: Collins.

——. 1953. *The Secret of Moon Castle*. London: Collins.

——. 1957. *The Famous Five: Five Go to Billycock Hill*. Bath: Chivers Press, 1998.

——. 1957. *The Mystery of the Strange Messages*. London: Collins.

——. 1958. *The Famous Five: Five Get into a Fix*. Bath: Chivers Press, 1999.

——. 1961. *The Famous Five: Five Go to Demon's Rocks*. Kent: Hodder and Stoughton, 1991.

——. 1986. *The Famous Five: And the Knight's Treasure* (told by Claude Voilier). Kent: Hodder and Stoughton.

——. 1988. *Six Bad Boys*. London: Random House.

Bond, Michael. 1958. *A Bear Called Paddington*. London: Collins.

Brett, Edwin J., ed. 1888–1990. *Boys of the Empire*. Vol. 1., 1888–1990. London: Boys' Empire League/Andrew Melrose.

Brunhoff, Jean de. 1931. *The Story of Babar the Little Elephant*. New York: Random House, 1961.

Buchan, John. 1928. *Prester John*. Boston: Houghton Mifflin.

Bulla, Clyde Robert. 1954. *Squanto: Friend of the White Men*. New York: Thomas Y. Crowell.

Burnett, Frances Hodgson. 1886. *Little Lord Fauntleroy*. London: Puffin Books, 1994.

——. 1905. *A Little Princess: The Story of Sara Crewe*. London: Puffin Books, 1994.

——. 1912. *The Secret Garden*. London: Puffin Books, 1994.

——. 1914. *The Lost Prince*. Philadelphia: J. B. Lippincott.

——. 1915. *The Little Hunchback Zia*. London: St. Hugh's Press.

——. 1920. *The White People*. London: Heinemann.

Cary, Joyce. 1939. *Mister Johnson*. New York: New Directions Books, 1939.

Churchill, Winston. 1898. *The Story of the Malakand Field Force*. 2003. www.blackmask.com.

Coleridge, Samuel Taylor. 1797. Kubla Khan. In *The Portable Coleridge*, edited by I. A. Richards, 156–61. New York: Viking Press, 1950.

Collier, Edmund. 1952. *The Story of Buffalo Bill*. New York: Grosset & Dunlap.

Conrad, Joseph. 1902. *The Heart of Darkness*. Harmondsworth: Penguin, 1973.

Cott, Jonathan, ed. 1983. *Masterworks of Children's Literature*. Vol. 5. New York: Stonehill Publishing.

Cunningham, Henry. 1887. *The Coeruleans: A Vacation Idyll*. 2 vols. London: Macmillan.

Dahl, Roald. 1961. *James and the Giant Peach*. New York: Puffin Books, 1988.

———. 1964. *Charlie and the Chocolate Factory*. New York: Puffin Books, 1988.

———. 1966. *The Magic Finger*. New York: Puffin Books, 1993.

———. 1970. *Fantastic Mr. Fox*. New York: Puffin Books, 1988.

———. 1972. *Charlie and the Great Glass Elevator*. New York: Puffin Books, 1988.

———. 1977. *The Wonderful World of Henry Sugar and Six More*. New York: Puffin Books, 1988.

———. 1978. *The Enormous Crocodile*. New York: Bantam Books, 1988.

———. 1980. *The Twits*. New York: Puffin Books, 1991.

———. 1981. *George's Marvelous Medicine*. New York: Puffin Books, 1991.

———. 1982. *Matilda*. New York: Puffin Books.

———. 1982. *The BFG*. New York: The Trumpet Club, 1982.

———. 1983. *The Witches*. New York: Puffin Books, 1985.

———. 1984. *Boy: Tales of Childhood*. London: Puffin Books, 1986.

———. 1986. *Going Solo*. New York: Puffin Books, 1988.

———. 1990. *Esio Trot*. New York: Puffin Books, 1992.

Dangarembga, Tsitsi. 1988. *Nervous Conditions*. Seattle: Seal Press.

Defoe, Daniel. 1719a. *The Life and Strange Surprizing Adventures of Robinson Crusoe, of York, Mariner*. London: Oxford University Press, 1972.

———. 1719b. *Robinson Crusoe*. New York: DK Publishing, 1998.

Denenberg, Barry. 1999. *Ben Uchida*. New York: Scholastic.

Diver, Maud. 1907. *Captain Desmond, V.C.* London: Blackwood.

———. 1908. *The Great Amulet*. London: Blackwood.

———. 1916. *Desmond's Daughter*. London: Blackwood.

———. 1921. *Far to Seek: A Romance of England and India*. London: Blackwood.

———. 1923. *Lonely Furrow*. London: John Murray.

———. 1931. *Ships of Youth: A Study of Marriage in Modern India*. London: Blackwood.

Eastman, Charles A. 1902. *Indian Boyhood*. New York: McClure, Phillips.

Farrar, Frederic W. 1985. Eric; or Little by Little: A Tale of Roslyn School. In *Masterworks of Children's Literature*, edited by Robert Lee Wolff. Vol. 5. New York: Stonehill Publishing.

Firmin, Peter. 1979. *Basil Brush in the Jungle*. Englewood Cliffs, N.J.: Prentice-Hall.

Forster, E. M. 1924. *A Passage to India*. New York: Harcourt-Harvest.

———. 1936. *Abinger Harvest*. New York: Harcourt Brace.

Fraser, George MacDonald. 1991. *Flashman and the Mountain of Light*. New York: Alfred A. Knopf.

———. 2000. *Flashman and the Tiger*. New York: Alfred A. Knopf.

Gobhai, Mehlli. 1969. *Lakshmi, the Water Buffalo Who Wouldn't*. New York: Hawthorn Books.

Gregory, Kristiana. 1997. *Across the Wide and Lonesome Prairie: The Oregon Trail Diary of Hattie Campbell*. New York: Scholastic.

Griffith, John W., and Charles H. Frey. 1996. *Classics of Children's Literature*. 4th ed. Upper Saddle River, N.J.: Prentice-Hall.

Henty, G. A. 1884. *With Clive in India: or, The Beginnings of an Empire*. Mill Hall, Penn.: PrestonSpeed Publications, 2002.

———. 1886. *For Name and Fame; or, Through Afghan Passes*. Mill Hall, Penn.: PrestonSpeed Publications, 2002.

———. 1894. *In the Heart of the Rockies: A Story of Adventure in Colorado*. Lake Wales, Fla.: Lost Classics Book Company, 1998.

———. 1909. *In Times of Peril: A Tale of India*. New York: Federal.

Hermes, Patricia. 2001. *The Starving Time: Elizabeth's Jamestown Colony Diary*. New York: Scholastic.

Hinton, S. E. 1967. *The Outsiders*. New York: Viking.

Holbrook, Stewart. 1952. *Wild Bill Hickok Tames the West*. New York: Random House.

Hughes, Thomas. 1857. *Tom Brown's Schooldays*. Mahwah, N.J.: Watermill, 1988.

———. 1985. Preface. *Masterworks of Children's Literature*. Vol. 5, Part 1: *1837–1900: The Victorian Age*. 6th ed. Edited by R. L. Wolff. New York: Stonehill Publishing.

Jhabvala, Ruth. 1972. *An Experience of India*. New York: Norton.

Johnston, Tony. 2002. *Sunsets of the West*. New York: Putnam's.

Kalman, Maira. 1995. *Swami on Rye: Max in India*. New York: Viking.

Keats, Ezra Jack. 1962. *The Snowy Day*. New York: Viking Press.

Kincaid, Jamaica. 1991. *Lucy*. New York: Plume.

Kingsley, Charles. 1878–1886. *The Works of Charles Kingsley*. 28 vols. London: Macmillan.

———. 1889. *The Water Babies*. New York: Children's Classics, 1986.

Kipling, Rudyard. 1894–1895. *The Jungle Books*. 2 vols. New York: Garden City, 1948.

———. 1901. *Kim*. Garden City, N.Y.: Doubleday, 1949.

———. 1980. *Complete and Unabridged*. New York: Octopus/Heinemann.

Lasky, Kathryn. 1996. *A Journey to the New World: The Diary of Remember Patience_Whipple*. New York: Scholastic.

Lester, Julius. 1996. *Sam and the Tigers: A New Telling of Little Black Samba*. New York: Dial.

Lewison, Wendy Cheyette. 1993. *Shy Vi.* New York: Simon & Schuster.

Low, Joseph. 1975. *Boo to a Goose.* New York: Atheneum.

Macaulay, J., et al., eds. 1899–1900. *The Boy's Own Annual.* Vol. 22. London: "Boy's Own Paper" office.

Mack, Edward Clarence. 1973. *Public Schools and British Opinion 1780–1860.* Westport, Conn.: Greenwood Press.

Mannoni, Octave. 1956. *Prospero and Caliban: The Psychology of Colonization.* London: Methuen.

Marryat, Frederick. 1829. *Frank Mildmay or The Naval Officer.* Ithaca, N.Y.: McBooks Press, 1998.

———. 1834. *Peter Simple.* New York: Henry Holt, 1998.

———. 1836. *Mr. Midshipman Easy.* New York: Henry Holt, 1998.

Murphy, Jim. 1998. *West to a Land of Plenty: The Diary of Teresa Angelino Viscardi.* New York: Scholastic.

Myers, Walter Dean. 1999. *Joshua Loper: The Journal of a Black Cowboy.* New York: Scholastic.

Naipaul, V. S. 1981. *Among the Believers: An Islamic Journey.* New York: Knopf.

Orwell, George. 1949. *Burmese Days.* Harmondsworth: Penguin. (Originally published 1934).

———. 1965. *The Road to Wigan Pier.* London: Heinemann.

Orwell, Sonia, and Ian Angus, eds. 2000. *George Orwell: The Collected Essays, Journalism & Letters: An Age Like This: 1920–1940.* Vol. 1. Boston: Nonpareil Books.

Pene du Bois, William. 1961. *Otto in Africa.* New York: Viking Press.

Rey, H. A. 1941. *Curious George.* Boston: Houghton Mifflin, 1993.

———. 1952. *Curious George Rides a Bike.* Boston: Houghton Mifflin.

———. 1957. *Curious George Gets a Medal.* Boston: Houghton Mifflin.

Reynolds, Quentin. 1951. *Custer's Last Stand.* New York: Random House.

Rinaldi, Ann. 1999. *My Heart Is on the Ground: The Diary of Nannie Little Rose, a Sioux Girl.* New York: Scholastic.

Roosevelt, Theodore. 1896. *The Winning of the West: Louisiana and the Northwest 1791–1807.* Vol. 4. New York: G. P. Putnam's Sons.

Rowling, J. K. 1997. *Harry Potter and the Sorcerer's Stone.* New York: Scholastic.

Sendak, Maurice. 1963. *Where the Wild Things Are.* New York: Harper & Row.

———. 1981. *Outside Over There.* New York: Harper & Row.

———. 1993. *We Are All in the Dumps with Jack and Guy.* New York: HarperCollins.

Shakespeare, William. 1609–1611. *The Tempest.* New York: Penguin, 1970.

———. 1612–1616. *King Henry VIII. William Shakespeare: The Complete Works.* Ed. C. J. Sisson. New York: Harper, 1954.

Spratt, Gladys M., ed. 1880–1950. *The Girl's Own Annual.* Vols. 1–70, 1880–1950. London: R.T.S.-Lutterworth Press.

Stevenson, Augusta. 1943. *Daniel Boone: Boy Hunter*. Indianapolis: Bobbs-Merrill.
——. 1945. *Kit Carson: Boy Trapper*. Indianapolis: Bobbs-Merrill.
——. 1948. *Buffalo Bill: Boy of the Plains*. Indianapolis: Bobbs-Merrill.
——. 1955. *Tecumseh: Shawnee Boy*. Indianapolis: Bobbs-Merrill.
Stowe, Harriet Beecher. 1852. *Uncle Tom's Cabin*. Harmondsworth: Penguin, 1966.
Thompson, Edward. 1931. *A Farewell to India*. London: Ernest Benn.
——. 1933. *So a Poor Ghost*. London: Macmillan.
Tousey, Sanford. 1936. *Jerry and the Pony Express*. New York: Doubleday.
Turner, Ann. 1999. *The Girl Who Chased Away Sorrow: The Diary of Sarah Nita, a Navajo Girl*. New York: Scholastic.
Van Riper Jr., Guernsey. 1951. *Will Rogers: Young Cowboy*. Indianapolis: Bobbs-Merrill.
Vaughan, Marcia. 1955. *Tingo Tango Mango Tree*. Morristown, N.J.: Silver Burdett Press.
Wilder, Laura Ingalls. 1935. *Little House on the Prairie*. New York: Harper.
Winders, Gertrude Hecker. 1953. *Jim Bowie: Boy with a Hunting Knife*. Indianapolis: Bobbs-Merrill.
——. 1955. *Jim Bridger: Mountain Boy*. Indianapolis: Bobbs-Merrill.
Wood, Kerry. 1960. *The Queen's Cowboy: Colonel Macleod of the Mounties*. Toronto: Macmillan.

Secondary Sources

Ahmad, Eqbal. 2000. *Confronting Empire: Interviews with David Barsamian*. Cambridge, Mass.: South End Press.
Ahmed, Leila. 1992. *Women and Gender in Islam: Historical Roots of a Modern Debate*. New Haven: Yale University Press.
Allen, Charles, ed. 1975. *Plain Tales from the Raj: Images of British India in the Twentieth Century*. London: Andre Deutsch.
Altick, Richard D. 1973. *Victorian People and Ideas*. New York: Norton.
Anderson, Benedict. 1991. *Imagined Communities: Reflections on the Origin and Spread of Nationalism*. London: Verso.
Ann Arbor Science for the People Editorial Collective. 1977. *Biology as a Social Weapon*. Minneapolis: Burgess.
Appleby, Joyce, Lynn Hunt, and Margaret Jacob. 1994. *Telling the Truth about History*. New York: Norton.
Ashcroft, Bill, Gareth Griffiths, and Helen Tiffin, eds. 1995. *The Post-Colonial Studies Reader*. London: Routledge.
Auerbach, Erich. 1953. *Mimesis: The Representation of Reality in Western Literature*. Princeton, N.J.: Princeton University Press.

Banton, Michael. 1978. *The Idea of Race*. Boulder, Colo.: Westview Press.

Barthes, Roland. 1953. *Writing Degree Zero and Elements of Semiology*. Trans. Annette Lavers and Colin Smith. Boston: Beacon Press.

———. 1979. *The Eiffel Tower and Other Mythologies*. Trans. Richard Howard. New York: Hill and Wang.

———. 1982. *Empire of Signs*. New York: Hill and Wang. (Originally published 1970.)

Bauer, Raymond A. 1952. *The New Man in Soviet Psychology*. Cambridge: Harvard University Press.

Bhabha, Homi K., ed. 1990. *Nation and Narration*. London: Routledge.

———. 1994. *The Location of Culture*. London and New York: Routledge.

Bixler, Phyllis. 1996. *The Secret Garden: Nature's Magic*. New York: Twayne Publishers.

Blyton, Enid. n.d. Foreword, *A Complete List of Books: Enid Blyton*. Edinburgh: John Menzies.

Brantlinger, Patrick. 1988. *Rule of Darkness: British Literature and Imperialism, 1830–1914*. Ithaca, N.Y.: Cornell University Press.

Brown, Dee. 1994. *The American West*. New York: Simon & Schuster.

Burgess, John W. 1933. *The Foundations of Political Science*. New York: Columbia University Press.

Butts, Dennis, ed. 1992. *Stories and Society: Children's Literature in Its Social Context*. New York: St. Martin's Press.

Castle, Kathryn. 1996. *Britannia's Children: Reading Colonialism through Children's Books and Magazines*. Manchester: Manchester University Press.

Chandler, Arthur. 1931. *Empire of the Republic: The Exposition Coloniale Internationale de Paris* at http://130.212.41.61/pef/1931a.html.

Davis, David Brion. 1966. *The Problem of Slavery in Western Culture*. New York: Oxford University Press.

Dawson, Graham. 1994. *Soldier Heroes: British Adventure, Empire and the Imagining of Masculinities*. London and New York: Routledge.

Derrida, Jacques. 1978. *Writing and Difference*. Chicago: University of Chicago Press.

Diver, Maud. 1945. *The Unsung: A Record of British Services in India*. London: Blackwood.

Dorfman, Ariel, and Armand Mattelart. 1983. *The Empire's New Clothes: What the Lone Ranger, Babar, and Other Innocent Heroes Do to Our Minds*. New York: Pantheon Books.

———. 1984. *How to Read Donald Duck: Imperialist Ideology in the Disney Comic*. New York: International General.

Duin, Julia. 1998. Victorian Children's Books Gain Latter-Day Following. *Washington Times*, 6 May.

Dykema-Vanderark. Playing Indian in Print. *Melus* 27, no. 2 (summer 2002): 9–30.

Eastman, Charles A. 1916. *From the Deep Woods to Civilization*. Mineola, N.Y.: Dover Publications, 2003.

Elliot, Michael. 2001. We Will Not Fail. *Time* (1 October): 18–31.

Femia, Joseph V. 1987. *Gramsci's Political Thought: Hegemony, Consciousness, and the Revolutionary Process*. Oxford: Clarendon Press.

Ferguson, Niall. 2003. The Empire Slinks Back. *New York Times Magazine* (27 April): 6, 52.

Fieldhouse, D. K. 1965. *The Colonial Empires: A Comparative Survey from the Eighteenth Century*. New York: Delacorte Press.

Fineman, Howard, and Martha Brant. 2001. Bush's Battle Cry. *Newsweek* (1 October): 24–26.

The First Team. 2001. *Newsweek* (3 December): 24–29.

Foucault, Michel. 1972. *The Archaeology of Knowledge and the Discourse on Language*. Trans. A. M. Sheridan Smith. New York: Pantheon Books.

Friedan, Betty. 1997. *Beyond Gender: The New Politics of Work and Family*. Ed. Brigid O'Farrell. Baltimore: Woodrow Wilson Center Press.

Fuller Timothy, ed. 1999. Cultures in the 21st Century: Conflicts and Convergences: A Selection of Papers Presented at a Symposium Celebrating the 125th Anniversary of Colorado College. Special issue of the *Colorado College Studies* 32. Colorado Springs: Colorado College.

Gates, Henry Louis Jr. 1985. *"Race," Writing, and Difference*. Chicago: University of Chicago Press.

Gatto, John Taylor. 2003. Against School: How Public Education Cripples Our Kids, and Why. *Harper's* (September): 33–38.

Gibbs, Nancy. 2001. If You Want to Humble an Empire. *Time* (14 September): 34ff.

Giroux, Henry A. 1999. *The Mouse That Roared: Disney and the End of Innocence*. Lanham, Md.: Rowman & Littlefield.

———. Youth Panic and the Politics of Schooling. *Z Magazine*. December 1999. Vol. 12/Issue 12, pages 27–31.

Gobineau, Arthur de. 1854. *Selected Political Writings*. London: Jonathan Cape, 1970.

Goode, Stephen. 2001. Harmon Details Terrorism Today: Christopher Harmon Interview. *Insight on the News*, 5 February.

Gott, Richard. 2001. Whitewashing the Real Evil Empire. Review of *Ornamentalism: How the British Saw Their Empire* by David Cannadine. *Guardian Weekly* 17, no. 23 (May): 15.

Green, Martin. 1990. *The Robinson Crusoe Story*. University Park: Pennsylvania State University Press.

———. 1991. *Seven Types of Adventure Tale: An Etiology of a Major Genre*. University Park: Pennsylvania State University Press.

Grewal, Inderpal. 1996. *Home and Harem: Nation, Gender, Empire, and the Cultures of Travel*. Durham, N.C.: Duke University Press.

Gunn, Katharine. 1990. Big Bill's Angela Brazil Stuff at www.kruse.co.uk/brazil.htm.

Hay, Elizabeth. 1981. *Sambo Sahib: The Story of Little Black Sambo and Helen Bannerman*. Totowa, N.J.: Barnes & Noble.

Helen Bannerman on the Train to Kodaikanal. 2001. *Pancake Parlour* at www.pancakeparlour.com.

Hochman, Baruch. 1985. *Character in Literature*. Ithaca, N.Y.: Cornell University Press.

Hochschild, Adam. 1998. *King Leopold's Ghost: A Story of Greed, Terror, and Heroism in Colonial Africa*. Boston: Houghton Mifflin.

Hunt, Peter, and Karen Sands. 1996. The View from the Center: British Empire and Post-Empire Children's Literature. In *The Nimble Reader: Literary Theory and Children's Literature*, edited by Roderick McGillis. New York: Twayne Publishers, 1996.

Huntington, Samuel P. 1996. *The Clash of Civilizations and the Remaking of World Order*. New York: Touchstone-Simon & Schuster.

———. 1999. Cultures in the 21st Century: Conflicts and Convergences. Address at Colorado College. Ed. Timothy Fuller, *Colorado College Studies* 32, February 4–6.

Hutchins, Francis G. 1967. *The Illusion of Permanence: British Imperialism in India*. Princeton, N.J.: Princeton University Press.

Isikoff, Michael, and Daniel Klaidman. 2001. A Matter of Missed Signals. *Newsweek* (31 December): 30.

Jagt, Arnold. 2002. Personal Character. *The Robinson Books on CD, G. A. Henty Collection* at www.henty.com/henty/s86p1056.htm.

JanMohamed, Abdul R. 1983. *Manichean Aesthetics: The Politics of Literature in Colonial Africa*. Amherst: University of Massachusetts Press.

Jones, Cornelia, and Olivia R. Way. 1976. *British Children's Authors: Interviews at Home*. Chicago: American Library Association.

Jones, David. 2000. Maharaja Duleep Singh. *Nishaan* (January): 46–51.

Jweid, Rosann, and Margaret Rizzo. 2001. *Building Character through Literature: A Guide for Middle School Readers*. Lanham, Md.: Scarecrow Press.

Kamenetsky, Christa. 1984. *Children's Literature in Hitler's Germany: The Cultural Policy of National Socialism*. Athens: Ohio University Press.

Kershaw, Sarah. 2002. Schenectady's Guyanese Strategy. *New York Times* (26 July): A18.

Khorana, Meena, ed. 1998. *Critical Perspectives on Postcolonial African Children's and Young Adult Literature*. Westport, Conn.: Greenwood Press.

Kingsley, Charles. 1892. *Sanitary and Social Lectures and Essays*. London: Macmillan (Originally published 1880.)

Kohl, Herbert. 1995. *Should We Burn Babar? Essays on Children's Literature and the Power of Stories*. New York: New Press.

Knox, Robert. 1850. *The Races of Men: A Fragment*. Philadelphia: Lea & Blanchard.

Kutzer, M. Daphne. 2000. *Empire's Children: Empire and Imperialism in Classic British Children's Books*. New York: Garland.

Lehr, Susan. 1995. *Battling Dragons: Issues and Controversies in Children's Literature*. Portsmouth, N.H.: Heinemann.

Lesnik-Oberstein, Karin. 1994. *Children's Literature: Children and the Fictional Child*. Oxford: Clarendon Press.

Lindqvist, Sven. 1996. *Exterminate All the Brutes*. Trans. Joan Tate. New York: New Press.

Loewen, James. 1995. *Lies My Teacher Told Me: Everything Your American History Textbook Got Wrong*. New York: New Press.

MacDonald, Robert H. 1993. *Sons of the Empire: The Frontier and the Boy Scout Movement, 1890–1918*. Toronto: University of Toronto Press.

MacLeod, Anne Scott. 1975. *A Moral Tale: Children's Fiction and American Culture 1820–1860*. Hamden, Conn.: Archon Books.

Mahbubani, Kishore. 1992. The West and the Rest. *The National Interest* 28:3–12.

Malarte-Feldman, Claire-Lise, and Jack Yeager. 1998. Babar and the French Connection: Teaching the Politics of Superiority and Exclusion. *Critical Perspectives on Postcolonial African Children's and Young Adult Literature*, edited by Meena Khorana. Westport, Conn.: Greenwood Press.

Marks, Jonathan. 1955. *Human Biodiversity: Genes, Race, and History*. New York: Aldine De Gruyter.

Maunier, Rene. 1949. *The Sociology of Colonies: An Introduction to the Study of Race Contact*. 2 vols. Ed. and trans. E. O. Lorimer. London: Routledge and Kegan Paul.

McGeary, Johanna. 2001. The Taliban Troubles. *Time* (1 October): 36–41.

McGillis, Roderick, ed. 1996. *The Nimble Reader: Literary Theory and Children's Literature*. New York: Twayne Publishers.

———. 2000. *Voices of the Other: Children's Literature and the Postcolonial Context*. New York: Garland Publishing.

Memmi, Albert. 1965. *The Colonizer and the Colonized*. Boston: Beacon Press.

Mill, James. 1840–1848. *History of British India*. 4th ed. 9 vols. London: James Madden.

Morrison, Toni. 1992. *Playing in the Dark: Whiteness and the Literary Imagination*. Cambridge, Mass.: Harvard University Press.

Morrow, Lance. 2001. The Case for Rage and Retribution. *Time* (14 September): 50.

Naidis, Mark. 1964. G. A. Henty's Idea of India. *Victorian Studies* (September): 58.

Neave, Dorinda. 1988. The Witch in 16th-Century German Art. *Woman's Art Journal* 9, no. 1:3–9.

Nodelman, Perry. 1988. *Words about Pictures: The Narrative Art of Children's Picture Books*. Athens: University of Georgia Press.

———. 1992. The Other: Orientalism, Colonialism, and Children's Literature. *Children's Literature Association Quarterly* 17, no. 1 (spring): 29–35.

Osterhammel, Jürgen. 1997. *Colonialism: A Theoretical Overview*. Trans. Shelley L. Frisch. Princeton, N.J.: Markus Wiener.

Pearce, Roy Harvey. 1988. *Savagism and Civilization: A Study of the Indian and the American Mind*. Berkeley: University of California Press.

Perrot, Jean. 1998. The French Avant-Garde Revisited: Or, Why We Shouldn't Burn Mickey Mouse. In *Critical Perspectives on Postcolonial African Children's and Young Adult Literature*, edited by Meena Khorana. Westport, Conn.: Greenwood Press.

Politzer, Michel. 1974. *Robinson Crusoé, My Journals and Sketchbooks*. Foreword by Andre Deutsch. New York: Harcourt Brace Jovanovich.

Pollitt, Katha. 2001. Put Out No Flags. *Nation* (20 September): 9

Quinlivan, Gary. 2002. Review of *Personal Character and National Destiny*, at www.paragonhouse.com/catalog/product_info.php?authors_id=56& products_id=66

Rabinow, Paul, ed. 1984. *The Foucault Reader*. New York: Pantheon Books.

Raghunathan, Abhi. 2002. Day-Care Agency Senses Sting of 9/11 Ethnic Bias. *Washington Post* (24 August) Virginia ed.: B1–B2.

Raskin, Jonah. 1971. *The Mythology of Imperialism: Rudyard Kipling, Joseph Conrad, E. M. Forster, D. H. Lawrence, and Joyce Cary*. New York: Random House.

Reimer, Mavis, and Perry Nodelman. 2003. *The Pleasures of Children's Literature*. Boston : Allyn and Bacon.

Review of *Desmond's Daughter*. 1916. *Times Literary Supplement* (25 May).

Review of *Far to Seek*. 1921. *Times Literary Supplement* (26 May).

Richards, Jeffrey, ed. 1989. *Imperialism and Juvenile Literature*. Manchester: Manchester University Press.

———. 1992. The School Story. *Stories and Society: Children's Literature in Its Social Context*, edited by Dennis Butts. New York: St. Martin's.

Roberts, Stephen. H. 1929. *History of French Colonial Policy, 1870–1925*. 2 vols. London: P. S. King.

Rose, Jacqueline. 1984. *The Case of Peter Pan, or, The Impossibility of Children's Fiction*. London: Macmillan.

Rosenthal, Michael. 1984. *The Character Factory: Baden-Powell and the Origins of the Boy Scout Movement*. New York: Pantheon.

Rudd, David. 2000. *Enid Blyton and the Mystery of Children's Literature*. London: Macmillan.

Said, Edward. 1979. *Orientalism*. New York: Vintage-Random.

———. 1993. *Culture and Imperialism*. New York: Alfred A. Knopf, 1993.

———. 2002. Impossible Histories: Why the Many Islams Cannot Be Simplified. *Harper's* (July).

Scott, A. O. 2002. A Hunger for Fantasy, an Empire to Feed It. *New York Times* (16 June): sec 2, 1.

Showalter, Elaine. 1990. *Sexual Anarchy: Gender and Culture at the Fin de Siècle*. New York: Viking.

Sidey, Hugh. 2001. Conversations with a Father. *Time* (1 October): 35.

Singh, Rashna B. 1988. *The Imperishable Empire: A Study of British Fiction on India*. Washington, D.C.: Three Continents Press.

Slotkin, Richard. 1992. *Gunfighter Nation: The Myth of the Frontier in Twentieth-Century America*. New York: Atheneum.

Sonheim, Amy. 1991. *Maurice Sendak*. New York: Twayne.

Spurr, David. 1993. *The Rhetoric of Empire: Colonial Discourse in Journalism, Travel Writing, and Imperial Administration*. Durham, N.C.: Duke University Press.

Starbuck, Edwin D. 1928. *A Guide to Literature for Character Training: Fairy Tale, Myth, and Legend*. New York: Macmillan.

Takaki, Ronald. 1993. *A Different Mirror: A History of Multicultural America*. Boston: Little, Brown.

Tatar, Maria. 1992. *Off with Their Heads! Fairy Tales and the Culture of Childhood*. Princeton: Princeton University Press.

Thomas, Evan, and John Barry. 2001. Beyond Bin Laden: Evil in the Cross Hairs. *Newsweek* (24 December): 10–20.

Thomas, Evan et al. 2001. Gunning for Bin Laden. *Newsweek* (26 November): 30–37.

Tidrick, Kathryn. 1990. *Empire and the English Character*. London: I. B. Tauris.

Touhey-Kiniery, Eileen. 2001. A Survivor Reacts. *Newsweek*. (24 December): 4.

Townsend, John Rowe. 1971. *A Sense of Story: Essays on Contemporary Writers for Children*. Philadelphia: J. B. Lippincott.

Tucker, Frank H. 1980. *The Frontier Spirit and Progress*. Chicago: Nelson-Hall.

Turner, Frederick Jackson. 1920. *The Frontier in America History*. New York: Henry Holt.

Walton, Anthony. 2002. A Dream Deferred: Why Martin Luther King Has Yet to Be Heard. *Harper's* (August): 67–72.

Webster, Wendy. 2003. Domesticating the Frontier: Gender, Empire and Adventure Landscapes in British Cinema 1945–1959. *Gender and History* (April): 15.

Wilson, Angus. 1978. *The Strange Ride of Rudyard Kipling: His Life and Works*. New York: Viking Press.

Winks, Robin W., ed. 1963. *British Imperialism: Gold, God, Glory*. New York: Holt, Rinehart and Winston.

Wolff, Robert Lee, ed. 1985. *Masterworks of Children's Literature*. Vol. 5, Part 1: *1837–1900: The Victorian Age*. New York: Stonehill Publishing.

Wolpert, Stanley. 2000. *A New History of India*. New York: Oxford University Press.

Wright, Bradford W. 2001. *Comic Book Nation: The Transformation of Youth Culture in America*. Baltimore: Johns Hopkins University Press.

Wooldridge, Adrian. 1999. Henty's Heroes. *Economist* (December 11–17).

Zakaria, Fareed. 2001a. Why Do They Hate Us? The Politics of Rage. *Newsweek* (15 October).

———. 2001b. How to Save the Arab World. *Newsweek* (24 December): 22–28.

Index

Africa, 70, 91, 94, 98, 99, 100, 101, 104, 105, 106, 111, 149
Ahmed, Leila, 25, 28
Aladdin, 68, 305, 307, 308, 309
Ali Baba & the 40 Thieves, 99
Alger, Horatio, 247
Allen, Charles, 118
Altick, Richard, 138, 147
American Adventure Series, 271
American West, xxxvii, 22, 39, 247, 249, 251
Amin, Qassim, 28
Anderson, A. M., 268, 269, 270
Anderson, Benedict, 24
Anderson, Marjorie, 211
Arnold, Mathew, 36, 142
Arnold, Dr. Thomas, 38, 138–147
Arnold, William Delafield, 36, 142, 143, 145, 147
Atkins, Jeannine, 101

Atlantic slave trade, 23
Avery, Gillian, 80

Babar, 88–94, 99, 101, 104
Babri Mosque, xiv
Baden-Powell, Lord, 34, 35, 45, 209, 219, 235, 241
Ballantyne, R.B. xxxviii, xl, 243, 250; *The Coral Island*, 165–170, 242; *Mr. Midshipman Easy*; 170
Bamiyan Buddhas, xiv
Bannerman, Helen, 83–85; *Little Black Sambo*, 83–86, 92, 100, 101
Banton, Michel, 33
Barrie, J. M., *Little White Bird*, 77; *Peter Pan*, 76–80, 95, 112, 150, 151, 245, 246, 257
Barthes, Roland, 42, 70, 86, 95
Batman, 295

Bauer, Elvira, 7, 311
Bauer, Raymond A., 30, 31, 63, 64
Beals, Frank Lee, *Buffalo Bill*,
    258, 262–264, 267; *Chief Black
    Hawk*, 271–275
Bettelheim, Bruno, 75
Bhabha, Homi, xxv
Billy Bunter, 202
Bin Laden, Osama, xii–xiv, xxv,
    xxx, 68, 86, 99
Bixler, Phyllis, 116, 126
black hole of Calcutta, 50, 188,
    190
Blake, Quentin, 103
Blyton, Enid, xli, 106, 124, 174,
    199–202, 216, 263
    BBC interview of, 211
    Claudine, 237, 238
    Claudine at St. Claire's, 227,
    228, 233, 238
    *The Famous Five and the
    Knight's Treasure*, 205, 219,
    220, 222
    Five Fall into Adventure, 206,
    208–210, 213, 220, 221
    Five Get into a Fix, 205, 207,
    208, 211, 212, 219, 221
    Five Get into Trouble, 205, 206,
    209, 210, 212–214, 220
    Five Go to Billycock Hill, 204,
    206–208, 211–213, 215
    Five Go Off in a Caravan, 204,
    207, 210, 222
    Five Go to Demon's Rocks, 210,
    211, 219
    The Five Find Outers, 216, 226,
    227, 243
    First Term at Malory Towers,
    228, 229
    Second Form at Malory Towers,
    229, 231, 236–238
    Third Year at Malory Towers,
    236, 237
    In the Fifth at Malory Towers,
    229, 235–238
    Last Term at Malory Towers,
    230, 231, 235
    The Secret of Killimooin, 220,
    222, 224, 226
    The Secret of Moon Castle, 205,
    209, 218, 219, 225
    The Secret Seven, 216, 224, 243
    The Six Bad Boys, 214
Boas, Franz, 28, 29
Bonanza, 252
Bond, Michael, 95
Boykin, Lt. Gen. William G.,
    xxxi, 248
Boys' Empire League, 43, 44
Boys of the Empire, 41–47, 49–54
Boy's Own Annual, 56
Boy's Own Paper, xl, 45, 48–55, 59
boys' papers, xl, 47
Boy Scouts, 39
Brantlinger, Patrick, 8
Brazil, Angela, 201, 202
Brent-Dyer, Elinor M., 201
Brer Rabbit, 87
Brooke, Rajah James, 223
Brown, Dee, 195, 279, 281
Bruce, Darita Fairlie, 202
Buchan, John, 4, 22, 39, 232;
    Prester John, 3
Buddhist *Jataka* tales, 66

Buffalo Bill's Wild West Show, 252, 264–267
Bulla, Clyde Robert, 268, 270
Bunyan, John, *Pilgrim's Progress*, 250
Burgess, John W., xx, xxi, xxii
Burnett, Frances Hodgson, 243; *The Hunchback Zia*, 137; *Little Lord Fauntleroy*, 115, 134–136; *A Little Princess*, 115, 116, 129–134, 140, 150, 209; *The Lost Prince*, 115, 136, 137; *Sara Crewe*, 117, 129; *The Secret Garden*, 65, 114–134, 137, 141, 213, 215; *The White People*, 137
Burnham, Fred, 40
Burton, Richard, 8
Bush, George W., xii, xv, xxii, xxiv, 26, 29, 35, 296
Bush, Laura, 29
Butts, Dennis, xli, 48

Canada, 263, 286
Carlyle, Thomas, xxviii, 2
Carroll, Lewis, *Alice in Wonderland*, 111, 112
Castle, Kathryn, 61
Castro, Fidel, xii
Cary, Joyce, 28, 36
Chamberlain, Joseph, 36
character building, 196
character determinism, 27
character education, xliii, 63–66
character ethics, 40
character training, 40
Cheney, Dick, 35

Childhood of Famous Americans series, 278, 284
Children's Literature Association, xxxvii
Churchill, Winston, xix, xxii, xxiv, 33, 113, 291
Clifford, Hugh, 223
Clive, Robert, 45, 46, 50, 186, 187, 218
Coleridge, Samuel Taylor, 82
Collier, 260, 261, 265, 267
comic books, 295, 296
Conde Nast Traveler, 96
Conrad, Joseph, 76; *Heart of Darkness*, i, xxvi, 6, 10, 70, 71, 75
Cooper, James Fenimore, 251
Croker, B. M., 232
Cromer, Lord, 25
Cunningham, Sir Henry Stewart, 36
Cust, Robert, 220
Cuvier, Georges, 9

Dahl, Roald, 111, 112; *The BFG*, 109, 110; *Boy*, 106, 108, 110; *Charlie and the Chocolate Factory*, 103, 104, 110; *Charlie and the Great Glass Elevator*, 110; *Fantastic Mr. Fox*, 109; *George's Marvellous Medicine*, 109; *Going Solo*, 105, 106, *James and the Giant Peach*, 109, 110; *The Magic Finger*, 110; *Matilda*, 109, 110; *The Twits*, 110; *The Witches*, 109, 110

Dangarembga, Tsitsi, *Nervous Conditions*, 201
Darwin, Charles, 6, 8, 81, 166
Daugherty, James, 252
Davis, David Brion, 23
Dawson, Graham, 311, 312
Dear America series, 297
Defoe, Daniel, *Robinson Crusoe*, xxvi, 151–167, 171, 250
Delamere, Lord, 223
Deloncle, Pierre, xxvi
Denenberg, Barry, *The Journal of Ben Uchida*, 297, 302, 303
Derrida, Jacques, 114, 314
Deutsch, Andre, 163
De Vargas, Pedro Fermin, 24
Disney, 68, 99, 194, 268, 294, 303–309
Diver, Maud, 33, 38, 188, 232, 238, 250; *Captain Desmond, V.C.*, 234; *Desmond's Daughter*, 72, 203, 233; *Far to Seek*, 235; *The Great Amulet*, 37; *Lonely Furrow*, 35
Dorfman, Ariel, 88, 90–92, 94, 303, 304, 309
Du Bois, Pene, *Otto in Africa*, 98, 99
Duke, David, 26
Dupleix, Joseph Francois, 45

Eastman, Charles A., 92, 284, 285, 290
Eastwood, Clint, xvi, 252
Evans, Dale, 249
Exposition coloniale et internationale, xxvi, xxvii, xxviii

Falwell, Jerry, xxxi, 26
Fanon, Frantz, i
Farrar, Frederick, 19
Farrar, Frederic W., *Eric; or, Little by Little*, 19, 149, 150
Farris, Michael, 194
Ferguson, Niall, 35
Fielding, Sarah, 201
Firmin, Peter, *Basil Brush in the Jungle*, 87, 88
The Flashman Papers, 149
Ford, Gerald, 297
Forster, E. M., 76; *A Passage to India*, xxvi, 25, 28, 38, 75, 118, 120, 147, 178, 238, 241; *Abinger Harvest*, 38, 41, 42
Foucault, Michel, 67, 294, 314
Fox, Mem, *Boo to a Goose*, 310
Fox News, 26
Fraser, George MacDonald, 149
Freud, Sigmund, 77, 79
Friedan, Betty, 311

Gadafi, Muammar, xii
Gatto, John, xlii, xliii
The Gem, 202
Gephardt, Dick, xii
Gilman, Sandra, 9
Girl's Own Paper, 56, 57, 200
Giroux, Henry, xliii, 304, 307, 309
Gobhai, Mehlli, 97
Gobineau, Comte de, 20–23, 25, 154, 173
Golding, William, *Lord of the Flies*, xxvi
Gordon, General, 223
Gott, Richard, 224, 239

Graham, R. B. Cunningham, 5
Gramsci, Antonio, 312
Grant, Charles, 128
Grant, George, 195
Green, Martin, 60, 150–152, 162, 250, 251
Gregory, Kristiana, *Across the Wide and Lonesome Prairie*, 301, 302
Greyfriars School stories, 55, 202, 243
Gunn, Katharine, 202
Gunsmoke, 252
Gupta, Brijen Kishore, 190, 191

Hannity, Sean, 26
Harry Potter, xv, xvi, 65, 115, 294
Hastert, Dennis, xii
Hastings, Warren, 218
Hay, Elizabeth, 83–85
Henty, G. A., xxxvii, xxxviii, xl, 4, 5, 22, 39, 150, 152, 186, 232, 243, 247, 250, 252; *With Clive in India*, 186–89; *In the Heart of the Rockies*, 195, 196; *For Name or Fame*, 190–193; *In Times of Peril*, 186
Hermes, Patricia, *The Starving Time*, 298
Herrnstein, Richard J., 9
Hilary, Sir Edmund, 60
Hinton, S. E., 221
Hitler Youth, 7
Hochschild, Adam, 21
Hodson's Horse, 146
Hogben, Lancelot, 28
Holbrook, Stewart H. 279, 280

Holwell, J. Z., 50, 191
Hughes, Thomas, *Tom Brown's Schooldays*, 109, 124, 137–150, 174, 175, 203, 240
Hume, David, 2, 3, 23
Huntington, Samuel, xvii, xviii, xix, xx, 26
Hussein, Saddam, xii, xxx
Hutchins, Francis G., 125, 126, 128, 129

Imperial Institute, 36
India, 69, 97, 98, 115–122, 124–129, 131–133, 149, 178–192
Indian Mutiny, 34, 117
Inglis, Alexander, xlii
Inglis, Fred, 68, 202
Iraq, xii, 96, 97
Islamic extremism, xv
Islamic mind, xxxi

Jabar, 68
Jan Mohamed, Abdul, xvi
Jefferson, Thomas, 23, 66, 290
Jhabvala, Ruth, 126
Johnston, Tony, 303
Jones, David, 89
Jones, Harold B., 63
Jweid, Rosann, 65

Kalman, Maria, *Swami on Rye*, 97
Kamenetsky, Christa, 7
Kant, Immanuel, 2, 3
Kasem, Casey, 307
Keats, Ezra Jack, *The Snowy Day*, 101
Keats, John, 69

Kidd, Benjamin, 3, 33
Kipling, Rudyard, xxvii, 76, 98, 99, 243, 250, 269; poems, i, 144, 166; *Jungle Books*, 171–173; *Kim*, 137, 181–186, 285; *Stalky & Co.*, 173–181
Kincaid, Jamaica, 201
King Leopold, 21, 57, 58
King, Martin Luther, 66
Kingsley, Charles, 114; *Sanitary and Social Essays*, 33; *Water Babies*, 80–82
Knox, Robert, xi, 8–20, 22, 23, 26, 52, 154, 173
Kohl, Herbert, 90, 92–94, 102, 196
Kutzer, M. Daphne, xl, 65, 126, 166, 184, 221, 242

Laskey, Kathryn, *A Journey to the New World*, 298
La tutelle coloniale, 89
Lawrence, Sir Henry, 217, 223
Lawrence, John, 46, 217, 223
Lawrence, T. E., 180
Lehr, Susan, 82
Lesnik-Oberstein, xl, xli, 114
Lester, Julius, 86, 87
Lewison, Wendy Cheyette, *Shy Vi*, 310
Lindqvist, Sven, 5, 6, 8, 19
The Lion King, 306
Loewen, James, 256–258, 267–270
Lost Classics Book Co., 193, 194
Lugard, Lord Frederick, 32
Lyautey, Le Marechal, xxvi

Macaulay, Lord Thomas Babington, 24, 200
MacDonald, Robert H., 34, 39, 40, 288
Mack, Edward, xliii
MacLeod, Anne Scott, 289
The Magnet, 55
Mahbubani, Kishore, xviii
Malarte-Feldman, Claire-Lise, 89–91
Malleus Maleficarum, 109–110
Manichean Allegory, xxii, 100, 165
Manifest Destiny, xxvii
Mannoni, Octave, 37
Marks, Jonathan, 12, 28, 29
Marlborough, Duke of,
Marryat, Captain, xxxviii, 39, 150, 252
Martino, Joseph P., 246
Mattelart, Armand, 303, 309
Maunier, Rene, xxviii, 233
McGillis, Roderick, xxxvii, xli
McInerney, Lt. Gen. Tom, xii
McMurty, Larry, 252
McVeigh, Timothy, 31, 68
Meade, L. T., 201
Memmi, Albert, xviii, xix, 154, 293
Mill, James, 128, 129
Mission civilisatrice, xxvi, 88, 90, 91, 295
Mistry, Rohinton, *Family Matters*, 200, 201
Montesquieu, Baron de, 23, 128
Moore, Thomas, 69

Morrison, Toni, 76
Morse, Jedidiah, 248
Mountbatten, Lord Louis, 223
Mulan, 305
Murphy, Jim, *West to a Land of Plenty*, 299, 302
Murray, Charles, 9
Muslims, xxiii, xxix, xxxi
Muslim solution, 26
Myers, Walter, *The Journal of Joshua Loper*, 301
My Name is America series, 297

Naidis, Mark, 232
Naipaul, V. S., 76, 99
Nazi Germany, 7, 21
Neal, Richard, xii
Neave, Dorinda, 74
Nesbit, E., 243
Newbolt, Sir Henry, 34
Nicolson, John, 34
Nodelman, Perry, xl, 68, 83, 103, 313, 314

Oklahoma City, 31
Oliver Optic, 194
Orwell, George, 55, 181, 202, 297; *Burmese Days*, 1, 37, 38, 148, 178, 222, 238, 240; *The Road to Wigan Pier*, 239
Osterhammel, Jurgen, 32
Otis, Jame, 194
Ottoman Empire, xxix
Oxenham, Elsie Jeanette, 201

Parascandola, Louis J., 171
Pax Britannica, 127

Payne, Harry, 90
Pearce, Roy Harvey, 290, 291
Pearson, Lester, xxxviii
The Pentagon, xiii
Perrin, Alice, 232
Pinkney, Jerry, 86
Pocahontas, 35, 76, 194, 268, 278, 305, 306, 310
Politzer, Michel, 163
Potter, Beatrice, 112
Preston Speed Publications, xxxvii, 191, 194
Princess Elizabeth, 58
Prophet Mohammed, xxxi

Queen Alexandra, 58
Queen Elizabeth, 60
Queen Victoria, 57, 58, 89, 265

Rackham, Arthur, 77
Reagan, Ronald, xi, 298
Reimer, Mavis, 117
Religious Tract Society, 45
Renan, Ernest, 184
Repton School, 107, 108
Rey, H. A., *Curious George*, 94, 95, 101, 104
Reynolds, Quentin, 280
Rhodes, Cecil, 146, 208, 218, 223
Rice, Condoleeza, xii
Richards, Frank, xl, 1, 55, 243
Richards, Jeffrey, xl, 48, 137, 250
Richardson, Patrick, 90
Rinaldi, Ann, *My Heart is on the Ground*, 299
Rizzo, Margaret, 65

Roberts, Pat, xxxi
Robertson, Pat, 26
Robertson, William, 290
Robinsonades, 165
Romantic poets, 69
Roosevelt, Theodore, 245, 266
Rose, Jacqueline, xxxviii, xl, xli, 76, 77, 114, 313
Rosenthal, Michael, 40, 207, 214, 219, 226, 235, 241, 242
Rowling, J. K., 294
Royal Diaries series, 303
Rudd, David, xli, 213
Rugby School, 38, 109, 138–142, 146, 149, 240
Russell, Bertrand, 30, 39, 146

Said, Edward, xxxi; *Orientalism*, xxix, xxx, xxxi, 68, 72, 102
Saleeby, Michael C.W., 207
Saturday cartoon shows, 296
Savi, E. W., 232
Schlesinger, Arthur M., Jr., xxxviii
Schlesinger, Arthur M., Sr., viii, xxxvii
Selous, Frederick Courtenay, 146, 218, 222, 223
Sendak, Maurice, *Outside Over There*, 73–75; *We Are All in the Dumps With Jack and Guy*, 76; *Where the Wild Things Are*, 70–75, 82, 100
September 11, 2001, xiii, xxx
Sesame Street, 95
Shakespeare, William, *Henry VIII*, 69; *The Tempest*, xviii, 155

Shelley, Percy Bysshe, 69
Showalter, Elaine, 112
Singh, Mehtab, 34
Singh, Prince Duleep, 89
Singh, Rashna, 34, 69, 75, 90, 232, 283
Sikh gurdwaras, xiv
Siraj-ud-Daula, 50
Sleeping Beauty, 307
Slotkin, Richard, 263, 265, 266
Smith, Captain John, 35, 76, 194, 305, 306
Snow White, 306
Social Darwinism, xvi, 26, 33, 81, 166, 171–173, 253, 290
Sons of Daniel Boone, 39
Sontag, Susan, 27
Southey, Robert, 69
Spencer, Herbert, 20
Spiderman, xv, xvi, 295
Spurr, David, 89, 275, 285
Starbuck, Edwin, 63, 64
Star Wars, xvi, 295
Steel, Flora Annie, 232
Stevenson, Augusta, *Buffalo Bill: Boy of the Plains*, 259, 260, 262–265, 267; *Daniel Boone: Boy Hunter*, 254–257, 261; *Tecumseh: Shawnee Boy*, 275–278
Stevenson, Robert Louis, 150, 162, 250
St. Jim's school stories, 55, 202
St. Nicholas, 284
The Story of Little Babaji, 87
Stowe, Harriet Beecher, xxviii, xxix

Stratemeyer, Edward, 194
Superman, 295
Sufi stories, 66
Swift, Jonathan, *Gulliver's Travels*, 250

Taj Mahal, xiv, 98
Takaki, Ronald, 254
Taliban, xiv
Tatar, Maria, xxv
"temperament is destiny," 129, 202
Thompson, Edward, 33, 34, 38
Thornton, A. P., 5
Tidrick, Kathryn, 140, 146, 214–218, 222, 223, 240, 241
Times Literary Supplement, 33, 34
Tolkien, J. R. R., *Lord of the Rings*, xvi
Tompkins, Jane, xix, 258
Touchstones, xxxvii
Tousey, Sanford, 261
Tucker, Frank, 246–252
Turner, Ann, *The Girl Who Chased Away Sorrow*, 301
Turner, Frederick Jackson, 286, 289
Twain, Mark, 150

Van Riper Jr., Guersney, 281
Vaughan, Alden, xix
Vaughan, Marcia, 95, 96
Victoria & Albert Museum, 50

Wallace, A. R., 19
Walton, Anthony, 66
Walton, Rev. John, xv
Warren, D. M., 248
Wa Thiong'o, Ngugi, 293
Wayne, John, xvi, 252
Webster, Wendy, 60, 250
Wellington, Duke of, 38
White Man's Burden, xxvii, 3, 131, 144, 166, 224
Wilder, Laura Ingalls, *Little House on the Prairie*, 104, 282, 283
Wilson, Angus, 178
Winders, Gertrude Hecker Winders, *Jim Bridger, Mountain Boy*, 277, 278
Wolpert, Stanley, 50, 188, 190, 191, 221, 224
Wood, Kerry, 286–288
Wooldridge, Adrian, 195
Wordsworth, William, 82
World Trade Center, xiii, xxx
Wright, Bradford W., 294–296
Wyatt Earp, 252
Wyss, Johann David, *Swiss Family Robinson*, 165

Yeager, Jack, 89–91
Young, Francis Brett, 4

Zane Grey, 252
Zumwalt, Admiral E. R., Jr., xxxvii

About the Author

Rashna Batliwala Singh was born and raised in India where she completed her BA (Honours) in English and Political Science at the University of Calcutta. She attained an MA in English from Mount Holyoke College and a PhD in English from the University of Massachusetts at Amherst. She is the author of *The Imperishable Empire: British Fiction on India* (1988), a pioneering work in the field, and has contributed to *Asian American Playwrights: A Bio-Bibliographical Critical Sourcebook* (2002).

Dr. Singh is the author of numerous scholarly articles and conference papers on issues in British colonial and postcolonial literature. She has taught in both India and the United States. In 2003 Dr. Singh was awarded a grant by the National Endowment for the Humanities to participate in an institute at Oxford University, and in 1998 she was chosen by the Massachusetts Council of International Education to lecture on "Perceptions and Representations of the Other" at various colleges in the state.